The Holocaust
and the
German Elite

The Holocaust
and the
German Elite

Genocide and National
Suicide in Germany,
1871–1945

RAINER C. BAUM

ROWMAN AND LITTLEFIELD Totowa
CROOM HELM London

6916259
DLC

7-8-82 JH

Copyright © 1981 by Rowman and Littlefield

First published in the United States in 1981 by Rowman and Littlefield,
81 Adams Drive, Totowa, New Jersey 07512.

First published in The United Kingdom in 1981 by Croom Helm Ltd,
2-10 St. John's Road, London, SW11

ISBN 0-7099-0656-0

Library of Congress Cataloging in Publication Data

Baum, Rainer C.
    The holocaust and the German elite.

    Bibliography: p.
    Includes index.
    1. Elite (Social sciences)—Germany—History.
2. Social values. 3. Social ethics. 4. Genocide—
Germany—History. 5. Holocaust, Jewish (1939–1945)
—Germany. I. Title.
HN460.E4B38   1981   305.5'2   80-25937
ISBN 0-8476-6970-X   AACR2

Printed in the United States of America

Contents

List of Tables

Preface

The Holocaust remains a unique historical experience in that we *should* never rest content with any explanation of it. Obviously, that is a normative conception of uniqueness. If we adopt it, only one limitation for research results. One should not write about it in a manner that restricts the readership to professional sociologists. This subject is far too important a part of our history to be addressed in the language of any specialist. Acknowledging the constraint, I have tried to write for the general readership. But otherwise the just mentioned notion of uniqueness is not incompatible with a search for scientific explanations. Such explanations may vary; they may conflict or complement each other. In any case, scientific work produces no "final solutions." It is inherently a restless activity, one that never reaches completion, and one in which each closing of a chapter generates the opening of a new one. This character of scientific work makes it compatible with our normative response to the Holocaust and provides justification, however precarious, to apply the tools of science to this part of our history.

Nonetheless, one must decide on a method of approach. One can regard the Holocaust as merely an instance in the long history of man's inhumanity to man, an extreme form of the oppression of a minority perhaps, but an event belonging to the general class of minority-host relations. In that case its unique features are left up to the work of others to elucidate; uniqueness only emerges as new aspects are discovered, aspects complementing in asymptotic fashion those already at hand. One cost of this procedure is that any one given study hides rather than reveals the unique character of the phenomenon. The alternative is to regard the Holocaust as a unique phenomenon not only in the sense of our response to it but also in cognitive terms. It entails the claim that the Holocaust has no acceptable—that is to say, critically important—parallels in prior mass murders in history. Or to put it more precisely, there are at least one or more aspects of the Holocaust for which one fails to discover historical antecedents. These aspects are of compelling interest to us. I have chosen the latter approach.

vii

Mass murder is not new in history; bureaucratized mass murder *sine ira et studio* is. The Holocaust was a bureaucratically administered program to eliminate an alleged political surplus population. Millennia of religious, social, and political anti-Semitism failed in generating a society-wide effort to kill the Jews that could stand in meaningful comparison to Germany's attempted "final solution of the Jewish problem" during the Third Reich. Moreover, while the history of collective violence is one replete with ample justifications covering both ideal and material interests, one searches in vain for any justifications of the Holocaust adequately related to the scope of this undertaking. We know that Hitler did not need Treblinka to legitimate his rule. We also know that only the pursuit of empire, the big show in modern German political history, provided the necessary cover for the "final solution," which was in fact a sideshow in the effort of the German people to become a superpower. We may not know much about the limits of Hitler's power, but when peasant women could beat up SA men over a religious issue in school policy and make them disappear for good, and when wives of Jewish husbands could "force" the Gestapo in Berlin in 1943 to release their spouses with the simple but publicly uttered demand, "Give us our husbands back" (Peterson, 1969:404–27; Leuner, 1966:103), then we do know enough to realize: (1) only a moral indifference so vast and so deep as to defy initial comprehension made the Holocaust possible; (2) that same moral indifference played a central role in Germany's suicidal drive toward empire; and (3) since the collective affairs of societies are primarily the affairs of elites, only an understanding of a hitherto unparalleled capacity for amoral role behavior among the members of German's elites can shed light on that aspect of the Holocaust that makes it unique for us. Making these three points and explaining how so much moral indifference could come to pass is the purpose of the book.

Work on separate portions of my effort has stretched over several years. Many have contributed, but I name only those without whose encouragement the book would not have been done. My intellectural debts to the work of Hannah Arendt and Talcott Parsons remain indelible. In essence, what I do in this book amounts to the use of some of the powerful theoretical tools Talcott Parsons gave us to provide empirical moorings to Hannah Arendt's unsurpassed insight into the nature of modern evil. Many years ago the Canada Council gave me a year off from teaching duties, one I spent to gain some familiarity with modern German social history. Martha Baum, my wife, is also my professional colleague. Her ability for empathy across cultures makes my life possible, not to mention my professional existence. This book appears under my authorship only because mine alone is the responsibility for its content; otherwise, her presence in it is more pervasive than another we co-authored. John Marx's interest in the topic has been unflagging over several years, and it is extremely gratifying to know that his interest will persist. No one can be an author without a publisher risking a venture with him; and so I owe a great debt to Jim Feather. Last but not least, while several of our secretaries in the department have helped with typing, it has been the angelic patience of Mrs. Mary Ann Knott that sustained the effort in the last few months. I owe completion of the book to her.

Pittsburgh, Pa.
August 1980

CHAPTER ONE

Introduction

> The wild grasses rustle over Babii Yar.
> The trees look ominous, like judges.
> Here all things scream silently and,
>   baring my head,
> Slowly I feel myself turning grey.
> —Yevgeney Yevtushenko

Words of poetry, so sparse and lean. They recall one instance in a sea of events that was the Holocaust. And so, they tell of an eddy in an ocean of suffering and pain, of dying and death so utterly meaningless and so vast as to dim all horizons. Words of poetry . . . only the outline of a theme but evoking a yearning for a symphony of remembrance and witness, one hitherto silent, not played publicly. Words of poetry . . . compelling us to remember what we cannot bear during the day yet cannot forget at night, urging us to see what we do not wish to acknowledge: that simply to know about the Holocaust, some unlimited desire for knowledge, is as inherently immoral as the unlimited pursuit of any interest. For who can be just curious about the Holocaust? Could one justify curiosity about history here? And if not, what ends are to be served by another book?

One answer is that if we are to overcome our inadequacy of mourning, perhaps even our inability to mourn (Mitscherlich and Mitscherlich, 1970), we must still learn what it is we need to commemorate. Apparently, the victims sensed that something utterly extraordinary was happening to them. Their will to persist, to survive as long as possible derived from an unquenchable need to give witness, to let a world that did not care to know, know after all (Donat, 1963; Steiner, 1967). At issue is the uniqueness of the Holocaust.

Hannah Arendt, more than any other student, described that uniqueness in her formulation of the banality of modern evil. Her suggestion seems to be that evil itself *can* be banal, thus appearing in a form radically

1

different from our traditional understanding of it. In its new cloth the victim still recognizes evil, but the perpetrator of it scarcely knows what he does. In her *Origins of Totalitarianism* and her report on Eichmann's trial, Arendt (1951; 1963) alerted us to the new situation in two ways. First, we should not assume that it takes psychopathology to be engaged in mass murder. Completely normal human beings can do it. Second, we can no longer trust that extraordinary action requires extraordinary motivation. Completely ordinary people can do the extraordinary, engage in mass murder, *without* first becoming extraordinary themselves through one or both of the traditional historical mechanisms that always transformed ordinary men and women into unusual characters: (1) conversion to charismatic beliefs legitimating their extraordinary actions or (2) response to an offer of material inducement so tempting as to prove irresistible. However indirectly, with these two observations Hannah Arendt hinted at a principle of adequate motivational causality as defining the boundaries of the human condition and behavior we call human by virtue of falling within them. The more unusual the behavior, the more extraordinary that motive must be. And where, in the past, we failed to discover either the power of charismatic belief or the powers of greed that lead men into temptation at the root of unusual behavior, we located the cause of it in psychopathology. That strategy reassured our common-sense trust in our notions as to the nature of human action. With the figure of Adolf Eichmann, a person neither sick, nor a "true believer" in race ideology, nor, finally, a person ever unusually rewarded in money, perks, or rank, but just an ordinary *Obersturmbannführer* and yet a central organizer of the Holocaust, Hannah Arendt invites us to acknowledge this page in our history as a step beyond the human condition.

In her view, "that step beyond" covered more than the systematic destruction of human life. Part of a radically new form of political rule, totalitarianism, the destruction of life deemed unworthy was linked to as radical a pursuit of the construction of some new human order. And destruction and construction were premised on a radical commitment to the proposition that, for modern men and women, the word "impossible" can and must be stricken from the vocabulary. Totalitarian rule involves the deliberate shattering of all hitherto accepted constraints on human action, and the pursuit of a fictitious world that proceeds by the institutionalization of uncertainty in social life. This hypothesis caused considerable difficulties in explaining mass murder as well as the nature of the disordered society of which it was supposed to form an inherent part. One main difficulty was her notion that normal human beings can act quite abnormally without being abnormal. The very idea that normal and ordinary people were involved tempts us, over again, to seek the explanation of extraordinary events in extraordinary motives. Even in the latest, and perhaps first truly sociological account of genocide, anti-Semitism plays a central role (Fein, 1979). Yet everybody knows that the Holocaust engine destroyed the Gypsies just as systematically as the Jews, and that hundreds of thousands of Poles and millions of Russians perished in it as well. But no one has ever heard of anti-Gypsyism. Additionally stressing the theme of normal human beings behaving rationally, Fein (1979) then argues for the needs of new political authorities to legitimate their power position as a causal factor and compares human destruction under National Socialism to the massacre of the Armenians under Turkish rule. Thus again one locates the Holocaust within the human condition, and so within the realm of familiar and even rational human conduct. I do not think Treblinka, the phenomenon of the pure death factory, belongs there. To imply that the Nazi regime needed mass murder to legitimate itself is contradicted by the fact that the nature of the "final solution of the Jewish question" was an official state secret in Germany at the time. Fein's legitimation thesis also requires us to forget that Hitler gained all the legitimacy he needed by ending the economic chaos of the 1930s in Germany faster and more effectively than any other Western government.

To avoid misunderstanding, I am not suggesting that anti-Semitism was irrelevant. The Holocaust is unthinkable without Hitler, Goebbels, Streicher and that minority circle of "pornographic anti-Semites" (Höhne, 1967:303) in strategic positions. There were true believers, they did hate with passion. What I am suggesting is equally well known. The Holocaust remains unthinkable also without the involvement of hundreds of thousands of normal people, neither true believers nor gaining materially in any way commensurate with their contributions to mass murder. In short, despite the many facts one can marshal to demonstrate the play of varied, numerous "material" *and* "ideal" interests within Germany and occupied Europe more generally, theoretical approaches to the Holocaust that rely importantly on either or both of these factors tend to conceal rather than reveal a third and at least equally important factor: our ability to respond with profound moral indifference to the fate of our fellow human beings in modern times. It is moral indifference, the ability not to care that gives the Holocaust a radically distinctive and modern face.

To some extent responding with moral indifference to the fate of our fellow men is built into the very fabric of modern life. When we hear about violent crime, about murder and rape, and see the victims on the television tube, then these victims and their fate remain for most of us most of the time just statistics. And as some wit remarked, a statistic is people with the tears wiped off. Also, treatment of others and of ourselves in a compartmentalized fashion where we pay attention to only one aspect of human existence, the work role, that of the patient, or the welfare recipient, is part and parcel of everyday existence. To an important degree the organization of modern social life demands that we treat each other as statistics. No doubt, that entails often more thoughtlessness than was possible in pre-industrial social orders. Our ability to treat each other as mere statistics *should* worry us. One simple glance at the nature of social bonds that enable us to treat each other with moral responsibility should suffice to make the point. Having a sense of moral responsibility about our fellow men means caring about them as persons, not just as useful role partners at work, or at play, or in any other special-purpose association. For as mere objects of utility we treat each other as exchangeable. The *social* preconditions for moral responsibility and indifference are anchored directly in the nature of the social ties we maintain with each other. Caring about another as a person is almost unavoidable when we maintain multidimensional bonds with him, knowing about him as a worker, a father, a voter, a neighbor, a football fan, and so on. The near-inevitability of responding to another with moral concern was a characteristic of traditional village life. Villagers could hate each other, love each other, or orient with ambivalence to each other. The one thing they were scarcely capable of was mutual indifference. Traditional society was also a house of bondage, of moral bondage, you might say. Tradition did not grant privacy to individuals; everyone had to be responsive to others, whatever the nature of their claims to attention. Modernity grants privacy and freedom, including that temptation of freedom not to care. More, not caring about another as a person comes easy when we know the other only in one role context; for modern men and women everywhere orienting to others outside the circles of friendship and kinship with detachment, with indifference, as if they were but statistics comes very easy indeed. It is a feature built into the fabric of freedom in differentiated, functionally specialized modern society. And so we have good cause to worry about remaining human, which is to say creatures with a caring moral concern for one another as citizens. Milgram's (1974) rigged obedience experiments provide sufficient reasons for concern. They showed that the vast majority of normal Americans from all walks of life, and so average men and women like you and me, are capable of inflicting severe pain on their fellow human beings, and just on the word of a university professor and merely in response to a bit of pharaseology like "the advancement of science." These experiments were called the Eichmann experiments, suggesting that we are not killers or Nazi medical doctors experimenting on concentration-camp inmates because we merely lack the opportunity.

Our thoughtlessness and ability to abdicate personal responsibility to some authority figure does constitute an element of analogy to obedience in the Third Reich. But an analogy is not an identity. And we should not use self-doubt to raise the question *Are We All Nazis?* (Askenasy, 1978). That is the wrong question, and confusion mushrooms from pursuing it. Askenasy is a thoughtful person, a scholar and a human being who cares deeply. But he slid down the slippery road from analogy to identity with terrible results. In his opinion, Babii Yar is just like My Lai, the Holocaust like Vietnam, and Goebbels' anti-Semitic pharaseology like any religion (all merely sacred cows). Then the heart cries out in pain; handwringing ensues about the old refrain of man's inhumanity to man, and the distinctiveness of modern evil, the institutionalization of moral indifference as a principle of governance that became a reality in the Third Reich, is lost again. The survivors made themselves survive so that we attend to that difference. It is not the fact of thoughtlessness in human life and suffering that is the issue. Raising thoughtlessness to a general principle of conduct is. We do no honor to the survivors and do not learn what it is we mourn by forgetting that difference.

The difference was clearly identified by Rubenstein (1975). It refers to the fact that in distinction to prior mass murders in human history, the *Holocaust Kingdom*, as some of the survivors referred to it (Donat, 1963), or *l'universe concentrationnaire*, as the French have called it, was a *bureaucratically* administered extermination of surplus populations in the service of an abstract goal, creating *Lebensraum* for Germans in a proclaimed New Order of Europe. And, I would add, it was possible *only* because the very impersonality of the bureaucratic spirit had been developed to a point where the pursuit of so abstract a goal, that identifying trait of genuine bureaucracy, no longer needed any morally compelling and therefore emotionally experienced legitimation at the level of concrete human beings who participated in its accomplishment.

Oppression and persecution, enslavement and killing belong to the human condition. But throughout human history, where man destroyed another, he never lacked ample, often impressively ingenious justifications for his action. These could range from a modest disguising of plain material interests as in American slavery (Cash, 1941) to the construction of an intricate demonology, counterposing the image of the Devil to that of God, and so completing the apperception of true good by a counter concept of true evil, as in the European witch craze (Trevor-Roper, 1969). But with the Holocaust Kingdom we encounter the *total* bureaucratic machine, disposable toward any end, *because* so many in Germany generated no effective demand for the legitimation of the "final solution of the Jewish question."

In Hobbes' (1881:91–96) original sociological model of hell we still find a very human portrait. For his "war of all against all" was not only plausibly motivated; it was indeed the hypothetical outcome of no less a source of human action than man's ability to reason, his rational pursuit of self-interest. Being a very "hard nosed" empirical realist, Hobbes argued that the simple realization of men's dependency on other men for what each wants *must* lead all to seek power over other men with all means, notably fraud and force; and where each acts according to the rational imperative of the maximization of power over other men, the eventual outcome must be suicidal where the lives of men become truly "nasty, brutish, and short." That human model of hell remains very instructive for an understanding of the domestic and foreign-policy conduct of the German nation. Consider, the modern nation-state of Germany was only born in 1871. Remember, it was born by the sword; a few successful cabinet wars between Prussia and other powers, culminating in the Franco-German conflict, led to the birth of the nation, abroad, at Versailles. Just a lifetime of an individual elapsed; seventy-five years later, in 1945, the nation that was born of war perished in one. Today there are two German states, the German Democratic Republic in the East and the Federal Republic in the West—not exactly a return to the many ministates of the German people early in the nineteenth century, but indicating a disastrous failure in modern nation-building nonetheless. During this short time, Germany struggled twice for world-power status. That was always the main show. In the First and Second World Wars the nature of the political regimes differed and so did the slogans, but the reach for world-power status was the same. The "splendor of Versailles in 1871" gave way to the "doom of Versailles in 1919." And one may gaze on modern German history as a veritable tale told by an idiot, like a collective psychodrama (Binion, 1976) where a people strains to undo itself twice over. Hitler promised the German people to undo the 1919 doom of Versailles and a Germany they would not recognize. By following him, the Germans also undid the Versailles of 1871, their birth, and made the prophecy come true. Only, the tools of psychoanalysis remain precarious instruments to study the history of a nation. One risks the creation of a myth, a myth of hidden reason where there was none; and a myth resulting from projection of that inner madness of which perhaps only intellectuals are capable onto hard-nosed businessmen trying to make profits, generals concerned with victory in battles, and above all bureaucratic functionaries engaged in the never-ending game of the advance and the defense of particular institutional interests. For understanding German national history Hobbes remains more relevant than Freud. At least leaning more on Hobbes, as I shall do, yields one clear advantage: It keeps our eyes glued to the main show and thereby reveals the truly diabolical character of the Holocaust, which is to be found in the fact that it was a sideshow.

The accomplishment of the Holocaust required many normal people. This industrialization of killing could not have been done by pathological monsters, seething with inner rage, nor by true believers, charismatically fired up to implement ideals, nor finally, by men and women tempted by others of status or material advantages they could not afford to turn down. Instead, it required sober bureaucratic functionaries or technicians (Steiner, 1967). And in their participation, which makes this mass murder different from all others and unique, we find *one* aspect of our history and therefore *one* feature of human potentiality that corresponds to a sociological conception of ultimate hell: the creation of meaningless suffering and the imposition of senseless death. Man's ability to exclude his fellow man from the human realm and to destroy him without any need to explicate to himself his deed, this is what is meant here as the realization of ultimate hell. This is what happened with the aid of the German state. Note that the destruction of German Jewry certainly was *not* the simple elimination of some foreign people under conditions of war. Rather, the Nazis first had to use the tools of a modern nation-state, its rational-legal authority, to exclude German citizens of Jewish ethnic origin *or* religious affiliation (*Glaubensjuden*, as Nazi bureaucratese referred to them) from the universe of moral obligations. And only having excluded them could they be led to slaughter. And their death, as well as that of so many others—the Jews of occupied Europe, the Gypsies, the leading strata of Polish society, the sick and no longer useful Russian POWs—served no institutional purpose. It had very little if anything to do with Hitler's role as a charismatic leader. Millions perished because of a profound moral indifference, one institutionalized in German society and already present long before Hitler appeared. Demonstrating that is my objective. If we can agree that it is human to kill, even on a grand scale, so long as either the passion of belief, or the powers of greed, or the forces of psychological abnormality are somehow commensurate with the scale of destruction, and agree on this point simply because the destruction of man by man looms so large in our common history, then we find that the few like Hitler who were true believers and who hated with passion belong inside the human condition. To them our normal moral repertoire of concepts and judgments, of sin and atonement applies. Potentially, Hitler can be forgiven, however weird his vision. But the many who just stood by or murdered with so profound an indifference placed themselves beyond and indeed outside the human condition. They cannot be forgiven because the language and thought of moral judgment in their very design apply only to the human condition.

The distinction, I am emphasizing here, between actions falling within the human condition and those falling outside it, or representing a step beyond it, has not received the attention it deserves. It was one central to the efforts of the late Hannah Arendt; hers was a focus not only on people but also on the social conditions under which they lived. Already in her *Origins of Totalitarianism* (Arendt, 1951) she emphasized the importance of recognizing that the killers were normal, average men. Thus she described the banality of evil as the distinctive feature of modern evil long before she actually coined the term, which she did in her report on Eichmann's trial in Jerusalem (Arendt, 1963). The meaningless destruction of human life was, in her eyes, part of the larger story of the modernization of societies. That is why she deemed a sociological approach appropriate. That story was one of whole societies bent on self-destruction, engaging in a kind of collective suicide, in which the very foundations of human order were subjected to some systematic step-by-step destruction. Whereas we used to think of beings as human insofar as they acted meaningfully—indeed, strove for meaning in their lives—she discerned in totalitarian elites role players on the order of experimental scientists, and so, people committed to trying out everything that some "fascinating theory" implies. The difference was one of selecting the experimental subject. Totalitarian elites experimented with societies. And their corresponding political credo was institutionalized cynicism, a cynicism so deep as to make the question of any serious meaning in their experimental play as superfluous as the alleged value of human life they extinguished. Destratification of social inequalities, or what she called the rise of "modern classless mass society," was Hannah Arendt's main explanatory variable. Loss of common sense (even the abandonment of an "instinct of self-preservation") and the organized pursuit of the implications of a fictitious dream—the totalitarian mystique, to use a term by Inkeles (1954)—were her intervening factors; and a society locked into a course of self-destruction, one that could only be stopped from the outside through war between nations, was her outcome variable. Now, her last point proved erroneous. Even her model of "totalitarian disorder" as a mode of governance was too systemic, assigning too much of a function to human destruction. In the case of Stalinism, the significant attenuation of the Gulag Archipelago since Khrushchev proved her wrong. But that is insufficient reason to abandon her central concern with the nature of modern evil. Yet this is precisely what has been happening. More of that in the next chapter. Here I comment only on three further matters. A more precise description of my subject matter is the first; what I do not cover and why, the second; and some difficulties in addressing the nature of modern, because banal, evil comes last.

My subject matter is moral indifference, not the moral indifference in German society in general but that prevalent among the elites. I want to explore and explain why so many in leading positions in the Third Reich participated in or tolerated the mass murder of the Jews, and of the Gypsies, when that organized mass murder of unarmed minorities neither served their ideal, nor their material interests; when in fact it threatened their institutional responsibilities, and so their status and material interests, through diverting manpower and material from the war effort. Consider, forced labor, and therefore slavery, was a fact in the Third Reich at war (Homze, 1967). And the enslavement of Jews and Gypsies, even their destruction through working them to death, would have contained this chapter of our history within the human condition. Slavery is an ancient institution, outmoded now. But it was once widespread, a real human institution, which means a legitimated one. And normally, so we are wont to believe, men and women never lack the imagination to relegitimate ancient customs when they deem them useful for their current aims. Parts of Auschwitz can be subsumed under the label of slavery because so many inmates worked there in factories. But neither its death camp, Birkenau, nor any of the other four pure death factories can be subsumed under any label familiar in human history. People in leading positions "knew" about the production of death. But they knew about it with their minds, seeing reality as some statistical abstraction. They did not acknowledge reality with their hearts because they did not care. They also "knew" that mass murder served only the private passionate hate of Hitler and a tiny Nazi Party minority of true believers in the racial myth, but they did not care to acknowledge that fully either. Yet without their willing cooperation or simple tolerance, the Holocaust would have been impossible. For them it was a sideshow, something you did not bother about while engaged in the big show, securing a place for yourself in the wonderland of the Nazi New Order in Europe. Let us not be misled by a misconception. Hitler's totalitarian state was not a power monolith where the will of one or of a few men turned the rest of society into robots, responding in total obedience like the circuits of a computer to the nimble fingers of two hands on the keyboard. Protest, under wartime conditions, almost stopped the euthanasia program of the mentally deficient and otherwise "undesirable." When the Jewish husbands of mixed marriages were to be deported from Berlin, their wives protested in demonstrations and had their husbands released and saved (Adler, 1974:307). But, so far as is known, only one other public demonstration against deportations ever occurred in Germany. And that remained fruitless. Germans simply did not care about the fate of the Jews (Adler, 1974:332). Further, the prewar years of National Socialism provide numerous examples of Hitler caving in to opposition against his policies whenever such opposition threatened his leadership *or* the big show, rearmament and preparation for war. In the Church conflict, in disputes over economic policies, and in challenges to the Army's monopoly claim over the nation's war machinery there were definite limits to Hitler's power (Peterson, 1969; Müller, 1969). So that history tells us that any serious opposition to Treblinka from any elite quarter critical in the big show—the Army leadership, business circles, the security apparat, the Churches—to say nothing of a combined protest, would permit us today to read the history of the Second World War just as it is, *except* those pages dealing with the Holocaust engine. They would be missing from the record. They are in it only because the German elites did not care about the fate of the Jews.

I am not directly concerned with moral indifference among the general population in Germany nor with that displayed by lower-level officialdom in the numerous government agencies handling Jewish affairs. The main reason is that the moral indifference among these people about the fate of the Jews, covering both the deprivation of all civil rights and their death, does not strike me as problematical. As to the general population, three reasons dictate this dismal perspective. First, the Jewish minority in Germany was so tiny as to make the experience of seeing a Jewish neighbor subjected to the loss of civil rights—becoming an outcast, losing his job, his home, and being shipped off—an exceedingly rare phenomenon. Jews made up but 1 percent of the population in 1871; by 1939, about two years before the deportations began, only about .33 percent remained (Steinert, 1977:133). Our "average man," even if he lived in Berlin or Frankfurt, where this minority was somewhat concentrated, would have had to look rather hard to meet a Jew personally. In Germany, for most people, Jews were mythical figures of Nazi propaganda, which is to say, they were abstractions, not real people; and in war particularly, propaganda abstractions do not touch us personally. Second, the fact of the physical destruction of the Jews was a state secret in Germany. For a person either favorably or neutrally disposed toward the Nazi regime hearing about the fate of the Jews "in the East" was a rumor. A rumor is not the truth. Third, since human death in wartime is nothing shocking at all but rather an everyday normal reality, there was no reasonable motive to follow up on rumors. You could even believe that rumor was fact, but then it remained a statistic, like the daily casualty bulletin from the front and from the bombing raids at home; and statistics do not arouse us. On the other hand, if you were an opponent of the regime, you credited the regime with atrocities anyway and had long become emotionally numb about it. As to lower officials who handled Jewish affairs, they handled paper, and so excessive a flood of forms recording the smallest detail of the stripping of Jews' rights and possessions as to turn the administration of people into the management of abstractions, or again statistics; and statistics are people with the tears wiped off. Such forms contained a name all right, but that, as in the nature of government forms, was the only human touch. The rest of the message was "bureaucratese" with references to laws, paragraphs, sections, and subsections, administrative decrees, or implementation decrees with their numbered sections and subsections (Adler, 1974). People whose job it is to apply procedure to the processing of other people, and so incredibly detailed procedures that demanded even the listing of the number of napkins in a Jewish household as the Nazi regime prescribed, literally do not see the people they process even if they stand right in front of them. For these sectors of German society, then, not caring was very easy—too easy, perhaps—and too obvious and familiar a feature of modern life to be worth investigating again.

My concern is with elites, the leading strata of German society in the economy, academe, government, and, above all, the armed forces. Their indifference strikes me as problematical first, because elites must be concerned with the legitimacy of their actions, almost by definition. Cracks in the legitimacy of behavior here translate themselves, almost automatically, so we normally believe, into doubts about the legitimacy of superior position. Being a member of an elite always entails a concern with tending the plants in the legitimacy front yard of the house of superior social position. This indifference to the loss of all civil rights of the Jews among elites strikes me as problematical. Second, whether as employers of slave labor, or as drafters of legislation, whether as railroad brass or as higher civil servants in the Ministries of Finance, External Affairs, and Internal Affairs, or finally, as Army commanders in the East, members of elite strata were close enough to mass murder to find out the truth. They were so close that not knowing took effort, if we postulate normal people possessed of just normal curiosity. Thus on grounds of both position and access to knowledge they should have cared. They did not. Finding out why not is the central focus of my effort.

In the third chapter I present an interpretive theoretical model to account for this profound and historically unprecedented moral indifference among the German elites. That model is one of the big show, Germany's repeated reach for empire, her double attempt to become a world power through waging war. And that procedure assigns the Holocaust its proper place, one so difficult to comprehend and accept precisely because it was a meaningless sideshow.

In subsequent chapters I turn to empirical evidence relating to the interpretive model. There you find data on value cleavages in German society; on the emergence of what I call "one-dimensional elites"; on the disappearance of social honor from social life, and the complete privatization of morals; on the ever-increasing militancy of social conflicts in Germany's history of modernization; and finally, on the loss of self-steering capacity in that nation, a matter that I treat as the sociological equivalent of Hannah Arendt's repeated emphasis of the abandonment of common sense under totalitarian rule.

Thus my effort does not "deal" with the Holocaust itself. I try to unearth the cultural and social sources of that profound moral indifference among Germany's elites that made it possible. Note that I speak here of a mere possibility that became reality. Nothing in the short history of the modern German nation-state made the Holocaust a necessity. But there was much in it that made it possible. On the critical question of my effort, which is whether the Nazis had to proceed to the final solution of their Jewish problem to maintain themselves in power, Helen Fein's affirmative answer is simply wrong, whatever the undoubted other merit of her work. The Holocaust was the realization of ultimate hell (Des Pres, 1976), ultimate because suffering, pain, and death on so vast a scale *without serving any* institutional interests remains unknown in prior human history. We should not use a commitment to social science as the study of recurrent phenomena to mitigate that fact. And that is why the question of how one does "deal" with such a subject must be addressed. This is not just a question of taste, which, here, is serious enough. It is a matter that goes much deeper. If we regard the Holocaust as a step beyond the human condition, we face issues relating to our identity, the nature of modern man in Germany and elsewhere, who we are and how we are to relate ourselves to the victims of our disregard. These are questions difficult to address in Western civilization apart from religion. I believe we are not yet ready to face them in religious terms. To illustrate, the question has been raised whether Auschwitz signals "The Beginning of a New Era?" (Fleischner, 1977). So far, I think, we must answer in the negative. And that confronts us with the problem that for modern men and women knowledge is one thing, acknowledgment of both the reality and the moral significance of what we know is another. In our day, the only really recognized knowledge is scientific. On a somewhat lower level, responsible journalism still inspires respect for common-sense knowledge. And for access to the morally relevant in our lives we tend to rely more and more on the administration of law. Religion we do not seem to use anymore for knowing about ourselves. Now, science, journalism, and the practice of law all share with the administration of the Holocaust one element: the professional cool, and so precisely that tool that we use to know but not to acknowledge the moral significance of what we know.

There are problems with our modern ways of knowing. They seem to be modes of knowing that blind us, modes of knowing that literally after tons of print somehow seduce us into not acknowledging the reality of what we know. Hannah Arendt knew. She was a courageous person, one not deterred by prevailing research conventions. But in sociology no one stepped into her footsteps, subjecting her seminal ideas to more rigorous tests. Let us consider some possible reasons why.

First, a social-scientific approach to the problem of moral indifference in the Holocaust itself poses moral dilemmas. One bears on the nature of the concern itself. That involves some subtle and not so clear distinctions among various motives of the murderer and/or the bystander, and worse yet, somehow the identity of their sons and daughters. Even though the victims themselves may have sensed something of the extraordinarily new in their suffering and death, common sense keeps pressing in on us, insisting that subtle differences in motives of the killer scarcely could have mattered to their victims. Solzhenitsyn (1975:91) goes so far as to express outright contempt for the idea that the presence of the pure death factory in the Holocaust Kingdom and its absence in the Gulag Archipelago has any moral significance whatsoever for the suffering victim. And so, the odor of self-indulgence, of a concern with the victimizers rather than their victims seems to cling to a concern with the nature and the causes of the banality of modern evil, our capacity for moral indifference. But then, no less than some survivors counsel us—indeed, urge us—not to be deterred by such implications. Langbein (1972) survived Auschwitz. He chose the title of his book, *Menschen in Auschwitz*, with deliberate care, telling us that a human community organized for the production of death, can be and was one where normal humans lived, nonetheless. Adler (1955), survivor of Theresienstadt, model camp to fool the International Red Cross, and transit camp for the selection and shipment of humans doomed to perish in the East, tells a similar story in his *Theresienstadt 1941–1945: Das Antlitz einer Zwangsgemeinschaft*. Literally translated, the German *Zwangsgemeinschaft* means force-based community, a community based on nothing but brute force, but a community where people cooperated, nonetheless. His later analysis of Gestapo files tells the tale of the exclusion of Jews from German society; freely translated, its title is *Administered Humanity* (Adler, 1974). It gives powerful evidence how bureaucracy in Germany developed to the point of a complete transformation from historical political rule with domination of man over man to the administration of things and with consequences undreamed of at the time of Saint-Simon. This brings to attention another moral dilemma in approaching this topic with the tools of social science. The world of science and that of the camps shared one element: orienting to one's conduct in a manner of objective detachment.

Steiner (1967) referred to the killers in Treblinka as technicians, and scientists are technicians as well. The very professional cool of the language of social science, its ugliness apart, strikes one as offensive when applied to so much suffering. Writing about the Holocaust and features of German society that relate to it demand some special language of taboo, one that while communicating what we comprehend does so in a mode simultaneously paying respect to the victims. I have no literary skills adequate to the task; perhaps noting this explicitly, as I do here, can excuse my deficiency somewhat. Even though poorly equipped, one writes because the topic is too important to make literary skills the decisive consideration.

Another limitation of a social-scientific approach is cognitive. These disciplines are designed for the study of meaningful behavior. Practically all theoretical concepts in our repertoire are linked to axioms stating that human action involves some striving for meaning. Max Weber's work as a whole, for example, was based on the assumption that some striving for comprehensive meaning in life is distinctive of the human species. Human behavior is deemed intentional or purposeful. Men and women relate means to ends they seek to accomplish, and evaluate themselves and each other in their conduct accordingly. That makes difficult the study of purposelessness, or of moral indifference as a feature characterizing a whole society. Imagining a given individual as an uncaring bystander is one thing, because we always discover that he cares about something after all. Envisaging a whole network of organizations as some free-floating bit of unleashed social energy, unanchored in purposes and slashing out violently in all directions, not so bad an image of Nazi Germany, is more difficult. The tools of social science were not really designed for such an image of reality.

Also, there is the problem of uniqueness. Sociologists do not study unique events, normally. And in regarding the Holocaust as merely another instance of man's inhumanity to man, we insult the survivor. Let us see how. In sociology it was perhaps only Max Weber who self-consciously committed himself to the sociological analysis of historical particulars. His basic strategy entailed working with universal variables, applicable to all societies, and seeking for a particular constellation of values on such variables as the explanation of a particular historical event. Most of us sociologists learn about this in graduate school with lengthy discussions about the nature of ideal-type concepts. Discussions notwithstanding, the study of unique phenomena is not exactly in vogue in sociology. Sociologists study recurrent phenomena; only that seems scientific. If the Holocaust appears in a textbook at all, it appears as merely an extreme case of oppressive ethnic-group relations, and Hitler is treated in one breath with so traditional a tyrant as Idi Amin (Goodman and Marx, 1978:293). The *de facto* commitment to science as a study of recurrent phenomena "forces" sociologists to disregard the witness of the survivors who sensed that something utterly exceptional and new was happening to them. They risked their very humanity in survival and did so only because of their unique fate. Never forget, you could survive in Treblinka *only* by becoming a tool of destruction (Steiner, 1967). Wittingly or not, a treatment of Nazi anti-Semitism as just another case of minority relations, however extreme, designates the survivor as a simple collaborator with the Nazis. That is not just false, it is also immoral. A collaborator is one who faces the ancient question of who shall live and who shall die in a situation where one expects that some will survive even if you do nothing. The Holocaust survivor faced a completely different dilemma, namely whether anyone would survive to give witness if you did nothing. And so he made himself do something, participate in murder, in order to survive and give witness, for your sake and mine. In Treblinka there was a lot of suicide at first. When an organization for survival and witness sprang up, the members deprived others whom they needed from committing suicide, that human way out of the dilemma. That does not transform people into angels. Nothing does. When life in Treblinka neared its end, guards and inmates fraternized with each other, sharing a common table, laughter and sorrow and each other, feasting into the night, only to return to the work of killing the next morning. They too coped as humans are wont to with ending a community (Steiner, 1967). Limited contemporary experience with terrorists has accustomed us to refer to such a phenomenon as "bonding" between captor and captive. But instead of debating the question of the Jews' collaboration in their own destruction, as some have done (Krummacher, 1964; Lendvai, 1971:191), the gift of the survivors' witness imposes on us another obligation. That is to seek comprehension of the realization of ultimate hell, however difficult the apprehension of unique evil may be.

Still, it is questionable, very questionable whether another book on this page of our history can make any difference. Much, very much has been written about the Holocaust. For example, covering only the years 1945 to 1968 and only material about the Germans and the Jews, one estimate listed 7,603 scholarly books and articles about the subject (*Der Spiegel*, 6/15/1970:131). In addition, we have millions of pages of court testimony and a huge amount of newspaper reports publicizing the trials. All of this knowledge has existed for decades, apparently without much public impact. Then, finally, one is almost tempted to say, the search for profit led to the production of a TV movie on the Holocaust. And that, if viewer reaction can be a guide, and I think it can, made the Holocaust part of our history, a reality, and so part of ourselves, certainly in Germany and probably elsewhere (*Der Spiegel*, 1/29/1979:17–34). The movie brought catharsis to Germans and many in America, transforming what had been known privately with the mind into a public and therefore widely shared acknowledgment of reality with the heart. This belated awakening to the reality of our recent history clearly refers more to the sons and daughters of the murderers and the bystanders, that "Gentile" world, than to the survivors of the Holocaust and their offspring, the Jewish community. But that scarcely diminishes one's concern with knowing something in distinction to learning meaningfully about ourselves. Apparently, it was neither the pursuit of truth through scholarship or science, nor that of justice by means of law, neither the pursuit of relevant common-sense knowledge through journalism nor, finally, the passage of time that brought the Holocaust home to so many. Instead, the pursuit of profit through mass entertainment proved the superior teacher. Perhaps I attribute too much message power to the medium here. As we know from the introduction of the Holocaust into the curriculum of public schools in New York City and the erection of a Holocaust memorial in New Haven, Connecticut, some public awakening in America preceded the TV movie. Nonetheless, with so much written material available for so long a time and so little response to it, one may ask: Do the "clinical" or "objective" ways of reporting truth, which we have come to insist upon as the only valid modes of knowing, only supply us with abstract knowledge where events and people become statistics, meaningful to specialists and their concerns, but meaningless to most of us as persons and citizens?

There may be a connection between the modern ways of knowing in their cloak of objectivity devoid of any emotion, and the way the event itself was experienced on the part of the murderer and the bystander, as well as, finally, the passage of time before we acknowledged the reality of the Holocaust. If we ask why it took so long for any visible public impact of the Holocaust to materialize after 1945, our first supposition points to repression of reality and the need for the passage of time to create more distance between ourselves and these events before we could face them. But that hypothesis implies guilt. A contrary opinion may hold that there was never guilt because, at the time when it happened, this mass murder was experienced as just an abstraction outside the circle of victims: Nothing was repressed in the first place because nothing to repress was apprehended; and it took time to gain access to the reality of the past. Perhaps it is far more easy for modern men and women to treat their fellow human beings as mere statistics than the teachers of methodology in the social sciences with their laborious modes of inculcating students with the need for and the skills of taking an objective perspective are inclined to assume. In any event, the comparative failure to teach us on the part of historical scholarship, law, and journalism remains impressive. The movie, in contrast, reduced the scale of these events to the level of plausible comprehension of family life, and so made history more real, revealing its moral significance. Moving pictures transformed mere statistics, concepts, rules of evidence, and the cool of professional journalism, abstractions all, into behavior of real concrete human beings, and so into beings with whom we share an identity, to whom we can react with feeling, and fellow human beings in whom we can see ourselves mirrored as murderers and murdered. And if we grant that grasping the emotional reality of history is a first necessary step in reaching a public and shared apprehension of its moral significance, then it remains a disquieting experience that we owe it more to the pursuit of profit through the marketing of pop culture, that alleged incarnation of contemporary triviality, than to our seemingly more responsible modes of knowing in scholarship and journalism.

And who am I to write about this part of our history? You should know because nothing provides a more powerful bias than caring much about one's subject matter. Let me use my reaction to the movie to tell you who I am. You may recall the scene where the physician's family leaves their apartment. The last thing that mother and daughter do is play the piano and sing a song together. It is the song of the Lorelei. Next to the national anthem, the Lorelei is the most German song. Certainly, every middle-class child learned it at some time. And it is a song expressing the mood of melancholia. Its opening line states *Ich weiss nicht, was soll es bedeuten, dass ich so traurig bin*; freely translated this means: "I do not know what makes me so profoundly sad." That scene moved me more than any other in that movie, one that did not tell me much new. And what does that tell you about me? I was born in Germany, in 1934, and into a middle-class family, a family that always did well, as subjects of the Kaiser, during the Weimar Republic, and during the Third Reich. My father served them all, all with the requisite loyalty as he thought fitting for a soldier and a higher civil servant. My mother had been graduated from the Dresden Conservatory of Music and I had stood often next to our piano, scarcely reaching with my head the height of the keyboard, listening to her, and sometimes singing with her, just like the little girl in the movie. And what was a typical German middle-class family, then and throughout the short history of the modern German nation-state? It was a life dedicated to "nationalism," career, and "*Kultur*," a combination in which only the middle term does not require quotation marks. For now we know: It was a nationalism perverted into its opposite, an uncaring disregard for the nation and its people, and a "*Kultur*" misused as an *Ersatzreligion* with

Beethoven and Goethe the vehicles of the total privatization of moral concern. So now you know who I am, and you may correct the angle of my vision accordingly. And as you do, remember one fact: It was not fanatics who enabled the German Army to walk across the face of Europe; the soberness and diligence of the middle-class folk did, and that German phenomenon, the cultural, noneconomic middle class in particular, these people with their pride in "*Kultur*" who apparently needed a TV movie to wake up to the reality of their deeds.

But not even here can we end this story about the troublesome relation between knowing and learning and properly coping with the witness of the survivor. Even though it occurred but yesterday, the Holocaust is history. That alone, once seen through the lens of the insight of Max Weber and Ranke, puts us in a double bind. From Max Weber (1919b) we learned that scientific truth, that last remaining form of truth in our time, is inherently devoid of any moral, religious, or aesthetic significance. If we are to use the truth for moral ends, we must bring to bear values from outside the house of science onto its products, values that we believe in as human persons, different from and additional to the ones we cherish in our role as investigators. But in order to evade the rampant revisionism, which indeed would make us historyless creatures, Ranke enjoins us to write history as experienced by those who lived it rather than as dictated by the needs of those who come afterward. Thus, from the point of view of the German bystander and some of the murderers at the time, one can describe what happened at Babii Yar with accuracy *and* a terrible simplicity. What happened there was this: Colonel Blobel with a few dozen men of one *Sonderkommando* of one of the four *Einsatzgruppen* operational in the East eliminated the Jews of Kiev—to be precise, 33,771 of them, men, women, and children. The *Aktion* took only two days. With proper attention to organizational detail, timing the loading and trucking of victims, just so; sparing off the executioners each hour, and working from dawn to dusk, that much could be accomplished. The operation was efficient (Musmanno, 1961:156–57). One day the Jews of Kiev were there; two days later, they were gone. And for the student of the moral indifference that made it possible, that is all that happened. If we are to grasp the nature of moral indifference, we must present it accurately, as flat and as cold-blooded and as objective as it was. In one part, and the one that counts here, even the history of the Holocaust, that realization of ultimate hell, must be presented in the form of a bureaucratic memo because it was accomplished by the tools of bureaucracy and in that spirit of impersonality that characterizes bureaucratic administration *and* objective scientific truth alike. Pursuing the truth farther here may produce only more words, words that do not touch and alter us because of the way they must be put down, and superfluous ones at that, mere additions to the millions that have already been spoken into the wind. Invoking Tolstoi's passion with the one question of moral signifi-cance—namely, how we must live and how we must die—Weber went so far as to assert the utter meaninglessness of scientific truth on the simple grounds that it could not answer that question. But in terms of common-sense truth, the hope for an answer to that question is the only tolerable reason for writing about this history, even a single line of it.

There is only very little one can do about these limitations of our modes of knowing. That little is to suspend the usual scientific ideal of efficient communication, at least for a moment. That little must be done. Given our only current form of understanding truth, the scientific one, if we are to understand better what were the causes of ultimate evil, and so what happened, and do so in order to advance our ability to mourn, we must select. And all selection from experience is abstraction. But let it come here as a second step. Our first obligation is to remember all those who perished, and especially the members of the *Judenräte*, and those who organized to survive who sensed their complicity and experienced throughout a terror of helplessness hitherto unknown to man. And only having stood there at the gates of hell, in silent imagination as best we can, exposed once again to that ultimate of evil of which we have been capable, may we permit ourselves the comforts of abstraction and a right to hope for learning. Toward this end, let us listen once again, to voices from the "Gentile" world. One belongs to a man, so rare then, one who acknowl-edged the reality he saw while it was in progress, and one who struggled and shouted but found no brethren to share the truth with and stop it. Appropriately, these voices have been quoted so often as to sound utterly familiar to the reader who cares about this part of our history. And so, in listening again, we enter into a kind of ritual, the form of remembrance we still strive to gain (Poliakov, 1954: 193–96, 125–26):

Kurt Gerstein:
   In January, 1942, I was named chief of the Waffen SS technical disinfection services, including a section for extremely toxic gases. . . . One day SS-Sturmbannführer Gunther of the RSHA came into my office, dressed in civilian clothing. I did not know him. He ordered me to get him 100 kilos of prussic acid and to go with him to a place known only to the truck driver. When the truck was loaded, we left for Lublin (Poland). We took along Dr. Pfannenstiel, occupant of the chair of hygiene at the University of Marburg. SS Gruppenführer Globocnik was waiting for us at Lublin. He told us, "This is one of the most secret matters there are, even the most secret. Anybody who talks about it will be shot immediately." He explained to us that there were three installations:
   1. Belzec, on the Lublin-Lwow road. A maximum of 15,000 people per day.

2. Sobibor (I don't know exactly where it is), 20,000 people a day.
3. Treblinka, 120 kilometers NNE of Warsaw.
4. Maidanek, near Lublin (under construction) . . .

The next day we left for Belzec. Globocnik introduced me to SS [Wirth?] who took me around the plant. We saw no dead bodies that day, but a pestilential odor hung over the whole area. Alongside the station there was a "dressing" hut with a window for "valuables." Further on, a room with a hundred chairs, [designated as] "the barber." Then a corridor 150 meters long in the open air, barbed wire on both sides, with signs: "To the baths and inhalants." In front of us a building like a bath house; to the left and right, large concrete pots of geraniums or other flowers. On the roof, the Star of David. On the building a sign: "Heckenholt Foundation."

The following morning, a little before seven there was an announcement: "The first train will arrive in ten minutes!" A few minutes later a train arrived from Lemberg: 45 cars with more than 6,000 people. Two hundred Ukrainians assigned to this work flung open the doors and drove the Jews out of the cars with leather whips. A loud speaker gave instructions: "Strip, even artificial limbs and glasses. Hand all money and valuables in at the 'valuables window.' Women and young girls are to have their hair cut in the 'barber's hut.' " (An SS Unterführer told me: "From that they make something special for submarine crews.")

Then the march began. Barbed wire on both sides, in the rear two dozen Ukrainians with rifles. They drew near. Wirth and I found ourselves in front of the death chambers. Stark naked men, women, children, and cripples passed by. A tall SS man in the corner called to the unfortunates in a loud minister's voice: "Nothing is going to hurt you! Just breathe deep and it will strengthen your lungs. It's a way to prevent contagious diseases. It's a good disinfectant!" They asked him what was going to happen and he answered: "The men will have to work, build houses and streets. The women won't have to do that, they will be busy with the housework and the kitchen." This was the last hope for some of these poor people, enough to make them march toward the death chambers without resistance. The majority knew everything; the smell betrayed it! They climbed a little wooden stairs and entered the death chambers, most of them silently, pushed by those behind them. A Jewess of about forty with eyes like fire cursed the murderers; she disappeared into the gas chambers after being struck several times by Captain Wirth's whip. Many prayed; others asked: "Who will give us the water before we die?" [A Jewish rite] SS men pushed the men into the chambers. "Fill it up," Wirth ordered; 700–800 people in 93 square meters. The doors closed. Then I understood the reason for the "Heckenholt" sign. Heckenholt was the driver of the Diesel, whose exhaust was to kill these poor unfortunates. SS Unterscharführer Heckenholt tried to start the motor. It wouldn't start! Captain Wirth came up. You could see he was afraid because I was there to see the disaster. Yes, I saw everything and waited. My stopwatch clocked it all: 50 minutes, 70 minutes, and the Diesel still would not start! The men were waiting in the gas chambers. You could hear them weeping "as though in a synagogue," said Professor Pfannenstiel, his eyes glued to the window in the wooden door. Captain Wirth, furious, struck with his whip the Ukrainian who helped Heckenholt. The Diesel started up after 2 hours and 49 minutes, by my stopwatch. Twenty-five minutes passed. You could see through the window that many were already dead, for an electric light illuminated the interior of the room. All were dead after thirty-two minutes! Jewish workers on the other side opened the wooden doors. They had been promised their lives in return for doing this horrible work, plus a small percentage of the money and valuables collected. The men were still standing, like columns of stone, with no room to fall or lean. Even in death you could tell the families, all holding hands. It was difficult to separate them while emptying the rooms for the next batch. The bodies were tossed out, blue, wet with sweat and urine, the legs smeared with excrement and menstrual blood. Two dozen workers were busy checking mouths which they opened with iron hooks. "Gold to the left, no gold to the right." Others checked anus and genitals, looking for money, diamonds, gold, etc. Dentists knocked out gold teeth, bridges, and crowns, with hammers. Captain Wirth stood in the middle of them. He was in his element, and, showing me a big jam box filled with teeth, said, "See the weight of the gold! Just from yesterday and the day before! You can't imagine what we find every day, dollars, diamonds, gold! You'll see!" He took me over to a jeweler who was responsible for all the valuables. They also pointed out to me one of the heads of the big Berlin store Kaufhaus des Westens, and a little man whom they forced to play the violin, the chiefs of the Jewish workers' commandos. "He is a captain of the Imperial Austrian Army, Chevalier of the German Iron Cross," Wirth told me.

Then the bodies were thrown into big ditches near the gas chambers, about 100 by 20 by 12 meters. After a few days the bodies swelled and the whole mass rose up 2–3 yards because of the gas in the bodies. When the swelling went down several days later, the bodies matted down again. They told me that later they poured Diesel oil over the bodies and burned them on railroad ties to make them disappear.

Hermann Graebe:

I, the undersigned, Hermann Friedrich Graebe, make the following declaration under oath:

From September 1941 to January 1944 I was director and chief engineer of the Sdolbunow branch of the Josef Jung Construction Company of Solingen. In this capacity I had, among my other duties, to visit the firm's projects. Under the terms of a contract with the army construction services, the company was to build grain warehouses on the old Dubno airfield, in the Ukraine.

On October 5, 1942, at the time of my visit to the construction offices in Dubno, my foreman, Hubert Moennikes, living at 21 Aussenmuehlenweg, Hamburg-Haarburg, told me that some Dubno Jews had been shot near the building in three huge ditches about 30 meters long and 3 meters deep. The number of people killed daily was about 1,500. The 5,000 Jews who had lived in

Dubno before the pogrom were all marked for liquidation. Since the executions took place in the presence of my employee, he was painfully impressed by them.

Accompanied by Moennikes, I then went to the work area. I saw great mounds of earth about 30 meters long and 2 high. Several trucks were parked nearby. Armed Ukrainian militia were making people get out, under the surveillance of SS soldiers. The same militia men were responsible for guard duty and driving the trucks. The people in the trucks wore the regulation yellow pieces of cloth that identified them as Jews on the front and back of their clothing.

Moennikes and I went straight toward the ditches without being stopped. When we neared the mound I heard a series of rifle shots close by. The people from the trucks—men, women, and children—were forced to undress under the supervision of an SS soldier with a whip in his hand. They were obliged to put their effects in certain spots: shoes, clothing, and underwear separately. I saw a pile of shoes, about 800–1,000 pairs, great heaps of underwear and clothing. Without weeping or crying out, these people undressed and stood together in family groups, embracing each other and saying goodbye while waiting for a sign from the SS soldier, who stood on the edge of the ditch, a whip in his hand too. During the fifteen minutes I stayed there, I did not hear a single complaint or a plea for mercy. I watched a family of about eight: a man and woman about fifty years old, surrounded by their children of about one, eight, and ten, and two big girls about twenty and twenty-four. An old lady, her hair completely white, held the baby in her arms, rocking it, and singing it a song. The infant was crying aloud with delight. The parents watched the group with tears in their eyes. The father held the ten-year old boy by the hand, speaking softly to him: the child struggled to hold back his tears. Then the father pointed a finger to the sky and, stroking the child's head, seemed to be explaining something. At this moment, the SS near the ditch called something to his comrade. The latter counted off some twenty people and ordered them behind the mound. The family of which I have just spoken was in the group. I still remember the young girl, slender and dark, who, passing near me, pointed at herself, saying "Twenty-three." I walked around the mound and faced a frightful common grave. Tightly packed corpses were heaped so close together that only the heads showed. Most were wounded in the head and the blood flowed over their shoulders. Some still moved. Others raised their hands and turned their heads to show they were still alive. The ditch was two-thirds full. I estimate that it held a thousand bodies. I turned my eyes toward the man who had carried out the execution. He was an SS man; he was seated, legs swinging, on the narrow edge of the ditch; an automatic rifle rested on his knees and he was smoking a cigarette. The people, completely naked, climbed down a few steps cut in the clay wall and stopped at the spot indicated by the SS man. Facing the dead and wounded, they spoke softly to them. Then I heard a series of rifle shots. I looked in the ditch and saw their bodies contorting, their heads, already inert, sinking on the corpses beneath. The blood flowed from the nape of their necks. I was astonished not to be ordered away, but I noticed two or three uniformed post men nearby. A new batch of victims approached the place. They climbed down into the ditch, lined up in front of the previous victims, and were shot.

On the way back, while rounding the mound, I saw another full truck which had just arrived. This truck contained only the sick and crippled. Women already naked were undressing an old woman with an emaciated body; her legs frightfully thin. She was held up by two people and seemed paralyzed. The naked people led her behind the mound. I left the place with Moennikes and went back to Dubno in a car.

The next morning, returning to the construction, I saw some thirty naked bodies lying thirty to fifty yards from the ditch. Some were still alive; they stared into space with a set look, seeming not to feel the coolness of the morning air, nor to see the workers standing all around. A young girl of about twenty spoke to me, asking me to bring her clothes and to help her escape. At that moment we heard the sound of a car approaching at top speed; I saw that it was an SS detachment. I went back to my work. Ten minutes later rifle shots sounded from the ditch. The Jews who were still alive had been ordered to throw the bodies in the ditch; then they had to lie down themselves to receive a bullet in the back of the neck.

(Signed) Graebe
Wiesbaden, November 10, 1945

. . . Here all things scream silently . . .

CHAPTER TWO

Why Moral Indifference?

An investigation of the cultural and social sources of a profound moral indifference among German elites remains a useful task for three reasons. One is that this indifference played a central role in Germany's persistent foreign-policy aspirations, the reach for empire. This was the main show. And however much the Holocaust was a "war against the Jews" (Dawidowicz, 1975) in that it amounted to a systematically organized effort to destroy them, it remained for Germans at all levels of society a scarcely known sideshow. If one cannot grasp with what profound moral indifference the German elites oriented to their own people and institutions, if one cannot appreciate how a modern people can go forth on a suicidal path in an overweening reach for success, one cannot apprehend the nature of modern sin, the creation of meaningless suffering and death. Another is that Hannah Arendt's (1951; 1963) theoretical formulation of this problem can be improved, and her seminal ideas need more follow-up than they have received. For at the core of her apprehension of modern sin stood the figure of modern man, the achieving personality, that creature of a middle-class upbringing who is, at any given moment in his life, never more than the sum of his occupational successes and failures. That means we are confronted with a personality type brought up to believe that one has to earn one's right to exist every day, a person forever incomplete, one who suffers status insecurity, and one who is restless, forever on the prowl for opportunities to prove his worth. Now, Europe knew a variety of fascisms (Weber, 1964; Nolte, 1965). There was a French variety and a Spanish one, the Italian type and the Romanian one, as well as others. But German National Socialism remains the case of middle-class extremism *par excellence*. And so it behooves us to inquire whether Germany, from the beginning of her existence as a modern nation-state in 1871, was a society ruled by people particularly stamped by this middle-class mentality, one that sees in self-advancement and careerism the sole purpose of life. If so,

24

we have the third reason for picking up the threads of inquiry where the late Hannah Arendt left them. Moral indifference—indeed, the institutionalization of an amoral public sphere—was a more important cause of the Holocaust than psychopathology, simple economic self-interest, or the forces of charismatic beliefs. Above all, one should guard against assigning a function to the Holocaust when the available evidence does not permit it. Treblinka did not serve to legitimate Nazi domination, as Fein (1979) has argued. False comfort lies in such a reconstruction of history. Instead we should realize that the middle-class spirit at issue here is a universal one, present to important degrees in all modern societies. Learning about its particular nature of excess is learning about possibilities built into the fabric of our own lives. Doing that is more worthwhile because more realistic than reducing the causes of this instance of modern genocide into some plausible motive sets after all. Demonstrating these assertions is the purpose of this chapter.

In a recent reminiscence about his country of origin and some people he knew, Peter Drucker (1978) gave us a very impressive description of the moral indifference that is our concern. He recalled three acquaintances. Being a nobody and desperately wanting to become a somebody, one turned into a "Monster"; he became an administrator of "the final solution of the Jewish problem." Being a somebody, but believing, erroneously, that staying at home and playing the game could grant one a chance to prevent the worst, another turned into a "Lamb"; he perished. In a third, a university professor (and a very distinguished one at that), Drucker identified the "Indifferent Man"; he only cared about adequate research funding—that is to say, about his career. And so, Peter Drucker (1978:87):

I have often wondered which of these did, in the end, do more harm, the "Monster" or the "Lamb," and which is worse . . . lust for power . . . or sin of pride. But maybe the greatest sin is neither of these two ancient ones; the greatest sin may be the new, the twentieth-century sin of indifference, the sin of the distinguished biochemist-physiologist who neither kills nor lies but refuses to bear witness, in the words of the old gospel hymn, when "they crucify my Lord."

What Peter Drucker still wondered about was a certainty for Hannah Arendt. In the mass death of the Holocaust Kingdom, to borrow a name from Donat (1963), and the Gulag Archipelago, to use Solzhenitsyn's (1973; 1975) term for Stalin's camps, she discerned distinctly modern phenomena because none cared "to bear witness when they crucified the Lord." Let us not be deterred by her treatment of Hitler's and Stalin's camps as identical phenomena for theoretical purposes. On that point she erred. Unless you define totalitarianism in terms of the ceaseless production and destruction of some surplus population, the persistence of totalitarian rule does not *require* the organized, state-administered destruction of human life. I shall briefly return to this point below. Let me note here that the removal of the Holocaust from the conceptual array of necessary system attributes that made National Socialism work puts into much sharper focus Hannah Arendt's correct identification of this mass murder as meaningless because it served no institutional purpose. Also important is the fact that no one in Germany pretended that genocide served some institutional interest. Evidence on this point will be listed below. But this feature separates the Holocaust Kingdom from the Gulag Archipelago. More people perished in the Archipelago; but that is hardly the point. There was never a pure death factory in the Archipelago. That made it possible for bystander and killer alike to discern some legitimating cover. The Gulag administration could formulate institutional purposes and claim to serve society. Imprisonment and forced labor under Stalin was said to serve a double purpose: re-education of "bourgeois" minds, and construction of socialist society. As Solzhenitsyn (1973; 1975) makes eminently clear, to the many who suffered and perished, such formulations remained a cruel joke. Nonetheless, for the administrators a legitimating cover, perhaps a mere fig leaf, but still some cover was provided. With it men and women on the outside could pursue their public responsibilities and their private interests. Treblinka only served death. No official institutional purposes were ever invoked. The Third Reich dispensed, and successfully so, with the need for legitimation, even so modest a one as a fig-leaf cover. Therefore, let us simply forget what Hannah Arendt had to say about the Soviet case and concentrate on the German one. What struck her as distinctive was the utterly anti-utilitarian character of the mass exterminations, one not attributable to charismatic beliefs. Nothing less than a motiveless destruction of human life, in organized and highly systematic fashion, seemed to be the essence of modern evil. Let us listen to Hannah Arendt for a moment and capture what it is that makes the Holocaust unique and different from all known forms of man's inhumanity to man. In the final stages of totalitarianism (Arendt, 1951: ix, 317, 411, 417):

an absolute evil appears (absolute because it can no longer be deduced from comprehensible motives); Neither tribal nationalism nor rebellious nihilism is characteristic of the masses; but "indifference" and "loss" of "self-interest" are. Our bewilderment about the anti-utilitarian character of the totalitarian state structure springs from the mistaken notion that we are dealing with a normal state after all—a bureaucracy, a tyranny, a dictatorship. . . The trouble with totalitarian regimes is not that they play power politics in an especially ruthless way, but that behind their politics is hidden an entirely new and unprecedented concept of power, just as behind their *Realpolitik* lies an entirely new and unprecedented concept of reality. Supreme disregard for immediate consequences rather than ruthlessness, and neglect of national interest rather than nationalism; contempt for utilitarian motives rather than unconsidered pursuit of self-interest; "idealism" i.e., their unwavering faith in an ideological fictitious world, rather than lust for power. . .

These are the features of modern mass murder that call for explanation.

And what about this problem definition of meaningless suffering and of men and women being moved toward world conflagration without legitimation? Do common sense and historical memory not immediately seduce us into rebellion against it? Do we not know that Hitler was the race ideologist *par excellence*, and that his movement preached the goal of the destruction of Jewry consistently from beginning to end? Have we forgotten that he sermonized about the creation of a Reich to last a thousand years? Do we not find an advocacy to murder the Jews quite openly expressed in *Mein Kampf*, in the propaganda serving the struggle for power, and, once in, legitimating the Nazis in power? Do we not find anti-Semitic sloganeering in the mobilization for war, in more than one of Hitler's Reichstag declarations, and finally, at the end, in Hitler's testament again (Bracher, 1970:199, 273, 397, 399)? Setting aside our own and contemporary preferences about the nature of reasonable beliefs, is this not sufficient evidence for the play of ideological forces and charismatic legitimations? And, since men do not live from idealism alone, do we not know about the Aryanization of Jewish property in Germany and elsewhere? With factories near Auschwitz, inmates for hire, enterprises in ghettos and camps, is it not obvious that the Holocaust Kingdom was a house of slavery? Surely, somebody must have gained economically? And to step beyond the German borders, do we not know about the very real social, economic, religious, and political anti-Semitisms in Poland, which under German occupation produced the *szmalcowniki*, those persecution racketeers on private account who drained the last zloty, piece of clothing, or crumb of bread from a Jew outside the ghetto or camp, only then, when practically naked and utterly useless, to turn him over to the Germans for disposal (Bauer, 1978:52–59; Gross, 1975)? Do we not know that such states created or enlarged under the tutelage of National Socialism as Slovakia, Croatia, Romania, and Bulgaria killed Jews on their own, or collaborated, more or less, with the Nazis for the sake of modern nation-building in those days (Fein, 1979:99–113; Lendvai, 1971; Chary, 1972)? Thus, is it not all too obvious that one can speak here of a variety of motives, if not indeed a surfeit of reasons for the Holocaust, rather than the absence of any?

One thing should be clear in response to this litany of questions just listed. If you find proof for an affirmative answer to all of them, Arendt's (1951; 1963) achievement in clarifying the nature of modern evil dissolves into metaphysical air, a mere speculation without empirical foundation, and one of little consequence. If you find proof for an affirmative answer to some of these questions, you reduce that achievement correspondingly. Research that yields affirmative answers returns our experience of the Holocaust right back into the familiar history of man's inhumanity to man. Hitler's exploits become a tale of classical tyranny, merely one that used the tools of the Industrial Age. And you might even add to the old reasons of man's inhumanity to man and see some cunning reason at work. The modern practice of mass death could "function" to keep an otherwise explosive population growth in check (Rubenstein, 1975). The fact is, most subsequent research has not focused on totalitarianism as institution-alized irrationality. No one, to my knowledge, has tried to test Arendt's hypothesis about the genesis of totalitarianism. Yet if we assume that nothing like Treblinka would have occurred in our time had it not been for the triumph of National Socialism in Germany, we must return to that country and its history. What, then, was the structure of Arendt's argument? Let me present an outline of it, one that I deliberately simplify to the sociological part and confine to the German case. This should make clear the task she set for the historical sociologist.

Hannah Arendt's Sociology of German Totalitarianism

De-stratification of social inequalities stands at the beginning and at the end of her analysis, occurring often between as well (Arendt, 1951:4, 169, 254–63, 306–40). Therefore, de-stratification of social inequalities figures as the most important cause of as well as identifying feature of a totalitarian polity. She starts her analysis with a quotation from de Tocqueville to the effect that it is "wealth without function" that is resented, and deeply so. As long as the French aristocracy was politically powerful as well as rich, the steep social inequalities in pre-absolutist France were quite tolerable. But when absolutism triumphed and rele-gated much of the aristocracy to relative political impotence *without* a corresponding reduction in their economic fortunes, then their wealth became intolerable to the poorer strata in society *because* it could no longer be seen and legitimated as a reward for the burdens of differential political responsibility. The result was resentment against the social order. Arendt illustrates the same de-stratification of inequalities in Germany at least twice. Imperial Germany developed a "cultural middle class" employed in the civil service of government and academe. These were bearers of cultural honor, one might say models of and for the morally sensitized person. But they lacked corresponding wealth and political influence. During the Third Reich she illustrates the point of de-stratified elites with the SS complex. As bearers of state secrets they had prestige, but they had no power, being mere instruments of but not participants in policy-making. It is important to note that the target of resentment is not social inequality as such. In Arendt's view it is a disordered unequal distribution of scarce and valued resources that is resented—indeed, hated with a passion. Let me elaborate that point. When political power no longer yields corresponding prestige, when the bearers of the highest prestige in society are relatively poor and when the wealthy command neither prestige nor political influence commensurate with their control over the nation's economic resources—when, in effect, there is a lot of inequality but no longer stratification at the top in society—then any privilege is seen as "functionless," no longer serving society but only the private interest of individuals. But the resultant anger at society is only one consequence.

De-stratification of inequalities among a society's elites also destroys the social nature of identity, both at the level of the individual and that of the national collectivity (Arendt, 1951:169, 364). Individual identity becomes radically individualized, or a matter of subjective consciousness alone. The answer to the question who we are is deprived of social anchorage. In a de-stratified social order, so her argument, it is no longer a set of social roles that tells us who we are. Instead, a sense of self is produced by the individual, through his own effort, and for his own enjoyment, as it were. Illustrated again with the cultural middle class in Germany, there occurred the manufacture of a sense of self from the consumption of art. The product was a radically subjectivist notion of the individual. Excluded from political participation during the Imperial period, not daring to challenge the *Junker*—and, I would add, not caring to—the German intellectuals celebrated the idea of the "innate personality," a sense of self not traceable to playing mere social roles, and so one uncontaminated by the sham of worldly affairs. But collective identity, the idea of a nation as a collectivity integrated by common and shared values, also falls victim to de-stratification at the top of society. The Nazi idea of a folk community was the exact opposite of a *Gemeinschaft*, of a people sharing values and caring about their implementation. That image of a human *Gemeinschaft* belonged to the past, an image of unemancipated man, one constrained by dead tradition. According to Reinhard Höhn, political scientist and theoretician of the New Order, the folk community of the future was radically different; it had to be a self-willed one, and one emancipated from the constraints of shared commitments. As he put it: "From the point of view of a folk community, every community of values is

destructive" (Arendt, 1951:363). For Hannah Arendt this double consequence of de-stratification, the "desocialized" sense of individual self and
the "decommunalized" notion of society, were very much related matters.
The heroic image of the modern individual fashioning his sense of self
creatively like an artist, living off society but not in it, and the figure of the
modern politician, creative like an artist and fashioning a social order,
these were corresponding mechanisms of modern identity constructions.

A third consequence of de-stratification at the top is the destruction of
common sense as a guide to the apprehension and the pursuit of
self-interest. Mass men and women, so Hannah Arendt (1951:316),
inclined to the construction of a sense of self by themselves and for
themselves, succeed so little as to experience a "radical loss of self-
interest," even to the point where our normally assumed instincts for
self-preservation wane. In a stratified society people have social identities,
identities shared with others through the medium of common sense, and
so a sense of self to which each individual is held to by others. That tells
him who he is and what he may reasonably want. But under conditions of
de-stratification, which force individuals into the pursuit of self-manufac-
tured identities, the tools of common sense fail in finding the elusive goal
because it has been placed beyond the reach of social control. And so,
fundamentally overburdened and isolated, a people must search for a
movement that provides parameters for action and opportunities to prove
and make oneself. Yet, given the anger against the social order in its
known form, such movements can be nothing other than a conglomerate
of terrifying negative solidarities (Arendt, 1951:315). Particularly for the
better-educated, politics becomes the more attractive the more terroristic
it is, and the more political leaders provide opportunities for the expression of emotion rather than for the discipline of cooperation.

The fourth and last consequence, and one flowing primarily from
institutionalization of commitments to the Reich as a social engine of
unlimited possibilities rather than a community integrated by shared
values, was a pattern of political domination without legitimation. In
Hannah Arendt's (1951:361–62) view, Hitler was *not* a charismatic leader.
Nazi rule employed propagandistic clichés, deliberately designed not to
be taken seriously by educated people, and it was a mark of elite status to
live, and above all to act, without the crutch of belief (Arendt, 1951:334,
384). The Nazi polity was *not* a monolithic dictatorship but a "system of
systemlessness." One cannot speak here just about a duplication of
functions and offices with a party office next to every governmental and
private-sector organization, but rather a multiplication of offices and
functions, all in competition with each other (Arendt, 1951:395). And
how did this near-Hobbesian state of nature maintain direction in terms of

foreign conquest? Terror and complicity in the practice of mass death here provided a triple service. Terror and complicity (1) prevented the Nazi movement from sliding back into a mere pork-barrel organization; (2) prevented the totalitarian polity from degeneration into a mere authoritarian regime; and (3) prohibited organization men throughout society from doing what otherwise comes naturally—namely, recommitting themselves to reason (Arendt, 1951:438, 456). For Hannah Arendt then, the Holocaust and Germany's reach for empire were connected phenomena. Nothing could be more erroneous than to see in the Holocaust the culmination of the long history of anti-Semitism. On the contrary, among the critical elites in German society, the Holocaust was a mere sideshow, the reach for empire was the main show; and both happened because de-stratified elites are elites without a capacity to care about the consequences of their actions.

What has happened to this hypothesis? Let us see.

Subsequent Research: Voices of False Reassurance?

I cannot pretend to review the literature on Nazi Germany and the Holocaust. There is too much of it. I can comment only on a limited variety of research. But unless these efforts are completely unrepresentative of the majority of effort on this page in our history, they permit the conclusion that Hannah Arendt's hypothesis has not been subjected to anything like the serious test it deserves.

Let me begin with stratification, a core concern of sociologists. Though lacking empirical foundations, theoretically de-stratification stood at the beginning and at the end of Hannah Arendt's (1951: ix, 4, 317, 411, 417, 426) analysis. It formed *the* independent variable for the emergence of mass society with its isolated individuals constituting, with deep resentment, a "terrifying negative solidarity" against society. Social inequality as such is *not* resented in this view. Resented is a disordered unequal distribution of power, prestige, and wealth. Though not as carefully specified as one might wish, de-stratification of social inequalities in society was very important in Hannah Arendt's hypothesis. All the other important features of totalitarianism—the loss of common sense, the isolated mass personality, the addiction to thoughtlessness, and the going along with slogans heedless of the consequences—followed from it.

But work on mass society took a different turn, examining issues not tied directly to different types of political regimes, and the invitation to inquire whether de-stratification may be a trend in modernizing societies everywhere has not been seriously pursued. Instead, mass-society analysis

returned to an older format inaugurated by de Tocqueville, where the
focus is on the role of intermediary power structures. Liberty and
democracy depend, according to this line of argument, on elites autono-
mous enough not to be swamped with mass demands and on an
underlying population experienced in the art of self-government on the
local level and in associational life and therefore immune to direct
mobilization from elites (Kornhauser, 1959; 1966). Following up on these
leads, Lepsius (1968) analyzed the collapse of Germany's intermediary
power structure under the onslaught of the Nazi movement and into the
first years of the Third Reich. But the analysis does not focus on
de-stratification as a causal factor; rather the focus is on gradual and
accelerating loss of legitimacy of such associations as unions and employers' organizations due to their ineffectualness in coming to grips with
economic chaos. In fact, that societies may be unstratified for very long
time spans as illutrated in the case of Tokugawa Japan, where the bearers
of top prestige in the country, the samurai, were also quite poor (Nishio,
1965), has not been a major research focus in sociology. In modern times
only Eisenstadt (1971) has paid any systematic attention to treatment of
stratification as a variable, distinguishing societies that are more stratified
from those that are less stratified. The discipline in general has acknowledged this only in terms of status crystallization, where the unit of
analysis is some individual, usually mobile, such as a black physician in
the United States who votes for the Republican Party and, as a consequence, experiences cross pressures. But the linkage of that phenomenon
to mass society has remained tenuous. Schoenbaum (1967) has been the
only one who asserted that the Nazis smashed the stratification order of
German society, making that the focal point of his understanding of
Hitler's social revolution. As we shall see later on, he exaggerated;
de-stratification occurred before the Nazis appeared. By and large,
however, the prevailing conventional wisdom is that inequalities in society
tend to be naturally stratified such that families with a certain amount of
control over prestige, for example, will have more or less commensurate
amounts of control over wealth and political influence, and any disturbances in this arrangement are seen as self-correcting (Kriesberg, 1979).
And the implied message here is a kind of moral and cognitive narcotic:
Don't worry, since de-stratification is improbable, Hannah Arendt's
concern with loss of common sense and unmotivated mass murder
remains improbable. More likely, there were reasons, and the Holocaust
was just another chapter in the endless history of man's inhumanity to
man.

A conceptual reintegration of this mass death into the stream of normal
human history also characterizes the broader literature on the more

immediate origins and the nature of Nazi totalitarianism. It was invited, in part, by Hannah Arendt, who assigned political functions to the destruction of human life, as mentioned above. Totalitarian domination demands killing, so a more precise version of this position, because only complicity in death among killers, bystanders, and potential as well as actual victims locks all irreversibly into the pursuit of what the totalitarian mystique may imply (Arendt, 1951:372; Poliakov and Wulf, 1955:185). If such a complicity theory were adequate to the facts (which it is not, as will become clear in a moment), an explanation of the rise of National Socialism would amount ipso facto to one of the Holocaust. But four objections must be raised against Arendt's oversystematized conception of German totalitarianism. Let me add here Friedrich's (1954) specification of the model to make more clear what the objections relate to. A totalitarian regime is one characterized by: (1) an overarching comprehensive ideology serving as an obligatory belief system for members of society; (2) rule based on systematic terror; (3) the rulers' monopoly control over all means of communication; and (4) the rulers' monopoly control over all means of violence. All of the four objections below should lead us to attend more rather than less to the problem of meaningless suffering and death.

First, the oversystematized model of totalitarianism is empirically false. One implication of the model is that camps served as training grounds for total domination, another is that the destruction of life was linked to the *Weltanschauung* as an overarching obligatory belief system, in this case the race ideology. Both are wrong. Political indoctrination in the SS was experienced as a crashing bore, and Himmler's instructions to give the respective courses were widely ignored (Höhne, 1967:146–49). When "Eiche's boys," those SS men with the allegedly proper training for total domination, left for front-line duty, their places as guards in Auschwitz were taken over by people no longer capable for front-line duty, people who came from all quarters of society, with little or no ideological training, and without any experience in guarding anyone. But life and death in Auschwitz went on as before (Langbein, 1972:318). Further, theories of fascism excel either in explanation or in description of what is to be explained, but never in both (Nolte, 1970:15–75), and worse, they do not pay enough attention to the details of mass murder. This has been clearly recognized only by Dahrendorf (1965:375–76): An explanation of the rise of National Socialism cannot claim to be one of the Holocaust because one cannot equate the two. Nothing in the broader history of the Third Reich at peace and at war *required* Treblinka. Sticking to the use of forced labor, or practicing only slavery would have deprived no SS functionary of career chances; it might have enhanced them instead.

Second, the model of totalitarianism has been falsified by Italian fascism, which Hannah Arendt correctly identified as an authoritarian regime. Mussolini's Italy had all four of the Friedrich characteristics of totalitarianism. But systematized terror was never developed to a point even approaching the awesome destruction of life under Hitler (Germino, 1959; Seton-Watson, 1967:702ff). More, despite the adoption of Aryan legislation, and so the introduction of the legal means to exclude Jews from society, the Military and Foreign Service elites of Fascist Italy actively intervened and sabotaged the final solution wherever they could, even to the point of staging a private invasion of foreign territory in order to save the Jews from Eichmann's net (Poliakov, 1949; Höhne, 1967:362–63). Already these two objections tell us: Neither in Germany nor in Italy did the four Friedrich features of totalitarianism form an interconnected system.

Third, the model certainly implies the impossibility of domestic reform significantly reducing terror, particularly in terms of the outright destruction of human life. For Germany this was true. But another indication of the looseness rather than the supposed systemic connections of the elements in Friedrich's model is the fact that Khrushchev inaugurated a significant attenuation of terror in Soviet totalitarianism.

Fourth and last, in sharp contrast to the historical evidence attesting to the important role of legislation as well as the endless implementation decrees in the exclusion of Jews from society, not only in Germany but among her satellites and allies in Eastern Europe as well, the model of totalitarianism implies the *complete* breakdown of the *Rechtsstaat*. One may hesitate to call the respective laws legitimate. But that is a different matter than arguing the absence of law. The Polish people, whether Jewish or not, were treated as absolutely rightless chattel and subjected to domination by pure terror (Gross, 1975). Conquered Russians met with a similar fate. But in Germany, "packing the Jews off to camps" was done legally, however illegitimately, and that legalized road to illegal murder was an indispensable facilitative mechanism in accomplishing the latter (Adler, 1974). This is not just a cumbersome detail, a matter of academic hair splitting between legality and legitimacy. For Hannah Arendt the distinction was critical. I would concur. It is only the modern state with its predominantly "rational-legal" rather than "traditional" or "charismatic" legitimacy base (Weber, 1922:215–66) that provides in the very foundations of its legitimation of authority the opportunity to separate legality from legitimacy and to rule illegitimately with the aid of law. That question will concern us further below in connection of the role of "ideal interests" or charismatic forces as a causal factor in the Holocaust. Let us not forget the internment of American *citizens* of Japanese origin in wartime America. That was possible in a stable democracy that did not lose its stability thereby. Such facts should make us more attentive to the nature of law in *modern* states and less certain about the supposed "systemic character" of any political regime—democratic, authoritarian, or totalitarian.

Other shortcomings of the early work on totalitarianism could be listed. These, however, should suffice to indicate that one is entitled to disillusionment with that model. The question is whether the nature of these shortcomings justifies simple abandonment and reconceptualization of the Nazi regime as an authoritarian one, a position to which Lepsuis (1978) has been moving rather closely, or whether they oblige us to concentrate even more fully on the "systemless nature" of this political system than Hannah Arendt did. I believe the latter is preferable, and I offer two considerations in support of this contention. If terror was neither as "systemic" or intrinsic, nor as irreversible as Hannah Arendt assumed, an explanation of totalitarianism does not provide an explanation of the Holocaust by itself; at best it supplies a better description of what needs explaining. And if the production of a profusion of conflicting policies characterizes a totalitarian mode of rule and, additionally in Hitler's Germany, impeccable National Socialists who opposed wholesale destruction retained their offices nonetheless (Arendt, 1951:337, 342, 401), two features in need of explanation become better defined. One is why a consistent destruction policy can emerge over time at all without getting bogged down in competing interests; the other is why in a system ostensibly committed to the leadership principle, hence to a monolithic command-obey structure, opposition resources are retained rather than wiped out. Both of these questions direct us to be cautious in assigning great importance to the role of ideology as well as any other traditional and familiar factor underlying human violence. But such caution has not been exercised.

Three obvious avenues to deprive the Third Reich of the diabolical character it actually had can be easily described. All of them involve the post-factum assignment of reasons for the destruction of human life that had none. One may take recourse to psychopathology; one may invoke greed; one may invoke the play of charismatic beliefs; or one may do all three. Two of these courses have been taken. And unsurpassed irony characterizes these efforts. When the ex-commandant of Treblinka, Mr. Stangl, talked with Gitta Sereny (1974) about his life, one overriding need colored all his recollections: the need to perceive some meaning, after all, in the unspeakable suffering he had wrought. But neither he nor Sereny could find one. As if to register this terrible truth, Mr. Stangl died the day after the last interview. Had he not, or read a little more before, he might have found solace and the reassurance he so desperately desired. Let us see how.

One of the earliest efforts to find reasons in mass death where common sense denied the existence of any commensurate with both scale and organization of so much destruction was the work on the authoritarian personality (Adorno, Frenkel-Brunswik, Levinson, and Stanford, 1950). But trust in this personality syndrome as a significant explanatory factor soon dissipated. The attribution of high F-scale values to practically all the German population seemed dubious. Authoritarian personality traits could be found in countries with stable democracies. And authoritarian attitudes are not related to authoritarian behavior vis-à-vis others (Heaven, 1977). So this version of national-character studies soon fell into disrepute. Curiously, the only research on Nazism ever to enter the pages of West Germany's main journal of sociology in the last twenty-five years was a study on the authoritarian personality (Steiner and Fahrenberg, 1970). The dismal result is twofold. No one claims the irrelevance of psychological factors, but no one knows either how to order them into some larger conceptual scheme where they might play their properly delimited role. And so, under different labels, more psychiatric and clinical in tone, the search goes on. And that means taking the psychological way out rather than pursuing the invitation of Hannah Arendt. Psychohistory may be said to be in vogue, indeed. So we get a portrait of Hitler as a "psychopathic god" whose sexual perversion might well have been due to monorchism (one undescended testicle) (Waite, 1977). Or we are told that Hitler's anti-Semitism can be traced to a double trauma, one due to the loss of his mother under the care of a Jewish physician (his mother died a painful, slow death, of breast cancer), and the other due to temporary blindness from a gas attack, which caught Adolf Hitler as a soldier in World War I. And thus rises the reason: Avenge the mother and do it with gas (Binion, 1976). Of Himmler we learn that he was a schizoid personality, rigid, and restricted in emotional experience (Loewenberg, 1971). Of Eichmann we are told that he seethed with inner rage (Selzer, 1977). And similar psychiatric disorders have been found among the main defendants at Nuremberg (Miale and Selzer, 1976).

The intention of such efforts seems to be much clearer than their yield in explanations. As to the former, the nimble intellectualization points to either madness or neurosis. Both provide false comfort. In the legal sense of not knowing the difference between right and wrong or the loss of capacity to refrain from doing wrong, Hitler's henchmen were not mad (Harrower, 1976). On the other hand, the lines between normality and neurosis remain hazardous to draw. The invitation seems to be to make psychiatric examinations a requirement of running for public office. The explanatory power remains obscure. For example, Eichmann's seething inner rage presumably explains his dedicated zeal, even if he enjoyed the fruits of his labor mostly vicariously. For Hitler, a man far more articulate in his hate for Jewry, no evidence of vicarious participation in destruction exists. Apparently, he never bothered to read any of the reports detailing the progress of the final solution (Fest, 1973:931). In contrast, he did pay concentrated attention and obviously derived satisfaction from the executions of his would-be assassins in the aborted coup of July 20, 1944 (Bracher, 1970:499). For the psychoanalytically inclined such differences *obviously* can be attributed to the structure of defenses, permitting vicarious participation in destruction in one case, and prohibiting it in another. If anything, Himmler was a person afraid of violence (Fraenkel and Manvell, 1965:166–77; Kersten, 1952). Discovery of such a trait in the chief administrator of the final solution then, presumably, points to overcompensation for doubts about his manhood as a plausible motive. The problem with the extension of psychoanalytic concepts from the scene of the couch to that of history and a whole society is that you can prove too much and disprove nothing. The accomplishment of the Holocaust took thousands of people from all walks of life, at all ages, and both sexes (Hilberg, 1961). Were they all neurotic? One need not be committed to skepticism as a virtue to doubt it. The inconclusiveness of such findings becomes rather glaring when you discover that for everyone with some psychopathological syndrome you find also others, equally involved or more directly so (Dicks, 1972), but neither sadists nor otherwise burdened with suggestive symptoms, and ordinary, normal people instead, people who just followed orders like Höss (1959), commandant of Auschwitz, or Stangl, commandant of Treblinka who, as he said (Sereny, 1974), managed to occupy himself so much with sheer administrative tasks as not even to reappear in the memory of his survivors (Steiner, 1967). More seductive than these examples is the practice of psychohistory that focuses simultaneously on the figure of the *Führer* and that of the German people as a whole (Binion, 1976). For leaders must find responsiveness among the led if they are to lead, and Hitler did retain almost unchallenged authority to the end. So we find a coincidence of private neurosis (of Hitler) and collective trauma about defeat in the First World War as the explanation of it all. Clear here are only two things. You can write an entire book on the basis of the writing and talking of Adolf Hitler. As to the response of the German people to his speeches, however, you have to rely entirely on conjecture. The result is the portrait of a truly charismatic marriage between Hitler and the Germans, and an indissoluble one at that, covering not only the reach for empire but the Holocaust as well. One wonders: Is such a psychoanalytically inspired complicity theory "the final realization" of the fondest dreams of Goebbels, dreams he could never turn into reality?

And what about greed? The forced emigration of German Jewry was considerably stalled by the simultaneous pursuit of expropriation (Adler, 1974). As late as December 1942, when the final solution was in full progress, Himmler obtained permission for the sale of exit visas to rich Jews (Fraenkel and Manvell, 1965:130). An economic interpretation would of course make very comprehensible this tale of mass oppression and mass death. If one could only show that it paid, one would be reassured simply because the footprints of the pursuit of material interest loom so large in history. I know of no author who assigns genuine importance to the Holocaust Kingdom as an expropriation and exploitation engine. Perhaps Tillion (1975:48–49, 164, 175) comes closest to a material-interest explanation. Noting the contradiction between exploitation and extermination, she concludes: One could profit from mass death by adopting a policy of extermination by labor. However, even this formulation puts too much emphasis on a rational pursuit of interests. The relevant facts can be conveniently reviewed under three headings: (1) the realization of the socioeconomic promises of the Nazi movement; (2) the gain from expropriations; and (3) the gain from "slave labor" in the concentration camps.

With their rhetorical guns aimed at international Jewish capitalism on the one hand and Jewish Bolshevism on the other, the Nazis mobilized support from the Protestant old middle classes in town and country alike. The small retail businessmen, the older crafts in tailoring, and the small independent farmer, all squeezed by big business on the one side and big labor on the other, were the core voters of the Nazi Party (Lipset, 1960:138–48). But these class interests were to be disappointed. As Schoenbaum (1967) has shown quite unequivocally, the movement in power realized exactly the opposite of the substantive economic and social-policy goals proclaimed before. Instead of a rejuvenation of the old middle classes in town one finds their disappearance from the economic scene; instead of strengthening the small farmer and stemming the tide of flight from the countryside, one finds increased urbanization; and instead of preserving or recapturing the "traditional" role of the female as a creature of "kitchen, kids, and church," one finds an accelerated pace of female inclusion into the labor force and into higher education. In short, rather than stemming the tide of modernizing change in Germany, the Nazi movement in power transformed German society more in the direction of the industrialized, urbanized, fluid, and mobile "Western" model of modern society than prior regimes (Dahrendorf, 1965). None of the "étatist" ideals of preserving the old middle strata were realized.

Expropriation, of course, benefited certain groups and individuals here and there, both outside and inside the Holocaust Kingdom (Adler, 1955:423; Langbein, 1972:158–68, 223ff; Sereny, 1974:212–32). Apartments and furniture left behind by those shipped off became prized objects for civil and military administrative personnel in the bomb-raked cities of the Reich and elsewhere (Adler, 1974; Hilberg, 1961). In Greater Germany the expropriation of industrial and business property by and large profited the banks (Hilberg, 1961:64). But persecution and extermination was a state policy. In Greater Germany and conquered Poland the goods seized were disposed of in the private sector, with the proceeds from sales becoming state income (Hilberg, 1961:156–61). Consequently, the rationality of the expropriation policy can be considered in terms of national income. And in those terms the gains proved exceedingly meager. A summation of Reich income prepared by Ministry of Finance officials after the war yielded a figure of about two billion Reichsmarks (Adler, 1974:544–45). Apparently this estimate remained incomplete. No figures for the Polish territories outside the Generalgouvernement were ever found (Hilberg, 1961:161). If we make a very generous allowance for this by substituting the value of expropriation in the Generalgouvernement for the missing item, we can raise the gross Reich receipts to 3.5 billion Reichsmarks. With a population of 86 million in Greater Germany of 1939 (which includes the Protectorate), that yields an increase of per-capita income by 40.70 Reichsmarks. So much for gaining from expropriation here. Indeed, it is highly doubtful whether there was any net gain. The administrative cost of expropriation and deportation in Greater Germany has never been separately calculated. But as shown by Adler's (1974) analysis of Gestapo files, it must have been phenomenal, pointing to a net loss in the operation rather than any gains. Two examples suffice to give some indication of the truly endless red tape involved. Just for the initial assessment of Jewish property a questionnaire 6½ pages long had to be filled out for every member of a Jewish household. These forms grew to a length of 8 pages by the date of deportations. And while the Jews themselves did the writing, Gestapo officials did the checking and filing. And that covered property down to a toothbrush (Adler, 1974:547–53). The "proper" disposition of a dormant bank account with a deposit of 32.80 marks, belonging to the estate of a Jew killed in action for the fatherland in 1916, could easily generate 20 separate exchanges of correspondence among over a dozen bureaus of government and the private sector, with the correspondence stretching over 2 years (Adler, 1974:707–13). Some of the Jews in Greater Germany were at least wealthy, but in Poland most were poor. There the economic consequences of the final solution must be assessed in terms of the losses from

Jewish labor, the gaining from the collection of their clothing (rags, mostly), and from the resulting savings in food. According to Hilberg's (1961:332) estimates, the operation in Poland was one of loss. Finally, since the property of Jews from countries that either retained an indigenous administration or were allied with Germany did not accrue to the Reich, the Aryanization of property hardly made the destruction of life a profitable enterprise for the Third Reich.

And what about extermination by labor of *Untermenschen*, whether Jewish or not? The Holocaust Kingdom was also a house of modern slavery. In contrast to most earlier forms, though, slavery in the concentration camps was peculiar in that labor power was treated as an expendable resource, not a scarce one to be husbanded with some prudence. The exploitation of labor in the concentration camps was organized on the assumption of an indefinite supply of inmates (Langbein, 1972:506–15; Rubenstein, 1975:48–67). While based on a new premise, that of the total expendability of man, a "traditional veneer" was maintained even here. Concentration-camp slavery was legally regulated in that a "regulation" designated ghetto and camp inmates as property to be rented to the private sector of the economy (Adler, 1974:540). The Third Reich also had a more traditional form of slavery, one where economic reason played a significant role. This was to be found in the forced-labor program (Homze, 1967). Furthermore, the SS was not just master of the concentration-camp universe. It was also deeply involved in the economy, in the private as well as the public sector; and in 1942, for example, the Administrative and Economic Head Office SS not only supervised 20 concentration camps but also 165 labor camps (Höhne, 1967:372). So far as available information permits a conclusion here, it is this: The practice of traditional slavery in the forced-labor program was economic, but slavery of the modern variety inside the Holocaust Kingdom with its ruling premises of an indefinite supply of labor power and the total expendability of man was quite uneconomic and more likely a loss- than a profit-yielding operation. Now, while the former has been established quite well, the latter is a matter I can only illustrate. There is no doubt the forced-labor program was not only just economic, it was also indispensable to the pursuit of the big show, the war of conquest (Homze, 1967). Inside the Holocaust Kingdom, in contrast, recurrent and deep intra-SS conflict between the advocates of exploitation in the Administrative and Economic Head Office SS (WVHA) and the champions of extermination in the Reichs-Security Head Office SS (RSHA) yielded victory to the latter (Höhne, 1967:298–403). Further, when "modern" slavery was practiced there, it could be more manpower-expensive than grade-school education. Unless conditions in Auschwitz during the summer of 1944 were quite misrepresentative of slavery in the Holocaust Kingdom in general, this "modern slavery" required a guard/inmate ratio higher than the teacher/pupil ratio in your neighborhood grade school—a ratio, in fact, comparable to or higher still than the professor/student ratio in university graduate seminars. Also, one finds little difference whether slaves were used for the production of goods and death, as in Auschwitz, or only for the production of death, as in Treblinka. Discounting one half of the inmates not even marginally useful for the production of anything, in June 1944 the guard/inmate ratio for the employable slave force in Auschwitz was one to ten (Reitlinger, 1961:261–263). The same ratio, one guard to ten inmates, was typical for Treblinka (Sereny, 1974:166–81). Now, however notorious the expense of education, teachers teach. They make some contribution to the final product, literacy or a Ph.D. Camp guards only guarded, normally.

It would be difficult to assert that extermination was profitable. And while such a "material interest" explanation has not been seriously proposed, the same cannot be said about the role of "ideal interests" in the Holocaust. Indeed, the introduction of a death factory was certainly extraordinary. And since by definition, charismatic authority rests on beliefs in the extraordinary qualities of a leader and the extraordinariness of his vision of social and historical reality, the search for some charismatic foundations of the Holocaust comes almost naturally.

To begin with, Hannah Arendt's position was quite ambiguous on this point. On the one hand, she consistently emphasized the strongly anti-utilitarian nature of Nazi ideology, the dedication to the construction of an entirely new and fictitious world, and the indispensable role of such beliefs in the Nazis' drive to realize omnipotence (Arendt, 1951:460–70). Anti-utilitarian beliefs are one defining criterion of charismatic authority (Weber, 1922:244–45). On the other hand, she explicitly refuted the idea that Hitler was a charismatic leader (Arendt, 1951:361–62). That refutation rested on three claims. First, while charismatic authority is specifically revolutionary, proclaiming some new revelation, there was nothing new in the Nazi gospel of hate the Jew. Anti-Semitism was old hat. Second, while charismatic communities are composed of believers who take ideas seriously, National Socialism was not a debating society. The Nazis cared about organization and action, not about some truths. Third, while charisma in social life is the manifestation of human responsiveness to ultimate meaning (Weber, 1922:1,115), Nazi ideology was not only relatively contentless, treating needs of beliefs in ultimate reality with contempt, it also saw ideas as sheer instruments for propaganda.

One can document this contempt for ideas quite easily. Early after the ascension to power, Hitler assured leaders of the Catholic Church that

Rosenberg's *Myth of the Twentieth Century*, the purported dogma of National Socialism, was but a private document not representing official views at all (Lewy, 1964:151–52). Later in the war it became even fashionable in higher-leadership circles to claim that one had never read this "Nazi philosopher" (Bracher, 1970:307). The party program with its explicit claim about commitments to positive Christianity was never abrogated. Nor was the Weimar Constitution with its guarantees of juridical and civil rights ever changed or abolished. Both were simply disregarded. For example, the Catholic Church was simply deprived of its newspapers, welfare, educational, and youth organizations; or a reform movement within the Protestant *Landeskirchen* for nationwide organization could be exploited for infiltration, even though Hitler had no interest in rekindling the state-Church struggle of Bismarck's *Kulturkampf* (Lewy, 1964; Conway, 1968; Helmreich, 1979). Leading Communists and Socialists disappeared permanently into concentration camps, while Jews, taken into "protective custody" in the wake of the engineered *Kristallnacht pogrom*, would be released again (Adler, 1974). The meaning of "positive Christianity" or "civil and juridical rights" could change from day to day. But neither the contentless nature of an ideology nor the contempt for ideas helps us much in clarifying the nature of this "charismatic" authority. Such real shortcomings relative to the requirement of ideal-type charismatic authority did not prevent Nyomarkay (1967) from identifying Hitler as a charismatic leader, even though the two main findings of his study attest to contentlessness. Hitler, so we find, always avoided settling any policy disputes among his followers as long as possible because he did not care about programs. Moreover, he only decided some issue when the festering dispute about policies threatened to spill over into disloyalty to himself.

Further, most contemporary polities rest on all three of Weber's types of legitimate authority. One finds in them rational-legal, traditional, and charismatic traces. Recognizing this fact has led Höhne (1967) to suggest a kind of division of labor in their use for the final solution. The exclusion of German Jews from society was accomplished by legal-rational means, as evident in the Nuremberg racial laws and the Aryan paragraph in the civil-service law. The collection of their property and their transportation to the East involved traditional authority in the form of routine implementations of legal decrees and regulations, as well as courteous cooperative patterns among officials of various government departments. The order to kill, orally transmitted through the channels of the Reichs-Security Head Office SS and shrouded in official secrecy, relied on Hitler's charismatic authority. The implication of this type of analysis is clear: At best, or if you prefer at most, killing the Jews served the internal legitimation needs of the Nazis in power. The distinction between internal and external legitimation needs of a political regime will occupy us below in assessing the work of Helen Fein (1979). She does not use that distinction; but it is one improving the chances of her claims to withstand empirical scrutiny.

In *Accounting for Genocide* (Fein, 1979) one finds a radical departure from Hannah Arendt's abiding concern with the nature of modern and banal evil. Instead, we find the Holocaust reintegrated into the normal if dismal history of man's inhumanity to man. For the German case of interest here, Fein's explanation is utterly simple: The final solution served the legitimation needs of National Socialism. To be sure, there is great merit in her book. A more sophisticated use of quantitative data and making the accomplishment of killing problematical in a way to account for failure and successes in mass murder are only two of her achievements. I am not reviewing the book here. My concern here is only her explanation with respect to Germany, one I find unsatisfactory. Fein's study design is geared to explain variation in rates of victimization, the percentage of Jews killed in those nations of Europe touched directly by Germany's second reach for empire in the Second World War. Basically her account proceeds in two steps. The first is to explain the exclusion of Jews from the web or universe of moral obligations in society, or to put it differently, their exclusion from the circle of people to whom the rules of the moral life apply, rules that when violated call forth guilt, shame, or both, but expiation anyway. The prewar success of an anti-Semitic political movement explains such exclusion. Note two features of this indicator of political anti-Semitism. First, it does not matter whether or not political anti-Semitism feeds on social, economic, and religious anti-Semitism. Second, it covers two different orientations to Jews; one of hate implying that one could rejoice in their destruction, and one of utter indifference to their fate. To Hannah Arendt this was an important distinction, one not to be glossed over. But in glossing it, Fein follows Poliakov (1954), who first used political anti-Semitism as a measure of moral indifference, only later to assign more motivational force for destruction to old legends that prowl the modern political landscape in the form of racism with devastating results (Poliakov, 1974). Second, to Fein, the norms of obedience to authority will hold, covering everything including killing people, unless those called to obey manage to define extant authority as illegitimate. Only where the order of genocide was opposed through delegitimating the source of authority whence it came did the Jews even have a chance to escape. In states with a successful prewar anti-Semitic movement and complete SS control, like conquered Poland, the final solution was crowned with near total success; hardly any Jews escaped. In states with neither of these characteristics, the final solution was a near total failure, as, for example, in Denmark. In between, all cases of varying degrees of the destruction of Jewry, the one critical variable is the delegitimation of authority ordering the Jews to doom. So it matters very much whether an indigenous political authority was maintained under German occupation, or whether the state was allied with Germany and what the rational interest of such political authorities were. Church protest, when done publicly, for example, could reduce collaboration with Germany because that undermined the authority of the indigenous administration; Belgium was a case in point. The changing fortunes of war could dissuade a government allied with Germany from further collaboration; or counter-authorities to an indigenous state administration could issue from abroad —some government in exile, for example. Whatever the details, my concern is with her explanation as it applies to Germany alone; and that is, ". . . two causes alone—prewar anti-Semitism and SS control—account for virtually all (86 percent) of the variation in Jewish victimization" (Fein, 1979:91). It is clear that this is an explanation only for someone who takes modern political anti-Semitism as unproblematical.

Fein simply abandons Hannah Arendt's concern with ultimate evil. This is apparent in two ways. First, Fein does not bother with motives leading to the exclusion of Jews. Social, religious, and political anti-Semitisms appear as simply different forms of hate; and hate in turn explains quite well the success in stripping the Jews of their civil and social rights. To hate is as human as to love, and both are as old forms of sociation as mankind itself. Consequently, there is nothing unusual, unprecedented, or unique about the Holocaust. Second, for Fein genocide is the outcome of perfectly rational interests in society. The Holocaust in Germany was an event exactly parallel to the Turkish massacre of the Armenian minority. Both were the consequence of "integral nationalist movements," of new political elites in need of legitimating their power position vis-à-vis elites they had replaced, and of attaining legitimacy in terms of the goal, building a homogeneous nation-state, which had led to their gaining a position of power (Fein, 1979:10–30). Instead of the abandonment of common sense, which was so important to Arendt, Fein returns to the role of common sense. The Nazis were the anti-Semitic political movement par excellence; they came to power under the banner of anti-Semitism; and in need to legitimate their rule, they proceeded to carry out their promise, eradicating the Jews once and for all. It is really quite simple, thank you. Treblinka and Auschwitz served "ideal interests," the needs of the new rulers of Germany to legitimate their position. To repeat, I do not wish to discount in any way Fein's scholarly contribution in bringing together so vast a range of material on the variable fate of the Jews under the impact of the Holocaust engine. But her treatment of Hitler's anti-Semitism in Germany, and that remains my concern here, I find unacceptable.

The question whether the destruction of Jewry was charismatically legitimated, and indeed served to legitimate the Hitler movement in power as Fein (1979:30) asserts, is anything but an easy one to answer with adequate empirical material. During the struggle for power we only know who the Nazi voters were. We have no survey data collected at the time telling us why they cast their votes for the National Socialist Party. A vote is a many-splendored statement, like the expressions of romantic love. A large array of different motives, expectations, emotions, and intentions may stand behind a checkmark on a ballot. So one has to rest one's case with inferences. Knowing the social and economic characteristics of the typical Nazi voter permits but inferences as to likely reasons for the voter's choice. To jump ahead a little, the knowledge we do have does *not* support Fein's assertion. A Nazi vote in 1932 was not a mandate to exclude Jews from German society, to say nothing of a call for Treblinka. Further, the National Socialist movement did not ascend to power on the basis of votes alone. The *Machtergreifung* (capture of power) did not even rest on voting support primarily. It was also the result of negotiations. And what we know about the parties who negotiated with Hitler points away rather than toward belief in Hitler as a charismatic leader, and away from rather than toward any concern with the so-called Jewish question. When it comes to the legitimacy needs of the National Socialist regime in power before and during the war, the question of whether exclusion and destruction of Jews were needed to maintain the regime in power not only demands some assessment of success and failure of the regime but also some grasp of the nature of the regime and the limited role that charisma can play in the governance of a modern industrialized nation. Once again, in balance, what is known here concerning these points denies rather than confirms Fein's legitimation thesis. This holds true even if one introduces a distinction between external and internal legitimation, one that she does not use, and one generating considerations with a greater potential to support her assertion.

External legitimation refers to the perception of the movement by outsiders, their knowledge and feelings about the movement or regime as right for them and deserving their support. Internal legitimation refers to the corresponding perceptions of the insiders, the members of the party, the SA, and the SS, and their convictions and feelings about possessing a right to rule. Only taking the model of totalitarianism for the reality; indeed, only confusing the propagandistic caricature of Nazi totalitarianism as a monolithic engine of the complete domination of every subject under it, covering every facet of their lives, with historical actuality make the distinction superfluous. But, as attested to by a few rebellions in camps and ghettos like Treblinka (Steiner, 1967) or Warsaw (Mark, 1975), this model was not even fully realized at the sites of destruction, to say nothing of everyday life under National Socialism outside ghettos and camps. If we can agree that Fein's legitimation thesis of the final solution depends on Hitler's role as a charismatic leader, we can turn to Weber's typology of legitimate authority and then confront the historical record with three questions: How much did National Socialism rely on charismatic authority? Was a promise to destroy the Jews relevant in the movement's rise to power? Was the final solution helpful in maintaining Hitler in power?

The Legitimation Thesis Rejected

Weber's (1922:215–66, 1,111–57) typology of authority or legitimate power rests primarily on different types of beliefs specifying why one owes obedience to others. Power may be legitimate in terms of commitments to the sanctity of custom, in which case one speaks of traditional authority. People in modern societies are not wont to ascribe the character of sacredness to mere custom. But that does not mean the absence of traditional authority. Two other features of traditional authority are of importance for finding answers to our questions. One, and a rare feature in modern life, is that traditional-authority relations are personalized. One owes obedience not to some office incumbent but rather to a superior as a particular person. This generates considerable tolerance for the issuance and acceptance of commands that look arbitrary at first sight. Given the personal nature of the social bond, the superior can privately explain, and he can appeal to a history of personal association claiming that he deserves trust where explanations fail. Second, traditional-authority relations generate obedience primarily out of sheer habit, and habit is not at all rare in modern life. Here Barnard's (1938:165–69) concept of the "zone of indifference" proves useful in describing the persistence of tradition in modernity. So long as commands reaching subordinates do not drastically contravene their understandings of the general purposes of the organization and as long as they do not importantly frustrate their private motives in working where they do rather than elsewhere, such commands are carried out without question because they fall within their "zone of indifference." That was Barnard's elegant way of describing thoughtless obedience. And a moment's reflection about the complexity of the division of labor in modern bureaucratic organizations should suffice to highlight the important role of sheer habitual obedience. Without it, without going along with what has been decided upstairs, hardly any large-scale organization could function. That, as we shall see, lends itself to complicity with the realization of ultimate evil.

Rational-legal rule is characterized by belief in procedure. Such a procedure may prescribe the negotiation of common purposes between rulers and ruled, the democratic variant; or it may prescribe going through proper channels, the authoritarian mode. Whichever, commands attain legitimacy by virtue of the observance of legal requirements. Whether belief in sheer procedural fidelity as a basis of legitimacy can satisfy Max Weber's (1904; 1905) methodological strictures of an ideal-type construct or whether it comes dangerously close to confusing legitimacy with legality need not detain us. Instead, it is important to note two features of rational-legal rule, the pattern that predominates in modern industrial societies. In contrast to traditional-authority relations so prevalent in preindustrial social orders, change in obligations, what citizens owe in obedience to government at various levels, is almost routinely produced. Laws, appropriation bills, implementation decrees, and regulations allocating responsible oversight powers pour forth from the governmental machinery of modern societies in a near-endless stream. New obligations can be produced and old ones abrogated. That means, first, if a given state were to operate entirely by rational-legal rule without any traditional or charismatic elements in a written or unwritten but living constitution it would lack the capacity to guarantee even basic civil and social rights, such as the Fourteenth Amendment of the United States Constitution, which prohibits any state from depriving any person of life, liberty, or property without due process of law. And second, given the fidelity to procedure as the legitimacy basis under rational-legal rule, the temptation to confound legitimacy with legality or confuse what is moral with what is legal is greater in this kind of authority relation than either of Max Weber's other two.

Finally, charismatic authority stands in contrast and in opposition to traditional and rational-legal authority. Born out of a condition of despair and hope, a belief that one owes obedience to another or to others is charismatic when: (1) it is based on extraordinary qualities of another person who (2) represents in his person an entirely new vision of the nature of man and society in the name of which he creates revolutionary obligations that do not recognize any limits as to his sphere of competence or jurisdiction of office; and (3) the belief binds the leader or leaders and the followers into a community of faith, which (4) is distinctively anti-utilitarian in character, leading the community not only to live off booty or gifts rather than regular work but also to disdain the pursuit of all manner of "worldly" interests in any regular fashion. Because of this anti-economic feature, charismatic authority not only depends on some

spectacular initial success changing the conditions of despair that gave rise
to it, but it is also subject to various forms of routinization in the direction
of either traditional or rational-legal forms of rule. Emphasizing the
revolutionary character of charismatic beliefs, Weber used the figure of
Jesus and His assertion: "The Scriptures say, but I tell unto you." Since
Weber's definition lacks somewhat in desired clarity when it comes to
belief in the extraordinary qualities of the leader's person as distinct from
the message he bears, perhaps the following rule suffices. For the better
educated or the more intellectually inclined who seek a new ethos to order
their whole life, charismatic commitments entail beliefs in substantive
propositions. For the less intellectually equipped or inclined, belief in the
leader's extraordinary qualities without any further intellectualization
may suffice. In that case one might operationalize this variant as belief in
the infallibility of the leader. What he demands is right and carries validity
without the requirement that the follower understand.

　　With these conceptual tools at hand, let us focus on external legitimation and the movement's rise to power, trying to find answers to two
questions: How relevant was charismatic authority? How relevant was
anti-Semitism to the movement's success?

　　A first clue to the marginal role of charismatic appeals can be gleaned
from Hitler's tactic to adopt "the legal revolution" as the means to attain
power. The abortive beer-hall *Putsch* of 1923 had convinced him that
Germans would not respond to any charismatic revolutionary message. At
the Army trial in Leipzig he swore that he would abide by the constitutional rules of the game only in order to change them, once in power. He
understood well to exploit the legitimacy of belief in procedure on which
rational-legal rule rests. Asserting, correctly, that the Constitution only
prescribed the rules of the game in political competition but not the
substantive aims pursued by the contestants, he promised to stick to these
rules and to change them only with the aid of constitutional means
(Bracher, 1970:211). For the outsider, reliance on legality meant protection against the specter of revolutionary charisma; but for his following,
the insiders, the attention remained focused on the revolutionary portion
of the phrase "legal revolution." Nonetheless, the compromise was crucial
in establishing the National Socialist Party as a credible contender for
power. Revolutionary charisma had never attracted Germans. Important
political change had always rested on following procedure and reliance on
the personalized bonds of trust in traditional authority. The 1848
democratic "revolution" had been a failure, but the contract among
sovereigns that Bismarck engineered as the basis of the confederation in
1871 had been a success; the 1918 "revolution" had been a failure, but the
compact between Army and Social Democratic leadership circles had
been a success in establishing Weimar democracy; the rightist authori-

tarian Kapp *Putsch* of 1920 had failed just like Hitler's 1923 episode. *Only* observing the niceties of legality could get you anywhere in Germany (Bracher, 1970:209–18). Indeed, in light of modern German history, where no revolution ever succeeded in a fashion uncompromised by elements of traditional and/or rational-legal authority, substituting the slogan "legality above all else" for the phrase *"Deutschland, Deutschland über alles"* in her national anthem would considerably improve its empirical veracity as an expression of national identity. Only because Hitler understood that, and in a manner superior to his opponents on the left, did he succeed.

And what about the appeal of anti-Semitism in the Nazis' rise to power? Unfortunately, no quantitative evidence about the role of anti-Semitism in Nazi ideology exists. An analysis of popular political writings and pamphleteering suggests that German society was literally drenched in anti-Semitism for a considerable time before the National Socialists appeared on the scene (Mosse, 1964:294–311; 1970). In stark contrast, the history of anti-Semitic movements and political parties from the closing decades of the nineteenth century to the Weimar Republic seems one of utter insignificance. There were many such movements; they had always remained tiny minority phenomena; they had never lasted for any length of time, flashing up for a few months on the political scene, only then to sink again into utter obscurity (Bracher, 1970:35–52). Throughout the longest portion of the struggle for power, Hitler's movement seemed to fall into the same pattern, remaining small in size and subject to rapid shifts in support and attention (Orlow, 1969). If there was a distinctive feature to the anti-Semitic part of Hitler's message it was its constancy and unwavering intensity, a gospel preached without regard to the changing fortunes of the movement during the struggle for power and into the Third Reich until the very end. As will be seen in a moment, that feature of utter constancy and consistency in professed beliefs tells us something about internal legitimation needs. As for external legitimation, the available evidence suggests that it was not anti-Semitism that brought Hitler to power, nor was it anti-Semitism that granted the movement legitimacy while in power. During the struggle for power and as long as elections were freely competitive—in short, until January 1933—the National Socialists never won more than just over a third of the popular vote. Their peak electoral support registered in the presidential and parliamentary elections of April and July 1932, respectively, when the National Socialists gained about 37 percent of the popular vote (Bracher, 1970:208, 212; Lepsius, 1978:70). What is more, in these elections, particularly the presidential one, where Hitler stood for the office of Chancellor of the Reich, the main campaign slogans never even referred to Jews. These campaigns were clearly fought about the fate of democracy.

The defenders of democracy threatened the electorate with the specter of the revolution; the attackers of democracy threatened the electorate with continuity in economic misery. The option was a vote for or against the democratic Weimar Republic and little else. The socialists went into the campaign with the slogan, "A Vote for Thälmann [of the Communist Party] is a vote for Hitler"; the conservative right deployed the slogan, "A Vote for Hitler is a vote for Thälmann"; the Communist Party put out the message, "A Vote for Hitler is a vote for Hindenburg [thus Weimar democracy]"; and the National Socialists bombarded the voters with the slogan, "A Vote for Thälmann is a vote for Hindenburg" (Arendt, 1952:264–65). It remains highly unlikely that anti-Semitism attracted votes to Hitler. Rather his mode of preaching the anti-Semitic gospel attracted more of the diverse forms of discontent—political, on the part of the old conservative right; social, on the part of the old middle class threatened in their status position by industrialization; and economic, on the part of almost all suffering from massive unemployment—than the Communists managed to attract (Lipset, 1960:139; Schleunes, 1970: 57–59). In light of the later Holocaust one must also emphasize, however: While Hitler did not gain votes with anti-Semitism, his otherwise well-known hatred of the Jews did not lose him any either. Nonetheless, these were the crucial elections. We know who the Nazi voters were; and we can infer what, in the main, led them to cast their votes for National Socialism and against democracy. The Jewish question had precious little to do with it. Hitler's support came from the old middle class. "The ideal-typical Nazi-voter in 1932 was a middle-class, self-employed Protestant who lived either on a farm or in small community, and who had previously voted for a centrist or regionalist party strongly opposed to the power and influence of big business and big labor" (Lipset, 1960:148). These people and their employed dependents, making up just under a third of the labor force in 1933, suffered the strains of de-stratification. For years they had been living on proletarian incomes while desperately clinging to the respectability values of a middle-class existence (Schoenbaum, 1967:4). *Presumably*, they wanted restoration of their economic fortunes, making their income once again commensurate with their claims to middle-class status. They wanted protection of their style of life. Their vote for Hitler was one for a world made safe again for the corner store owner and the small, independent farmer. Of course, they were not the only ones casting their fate with Hitler. But the rest must have done so primarily out of economic distress. Germany's economic chaos during the Great Depression of the thirties was so much larger than in other industrialized nations, and the rising curve of the Nazi vote so closely paralleled that of the national unemployment rate (Kaltefleiter, 1968:37) that it remains a difficult task indeed not to reduce Hitler's rise to power entirely to economic conditions in a nation on the brink of complete collapse. In 1932 almost 44 percent of Germans found themselves unemployed, a rate twice that of Britain and Sweden, more than twice that of France, and almost double the U.S. rate; relative to 1929, total industrial production in Germany was down by 42 percent, consumption-goods output down by over 20 percent, gross national income down by 38 percent, wage and salary income down by 39 percent, property and proprietorship income down by 39 percent, and public-transfer payments up by a mere 9 percent (Lepsius, 1978:52–59). In light of these facts and the steadily deteriorating economic situation they reflect over a three-year period, it is amazing that a majority still voted for Hindenburg as Reichspräsident on the second ballot in 1932 (Lepsius, 1978:39); for that was, after all, a vote for a system of rule, democracy, so obviously unable to cope.

Keeping in mind that almost two thirds of the electorate never gave their vote to the National Socialists as long as free elections prevailed, what about the role of Nazi ideology among the rest? If one can speak about an ideology of the Nazi Party at all, rather than just propaganda, that ideology boiled down to antimodern rural romanticism (Schoenbaum, 1967:154). Borrowed from the German folk movements of the nineteenth century, there was nothing revolutionarily charismatic about this message. It too was old hat. Beyond this the Nazis promised to smash "the chains of Versailles." Essentially that meant three things. One promise was a Greater Germany, realizing the aspiration for the "greater German solution" to national unification, the one Bismarck had sacrificed by leaving Austria out of the modern nation-state. Another—and of course a very obviously connected—objective was to make Germany a world power, undoing the defeat of 1918. And the third element was to risk war in obtaining these objectives and make sure that no alleged "stab in the back" or internal revolution would ever frustrate Germany's reach for world-power status again. None of these ideas were new, none the distinctive trademark of National Socialism. If anything, their message was antirevolutionary. What was distinctive was the way the National Socialists packaged old ideas. They poured the old wine into the new bottle of racism. But the figure of the mythical Jew had nothing whatever to do with any concrete historical Jew of a religious or ethnic character. The mythical Jew represented the radical militancy of National Socialism in pursuing Germany's historical mission in providing a third alternative to the rampant liberalism of the West and the class dictatorship of the East. Racism meant being antiliberal, anticapitalist, and anticlass, the latter in the sense of a declaration of war against classwar. In this fashion they offered a multiplicity of appeals, promised everything to everybody, and so nothing in particular to anybody. Every outsider could envisage what he wanted, including the belief that Jews were not at all even Hitler's own favorite target (Schoenbaum, 1967:29, 33–42, 154; Bracher, 1970:22, 155).

A similar irrelevance of the Jewish question characterizes the way the movement came to power. That was due to negotiations among representatives of the Army, big business, Reichspräsident Hindenburg, and Hitler. Falling into the groove of rule without parliamentary support and on the basis of emergency decrees already in force for about two years, the groups that heaved Hitler into the position of the chancellorship could not care less about the Jewish question. Theirs was the pursuit of the establishment of an authoritarian regime. They believed they could use Hitler's mass-support basis and get rid of him again. The Army pursued its institutional interest, rearmament; the business community was interested in controlling labor, reversing some of the social legislation, and getting rid of restrictions imposed by the Versailles peace treaty (Bracher, 1970:184–218; Lepsius, 1978:71–74). In these negotiations it was not charisma that brought Hitler to power. It was a mixture of traditional authority epitomized in personal fealty to Hindenburg and an adroit manipulation of the procedural rules of constitutional rational legalism, permitting the exercise of executive powers or rule by emergency decree without parliamentary support. What is more, even long after the polity had become a totalitarian one, Hitler continued to observe the legal niceties. The Enabling Act, granting unrestricted powers, was routinely renewed, "as required by law," by his puppet parliament until 1943. But not even that proved sufficient in using the means of a modern society. A legal basis for total power had to be established as well. In 1942 the Reichstag passed a law granting Hitler the right to use any means he deemed useful, and means "unrestricted by any existing law," to make everyone do his duty in the service of victory. By this act Hitler became the supreme legislative and judicial authority in the state, and rational legality was the tool to transform the arbitrariness of traditional rule into its totalitarian version, which is one freed from any constraint (Adler, 1974:992–93). What this shows is not hate of the Jews or other *Untermenschen* categories. This shows a grand declaration of moral indifference in the selection of means "to make Germany great again." In Weber's terms the only charismatic element was the grant of absolutely unrestricted power to Hitler. One could describe this as a kind of charismatic commitment to unbelief, some ideological fervor to believe in nothing but expediency. Yet this too had to be cloaked in legality, which seemed to provide just sufficient reassurance among a people basically averse to any revolution.

Once in power Hitler did, at first, succeed beyond all expectations. The military occupation of the Rhineland, the annexation of Austria, the Munich agreements, these were modes of "smashing the chains of Versailles" in a grand style. It was similar on the domestic front. The National Socialist "battle for the creation of jobs" took exactly three years to achieve overwhelming success. In 1932 Germany had about six million unemployed, a misery affecting every second family in the nation; by 1936 there was a labor shortage. That initial spectacular success before the war gave the National Socialist regime all the external legitimation it could conceivably need (Bracher, 1970:369). Once at war, the regime could rely on traditional conceptions of authority for compliance with and tolerance of evil so vast as to defy the powers of normal speech.

These facts attest to a widespread moral indifference about the *de facto* destruction of the *Rechtsstaat*. But none support Fein's (1979:29–30) contention of National Socialism as a movement of integral nationalism that had to proceed to genocide because the new elite in power needed legitimation in terms of the anti-Semitic formula they had propagated. Neither the Holocaust, nor the truly complete anomic hell the German occupiers of Poland had unleashed on the Poles (Gross, 1975), nor the fate of thousands of non-Jewish victims inside and outside of the Holocaust Kingdom was dictated by any political-system need. These unspeakable crimes against the human condition were the realization of a possibility not the result of any political necessity. What is more, Fein's legitimation thesis of Jewish genocide remains historically incorrect for Germany. Her problem of national integration had always focused on inclusion of the Catholics and the working class. Bismarck's *Kulturkampf* and anti-Socialist legislation should suffice as evidence for Imperial Germany. Yet insecurity about national integration continued to focus on these two groups, and not the tiny minority of the Jews, which in Germany was an overassimilated one at that (Bokolsky, 1975; Schoeps, 1970). By the time Hitler appeared on the scene, these two groups still figured as potential enemies of the Reich. Even though Hitler himself was adamantly opposed to warming up the *Kulturkampf* again, "political Catholicism" and communism were the main figures on Heydrich's enemy list; and if the Düsseldorf Gestapo files are not entirely misrepresentative of Gestapo practice elsewhere, then it is clear that not the Jews but Catholics and Communists were perceived as the important enemies of the Third Reich (Mann, 1978).

Finally, moral indifference to the fate of the Jews rather than hate also emerges from what little is known about the reaction of the population at large to anti-Jewish measures. Fein's assertion that Jewish genocide served the legitimation of Nazi rule is also contradicted by two more facts. First, the exclusion of Jews from society, stripping them of civil and social rights, was accomplished by means of legislation—that is to say, through reliance on rational-legal, not charismatic authority. Second, in Germany the destruction of the Jews remained a secret.

Starting with prohibiting the employment of non-Aryans in the teaching profession and ending with denying to Jews the protection of the courts, stripping the Jews of membership rights in Germany was a legal process involving legislative acts, implementation decrees, and regulatory decrees specifying the tasks and responsibilities of various state administrations. This process took eleven years without ever resolving all doubt as to who was a Jew (The Jewish Black Book Committee, 1946:106–7; Hilberg, 1971:97). That an excessive legalization of the illegitimate can effectively substitute for a deficit in charismatic legitimacy has been shown by Adler's (1974) analysis of Gestapo files pertaining to the exclusion of the German Jews from society. All the regulations and orders given to the Jewish community councils were formulated in a language as if the self-administration of the civil death of the Jewish community was something completely normal, as proverbially normal as taxes and death. On both sides of the fence—the Gestapo officials who processed the files, and the Jewish community agencies who produced the statistics—the striking feature remains rational legality, the administration of things, all conducted in the classic spirit of bureaucracy *sine ira et studio* (without passion and bias). This sense of normality was quite easily maintained as long as the goal was emigration, until October 1941, even though emigration was dictated by the state, and even though it entailed expropriation. Subsequently, when the official goal became resettlement and the actual one death, the cooperation between the Jewish community and the Gestapo remained perfect. By that time both parties were almost unconscious of the ethical nature of their activity. They could easily suffocate the voice of conscience in the formal procedural aspects of administration, which did not deal with people but with matter. Furthermore, the sheer volume of paperwork increased steadily (Adler, 1974:3–32, 374). No mayor, no county administrator, no head of the local internal-revenue office could remain ignorant of the process of exclusion. The civil death of German Jewry was widely known in Germany. But its very legality helped all, persecutor and victim alike, in stifling the voice of conscience about the illegitimacy of their action. Processing emigration and expropriation forms, with endless citations of laws, decrees, regulations, and paragraphs were activities that for bureaucrats fell within their

"zone of indifference." Everything looked rather familiar. The expropriation of their property could be seen as the administration of an amended
emigration tax, based on a law passed in 1931 by a democratic regime.
And however forced their emigration, they were no longer citizens, and
"foreigners", after all, enjoy residence rights only at the pleasure of the
state. German civil servants, it must be noted, always thought of
themselves as serving the state, some vague conception of law, and not a
government. That is why the exclusion of the German Jews could rest on
a mixture of rational-legal and traditional authority. The whole process
attests to a neat reversal of one of Merton's (1957) categories of deviance.
Normally, so we are wont to believe, bureaucratic ritualism, going
through the procedural motions without caring about the ends to be
served, interferes with goal attainment. But, as amply shown in Adler's
(1974) analysis, when the ends lack legitimacy, bureaucratic ritualism can
be a potent tool in attaining them. In Germany ritualism led to the
accomplishment of hell.

As for the general public in Germany, what do we know about their
reaction? The closest thing to public-opinion surveys in the Third Reich
were the "public morale estimates" *(Stimmungsberichte)* of the domestic
branch of the SS intelligence apparat (Boberach, 1965). Popular reaction
to the introduction of the segregation badge (a Star of David Jews had to
wear on their clothing) was reported as mostly indifferent and mildly
supportive. Some Germans registered surprise about how many Jews
were still in the Reich; some expressed worry about retaliation abroad.
Perhaps Germans in foreign countries would be forced to wear a swastika
and so made to suffer (Steinert, 1977:135). But by September 1941, when
the badge regulation was implemented, and so after almost nine years of
unremittent Goebbels' propaganda, it was also quite clear that the German
population cared far less about anti-Semitism than their *Führer* did.
Germans at large worried about the bombs, about food, and about the
fortunes of war. Theirs were the concerns of normal, average people, not
those of members of a charismatic community bent on liberating mankind
from the curse of the Jewish bacillus (Boberach, 1965). These were
reactions to the exclusion of the Jews, and they remained those of
indifference rather than the alternatives of enthusiastic support or protest.
When it comes to knowledge about mass murder, the available evidence
points to ignorance. While the reality of the final solution was common
knowledge in Poland by 1942 (Hilberg, 1961:315), Adler (1974:473–85)
maintains that it remained more of a secret in Germany than anywhere
else. A public acknowledgment that one knew made one liable to a crime
listening to foreign broadcasts. Given the euphemisms about "resettlement" or "deportations" in Gestapo correspondence, a lower-echelon

Gestapo official who had never served outside Germany since 1939 could afford to remain ignorant. In addition, the Gestapo was not recruited primarily from Hitler's movement. The middle-and lower-level officials were simply assigned to Gestapo duty from other branches of the police apparatus without any ideological indoctrination (Adler, 1974:1,035). Members of the Jewish community lived in isolation, and that means a life of rumor. But refusal to cooperate with rational-legal authority would require knowledge about murder rather than rumor; and given the flood of paperwork, protest or sabotage would have required an unusually sensitive moral conscience, one willing to assume personal responsibility with possible consequences, rather than the directly visible and known consequences of one's compliance. Perhaps the best indicator of the prevailing ignorance in the German-Jewish community remains the Gestapo correspondence with the Jewish agencies. The enforcement of compliance with administrative decrees rested almost entirely on the stick. There was never any concealment that all Jews would be deported. And there were constant reiterated threats of "dire consequences," immediate deportations, and the death penalty (Adler, 1974). Presumably, had the parties addressed known that death stood at the end of the road of obedience to state authority, such threats would not have been effective. The only evidence about knowledge comes from the German lower class. They called a spade by its name (Boberach, 1965:63), but everywhere else in the Third Reich euphemisms veiled the fate of the Jews.

If Fein's thesis of genocide serving the external legitimation needs of the regime fails, what about the internal legitimation needs of the regime? To begin with, a somewhat better case of Hitler's role as charismatic leader can be made in his relation to the insider, members of the party, the SA, and the SS. During the struggle for power Hitler succeeded in no less than three internal "seizures of power": (1) In 1921 he obtained recognition as the sole leader of the party unrestricted by formal regulations. (2) In 1925, on his release from prison, he denounced all party organizations that had survived or formed in his absence and found acceptance as the only valid embodiment of the party. (3) In 1926, when North German party leaders insisted on specifying the party program in a "socialist direction," he gained a monopoly right over all questions of policy. With these three power seizures his unrestricted personal authority became fully established and sufficiently so to overcome any subsequent challenge from inside the movement (Lepsius, 1978:62–63). If one were to accept this claim literally, it would follow that anti-Semitism served no conceivable internal-legitimation need *at any time* after the year 1926. It was Hitler's right to switch on anti-Semitism, or to switch it off, depending on how he felt. But not only the store boycott of 1933, but also the very "zigzag road to Auschwitz" afterward indicate clearly that the exclusion of Jews from society, though not their physical destruction, did serve some internal-legitimation needs on the one hand, and prevented the party from sinking into a mere job-sinecure bureaucracy on the other. In the store boycott of 1933, for example, a committee had to be formed to control SA street violence after it had broken out. Further, mutually reinforcing commitments to anti-Semitic actions kept the party alive as a movement (Schleunes, 1970). That anti-Semitic radicals within the party occasionally egged each other on also emerges from Adler's (1974) analysis of the exclusion process in Germany. Here and there, the impetus to take action against the Jews, and get on with it, as it were, did come from lower party officials in the countryside (Adler, 1974:699–703, 726, 733–38, 755, 797, 804). Still, these voices of hate from the bottom were not critical. The Gestapo ignored them often, following up on suggestions from that quarter only if they fell in line with policies received from the top.

In addition, we have at least six categories of evidence that deny that the Holocaust engine was set in motion in order to satisfy internal-legitimation needs of the National Socialist regime. Some of these pertain to the nature of social class support, others to Hitler's compromised charisma, and yet others to anti-Semitism directly.

First, and most important in refuting Fein's contention, German Nazism was a middle-class phenomenon and one appearing in a society without any Jewish minority worth mentioning. In stark contrast, fascism in Hungary and Romania, for example, was a lower-class phenomenon (Mosse, 1978a:111). In the less industrialized countries of Eastern Europe more generally, where socialist or Communist parties had hardly gained any ground yet in mobilizing lower-class discontent and where Jewish minorities were of a considerable size, fascism could have a real anti-Semitic basis, one drawing on very concrete material and "ideational" conflicts and interests. There hate of the Jews lacked neither in ethnic and so "nationalist aspirations," nor in religious or in economic bases. But in Germany, National Socialism was a phenomenon of centrist extremism (Lipset, 1960) in its voting base, and one of middle-class extremism at the level of elites; for, as will be shown in subsequent chapters, Germany was a country with one-dimensional elites. Insecure in their sense of legitimacy, they were mobilizable for building an empire as a means to gain status security. What appealed to them in the Nazi *Weltanschauung* was the historically familiar theme of aspiring to successor status to the Austro-Hungarian and Russian empires and the fact that this aspiration was preached in a completely unsentimental fashion (Michalka, 1978). Jews, on the other hand, were a matter of utter indifference to them, as were the fates of other peoples, including that of the Germans, who were to them merely material for their own success strivings.

Second, two pieces of evidence suggest that party members reacted with indifference or even with disturbance rather than with enthusiasm to the news of the slaughter. One small "private survey" in 1942 tried to ascertain the level of support for the final solution. Müller-Claudius managed to collect opinions from sixty-two individuals, mostly party members, and mostly upper middle class in terms of their occupations. He found 5 percent registering enthusiastic approval, 5 percent categorical disapproval, and 90 percent indifference or confusion (Poliakov, 1954:282). But Bormann's language regulations for internal party communications provide a broader basis to reject the internal-legitimation thesis. When returning soldiers from the East spread the news about the activities of *Einsatzgruppen*, the administration of the truth became an official task of the party. And the manner of this administration tells us that telling the truth proved damaging to the maintenance of support for the regime, even within the party. This is clearly evident in Bormann's turn-around in issuing the pertinent language regulations. The first, issued in October 1942, ordered that the truth be told, confidentially and within the party, of course. But only six months later that order was reversed. The discussion of the extermination of the Jews inside the party was forbidden. Permitted was only the message that "a complete mobilization of Jewish labor for the war effort" was under way (Steinert, 1977:141, 144).

Third, the anti-Semitic radicals in both party and SA who figured as instigators of anti-Jewish actions early in the regime became politically irrelevant later on with the rise of the SS complex, inaugurated with the murder of Röhm in 1934. Neither the number nor the prominence of "true believer" anti-Semites in the movement as a whole sufficed to argue that genocide served internal-legitimation needs. If one designates as "true believers" those committed to the radical myth of National Socialism to the point of actually demanding the killing of the Jews, then one finds only a tiny group of "pornoneurotic" anti-Semites, even in the party a minute minority, and one in existence only before such talk became reality (Höhne, 1967:303). Grouped around Streicher and Hitler, that is where the idea of the final solution originated. But it would be very hard to argue that Hitler needed the support of Streicher to maintain himself in power. Furthermore, while Streicher had a race ideology with substantive beliefs, that was only partly true of Hitler but not to any serious degree of his movement. While ideas and their ethical implications are the main guides to action of any genuine charismatic figure, Hitler considered ideas and "ideals" as pure propaganda instruments for modern political leadership.

And his own eyes were always on the main show, Germany's drive for hegemony in Europe (Fest, 1973:184 esp.). However instrumental his approach to mere ideas, though, hatred of the Jews did play an important role in Hitler's own conception of himself as the missionary figure leading Germany to ascendancy. Acting on his emotions by actually proceeding to make Europe *"judenrein"* reassured him in his commitment to his "philosophy of history" as a ceaseless Darwinian struggle among people. It convinced him that he could be ruthless enough to deserve unabridged power in the foreign-policy sector. But it is also important to realize that this bit of personal anti-Semitism served a legitimation function of Nazi domination to a minuscule point of near-autistic proportions. No one else cared about this aspect of the *Führer*. Certainly what Speer (1969) told us about daily life in the entourage of Adolf Hitler points to the kind of household where searching for charismatic forces would be like looking for a needle in a haystack. Among a somewhat wider circle of associates one finds at best two figures who regarded Hitler as a genuinely charismatic leader. Hess believed in his infallibility; and Rosenberg believed in the racial myth, but curiously, not to the point of the extermination of human life that did not fit into the projected Reich. Commitment to sheer conquest, to organizational expansion, and to expediency as the only relevant standard in the exercise of power characterized all the other principal associates. Göring believed in office accumulation. Goebbels' only conviction was that everything could be organized; his was a commitment to the sociological principle of "reality construction." Bormann and Himmler remained pure functionaries all their lives, believing neither in the infallibility of their leader nor in any dogma whatever (Bracher, 1970:304–12).

Fourth, if neither the party nor the inner circle of Hitler's associates support the internal-legitimation hypothesis for the Holocaust, the same is true for the SS, executor of the final solution. The SS was the only official voice in National Socialist Germany ever to denounce publicly so "crude, primitive, and emotional an anti-Semitism" as calls for the physical extermination of the Jews (Höhne, 1967:301). Furthermore, the SS, a self-declared aristocracy of the New Order, based its claims to superiority on an ideological commitment to the end of all ideology. Their trademark of the new man was the ability to live and act without the crutch of belief. But while Arendt (1951:385) still thought that a genuine belief in unbelief, in a serious commitment to the idea that the acid test of being elite resided in the conviction that all legitimation of conduct is irrelevant was so extraordinary as to demand extraordinary socialization in the *Ordensburgen*, subsequent data showed that ideological training was despised, orders against church weddings were simply disobeyed, and a simple idolatry of achievement values sufficed for carrying out orders (Höhne, 1967:146–49). When Heydrich recruited for the *Einsatzgruppen*, he had to scrape the bottom of the barrel of still-available manpower; the aims of the special mission remained concealed from the officers until the day before departure to the East, and the rank and file only learned reality on the scene (Höhne, 1967:328–30). None of the *Einsatzgruppen* chiefs were believers in the race myth. They ranked among the most highly educated of the Nazi elite. Their Ph.D.-certified intellectualism despised the very idea of believing in an ideology. They also came, in part, from that group of SS intellectuals who had opposed the night-of-crystal *pogrom* in Germany on grounds of its sheer stupidity. Not belief but commitments to advance their careers sent them on their mission of death (Musmanno, 1961; Höhne, 1967:313, 327). None of the commanders of the most notorious death factories, nor transport chief Eichmann were "true believers" (Sereny, 1974; Höss, 1959; Höhne, 1967:307; Arendt, 1963). And this was true of Heinrich Himmler himself. In a posthumous publication of his secret speeches one finds that it was the rare occasion indeed when he spoke about the final solution in those terms of heroism one would expect of a servant of charisma. And on one of these occasions, his speech to party leaders in Posen in 1943, we can use his own voice as testimony concerning the absence of internal-legitimation pressure as a factor in the final solution. Said Himmler, "I dare to claim that if you take the number of applications for exceptions [from deportation and death] as an index of prevailing opinion, more 'decent' Jews must live in Germany than the total number enumerated. . . . I mention this only because you know yourself from your experience in your districts that each respectable National Socialist knows his 'decent' Jew" (Smith and Peterson, 1974:169). On another of these rare occasions, his speech to SS leaders in Posen in 1943, Himmler expressed his utter indifference to the fate of the conquered humanity in Eastern Europe as follows: "Whether other nations live well or starve to death is of interest to me only insofar as we need them for slaves for our culture; otherwise it does not interest me. Whether ten thousand Russian women collapse in constructing a tank trench interests me only with respect to whether or not the trench gets done" (Fraenkel and Manvell, 1965:131). Neither the decimation of the Slavs nor the extermination of the Jews were questions of ideology for Himmler. They were surplus populations to be removed in the service of an abstraction, *Lebensraum*. But we also know from his masseur and intimate Kersten (1952) that Himmler constantly engaged in attempts to decriminalize and miniaturize his work of death. Himmler too tried to evade reality. I would attribute it to the absence of charismatic beliefs. Thus rather than demands for the destruction of Jewry, to say nothing of other *Untermenschen* categories, to justify National Socialist rule, one finds also widespread efforts to keep the destruction a secret. Even internal communications used euphemisms and "justifications" in terms of traditional common-sense reasons. Among them one finds mention made of the need to prevent epidemics, to combat partisans, to secure the rear area of the Army, or preventive measures against collaboration with the enemy. What one never finds in these internal reports is that kind of pride in the accomplishment of a mission one would expect of "true believers" (Höhne, 1967:337). Instead silence and concealment of the truth pervaded ghettos, "model camp" Theresienstadt, and other camps alike; and killers and their victims avoided facing reality as much as possible (Hilberg, 1971:89–106; Höss, 1959:205; Langbein, 1972:353; Goldstein, 1949:108–10; Adler, 1955:118; Sereny, 1974:213).

Fifth, Fein's legitimation thesis about Jewish genocide requires a treatment of National Socialist rule as one resting importantly on legitimacy beliefs. By and large, this is not true. Instead the Nazi regime was "rule by constellation of interests" (Weber, 1922:941–48). That form of governance evokes obedience not by virtue of a sense of obligation to obey but because obedience is perceived as paying off better than resisting. Hannah Arendt's (1951) original portrait of Nazi rule as a set of competing power hierarchies, "bounded" into what she called an "onion structure," has only been revised in a direction farther away from the model of an internally well-structured dictatorship. Even the onion structure proved too much of a structure for the institutionalized chaos of reality. Hüttenberger (1976) proposed the highly descriptive term "polycracy" as the most adequate label to capture the historical reality. Polycracy means that domination of society results from a shifting-interest constellation among several competing "power complexes." The relations among such complexes as Army, big business, and party that had brought Hitler to power were governed by "compacts," contractlike arrangements in one part and informal friendship pacts in another, connecting persons and their organizations with control over separate power resources. The authority relations within a given complex were also a mixture of tradition and modernity. On the one hand, one operated with rational legality and the style of military orders, but on the other hand, the members of a complex gave their leader that arbitrary power to deploy them for tasks of various kinds that was once typical of feudal vassal-lord relationships. As the Third Reich moved through its short history both number and prominence of complexes changed, but the nature of the compact-governed interrelationships did not. During the war the most important complexes were the SS state-security complex, the party front organizations complex, the labor-front complex, Speer's Armaments Ministry complex, and Goebbels' Propaganda Ministry complex. And compacts and shifting alliance patterns governed their relations. True, Hitler was not openly opposed by any complex leader. But this absence of opposition to his policies did not rest on belief in the *Führer's* infallibility nor on any kind of ideology with a substantive revolutionary content, but rather on the principle of expediency. A player who wanted to stay in the game (and all of them wanted that) pursued tasks as dictated by the immediacy of the interest constellation in which he found himself. The dynamic elements in this constellation were above all the party and the SS. Conceived as nothing but an agitation apparat, the former encountered the prospect of unemployment after the seizure of power. Conceived as nothing but an instrument of terror for the destruction of the domestic political opposition during the struggle for power, the SS faced similar dismal prospects after all serious contenders had disappeared into the concentration camps. Both of these complexes could justify their existence only through growth beyond their original functions. The war and conquest in the East provided the field of activity that the pursuit of material and status interests demanded. In short, polycracy or "rule by interest constellations" characterized the Third Reich far more than rule by virtue of beliefs in legitimacy. It was not the legitimacy needs of the regime that doomed the Jews—and the Polish intelligentsia, the Gypsies, and the Russian POWs—but rather a profound indifference to the suffering of any individual or groups.

The characterization of Nazi Germany as a polycracy is based on fairly extensive empirical evidence. That the Third Reich was a "system of systemlessness," as suggested by Hannah Arendt (1951:395), has been borne out by separate studies covering such areas as the foreign labor program (Homze, 1967), the Nazi Party (Peterson, 1967), the SS complex (Höhne, 1967), and the conduct of economic-development policy in the Balkans (Orlow, 1968). Conquest of resources, empire building, and competition for tasks and prerogatives characterized rule according to the "leadership principle." So long as implementation of the final solution served the interests of the SS state-security complex, it was done; it was halted when it no longer served these interests (Höhne, 1967:525). In all of these near-chaotic relationships no one cared about the Jews, as no one cared about elimination of other groups. Not legitimacy needs of the system, but a profound indifference to human life characterized the leadership of the Third Reich. While one cannot substantiate the claim of complicity in Jewish mass murder as a strategy (Arendt, 1951:372; Poliakov, 1954:247; Poliakov and Wulf, 1955:185) designed to keep the killers at their tasks, the utter ruthlessness of the pursuit of "total war" brought about a similar effect. But it was not the racial myth and its implementation, it was the pursuit of an empire "regardless of the means" that brought that about. Goebbels understood this well. In 1943 he stated: "As far as we are concerned, we have burned all bridges behind us. . . . We are now forced to the ultimate, and we are therefore determined in its pursuit. We shall either become the greatest statesmen history has ever known or its greatest criminals" (Bracher, 1970:309).

Sixth, that it was not hate of Jews and other *Untermenschen* but indifference to their fate that manifested itself in mass exterminations has also been noted by some survivors (Wiesel, 1960). What we know about the response of various elites in German society to the negative population policies tends to corroborate that impression. The top leadership of the Army provided indispensable aid to the Nazis, not only in their rise to power but also in the process of totalitarianization of their polity after 1933. A few examples of the post-1933 period must suffice here to make the point. It was the Army that backed Hitler and his then still tiny SS in the defeat of the so-called Röhm *Putsch* of 1934. On that occasion the Army armed and housed the SS units, provided transportation, promised to stand at alert should the mighty SA manage to fight back, and even guarded the Munich party headquarters where Hitler addressed the remaining SA leadership afterward. Two generals—Von Schleicher and Von Bredow, the former together with his wife—were murdered during those days. But the Army elite found that acceptable according to the slogan, "Where you shave wood, some chips will fall." Shortly afterward, on the death of Reichspräsident Hindenburg, the Army leadership ordered the troops sworn to Hitler personally without being asked to by Hitler. Further, the Aryan paragraph for civil-service employment was applied by them, again without external pressure. Seventy officers were fired, or were pensioned off. During the Polish campaign the Army simply caved in to SS pressure and yielded administrative authority to them and the party in the conquered territory, which was certainly a breach with traditional practice. And while the Army resisted similar takeover attempts on the part of the SS later on in occupied Western Europe, the Army's complicity in the systematic destruction of political surplus populations was by then well established. And in all of this compliance with the new master it was not succumbing to National Socialist convictions, which was the cause, but rather the deliberate pursuit of political adjustment to the New Order, a policy guided strictly by narrow institutional interests. And at first, that policy payed off. Under the Versailles peace treaty the strength of the German armed forces had been limited to a force of one hundred thousand men. By 1939 the Army had grown to seven hundred thousand men. That is what "smashing the chains of Versailles" meant to the Army leadership

(Müller, 1969). When the final solution was set in motion, the generals were very well informed indeed. But a "compact" was arranged between Army and SS that left most of the dirty work to the latter. That compact was opposed openly and strenuously by exactly one general, Blaskowitz. But as with the other few, so very few, who ever opposed the slaughter of whole populations on moral grounds, this one Army general was simply transferred (Höhne, 1967:281–83; Hoffmann, 1970:189, 309; Buchheim et al., 1965).

Moral indifference reigned in the German Churches. On the Protestant side one finds both: abject cooperation with the New Germany in the attempt to establish a nationwide official state Church, and a "confessing Church," which opposed National Socialism. Significantly, though, that opposition was self-consciously nonpolitical. The members of the Confessing Church opposed the preaching of a godless heathenism on the part of a few party zealots; they did not oppose the exclusion of the Jews from German society or the disappearance into the concentration camps of many Communists and Socialists (Conway, 1968; Helmreich, 1979: 133–236, 303–46). While the Catholic Church in Germany fiercely resisted the application of the Aryan paragraph to its own domain and nowhere proposed to exclude non-Aryan Christians from Church services as did two of the Protestant *Landeskirchen*, a profound indifference to the fate of the Jews also characterized the Catholic Church leadership. They fought a losing battle against the loss of their educational, youth, and communal-welfare organizations and their newspapers. But in each protest they reaffirmed their loyalty to the German nation as if they were still in the throes of Bismarck's *Kulturkampf* and had to prove that Catholics were "good Germans" too. The German Catholic Church as an organization did nothing to save the Jews or the Poles (Lewy, 1964). And what about that ultimate pillar of German cultural respectability, the university professoriate? Silence, escape into professionalism and sycophancy characterized academe (Bracher, 1970:271–98; Beyerchen, 1977). The same holds true for the paragons of modern techniciandom, the business elite (Schweitzer, 1964; Rubenstein, 1975:48–67). Finally, even in the German resistance circles, moral revulsion against the Holocaust was a secondary concern. Here it was only a small group of students at the University of Munich, the "white rose," and so the voices of some late adolescents, who protested the barbarism of the German people from nothing but moral considersations. A moral concern about the *Untermenschen* policy in practice was not even the all-consuming, overriding passion of that man who came to plant the bomb that failed to destroy Hilter (Müller, 1970 [?]). And the most extensive history of the German resistance movement ever written discovered exactly one person in it for whom the final solution was *the* "decisive existential experience" (Hoffmann, 1970:381).

In conclusion, let us note that no book on the legitimacy sources of National Socialism has been written. It would take a book to prove my contention that neither external nor internal legitimation needs ever called for Treblinka. Nonetheless in Germany, the facts I have reviewed, and all have been known for a long time, simply do not support Fein's (1979) correlations. Insofar as the National Socialist polity depended on legitimacy rather than resting, in the main, on interest constellations, the foregoing remarks can be summarized in the following fashion. It was adopting a tactic, the "legal revolution" that was necessary for Hilter to become a serious contender for power. The rational-legal component of that phrase *adapted* the National Socialist movement to a people quite averse to revolutions. Interpersonal trust and arbitrariness, these two features of traditional authority, characterized the "compact" relations that served the overriding *goal-attainment* aspirations of the Nazi leadership: to gain unrestricted power and to maintain it. A perverted rational-legality coupled with extreme bureaucratic ritualism made available the tools of law for the attainment of illegitimate ends, the exclusion of the Jews from German society. Insofar as the drive for world-power status and empire on the Continent rested on any legitimacy beliefs, it fed on a traditional source of authority, the Greater Germany solution not attained by Bismarck. Thus the core element of political *legitimation* of the nation's efforts were traditional, sanctioned by the democratic voices of modern nation-building, voices from the past crying out for fulfillment. And finally, the *integrative* force that held these disparate elements together to the bitter end was not belief in the charismatic qualities of the *Führer* but rather that temptation of the modern mind that relegates all belief to the realm of superstition and devotes itself to the idolatry of secular achievement. Genocide served the private need of Hitler, a need he indulged in only after he realized that the big show, the drive for empire, was doomed (Haffner, 1978). The German elites participated or stood idly by for no other reason than expediency in advancing the interest of some "power complex." That degree of expediency presupposes the complete withdrawal of any moral caring concern from the public sphere of our lives. If we are to understand Treblinka better in order to gain a more mature ability to mourn, we need a theory about moral indifference, one that tells us why nobody cared when "they crucified my Lord."

CHAPTER THREE

On the Cultural and Social Sources of Moral Indifference in a Nation That Failed

What elites in German society cared about most was a powerful nation-state. In light of that professed aspiration, the history of the modern German nation-state looks like a tale told by an idiot. January 18, 1971, marked the Centennial of Germany as a nation. But there was no unified nation left to celebrate the occasion and no cause for celebration. As *one* nation-state Germany died a violent death before reaching her one-hundredth birthday. The German nation-state was created during the second half of the nineteenth century by a series of successfully conducted cabinet wars, the Schleswig-Holstein dispute, the Austria-Prussia conflict, and the war against France. Engineered on the model of conflicts prevalent among eighteenth-century monarchs, these wars were followed by two poorly engineered but also modern total wars ending in defeat. The closing of the second, in 1945, marked the beginning of the end of Germany as one national society, at least for the time being. Instrumental warfare stood at the beginning of her short history. Ideological warfare was the major means for her double attempt to attain "a place in the sun." And war too marked her end. Truly, the Germans paid a visit to the history of nation-states that was comparatively short, exalting for few, nasty for some, and brutish for many.

This was not necessary. In analyzing modern German history and the evil it wrought one must be wary of imposing some myth of causal-sociological destiny on it, for we confront but a possibility, albeit one that happened. And because our interest in that history is focused primarily on the evil realized, one that hitherto remained unique, we are justified in concentrating on German society. Wars are international events, but no foreign power dictated to Germany the mode in which she waged her last

66

one nor the essentially identical goal, the reach for empire or *Lebensraum* in Central and Eastern Europe, she pursued in the First World War as well as in the Second World War (Fischer, 1967).

As manifest in the Holocaust Kingdom, Germany's second war of conquest was so extremely brutal that only a study that sheds some light on that profound moral indifference among Germany's elites that made it possible promises some approximate understanding of this page in our history. That moral indifference can be specified. It amounted to a double commitment. One was a commitment to the idea that in a modern society the public sphere is necessarily an amoral one. The other was a conviction that the "human resources" of a modern society have to be used just like nonhuman ones in one critical respect—namely, unrestricted by any absolute constraints, whether sacred or secular in nature. Undoubtedly, these two features are to some extent inherent in any modern society, which is why modern German history has some universal significance. But only among the German elites were these convictions practiced with that consistency that made possible industrialized genocide and national suicide. That is why German society demands our attention if we are to learn about modern evil. I start with an outline of the sequence of preconditions, intervening factors, and consequent variables that made possible so extreme a level of moral indifference.

1. Prior to and during the early phases of nation-building the population that came to form the new nation was one characterized by deep value cleavages, dividing the people into different value communities by region, social class, and urban and rural ways of life. The nature of these cleavages was such as to provide few, if any, cross-cutting ties. Germans were ethical strangers to each other. (This precondition is treated as an empirical given, not itself subject to explanation.)

2. A temporal coincidence of nation-building and industrialization produced unusually severe integration problems, which made the following developments below more likely than they would have been otherwise. (This intervening factor is treated as an empirical given, not subject to explanation.)

3. Given the two features just listed, the Prussian legacy of rule by interest constellation became the German one. Obedience to state authority was always primarily a matter of expediency. Elites in German society obeyed because that paid off better than resistance. Only secondarily did obedience also flow from a belief in the legitimacy of state authority; and when it did, that belief was among the "weakest" of Weber's (1922: 212–301) three types of legitimacy beliefs, the belief in fidelity to procedure, the one on which rational-legal authority rests. Rule by interest constellation was the more prevalent pattern in German society.

That pattern laid the foundation for moral indifference among the elites, for in this mode of governance elites pursue the interests of one particular institution, the one where they are employed. They treat the policies pursued by other institutional elites as a matter of indifference *unless* those policies are seen as directly impinging on their own institutional domain.

4. Precondition, intervening factors, and rule by interest constellation led to the emergence of destratified or one-dimensional elites at the national level of society. Instead of a nationwide upper-class establishment, uniform in lifestyle and outlook, and cohesive in its interests, Germany developed peculiar elites with command over but one of the socially recognized scarce resources rather than over several. Superior wealth in the nation did not insure superior political influence at its center. People in the highest state offices were, more often than not, relative paupers. The German elites can be described as a conglomerate of the "merely rich," the "merely powerful," the "merely prestigious," and the "merely cultivated," an elite credited with superior moral wisdom. Compared to an upper-class establishment of a multidimensional kind with control over all four of these resources, elites in German society were typically suffering relative status-deprivation. That turned them into a "cartel of anxiety" (Dahrendorf, 1965:297). Such status deprivation deprived these elites of the very tools required for the assumption of moral responsibility. In common parlance, moral responsibility means assuming accountability for the consequences of one's conduct that arise beyond one's intentions and outside that sphere of action under one's own direct control. Normally, persons in elite positions in the business community, the armed forces, or the national government are expected to be committed to moral responsibility for the broader national welfare. One expects them to have a genuinely caring concern of the nation's well-being, a concern that transcends the narrow institutional domain of their employment. But in Germany, with her development of one-dimensional elites, this expectation became significantly attenuated. A very rich Rhenish manufacturer, for example, who lacked the kind of political influence in Berlin even halfway commensurate with his extraordinary wealth, could not assume responsibility for the political consequences of his contribution to the nation's economic development. He could not because he lacked the proper tool, political influence. As a consequence, the assumption of moral responsibility in the wider sense of the term I have in mind here remained for him an adolescent pipe dream, something that education for elite status weaned you from rather than trained you for. Next to de-stratification at the top of society, Germany also developed a pattern of "negative integration" in the form of segregated subcultural communities at the bottom. People did not live in isolation from each

other, as the model of modern mass society and big-city life suggests. Instead they lived in subcultural enclaves of their own kind, avoiding intimate contacts with ethical strangers in other such enclaves. Not the alleged insecurity and loneliness of isolated masses but the political organization of segregated subcultures provided the fuel for the practice of mass politics.

5. Engaged in relentless resource competition with each other, Germany's one-dimensional elites mobilized a variety of segregated subcultures against each other. The pursuit of pseudonationalist aims of expansion abroad based on shifting interest constellations and fed, in turn, by the politics of agitation and propaganda at home became Germany's characteristic style of governance. Three distinct though related phenomena went into it. Domestic conflict increased in militancy; and the ability to regulate social conflicts declined, step by deathly step, as one moves from Wilhelminian Germany over the Weimar Republic to the Third Reich. Nationalist rhetoric inflated to a point where, in the Third Reich, it became a role expectation for persons in elite positions to believe in nothing. A kind of ideological commitment against mere ideology developed, and it was this commitment to unbelief that came to express a level of moral indifference deep enough to permit the industrialized destruction of political surplus populations. Finally, that commitment to unbelief also effectively destroyed all remnants of prestige, that tool of generalized persuasion (Parsons, 1963a) that normally govern the relations among elites in modern societies. With prestige destroyed, the German nation lost all self-steering ability. Too indifferent to care about genocide, elites in German society also became locked into a policy of national suicide.

So much for an overview of the argument. The following discussion of it identifies the parts by the corresponding number in the outline.

The Meaning and Salience of Value Dissensus in Society (1)

There can be little doubt that Germany's elites desired a viable and powerful nation-state. The virulent nationalism of the Wilhelminian era, the ice-cold distance that fashionable *Vernunftrepublikaner* maintained vis-à-vis the Weimar Republic, and the propagandistic nationalism of the Third Reich should suffice as evidence. There can be little doubt also about the capacity of the German people to mobilize their resources. Two major wars within one generation attest to it. But the history of her double attempt at hegemony in the Occident also attests to one indisputable outcome: utter failure in national aspirations. Germany is an instructive case in how a people neither niggardly endowed with natural nor with human and cultural resources can utterly fail in meeting the challenge of modernization. That challenge concerns primarily the increasingly problematical nature of formulating realistic goals for society, one attributable to the growth of scientific knowledge, technology, and wealth. Extending on Max Weber's (1919a) observation, the dilemma of modernity can be succinctly put as follows: Neither scientific knowledge, nor its application in technology, nor its organized routinized exploitation economically can tell men *what* they should do. More knowledge, greater technological capacities, and ever-rising levels of wealth expand the means at the disposal of men. To be modern means to live with the conscious apperception that nothing is "obviously impossible." Indeed, as man's capacity to change the world, notably his society, increases, so does the need to set goals for societal transformation. No longer living in a communal "reality construction" where the extant and the meaningful coincided as a given of the human condition, modern man is faced with the dilemma of a conscious choice among frequently contradictory ideals if he is to create a meaningful existence. So long as ideals belong to the realm of the hypothetical rather than the realizable, commitment to intrinsically contradictory ideals poses little problem. Once ideals move into the realm of the attainable, the sorting out of priorities becomes crucial if a sense of authenticity in one's commitments to ideals is to be maintained (Taviss, 1968). And so the assumption of responsibility for the wider consequences of one's conduct, that classic burden of elites, grows more difficult because extant social conditions become evaluated relative to multiple alternatives of what could be. Societal success—that is, actually attaining national objectives—becomes, in large measure, a straight function of formulating realistic models of the good society to build, eliminating the unrealistic from political relevance in the nation, mobilizing just sufficient support for the former, minimizing the alienation of disappointed aspirations, and utilizing the support mobilized to coordinate diverse efforts in the realization of publicly sanctioned goals. Roughly, that was Max Weber's (1919b) view of modern politics as a vocation. But let us emphasize one element he did not stress enough. The ability of politicians to formulate realistic models of the good society presupposes some consensus on shared societal values in society, minimally among its elites. That precondition was not met in Germany. As Hintze (1962) observed, when it comes to shared values, Germany had no Germans; she was a nation only in a formal sense, and one composed of value subcommunities segregated by class, region, and religion. While his was an impressionistic judgment, what significance can one attach to value dissensus?

If textbook adoption (Goodman and Marx, 1978:93) is a measure of fame and recognized utility, Clyde Kluckhohn's (1951:395) definition of values must be counted among the famous and useful. Accordingly, a value is "a conception . . . of the desirable which influences the selection from available modes, means, and ends of action." The cognitive element (conception), the affective one (desirable), and the need to choose and justify one's choice (selection) are all equally important in this definition. Some of these ideas are common sense—for example, the reference to knowing and feeling. Others are less obvious—for example, the nonidentity between the desirable and what men and women often desire. A brief elaboration is in order.

Values are fairly abstract codes or standards for evaluating conduct. By virtue of their abstract nature, they display persistence through time and applicability to a wide range of social situations. Broad as it is, Kluckhohn's concept covers at least three distinct sets of codes: (1) moral ones, bearing on questions of right and wrong; (2) aesthetic standards defining the appropriate and the inappropriate, matters of good and bad taste; (3) codes bearing on reality assessments, distinguishing the true from the false. My interest here focuses on the moral dimension and the fact that knowing and feeling are involved. Just knowing what is right and what is wrong hardly ever deterred any of us from criminal activity. Feelings of what is right and what is wrong are the primary forces that keep the many on the straight and narrow. This already emphasizes the distinction between the desirable and what in fact we often desire. Values are beliefs about what we *ought* to do; they are *felt* and acknowledged obligations to others and to ourselves. One becomes conscious of values particularly when inclination (what we want to do) and obligation (what we ought to do) conflict. My inclination on a given morning may be to go fishing; but a glance at my wife across the breakfast table makes me go to the office, after all. There may be a common standard, "responsible adult," which defeats inclination. At home such a standard would be expressed in terms of family norms, the obligations one owes as husband, father, or lover. Family obligations are typically diffuse, and disappointing one may have widely ramifying implications. Suddenly not going to work may indicate I am a poor provider, someone who cannot even be relied upon to pay the rent; also, it may show I do not care for the children and, perhaps, don't even love my wife. At the office, organization norms come into play. Showing up there, however reluctant at heart, preserves my image as a reliable associate and keeps the absenteeism rate down. It is not love that matters there; reliability and punctuality count instead. However trivial and trite the example, the norms involved are different but the value standard "responsible adult" covers both. Norms, then, are role-set specifications of more abstract beliefs called values. Values are one thing, norms another. That point deserves some emphasis, for failure to keep the distinction in mind has led to an erroneous piece of conventional sociological wisdom. That is the notion that only small societies with a very low division of labor—hunting and gathering tribes, for example— are integrated by shared values of their members. Any modern, complex, and highly differentiated society, so it is held, is necessarily characterized by diversity of values among the population, or value pluralism (for example, Goodman and Marx, 1978:92). For American society in particular, the claim about value pluralism is additionally buttressed with reference to religious and ethnic diversity that did not melt into one common American pot. At the same time, though, and in the same breath, as it were, it is also asserted that there are American mainstream values shared by all Americans regardless of ethnic or class status, and regardless of religious or regional affiliation. Such common American values are achievement and success, pragmatism, humanitarianism, and, most importantly, a deep commitment to norms of distributive justice that have direct moral significance. It has been found, for example, that all Americans deeply believe that only a society that allows income inequality can be a moral one. They reject the possibility of real income equality as immoral; and they believe that the prevailing inequalities come pretty close to what they ought to be with the qualification that equality of opportunity has to be improved (Goodman and Marx, 1978:92, 277; Alves and Rossi, 1978). Thus claims about some necessary value pluralism in modern complex society stand next to, and in apparent splendid isolation from, assertions about common and shared values throughout modern society. Some values are shared, others are not, so it seems. While this may be empirically true, there remains confusion in the argument.

As to values, there is nothing in the model of modernity that demands value pluralism. Relative to the United States, Sweden is a modern society; but one finds far greater homogeneity in values in Sweden than in the United States (Tomasson, 1970). How homogeneous or heterogeneous, how much value consensus or dissensus characterizes a modern society can be treated as an empirical question. It is different with respect to normative diversity. That is not just an empirical question. Complexity in the organization of society and normative diversity are matters linked by definition. When applied to society, such terms as "complex" or "highly differentiated" refer to (usually functionally specialized) role sets, as, for example the neolocal nuclear family on the one hand, and the bureaucratic formal organization on the other. And, commonly, one defines roles in terms of normative role expectations. The very idea of specialized roles then entails the idea of specialized norms. Hence, normative diversity is a specification of what we mean by societal modernity. In distinction to values, norms define obligations and rights in concrete social settings. At this normative level, then, what is right in one context can very well be wrong in another. Insisting on impersonal norms of obligations in a bureaucracy is right, at least according to the normative design of formal organization. But transferring the spirit of impersonality to the family would be wrong, at least according to its prevailing normative design. A modern bureaucracy and a modern family are social organizations characterized by antithetical norms (Parsons, 1968a). In the former you have to earn your right to belong every day; in the latter "home is where they've got to take you in," as we say.

This does not mean that values and norms are independent of each other. Though their relationship is anything but well understood, norms are usually thought of as situation specifications of values, where the situation is any given specialized role set in the division of labor in society. However inadequately understood, shared values play a very important role in modern society. They provide the principal elements of an effective excuse culture. Since modern men and women are condemned to play many roles in diverse settings, the potential for role conflict is far greater than in simpler societies. And when an individual is subjected to competing loyalties and obligations—to company, career, community, or family—it is reliance on common values that enables him to offer acceptable excuses. This may not do much to reduce the pain of disappointed expectations, but it takes away its bitter social edge, the right to express moral indignation. An acceptable excuse is, after all, the invocation of a standard for choosing that compels respect. Without some shared values acceptable excuses could not be manufactured at all. And, however intuitively, this tells us something useful. Wherever we find much value rhetoric, pervasive professions of "idealistic" concern about values, we can be pretty sure to encounter a real situation of great uncertainty about shared values. On this point the old adage, "Where there is a lot of smoke, there is some fire," may serve us well. If values play their role in choosing among alternative modes, means, and ends of action, as Kluckhohn held, a political culture literally drenched with "idealisms," or constant appeals to higher purposes coupled with strong reluctance to admit to mundane material interests, very likely is the political culture of a people utterly uncertain about any shared values. In contrast, a political culture of pragmatic interest bargaining where, whatever the invective used, the shout most frequently heard is the simple declarative "Let's deal" is sure to be a culture with many shared values utterly taken for granted and simply not worth discussing.

Another useful consideration is the finding that values are held as systems of beliefs. They do not just coexist in isolation from each other

(Rokeach, 1968:1–21). There is then an architecture or inner coherence to the beliefs that guide human action. Nonetheless, some beliefs cohere better than others. And the findings just cited show that coherence probably varies positively with the emotional intensity, or a person's degree of identification with values. Another way of describing that aspect of values is to say that core values are those more intensely held and more connected to whole sets of values; peripheral values are those less intensely held and less connected. Now, a sociologist is more interested in core values for the simple reason of their identity-conferring character. From a purely psychological point of view, a person can of course adopt any conception of some desirable, including the private and hidden conviction that one is a genius, shared by no one else. But for sociological analysis, most notably the analysis of social conflict, the focus of interest is on core values internalized in personality, on the one hand, and institutionalized in social relations, on the other. Put another way, sociological interest is focused on those core beliefs that people use to legitimate action when the purely normative, habitual cake of custom no longer suffices to make some behavior mutually acceptable. Therein lies the danger. Legitimating behavior is justifying it with abstractions. But the concrete human beings with their concrete needs often simply vanish from the scene of legitimation talk.

Identity symbols tell us who we are supposed to be and are, in part; they refer to conceptions that we hold ourselves, are made to cling to by others, and make others cling to in turn. Identity symbols come in great variety, covering cultural objects, social ones, and physical objects. If a mother who is a music lover were one day to designate to her child the Beatles or Beethoven as simply noise, the child might find that funny, at first. But if the mother were to persist in this new definition of the situation it is a fair guess that the child would react with anxiety. The same would occur with changing names or the meaning of furniture. If little Mary were to become Nancy, and perhaps Elizabeth the next day; if a chair were a simple object to sit on one day but could become an object of prayerful devotion, to be gazed at but never touched, the next, little Mary's world would be rather upset. These trite observations only serve to make the obvious point that our identity, or sense of self, has multiple points of anchorage. And as we are identified with objects on many levels of reality, the student of values must choose some.

Although the empirical data on German values in Chapter IV are based on quite a number of conceptions of the desirable, the illustration here can do with just two, "conceptions of the good society to have and strive for" and "conceptions of the good person." The former entails obligations to society, the latter obligations to self. Both illustrate the nature and significance of values because one can draw on findings descriptive of national differences. For example, a conception of the good society to realize may stress hierarchy or egalitarianism. This distinction served Lipset (1963) well in analyzing differences in the functioning of democracy even within Anglo-Saxon culture. He showed, for example, that British democracy rests on patterns of deference to one's betters. In contrast, Australian democracy rests on the egalitarianism of "Aussie mateship," a lower-class export from the mother country that became a dominant value "down under." Similarly, a conception of the good society may rely heavily on universalist or more particularist notions of the significance of others. When American businessmen meet as strangers in some airport lounge, they use their rank in the firm to define who they are. For Americans whether you work for IBM or GM is a secondary consideration. What counts is rank—vice president, plant manager, and the like— for rank indicates generalized level of competence. As Nakane (1970) has shown, Japanese managers meeting under similar circumstances focus almost entirely on the company they work for, and for them rank is very much a secondary consideration. In Japan you are a Mitsubishi man or a Toyota man. There it is not rank within a bureaucracy but affiliation with a particular corporate family that defines who you are. Another person gains manageable social significance not by belonging to some universal prestige or competence category, a freely disposable piece of marketable labor power; rather, significance is attached to belonging to "their people" as contrasted with "my crowd." Presumably, the patterns of lifetime employment so prominent in Japan and so counterintuitive to American notions of sound management and worker motivation, are anchored in particularist notions of the conception of the good society. Such an interpretation of crossnational differences in business practices gains in plausibility when one can show that particularist conceptions of the good society in Japan antedate the modern period of industrialism, as Nakane has done. One deals here with core societal values, beliefs of great historical persistence to which Western technology and forms of organization were adapted, thus contributing to continuity in collective identity of a nationwide character. No matter what the nature of the common social problems emerging in all industrial societies, whether they be labor-management relations, consensus construction in democratic polities, or taking care of the elderly, the Japanese, as is well known by now, always manage to find solutions radically different from those adopted in North America and Western Europe (Palmore, 1975; Dore, 1973). Finally, let me use an example from a small-sample survey study, conducted in the 1950s, of the values among American and West German middle-class boys (McClelland, 1964: 62–92). The advantage in this instance bears on the coherence of values classifiable under the rubric "obligation to society" and those under the label "obligation to self." The American image of the good society is somewhat akin to a voluntary association, where people join in order to accomplish something together. So one owes to society membership in groups, joint activities, and sensitivity to the opinion of others. What one owes to the self amounts to three things primarily: self-fulfillment, achievement or success, and the fullest development of all one's potentialities. The obligation to society, then, being a joiner, can act as a social control to American individualism. Among West German boys, in contrast, obligations to observe the dictates of an explicit code of decency or propriety is the main obligation to society. Accordingly, their highest obligation to self is self-control, even to the point of taking pride in doing well what one must do but has little inclination doing. The meaning of individualism is also quite different in the two cases. Americans, joiners and other-directed, find security in being average men in some group at any given moment in time. Thinking and feeling like your peers make you normal (Zborowski, 1953). The American sense of individual self-direction derives from being members of many groups and changing group affiliations over time. Nonetheless, at any given moment in time, American individualism is a kind of "groupie" individualism. Belonging to a group, feeling and thinking like everyone else, gives you security, makes you an average man, and so assures you normality. To less kindly German eyes, such normality looks like banality. Such "individuals" appear as superficial social conformists, happy fools incapable of grasping the tragedy of all social constraints. The German sense of individualism is more focused on the isolated self. There is greater involvement with individualistic tasks, done by the self, for the self, and through the self. German individualism does not involve so much doing anything in particular or different from others. Rather, it is oriented to deriving some unique meaning from what one does. Being an individual amounts to bearing the burden of social obligations and constraints without breaking the essential loneliness (a term with positive connotations in German) of truly subjective consciousness. German individualism is more radical than the American version. The barrier between social and private experience is greater in German individualism. That barrier is bridged by clinging to an explicit code that tells one what one's duties are. Nevertheless, individualism demands that one find "one's own position" in adherence to a code. To the skeptical eye of an American, this German individualism with its constant harping about some subjective meaning of objective necessity, this "idealist" elaboration of mundane generalities must surely look a little like nuttiness, especially since it seems quite divorced from *doing* anything in particular or acting in ways different from ordinary ones. Nonetheless, such value differences have their manifestations. McClelland tells us that experimental psychologists induce frustration in their subjects in nationally specific ways. The American will block some striving for achievement, generating frustration through interference with self-actualization. His German counterpart produces frustration by demanding too much of his subjects, by setting goals that, despite explicit explanations and seemingly credible ones because they come from an expert, cannot be attained because of lack of adequate means in the situation. Frustration in Germany results from *Überforderung*, the receipt and the acceptance of impossible performance demands. The German will try, so says McClelland, because commitment to explicit codes of duty demands it. If so, the very fact that such internalized codes are fairly abstract eventuates in a latent sense that society tends to demand too much of individuals. And so the expression of self-pity should surprise us less than the prosecutors in the *Einsatzgruppen* trial, who were flabbergasted when learning that some of the commanders of the extermination squads pitied themselves more than their victims (Musmanno, 1961). In America beliefs about obligations to society and to self and the meaning of frustration are different. That meaning has little room for self-pity. The German meaning of frustration has much room for it. Let us note here only that the empirical study of values prevalent in whole societies has rarely been done in ways even modestly meeting basic standards of reliability.

This brief introduction to the nature of values that interest us serves to make only two points.

First, the values of interest are those of a social identity-conferring character. That means when members of groups with different values encounter each other they experience culture shock, the discovery that the other is an ethical stranger. What appeared self-evidently human loses the character of the self-evident. That other has a head, hands, and feet like yours and mine. But many of his important moral beliefs, his sense of obligation to self and to society, and so his very conceptions of what makes human life meaningful differ. As demonstrated in the next chapter, in nineteenth-century Germany it was groups with such different beliefs about "the good society" that were led together to form a modern nation-state. There was practically no consensus on what the national society of the Germans should be like.

Second, identities are not matters for negotiation; interests are. The bloody history of Northern Ireland reminds us that men and women who speak the same language, never ascribed racial characteristics to each other, but rely on contrasting religious affiliations in their commitments to collective identities can be governed without consensus but unending tensions spreading from generation to generation over hundreds of years (Rose, 1971). Value dissensus in Germany had different consequences, but the "Irish troubles" tell us how serious commitment to values is. More, over time as one confronts the ethical stranger, self-consciousness about value differences tends to rise, at least among the educated. That makes compromising about commitments more rather than less difficult. Believing in some substantive principles that give structure or coherence to our obligations to self and society and holding each other to such beliefs are not like taking a taxicab ride, to be entered and left where and when one pleases. The acquisition of a social identity takes half a lifetime or more, so the cultural psychoanalysts tell us (Erikson, 1959). Whatever little we may know in this area suggests that identities, individual and collective ones, cannot be negotiated and renegotiated like some commercial contract serving the mutual adjustment of interests. For most practical purposes during the short history of the modern German nation-state, the ethical strangers who gathered under its flags were stuck with their contrasting group-identity equipment.

While the forging of a common national identity out of diversity is always a difficult and time-consuming task, in Germany nation-building and the emergence of industrial society occurred during the same time. That made the construction of value consensus concerning the new nation impossible.

The Temporal Coincidence of Nation-building and Industrialization (2)

While some stirring for national unification occurred already in response to the appearance of Napoleon's armies, the onset of a more determined struggle for modern nationhood can be dated with the creation of the German Customs Union in 1834. This is significant. Material interests, not ideal ones, were the forces that gave birth to the first political steps toward national unification. The birth of the nation, in 1871, was a contract among sovereigns. In content it was an extension or generalization of the Customs Union for the conduct of foreign policy. And if we date the onset of industrialization in Germany with the great railway construction boom, that occurred in the late 1830s and early 1840s. Already by the 1880s the wealth of the nation derived from the industrial sector of the economy (Reinhardt, 1962). Nation-building and industrialization call for the forming of new patterns of collective identities and the shifting of political allegiance from regional centers to the new national one. In addition, due to a host of social problems that can no longer be solved in the family or at the local community level, industrialization eventuates in pressures for the inclusion of the lower strata into the political process. In Germany one can speak of an integration crisis with three separate sources. One was the sheer coincidence of nation-building and industrialization; another was the unusual speed of industrialization; and a third was regional unevenness in the rate of industrializing economic life. Let us take a brief glance at changes in economic life and then examine their political implications, with value dissensus as our background variable in mind.

In the areas covered by her later national boundaries, Germany passed Rostow's (1960, 1963) takeoff into sustained economic growth during the late 1850s. Relative to England, she industrialized definitely late. Relative to France, Belgium, and the U.S.A., she lagged by some twenty years. Industrial takeoff preceded national unification, and the period of Germany's "secondary phase" in industrialization, one of exceedingly rapid advance, coincided with the first decades of her newly founded nationhood (Born, 1966). Thus Germany was a latecomer economically. She was also a latecomer as a nation. But while she profitted from her first latecomer status, she only suffered from her second one (Plessner, 1959:83–91). Indeed, the very benefit of economic latecomer status contributed its share to her continuing failure to build a viable nation.

The success story of Germany's late and rapid industrialization is sufficiently known at least in its external aspects to warrant no more than providing a few highlights. During her "secondary industrializing burst," from 1870 to the beginning of the First World War, the population grew from nearly 41 million to 67.5 million, a process profoundly altering the structure of employment opportunities (SJDR:1912*). Urbanization was very rapid as forty big cities emerged within four decades (SJDR:1880, 1895, 1913). And although a residential shift of two thirds of the population who lived in rural communities in 1871 to two thirds who lived in urban ones by 1913 (Born, 1966:273) exaggerates the message because urban community in this statistic covers relatively small towns, by 1920 about one fifth of the population was concentrated in and around metropolitan centers more in line with the contemporary meaning of that term (SJDR:1913). By 1907 employment in industry and trade passed the 50 percent mark, while that in agriculture was approaching one third (SDR211:69–85†). From the mid-1870s to 1907 employment in the capital-goods sector grew by about 170 percent (Bechtel, 1956:281), while the white-collar salariat increased by 94 percent during a span of thirteen years covering the 1880s and 1890s alone. Just how fast Mills' "new

*SJDR = *Statistisches Jahrbuch fur das Deutsche Reich.*
†SDR = *Statistik des Deutschen Reichs (followed by volume number).*

middle class" appeared on the scene is well reflected in the white-collar-to-blue-collar ratio: This was 1:30 in 1870 and 1:9 in 1914 (SDR 211:95–96, 303; Born, 1966:281). Already by the 1870s Germany's exports ranked second only to those of the United Kingdom (Born, 1966:271), and by 1910 Germany's output in heavy industry exceeded that of her British rival considerably (Pulzer, 1964:23). Perhaps the best short way to communicate the explosive rate of Germany's secondary spurt at industrialization is to recall that 958 joint stock companies were formed in a single 3-year span during her *Gründer* (founding) period in the 1870s (Passow, 1922).

More important than figures can indicate easily was another development. Germany not only caught up rapidly with her industrial reference-group societies, she also innovated and outdistanced her rivals in the rationalization of production and organization. New industries in chemicals, optics, and the electrical field appeared. These gained predominance over the European competitors already before World War I. Her tariff policy of 1879 marked the beginning of the growth of cartels. Huge combines with a quiet managerial revolution appeared that put the German economy on an organizational footing second to none in the world. The new corporation seemed to know only one law: continuous growth and expansion. Soon Germany's narrow domestic raw-materials base threatened to become a bottleneck for further wealth production. This was to be overcome through economic penetration abroad. German industrial enterprise expanded toward the southeast, starting a Baghdad Railway project, linking up with Russian banks, and creating an oil company that was to compete with Standard Oil and Royal Dutch Shell. Imports of raw materials shifted to South America, while exports to the European countries grew with the consequences of serious payments imbalances calling for adjustment (Bechtel, 1956:296–309, 419–25; Fischer, 1967:11–19).

To the extent that rapid economic change contributed to the integrative problem at the beginning of her history by throwing people of very diverse origins into the new common-city environment, this impact also showed geographic variation in Germany. During the Empire, Upper Silesia, Saxony, Brandenburg-Berlin, the Rhineland, and Westphalia were the industrializing regions. Northeastern Germany and the Deep South remained essentially agrarian. Throughout modern history, the former areas constituted industrial society while the latter remained more backward. This uneven development reinforced interregional tensions, which in the main derived from differences in cultural and historical development.

The net effect of this regional unevenness made Prussia economically

more advanced than the South. However, containing the least as well as
the most economically developed areas, Prussia herself was also more
unevenly developed than the South. For the Empire, even the barest
minimum of data can serve to describe this economic contrast between
Prussia and the South—that is, the states of Bavaria, Baden, and
Wuerttemberg—quite well.

Prussia had about twice as much urbanization as the South, and the
growth of Prussia's industrial blue-collar labor force was also higher (SDR
111:303). Relatively more people worked in large firms in Prussia
(Neuhaus, 1913:122, 254). Her agricultural labor force was relatively
smaller than the southern, but Prussia also had the regions with the
highest proportions still in agricultural employment. The proportion of
the industrialized labor force with secondary employment in farming, on
the other hand, was still larger in the South. Prussia not only experienced
higher geographic mobility among her proletariat, but also her total labor
force was much more mobile than that of the South (Neuhaus,
1913:236–37). Inside Prussia people were rapidly moving out of East Elbia
and migrating straight across the full width of the country to the urban
areas in Westphalia and the Rhineland, though some of this flow
proceeded only as far as Berlin. No comparable mobility productive of a
mixing of people with variant cultural background and speech patterns
occurred in the South. In terms of the distribution of the industrial labor
force the Prussian-southern difference was still considerable in 1928
(Neuhaus, 1913:173–75, 179; Pfohl and Friedrich, 1928:CX58a).

Thus in the South industrialization was not only slower, the new urban
dwellers there also came from the nearby rural environs. The integration
problem concomitant with industrialization was therefore a much smaller
one. Given a slower rate of economic development and entailing a much
more homogeneous population in language, religion, and outlook, coping
with the new class relations could draw on a common historical experience
of sorting out opposed claims to rights among estates. Class conflict could
become only a somewhat different and newer version of the older
principle of "insisting on one's good old rights." The Southerners could
adapt the "parliamentarism of estates" where the *rights* of trader, peasant,
clergy, and prince had often clashed to the democratic regulation of
conflicts involving the clash of *interests* among worker, owner, and
government. Some *modus vivendi* on basic rights not to be tampered with
had been worked out before the modern dynamics of interest opposition
became a problem. Consequently respect for and some agreement on basic
rights made it possible to accept the reality of social conflict, if not as
something desirable then at least as something natural and, in any case,
unavoidable. Such orientations make the development of conflict-regula-

tion mechanisms more likely than morally tinged aversions against social conflicts. It is not difficult to think of democratic politics as one conflict-regulation game writ large. In Germany political development in this democratic direction was confined to the South, and this increased the tensions associated with perceived value differences vis-à-vis the Prussian North.

As has been shown above, the social composition of the new industrial society in Prussia was quite different. But the Prussian political tradition was also completely different from that prevailing in the South. Whereas the South had a history of a town-based aristocracy with some absentee land ownership, the Junkers had always sat on their estates. While the landlord-peasant tie was therefore relatively tenuous in the South, the Junkers extended the landlord tie into the modern era, exercising some feudal control over contract-based wage labor. The punctiliousness and regimentation of *Gutsherrschaft* was also reinforced by the central institution of preindustrial Prussia, the Army (Büsch, 1962). These East Elbian agrarian workers brought with them to the factories a valuable normative resource that in no small measure helped the rapid industrialization in the North of the country. What they had learned in the Army, obedience to impersonal authority, they could use in the factory. In many respects the idea of the Army as a school for the nation (Höhn, 1963) retarded democratic development in Germany's political life, but its teaching contribution to rapid economic development and to bureaucratic development in all public sectors should not be underestimated.

Politically Prussia symbolized to the continental powers of the prenationalist age something similar to what America represents socially to the world today: products of nothing but achievement. Unlike the American case, where a common escape from discontent provided at least one tie among many, there was nothing "binding" in Prussia except political authority. There was little in religion, cultural tradition, economic modes of making a living, language, or ethnicity that could tie together Prussia's various population components. The Prussian state was an early prodigy of modernity, a phenomenon "deliberately willed into existence" by a small oligarchy applying itself with Calvinist zeal to systematic conquest (Kayser, 1961). Before Napolean, Prussia had been more an army with a civilian support base than a society with an army to defend it. This tradition of ruling over "subjects" whose disparate heterogeneity in almost every conceivable respect had proved quite irrelevent for effectiveness for a considerable period even after Napolean, was still alive at the beginning of Germany as a nation-state. In terms of diversity the Prussian legacy became Germany's burden. As a political entity, Prussia, which constituted the largest part of the Empire, remained as checkered as it had always been. This state included Silesians and Rhinelanders, Masurians and Westphalians, Saxons and Pommeranians as well as other regional groups. It also comprised Catholics, a variety of Protestants, and a tiny minority of Jews. In addition, there were many tongues, distinct dialects nearly impossible to understand without learning, and many of her subjects were not verbally fluent in High German, its teaching in the schools notwithstanding. Last, there were also genuinely unassimilated foreigners: Alsatians, Danes, Poles, and Russians. Rapid industrialization brought all these disparate groups into contact with nothing more to sustain them than order imposed from above and their own community organizations below. Since Prussia made up two thirds of the Empire in area and population, the Prussian integrative problem became the German one; her "solution" to that problem became the German one as well.

Pseudonationalist Rule by Interest Constellation (3)

With so diverse a people so rapidly thrown together into the new industrial social order, the most likely political outcome was rule by interest constellation rather than the emergence of a political regime where authority rests on shared legitimacy beliefs. This development was the more likely since rule by interest constellation had characterized the Prussian state for a century and more. Further, Prussia not only made up the largest part of Germany; German unification had become a reality under the leadership of the Prussian state. If we are to understand German political life we must remember Prussia's style of governance.

The ruling house of Prussia, the Hohenzollern, were Calvinist, and that gave their patrimonial rule its peculiar twist. Ever since Prussia began to make a name for herself in Europe, her monarchs were modernizing monarchs. They looked on their domain somewhat in the spirit of a corner grocer anxiously watching his accounts. Their understanding of a king's duty was to make the domain grow: economically, and so they sponsored commercial and industrial development; in population, and so they maintained a systematic immigration policy; politically, and so they bureaucratized civil and military taxation; and territorially, and so they acquired land by negotiation or wars of conquest (Kayser, 1961). Instrumental rationalism in the choice of means to accomplish these ends grew among them in stepwise fashion with the secularization of the Protestant Ethic. The more "enlightened" the king, the more purely instrumental-rational his orientations to means. Further, already in the eighteenth century these Prussian monarchs were completely convinced of the indivisibility of domestic and foreign policy, something that on theoretical if not practical grounds has only recently been recognized as an inevitable aspect of modernity (Morse, 1976). But whether the Prussian monarchs focused their energies on the rationalization of finance administration, Army organization, commercial, crafts, and industrial development, on immigration policies, or on warfare, their guiding standard was always the chance for success relative to the prevailing interest constellations at home and abroad (Dietrich, 1966; Schoeps, 1966). Therefore, Max Weber's ideal-typical traditional authority in its narrower meaning with a commitment to "the sanctity of custom" was not a feature of Prussian domination. Prussian domination had always rested on a mixture of legitimacy sources. Predominant in that mixture were the ruler's right to arbitrariness of traditional patrimonialism, and rational legality. Since the late eighteenth century and increasingly so during the nineteenth, the weight of rational legality grew and so did a tendency to substitute for legitimacy beliefs simply success in satisfying the interests of powerful groups on whose support the monarchy depended. Remember, rational-legal rule is based on the weakest of the three legitimacy beliefs in Max Weber's triad, involving legitimation by procedure alone. The driving force in Prussia's development toward reliance on rational legality and rule by interest constellation was the struggle between ruler and administrative staff (Kehr, 1965). And in Prussia, that meant confrontation between a Calvinist ruling house and predominantly Lutheran landed aristocrats, the Junkers, who, in contrast to the Habsburg Empire, never let go of participation at the political center (von Preradovich, 1955). As a consequence, "system affect" (Almond and Verba, 1963) or identification with political institutions in a personal and emotionally meaningful fashion involving deep commitments to some substantive moral ideals remained a romantic and an un-Prussian notion. Prussian instead was to rely more on governmental effectiveness than on any legitimacy beliefs and an early commitment to the notion of the interventionist state where you have to earn the right to rule every day. Rule was intolerable really only when it did nothing.

Under the leadership of Prussia the move toward a unification of the Germans into a modern nation-state relied heavily on this Prussian tradition. Throughout the history of unification, a constellation of political and economic elite interests had been decisive for the outcome. The voices of the people, more idealistic, and mostly democratic since 1848, had not carried the day. Rule by interest constellation and rational legality became the dominant pattern also in the new Germany. But while social historians tend to rest content with a Bismarck legacy as an explanation (Wehler, 1973), sociologists feel compelled to complement it with factors going beyond any given individuals, no matter how prominent or influential.

If one can demonstrate that Germany had no Germans in terms of shared societal values or morally compelling models of the good society, it follows that rule by interest constellation and a highly positivist form of rational legality had to be the outcome, at least until some greater consensus on societal values emerged. What is more, Germans took it for granted that command over political power would be quite decisive in the outcome. At least among the educated strata in society we can use the fact that Max Weber was a political insider in his orientations (and an outsider only in the sense of office incumbency) to make that point (Mommsen, 1974a). In his inaugural lecture at Freiburg University, Max Weber declared: "It is not *how* people will live in the future [not their welfare] which stirs us when we think about the conditions lying beyond our own graves, but rather *who* they shall be. Neither peace nor the pursuit of happiness but the *eternal* struggle for the preservation and development of our national identity are the goals we have to bestow on our children" (Weber, 1895:12, 14). The First World War had done little to forge a national identity. Again we can lean on Weber (1917a:392–93) as a witness. Among the educated in Germany, there prevailed a conviction that power would decide which of the different value traditions of the German people—Prussia's military ethos or southern civility, Rhenish egalitarianism or Hanseatic city patricianism—would survive. And this belief made political participation inherently ideological and a fearsomely dangerous game. The resulting orientation to politics was deeply ambivalent. You had to participate, lest the others' values would win out. But you also had to find some mode of constraining politics because fights about identity cannot remain unbloody for any length of time. Without power you risked elimination from the stream of history; with power you risked civil war. Once again we can draw on Weber's ambivalent orientation to the state, his understanding of culture and its relation to individual and collective identities as representative of the worries prevalent among Germany's educated elites. Let us listen to Weber's "convictions" and realize the depth of ambivalence: (1) The bearers of ultimate values are individuals; yet also, all modern culture (the production, realization, and preservation of values) is inevitably nationally bound and manifest in international competition. (2) A state in whatever constitutional form is a mere piece of machinery and it is irresponsible to infuse it with absolute value commitments; yet also, the "power state" (*Machtstaat*, a powerful nation-state) is an end in itself, not only for the realization of a particular national culture, but also for the preservation of different forms of ethical life in the world without which all alternatives, including the idea of freedom, would simply petrify in an all-encompassing bureaucratic cage. (3) Attempts to stem the tide of leveling in modern life by political means is irresponsible political romanticism; yet also, constant struggle against the possible triumph of pure instrumental rationalism in social life is a leader's highest political duty (Mommsen, 1974a:427; Mommsen, 1974b:139).

Recall what was said above. This spanking-new modern German nation-state was born out of the womb of an economic silver spoon. She had passed the threshold of a capacity for sustained economic growth already in the 1850s, almost twenty years before unification; and already during the first years of her nationhood she experienced a secondary spurt of economic modernization with the appearance of huge joint stock corporations with their professional managers and the differentiation between ownership and control over the means of production. In terms of national product, Germany was awesomely rich and a giant among her continental neighbors. More, hers was also an impressively advanced technology; and, finally, if the capture of Nobel prizes can serve as a measure, she was also the recognized leader in scientific achievement, a prominent position she maintained until the First World War (Ben-David, 1971). In all conceivable respects, then, the means to build the good society that ought to be realized were available in ample supply. But as Weber (1919a) was so insistent in reminding his student audience, neither science and technology, nor wealth and power, nor any instrument in the impressive arsenal of modern secular intelligence can tell man what, so wonderfully equipped, he most desperately wants to know: how to live and organize life in meaningful ways or how to achieve a social existence that the ghosts of an inner-worldly ascetic religious tradition compel us to experience as meaningful *only if*, at the end of life, it grants us a sense of contentment in facing death.

Indeed, educated men and women in Wilhelminian Germany had good cause "to yearn for synthesis" and "to show a deep aversion against social conflict," these twin features of German political life that Dahrendorf (1965) identified as the main causes in the failure of democratic development. They had good reason to adopt these twin features as their basic orientations to political life, for the house of the nation as a value-based community was yet an empty one. Only the future would decide its content; and all the contending parties had impressive resources at their disposal to determine the outcome. One cannot explain these twin quintessentially German political orientations by saying the elites exploited them for the advancement of their status and material interests. True, that describes what they did as well as the fact that political domination in Wilhelminian Germany took the form of rule by interest constellation. But the elites did not produce these orientations in some simple, direct, willful manner. Instead, these orientations were an unavoidable consequence among people born into a society with profound value differences and into a class that taught one to care about values. And while the distinctive style of political participation they developed was anything but unavoidable, their heritage of value dissensus makes it at least understandable. That style was a mixture of a lofty rhetoric of Hegelianism and the practice of mass politics with huge agitation and propaganda machines constantly threatening already insecure elites suffering legitimacy deficits. The praise of Hegel's idea of the state responded to "the yearning for synthesis" by attenuating the fear of conflict. The practice of mass politics produced conflict and heightened anxieties about it. Save for one feature and its implication, Dahrendorf's (1965:234–36) description of the German idea of the nature of the state serves us well. Let us listen.

In the rhetoric of political participation, the legacy of Hegel meant three things. First, the state "stood above" all particular and conflicting interests in society. All rights, a chance for peace and order, emanated from above. Second, the state was law. But legality meant normative regularity and not substantive ideals with any value content. The constitution would change, as it did so frequently, but administrative law stood firm like the Rock of Gibraltar in the turbulent waters of history. Third, and the decisive element in the equation, each nation in the world was to be understood as the potential bearer of a moment in human ethical evolution, either making its contribution or failing to do so. And who wants to be a failure?

This idea of the state in Germany needs correction on only one point, the first, and only in one respect. No doubt, serving the state in Germany was not experienced as service to a particular administration or even a particular type of political regime, monarchical, democratic, or totalitarian. Whatever the changing legitimacy symbols, one served the state as a legal creature. But Dahrendorf's account implies endorsement of the old claims about Germans being peculiarly "traditional" and somehow addicted to the fetishism of obedience at all costs (Weber, 1906, 1917b:1,385–92). No such traditional, passive, and obedient a portrait of the German burgher satisfies when we realize that one generation could be mobilized for total war twice, and when we consider the considerable disobedience to the authority of the state during the Weimar period (Merkl, 1975). Instead, one should emphasize that Germans could always be mobilized for mass politics because they realized that their state was only tenuously grounded in any legitimacy beliefs and ruled by interests instead. Nonetheless, at the level of elites, the third feature, Germany's cultural mission into the world, was the decisive one for the nation's pseudonationalist practice of politics. That was a pseudonationalism for two reasons. On the one hand, this claim to a culture mission—whereby a powerful German nation-state would provide a third alternative to Russian autocracy in the East and rampantly exploitative capitalism in the West, whatever authenticity one may ascribe to it—also effectively covered up what the domestic struggle was really about, namely, massive status and economic-interest politics intricately intertwined with struggles about which of the different value formulas in Germany would come to predominate. On the other hand, this was a pseudonationalism because, with their Hegelian rhetoric about the nation's mission and its haunted national identity, the German elites struggled with each other about values, these *abstract* conceptions of the desirable; and they fought about those abstractions in a fashion where any caring concern with the concrete lives of concrete human beings, their fellow citizens, simply vanished from the horizon of their attention. There was, it seems, a direct connection between their "idealism," one in which genuine and deep commitments were focused entirely on necessarily abstract conceptions, values, and a radical disregard of the fate of human lives. The latter, ethical strangers for the most part, were treated as if they were but immaterial statistics, and material to be used in the struggle for the attainment of a national identity. Demonstrating this unholy alliance of German political action with its idealism and mass agitation will take up three chapters. Here brief illustrations must suffice.

In Wilhelminian Germany the most important interests were those of iron, heavy industry, and rye, the landed Junker nobility. Contrary to Kehr (1965:51–63, 111–29), Moore (1966:433–83), and Fischer (1967: 16–19), this was a highly unstable interest coalition. What tenuous coherence it had, for however short periods, it owed to representatives of the German professoriate (Barkin, 1970). Both of the coalition partners presented themselves as nationalist. Industry pushed a fleet construction program, one regarded with disdain in Army circles because it needlessly challenged Britain and, domestically, threatened the traditional predominance of the Army in Germany's armed forces. Now, while Prussian Junkerdom was far more represented in the Army than in the Navy, in their eyes a toy for an immature and insecure monarch, they nevertheless sided with industry in pushing their own interest: tariffs on grain imports from Russia. On both sides the slogans were "nationalist"; world political power status on the one hand, food autarchy for that power on the other. The slogans barely covered the massive material and status interests of the new industrial and the old agrarian elites. And only a "scientific debate about" and a fierce polemic against the inevitable commitment to industrial society on the part of prominent professors, like Sering and Wagner, could hide to many that a professed national idealism was utterly compromised by a ruthless pursuit of economic interests. Heavy industry needed defense business and succeeded; agrarian interests of the Junkers needed state subsidies in one form or another, and they succeeded. Ground between these two stones of elite interests, wages of the many remained modest at home, and Germany steered a collision course with Britain and Russia abroad.

The critical alliance yielding to the Weimar Republic what stability it had was one between the Army leadership and the Social Democrats. In exchange for obedience to the new democratic constitution the Army received a guarantee of autonomy in its own sphere. Into this pact went the betrayal of commitments to socialism on the left and collaboration with and support of democracy rather than efforts to restore the monarchy on the right (Eyck, 1962; Müller, 1969). Finally, the demise of democracy and the establishment of totalitarianism were also changes due to an interest constellation. Here big business, the Army, and the conservative right were the principal partners (Müller, 1969; Bracher, Sauer, and Schulz, 1960), and we shall see below just how deep a moral indifference about the fate of millions in Germany that cooperation brought.

But large segments of the German population did not only live in contact with ethical strangers with whom they maintained the impersonal bonds of the market. They also lived with "their own kind" in subcultural communities, the most prominent of which were well organized politically. These communities lived in a segregated style or "patterns of negative integration" with each other. Three reasons compel us to pay attention to this phenomenon. First, the image of modern mass man, living in isolation from all others in the anonymous big city, was more myth than reality in modern Germany. Second, these negatively integrated communities could fall prey to agitation and propaganda politics in the course of which one could try to use the law for nothing less than the "creation of new men," subjecting people to forced "Germanization," for example. Third, unless some elite had an institutional interest stake in some minority, the latter might find itself without any protector. If, under those conditions, some constellation of interests arose that deemed it useful to declare the minority superfluous, rational legality could be mobilized in the service of their eradication, whether in the form of forced acculturation or emigration.

Before the First World War the two most notable subcultures in negative integration were the Socialists and the Catholics (Roth, 1963; Ritter, 1954). A person could be born into either, live out his life within the community without ever having intimate contacts with others on the outside, and die within its boundaries. Both of these communities used a richly endowed, complex, and interlocking organizational network to preserve their particular values and ways of life. The organizations were of an educational and recreational kind, covered credit organizations, unions, and a political party. Drawn to the factories in the Rhineland, the Polish community in Germany acted in similar style, adding a Polish Episcopate for good measure (Wehler, 1966:436–55). More, insofar as analysis of aggregate voting data permits, negative integration was what most political parties produced in Germany, right up to the end of the Weimar Republic (Lepsius, 1966). Even the Nazis with their policy of *Gleichschaltung* produced more the appearance than a reality of centralized coordination. Since the story about the Socialist and the Catholic subcultures is well known, let me use the Polish example to describe what it meant to live in negative integration in the Kaiser's days.

Following Wehler (1966:436–55), in the decade preceding the outbreak of the First World War, nearly 500,000 Poles lived in Germany's western "coal and steel pot," the Rhur area. While far more concentrated, the size of that community was about as large as that of the Jewish community in Germany. The Poles' Church organizations grew from 100 in 1893 to 240 in 1914. Against some resistance in government circles, they secured the appointment of a Polish bishop. The organizational pluralism and communications media of the Polish community grew steadily. In 1894 they formed a national association to coordinate the interest representation of all the Poles in Germany trying to forge an interest bloc that was to reach from the western to the eastern boundaries of the nation. Another major contingent, of course, lived in the eastern part of the country, both in its northern agrarian section as well as in the industrialized Silesian South. The Polish miners in the West formed their own union in 1902. This organization gained a membership of nearly 5,000 by 1907. In 1913 they succeeded in linking up their union activities with the miners' union of the Poles in the East. With this federation they created a workers' organization with 75,000 members, expenditures of 1 million *Mark*, and a special biweekly newspaper. The Polish community maintained two additional newspapers for its general membership, *Wiarus Polski* and *Nauka Katolitika*. By 1914 the organizational proliferation of the western community was reflected in 100 singing clubs, 125 sports organizations, 18 educational associations, and a scholarship fund. Politically, the Poles in the West started out by supporting the Catholic Center Party. With the Poles own activists leaning toward socialism, this did not last long. But the German Socialists failed to attract them. More interested in doctrinal purity than gaining extra votes, they proclaimed a radicalism that was apparently too much for pious Poles to swallow. As a result, the western Poles sent their own representative to the Reichstag in 1912.

Throughout the nineties of the last and into the early teens of the present century, the Prussian and Reich governments constantly interfered with Polish political aspirations: Concerned with the prospect of permanently unassimilated foreigners in the polity of a nationalist age, they also attempted to break down the solidarity within the community in the hope of speeding up "Germanization." Their policies showed limited success in the former but complete failure in the latter objective. The governments' instrument in trying to solve the Polish question involved the use of three bodies of law: mining safety regulations, old anticoalition statutes of the Prussian state, and a newer German Associations Law, the *Reichsvereinsgesetz* of 1908. In the mines, Prussian officialdom faced no effective opponent. Here they succeeded in making any promotion to supervisory jobs contingent on fluency in German. Their zeal in pushing assimilation even led them to violate the basic intention of safety regulations. They forbade the display of warning signs in the Polish language. But their attempts to prohibit outright any public assembly where Polish was spoken failed miserably. In the West, the possible inclusion of Church services in the term "public assembly" mobilized the Catholic hierarchy and the Center Party to opposition. In the East, the prospect of simply outlawing the long-standing practice of Polish electoral rhetoric in party campaigns met with opposition from Polish noble colleagues of the Junkers and higher-level bureaucrats worried about rural rebellions. As a result, the Associations Law was compromised, permitting the use of a foreign language in public assembly for another twenty years in all areas where at least 60 percent of the population spoke a foreign tongue. This illustrates nicely how a multiplicity of separate institutional interests came together to protect those of the Polish minority. Polish representatives in the Reichstag and so this voice of direct representation aside, one finds here: (1) pressure on the part of unions on German managers; (2) pressure by the Polish Episcopate on the German Catholic hierarchy, on the Center Party, and on top regional bureaucrats, the Prussian *Oberpraesidenten;* and (3) friendly persuasion among friends in elite circles where Polish nobles obtained support from their German Junker hunting companions for the welfare of Poles in the Reich. But interest constellations in Germany were never stable. The life chances of negatively integrated minorities remained precarious. When the Jewish question emerged to political prominence no interest constellation formed to protect that minority.

This German style of politics, which combined a lofty idealism with domination by interest constellation, only laid the foundation for moral indifference among the elites in society. Under such conditions, the cardinal rule guiding elite conduct in the political process was a very simple one: Unless a policy pursued by another elite was seen as impacting on the interests of your place of employment, it remained a matter of indifference. Moral responsibility usually means caring about the wider consequences of one's conduct; it means anticipating unintended consequences and a readiness to cope with them also when they fall outside one's institutional domain. But that formulation presupposes stratification in society, including the elites of a nation. In Germany, however, much speaks against the development of such elites. Paying attention to the kinds of elites that emerged in the unified nation can shed considerable light on the question of why moral indifference among them took so extreme a form. One point needs emphasis, though. My interest here is not focused on local elites at the community level, nor am I interested in regional elites, as, for example, especially powerful or influential families in Bavaria or the Palatinate. Of sole interest are elites with nationwide significance, elites with so much control over one or another scarce resource in society that one would normally expect them to exercise considerable influence at the political center, the Reichs government in Berlin. All theoretical speculation and the evidence supplied in this book about elites refer to these national ones; nothing I say relates in any way to local or regional elites.

The Emergence of De-stratified Elites (4)

Stratification is to society what the ability to exercise will power and self-direction is to an individual. Saying this points to an analogy, of course, and not to an identity, but a useful analogy it is. Stratification is the concentration of control over all socially recognized and unequally distributed scarce resources in society, such as wealth, prestige, and power (Parsons, 1964). Having such resources available in concentrated fashion and under the control of the few enables a society to act as a corporate entity. That is one reason why Parsons regarded stratification as an evolutionary universal. Once invented, as it were, stratification tends to be adopted everywhere simply because the resulting superior ability for a society to act in concert, as an organized collectivity, particularly in relation to other societies, proves irresistible. More, such *organized* inequality, whereby some families have immensely more of all the good things in life than others, must be legitimated. Such legitimation tends to be community-building, providing a sense of collective identity over and above one's family, occupational, religious, and other social identities.

Such a new and wider collective identity—a sense of we-ness transcending more particular ones, and so a citizen identity crosscutting all others— tends to be invented because the few and the mighty try to legitimate their general superiority over all others by the assumption of superior responsibility in the use of society's resources. There arises the voice of leadership, the claim that superiority is deserved because it is exercised in the interests of all members of society regardless of their endowment with the good things in life. The main reason for this mode of legitimating stratification is that stratification tends to emerge from various forms of expropriation often under the duress of force or fraud. Who believes such legitimation claims and with what degree of conviction varies, of course. That is not an important consideration at the moment. Important is to keep in mind that stratification "creates" the idea of society as an organized corporate actor, a social system with potentially immensely more clout at its disposal than a society with so little surplus as to forestall the unequal distribution of anything.

In a stratified elite this claim to legitimacy is at least matched by their actual control over the most relevant scarce resources. Stratified elites are multidimensional ones. They do have superior control over wealth, political power, and prestige. And to the extent that their claims to legitimacy find acceptance, they also have acknowledged superior moral standing in society. The incumbent of a stratified elite position in society *is* endowed with control over all relevant scarce resources; and that multidimensional basis of superiority provides at least plausibility to the legitimacy claim of the assumption of superior responsibility in their use. After all, you can only assert responsibility for matters at least partially under your control.

Stratification in the sense of the systematic, organized unequal distribution of scarce resources in society whereby families control more or less of all socially recognized and valued resources is by no means as universal, or "normal" as most sociology texts suggest. In many traditional empires countrywide strata were rare. In China there was only one, the literati; for millennia in India, there was none at all; prerevolutionary Russia had no countrywide strata. In these societies, for very long periods of time, stratification was only a local phenomenon. And if a member of some given multidimensional rank position that gave him a clearly understood "standing" in the eyes of his local compatriots moved to another community, he found no social recognition of who he was there (Weber, 1916; 1916–17; Dumont, 1970; Eisenstadt, 1971:87–120). An interesting example of elite de-stratification occurred in Japan. Two hundred years of Tokugawa peace there had brought about a situation in which a feudal warrior caste, the samurai, had become relative paupers due to unemployment as warriors and their transformation into finance administrators. The rich in the country were the merchants. Nonetheless, both groups retained their traditional role as bearers of highly differential prestige. The samurai were among the highest prestige bearers; the merchants had the lowest of all, comprising a definitely disprivileged group, their wealth notwithstanding. This situation lasted until the eve of the Meijii Restoration, Japan's push for modernization. And in Japan, modernization brought about re-stratification of the elites as ex-samurai became managers in industry. That new role brought realignment between prestige and wealth (Bellah, 1957; Nishio, 1965). Thus, in the case of Japan, one encounters a situation of elite de-stratification in the period preceding modernization, and modernization brought re-stratification. As will be shown in a separate chapter below, the German situation was the reverse. Here, modernization brought about de-stratification of premodern elites who had been more stratified. At this point the reason for this pattern of social change is the issue.

Everywhere modernization brings with it the inflow of formerly passive groups as participants in new institutions such as the national economy, a more centralized state and, finally, the modern nation-state. Everywhere too, modernization brings new skills and new experts in these skills to national prominence. Thus new elites arise such as the industrial entrepreneur or manager, the new politician as someone skilled in mobilizing masses for political support, and the new professionals, the academically certified experts. To begin with, these new elites do not form a "circle of one's betters," or some diffuse upper-crust stratum. After all, initially they possess but differential control over one of society's scarce and unequally distributed resources, the very one that calls for new ways of management and at which these newcomers excel. Normally, when modernizing change ensues, these newcomers are one-dimensional elites. Concerning the fateful history of elite stratification, and therefore the very chances of a new nation to become an organized corporate actor with self-steering ability, the question is whether the universal striving for status consistency among these new elites will succeed or not. Other things being equal, such striving will be more successful in a society with common values (as, for example, Japan) than in one with deep value cleavages. In the former case, the claims for more diffuse rewards advanced by the new elites will fall on relatively fertile soil because those who make them can appeal to a consensual image of the good society, a society to which the new elites make a differential but commonly valued contribution. No doubt, value consensus in Japan was only one factor. They legitimated modernizing change also in terms of avoiding colonization from Western powers. That probably was a very important secondary factor in the development of stratified elites. But in Germany, where a far greater value dissensus prevailed and no foreign power posed the threat of subjugation, claims for entitlement to diffuse rewards fell on relatively deaf ears. Coming out of a history with more stratified elites in her separate parts before national unification than Japan, in Germany modernization probably brought about de-stratification among those groups that rose to national eminence. I shall endeavor to provide evidence later on that this in fact happened. A few examples may suffice at this point.

Dahrendorf (1965:297) noted that Germany was ruled by a "cartel of anxiety," at least during the Weimar period and after the Second World War in West Germany. The theme of insecurity in this formulation is highly useful for an understanding of the dynamics of mass politics in Germany. But the condition he described was very likely far more general, characterizing the national elites of the German nation throughout its existence from 1871 to 1945. The absence of a more diffuse national elite or some nationwide stratum of "one's betters" has also been noted by Zapf (1966:185–200). As in other European societies, industrialization produced a group of the "merely rich," the new industrial bourgeoisie who typically lacked prestige corresponding to their enormous wealth. But unlike other societies in industrialized Western Europe, notably Britain (Moore, 1966:36–39, 56–101), in Germany industrial entrepreneurs or managers never gained a level of prestige comparable to that of the military and the higher civil service. Further, several one-dimensional elites emerged, and their striving for status consistency remained largely a failure.

The early nineteenth century produced a one-dimensional cultural elite in Germany. Under the triple influence of German idealism, economic dependency of the Church on the state, and a property franchise that excluded the urban, educated strata from the vote before the formation of the Reich, sectors of the middle class developed an ideal of the cultivated man based on educational, philosophical, and artistic criteria that involved ideals with little bearing on practical, political, and social problems. Concentrated among the administrative and judicial bureaucracy, the professoriate, the clergy, and the free professions, the educated came to form a quasisecular cultural elite that succeeded in symbolizing "superior morality" (Ringer, 1967; 1969; Röhl, 1967b). Thus already prior to nation-building the Germans, particularly in the Prussian areas, had allocated superior virtue to one group—a cultural elite—while reserving power, wealth, and prestige to another still associated with the royal courts.

With rapid industrialization during the later nineteenth century, wealth became dissociated from the triad of prestige, power, and wealth that was still extant at the beginning of the century. The emergence of a capitalist class signified the appearance of the merely rich, who did not command prestige, political power, or virtues in amounts corresponding to their wealth (Zunkel, 1962). Yet throughout the century nobility remained a near-requisite for participation in court life. Contrary to appearances, however, the implied fusion of prestige and power was already under severe strain. During the Bismarckian and Wilhelminian eras monarchical constitutionalism in practice alternated between bureaucratic dictatorship and "personal rule." With varying ebb and flow but in one direction, prestige became gradually dissociated from power. A group of the merely prestigious appeared, the Junkers. They had not only lost their economic pre-eminence to the capitalists, they also now increasingly faced a government whose policies of modernization deprived them of the near-monopoly of the military officer corps they had held earlier. Thus the association between prestige still incorporated in nobility, the military, and the court, and power, now more and more lodged with the ministerial bureaucracy and/or the monarch, gradually became a façade before the First World War. With defeat in the war, this aspect of a unified ruling stratum was destroyed as well (Rosenberg, 1966; Kehr, 1965; Büsch, 1962; Lowie, 1945).

Unfortunately the separation of power and prestige was not as clear-cut as such a summarized account may pretend. First, while a group of the merely prestigious did emerge with the Junkers and the officer caste, neither the ministerial bureaucracy nor the monarch can be said to have lost prestige. Second, some prestige shifted to the cultural elite, particularly to its publicly most visible sector, the professoriate. The latter succeeded in translating some of the cultural eminence into political influence. As indicated above, they did this by becoming the spokesmen for the famed though instable iron-and-rye coalition through propaganda activities connected with the fleet-construction program and the volatile tariff questions. With that they not only gained prestige, they also became identified with the monarchical regime. As a result the loss of the First World War constituted a first blow to maintaining their stratification assets. Subsequently, prominent members of the professoriate became identified with the Weimar regime through their participation in constitution-making. But this hardly amounted to any significant re-stratification. The cultural elites in civil and judicial bureaucracy, and the prestigious in the Army failed to identify with the Weimar regime. During the Weimar years, power rested with party oligarchs, mass organizations, and the President (Eyck, 1962). The last remnant of elite stratification was a tenuous tie between virtue and prestige incorporated in a minority of the cultural elite, professors and members of the free professions, who managed some political influence. The rise of the Nazi movement signaled the destruction of this last connection. Aided by the merely rich and abetted by the merely prestigious of the Wilhelminian era, the Nazi ex-plebes made "Germany awake." They displaced the old cultural elite, already delegitimized through association with two failing political regimes, and successfully advanced a populist-based monopoly claim to a "new morality." By successfully defining the old middle strata as bourgeois and therefore corrupt, the Nazis removed the *Bildungsbürgertum* from elite status for good. Henceforth the educated middle strata retained prestige based solely on the utility of technical expertise. Claims to represent superior morality, however, became an attribute competitively sought by new groups in the party and its many organizational offspring (Schoenbaum, 1967). Such separation between prestige and virtue was effectively symbolized in the collapse of the middle class and conservative parties during the last elections of the Weimar regime. Though it maintained significant inequalities along all four dimensions of rank, Nazi Germany never reconstituted social cohesion among her elites. In fact, the very dynamics of a totalitarian regime depend in no small measure on the absence of such elite stratification. During the Nazi era, technical expertise was appreciated, and used. Similarly appreciated and used were wealth, claims to represent the "new morality," and power. But possession of one of these resources could not be used reliably for the attainment of another, nor for making a successful claim to "generalized superiority."

If one asks why this happened, consciousness about the value dissensus and an anxiety-ridden concern with the question of which of the various value formulas in Germany would gain supremacy provide the most plausible answers. The educated in Germany knew that theirs was a nation in a formal legal sense only, one that still had to struggle for national identity (Plessner, 1959). This meant that the public sphere was, for better or worse, a *tabula rasa*, a scene of human endeavor still to be filled with moral standards of relevance. That consciousness of a hitherto amoral public sphere effectively stifled attempts at building multidimensional elites. The idea of the morally empty public realm supplied an appearance of reasonableness to the absence of elite stratification while defining claims to general superiority as illegitimate expression of selfish interests. Weimar may have witnessed attempts at an "absurdly pure democracy" in a society shot through with authoritarianism (Eckstein, 1961). The conception of a public sphere devoid of any intrinsic morals points to a longer-lasting "absurdity"—namely, an absurdly pure commitment to the division of labor. Wielding political power, exercising some professional skill, commanding the disposition of wealth, or having a superior insight into problems of ultimate meaning in life were simply

seen as involving different jobs. Why should excellence in one go together
with excellence in another? Did that not deny the essentials about the
division of labor? Why should one *not* be obedient to one, properly
instituted political authority, while reserving prestige allocations to
another, properly certified professional expertise? And why should one
not reserve one's moral esteem for a third group, men and women of
cultivation and proven accomplishments in science and the arts, and agree
to reward with enormous income those best in generating wealth in the
first place, the new industrial managers? Why, indeed, should the wealthy
also be the more prestigious, or the powerful *also* the more morally
sensitive? These were meaningful questions in Germany, and one could
answer them in a way that withdrew legitimation from the very idea of a
more diffuse "establishment" at the top of the nation. That could be done
because what kind of a nation or society was to be built there remained an
open question. Where there was little agreement on relevant value
standards, the question of which occupations made more or less important
contributions to society as a whole could not be answered at all. Certainly,
everyone could appreciate that medical training, for example, was more
expensive than that of a plumber. But that remained a simple fact of
common sense and provided no reasonable basis whatever for an argument
that doctors were somehow more important to society as a whole than
plumbers. After all, most people, most of the time, are not critically ill.
But most people live in the new metropolitan environment. Imagine what
would happen in such an environment without the plumber or his more
sophisticated brother, the sewage engineer—filth, rats, and contagious
diseases more terrible than the medieval plagues, obviously. You could
just as well argue that plumbers were more important to society than any
other occupational grouping. The point of this trivial example is a simple
one. Where there was as little agreement on societal values as in Germany,
the query concerning which occupation made the most important overall
contribution to building the good society could find no answer.

Finally, a conglomerate of one-dimensional elites has good reason to
experience itself as a "cartel of anxiety." This has to do with the nature of
prestige and its uneven distribution among the elites. In giving prestige to
another, we trust that his judgment about what is in our best interest is
superior to our own. On this basis of trust we let ourselves be influenced
in what we do. Prestige is of course differentially allocated to positions in
society; some have more of it than others. But the greater significance for
present purposes is that the prestigious command a medium of influence, a
language of trust to which we listen when in doubt (Parsons, 1963a). In a
situation with one-dimensional elites, and with four kinds as I have used,
there are three that are deprived of influence. The "merely rich" have raw

economic power; they are nothing but capitalists in the pejorative sense of the term. The "merely powerful" have nothing but the tools of coercion at their disposal; they tend to be seen as near-tyrannical. The "merely virtuous" have nothing but moral sensitivity to offer; they appear as adolescent idealists in the pejorative sense of that term. These elites cannot assume moral responsibility in the broad sense of accountability beyond their narrow service sphere because they lack the basic tool, influence or superior persuasive power with which to correct the behavior of other institutional elites. Deprived of the principal means of moral responsibility, they tend to renounce the latter and develop a perverted kind of "responsibility ethic" (Weber, 1919b), which confines their sense of responsibility to short-run consequences of their action for the institution they serve. One may remember what it once meant to assume broader moral responsibility, one may be nostalgic about it and even sense that only the acquisition of prestige could attentuate one's present status anxiety. But sheer consciousness that prestige sits somewhere else transforms such considerations into mere futile "yearning for synthesis." And what about the military and the upper civil service in Germany who monopolized prestige? That very monopoly denatured prestige itself. On the one hand, underpaid and squeezed in their attempts to maintain a proper lifestyle, they looked like fossils from a preindustrial age. On the other, these "merely prestigious," lacking in power and in wealth, had no tools for demonstrating what superior judgment could accomplish. Eventually, their symbol of prestige, the uniform, became an empty one, a mere show, of little further consequence. The bases for the assumption of genuine moral responsibility became impossible for them as well. As a result, many continued to claim moral responsibility for the nation's fate. But that claim only served their struggle for status consistency. It had to become nothing but a propaganda tool.

If one assumes that a striving for status consistency is a universal one, such new and one-dimensional elites will keep on struggling for the scarce resources they lack. They will do so in order to earn greater legitimacy for what they possess already. But in the absence of value consensus in society such struggles acerbate the relations between elites. Value dissensus fuels the denial of entitlement in rewards beyond those relevant to the narrow service sphere provided. In response, the striving for status consistency should lead the one-dimensional elite to try to "earn" respect and trust by encroachment onto the institutional domain of another, traditional still or already modern. Such encroachments should not only intensify conflicts between elites, they can also be expected to lead to the systematic destruction of all vestiges of prestige and society's inability to regulate conflict. Chaos in conflicts is the last feature of German political life we must pay attention to if we are to understand why moral indifference among the elites could develop to the point of indifference about mass murder.

Mass Political and Unregulated Social Conflicts (5)

In referring to the prevalence of Social Darwinism, the linkage between industrial and political conflict, and the mixing of domestic and external affairs in politics, Reinhard Bendix (1965:272) once characterized German political life as an "unholy mixture of cynical *Realpolitik* and pretentious romanticism," and one that became a liability for the German nation since the early nineteenth century. While it is easy to agree with the description, neither ideology nor class conflict alone suffice as explanation. French politics can be highly ideological; class conflict in that society never seems to escape from the history of different responses to the French Revolution (Hoffmann, 1963:1–117; Crozier, 1964). Paradoxes may puzzle the observer of the French political scene; but France has never aroused as much concern and fear as Germany. One reason for the difference has to do with the relation between stratification and conflict organization, and the explosive dynamics that spring from it. If we assume that Germany was saddled with de-stratified elites, her severe integration crisis as well as the inability to regulate domestic conflicts would appear to be related phenomena. Alternatively, Germany's unholy political mixture can also be located in the relationship between stratification and conflict organization. Let us see how.

Following Galtung (1966) one may define stratification as the extent of status consistency prevailing in a society. Note that this formulation refers to stratification as a variable. Some societies may be more stratified than others. Let me take the hypothetical case of a society in which only two scarce resources or only two vertical dimensions of rank are recognized to illustrate what this means. Suppose then that wealth and power were the only unequally distributed resources. Every member of that society can be ranked as standing high or low on but two dimensions of ranking, the totem poles of wealth and power. Individuals who rank high on both, the wealthy and powerful, are the top dogs. Similarly, individuals who rank low on both, the poor and powerless, are the underdogs in this society. Both are said to be status-consistent groups. Other things equal in this hypothetical case, should conflict break out, we know who will fight whom. The underdogs will attack the privilege of the top dogs, and the latter will defend it. We also know what the fight is about; it is one about the unequal distribution of wealth and power, both simultaneously.

Keeping in mind that stratification is a variable, that a real society can be more or less stratified, this tells us about three consequences that flow from stratification. All three are important prerequisites that must be met if social conflicts are to be successfully regulated. Stratification provides order to conflict in society. First, it renders behavior, interaction, and relationships predictable, including who will fight whom and about what. Without the knowledge one could not even begin to design rules for the conflict game. In industrial disputes this has been easy. Everyone knows labor and management fight there.

Second, stratification brings temporal stability to conflict alignments. Underdogs and top dogs don't just fight each other today; so long as they stay who they are, they will keep on confronting each other. Subjecting conflict to regulations, to rules and procedures, presupposes stability of the parties involved and, broadly put, what it is they fight about. Were that to change every day, no one could ever hope to get beyond the constant design and redesign of rules for the game. Only behavior that shows some regularity lends itself to regulation.

Third, stratification provides effective organization for conflict. As Marx (1852) discovered when considering the dismal failure of the Paris *Lumpenproletariat*, it is far more easy to organize the status consistent for collective action than people coming from very different social backgrounds. A *Lumpenproletariat* is composed of dropouts from all kinds of positions in society. They are far too diverse in social identities for effective organization. Before the fight gets under way in earnest, they fall apart again under the sheer weight of their heterogeneity of origin. And to draw on collective bargaining as an instance of successful conflict regulation again, we know that social machinery is necessary to apply rules of regulation. Unions acting for labor, and industry representatives acting for management are indispensable for effectiveness in conflict regulation. Thus stratification provides order to conflicts in three separate and distinct ways. The more stratified a society is, the more order in its social conflicts prevails. But stratification also produces liabilities in the chances of successful conflict regulation. Stratification also increases the intensity in conflicts; the more a society is stratified, the more intense its conflicts will be. In our hypothetical case of but two dimensions of ranking, power and wealth, top dogs and underdogs inevitably confront each other about two inseparable issues at the same time, the unequal distribution of power and wealth. In the real world with many more dimensions of ranking— ethnicity, regional origin, religious affiliation, and so on—a 100 percent stratified society yields the specter of a people divided into one ruling class confronting one underdog mass on the inevitable eve of revolution because their conflict is one simultaneously about wealth, power, ethnic ranks,

South versus North, Protestant versus Catholic, and so on. If there is to
be a chance for regulating conflict, more than order is necessary. One
must also be able to separate issues. That is where the status inconsistent
come into the picture.

Status inconsistency characterizes persons who rank high on one
dimension and low on the other—say, the rich and powerless, or the
powerful but poor. The status attributes of these people crisscross those of
top dogs and underdogs. The rich and powerless share the high-wealth
status with the top dogs; they also share the status of powerlessness with
the underdogs. Note that top dogs and underdogs share no status at all.
And so, note as well that the rich but powerless literally hang in between
these two groups, sharing one status characteristic with each of two sets of
persons who in turn share nothing. That is why one also refers to the
status-inconsistent people in society as the cross-pressured, calling attention thereby to the psychological bind in which they find themselves.
Being rich, they share the corresponding economic interest with the top
dogs; but also being powerless, they share that corresponding political
interest with the underdogs. With their conflicting group loyalties on the
one hand, and their internally conflicted social identities on the other, the
cross-pressured are said to have a position-determined interest in the
regulation of conflict in society (Dahrendorf, 1959; Lipset, 1960). The
general reason for this assertion is very simple. Regulated conflicts permit
the status inconsistent to maneuver better. When there are rules of the
conflict game and people actually abide by them, you know when the
conflict starts, when it ends, who the losers and the winners were, and
what was lost and won. All of this is far more difficult to discern in
unregulated conflicts. The status inconsistent, then, have more of a stake
in conflict regulation because they want to throw their support to that side
whose victory preserves what they have (wealth in the example of the rich
but powerless) and enhances their control over the resource they lack
(power in my example). Underdogs have nothing to lose, save their lives;
they can only gain from conflict. Top dogs have nothing to gain from
conflict; they can only lose. These considerations lead the status consistent
toward intransigence, and militancy in confrontations. But the status
inconsistent, with their fear of loss *and* hopes for gain, are attracted to the
arts of compromise, to negotiation, and so to conflict regulation in general.
Thus, the more cross-pressured people there are in a society, the greater is
that society's supply of socially structured interests in the regulation of
conflict.

In the simple hypothetical case where people are ranked only on wealth
and power, it is readily apparent that stratification and crisscross vary
inversely and in zero-sum fashion with each other. The more a society is

stratified, the fewer cross-pressured people one finds in it, and vice versa. But this inverse relationship between stratification and crisscross also holds true in the multivariate case with as many dimensions of vertical ranking a people may use (Galtung, 1966). The social preconditions necessary for the successful regulation of conflict are therefore inherently contradictory. One needs order in conflicts, and stratification supplies that. One also needs an adequate supply of the cross-pressured, and stratification tends to eliminate that supply. In its impact on society's capacity for conflict regulation, stratification has a kind of Job effect, for as is said of the Lord in the Old Testament (Job 1:21): *What stratification giveth with one hand, order in conflicts, it taketh with the other, cross-pressured people.* It also follows that partial stratification that yields some requisite amounts of both, order in conflicts and a supply of the cross-pressured, is the condition most favorable for regulating conflicts.

The above reflections on the relationship between stratification and conflict organization rest on two simplifying assumptions. One is that all scarce unequally distributed resources on which the members of society are ranked are of equal worth and will be equally desired. The other is that scarce resources can be freely exchanged for each other—as if one could trade money for power, for example. In most cases neither of the two hold in the real world. In reality, status dimensions, the totem poles of wealth, power, prestige, and so on, tend to be rank-ordered themselves, making control over some dearer than that over others. Further, exchange of resources tends to be normatively regulated, permitting trade between some scarce resources in a fairly free manner, tightly regulating it with respect to others, and prohibiting it altogether for yet others. These are issues specified by the value system prevailing in a society. That is why they need not deter us at the moment. In the case of Germany, we shall see below what the different value formulas prescribed. In the nation as a whole, one shot through with value dissensus, there was little effective regulation about these matters.

Granted the emergence of one-dimensional elites in German society, the theoretical reflections just presented yield three hypotheses concerning the nature of their relationships. First, since stratification provides order in conflicts, the relations among one-dimensional elites, these de-stratified social creatures, should have been chaotic. Second, since by definition one-dimensional elites are cross-pressured ones, they can be expected to reveal a genuinely fetishistic commitment to "procedure above all." But third, over time and unless processes of re-stratification among them attenuated the disorder in their conflict relations, one would expect increasing militancy in their relations and the substitution of procedural legality for morality as the struggle for status consistency goes on and on without any resolution. And such substitution of legality for morality should eventually destroy any belief in substantive moral commitments as relevant in one's public roles. That means the complete privatization of moral beliefs. Their relevance shrank to applicability in the circles of friendship and kinship. In the public realm all value appeals became mere propaganda that nobody who was a somebody was expected to believe anymore. But in such a development the elites also inflate influence, the general language of persuasion in society, to the point of worthlessness. Then not trust but mistrust became the general orientation expected of a good administrator. And with values withdrawn from effective public circulation and with influence destroyed, the only thing that men in elite positions could still "trust" was power, and a power in its raw form of control over the means of coercion. Mere power technicians in this form are essentially amoral men, people who deprived themselves of the collective ability to realize any morally caring concern for the welfare of their own society or that of any other. Again, documenting that chaos in conflicts that pushed Germany's "unholy mixture of cynical *Realpolitik* and pretentious romanticism" to a point where the goals pursued became utterly unreal and the romanticism turned into complete moral indifference about the fate of concrete human beings, whether German, Jew, or Slav, will take up three chapters. Here a few illustrations must suffice to make these hypotheses plausible.

Already during the first days of her national existence Germany's burgeoning economy produced sufficient surplus to permit the appearance of mass-based propaganda organizations deployed for the manipulation of public opinion and the generation of alleged populist demands. These organizations were nationwide, with many full-time officials who even enjoyed pension rights. Excellent organization, skillful emotional appeals in print and demagoguery—in short, deployment of all the paraphernalia of modern propaganda campaigns, which the Nazis were to evolve into a high art of political-support mobilization, occurred already during Wilhelminian days. For Germany this form of communications development was more important than that reflected in such standard indicators as transport and telephone links, or flows of mail, which also, incidently, showed that she was second to none in Europe already before World War I (SJDR 1912:32). On the propaganda front the Industrial Association and the Agricultural Association, instruments of the iron-and-rye coalition, were perhaps the most important. But there were other important voices that could not be ignored, as, for example, the Fleet Construction Association, the Pan-Germans, the Arms League *(Wehrverein)*, and the Colonial Society. At the turn of the century in Germany's halfway house of parliamentarism, these organizations provided a service usually assumed by political parties in more developed polities: support mobilization for some national policy. Moreover, more than once these organizations succeeded in pressuring the executive and in "leading" the Reichstag. Typical of such organizations is the absence of any valid *and* accepted quantifiable measure of actual support—as votes or seats in parliament, for example. This provides them with an opportunity to produce the appearance of integration at the national level. The German organizations frequently succeeded in presenting as a manifest national-interest policy, enjoying wide support, what in fact was no more than a conglomerate of unassimilated conflicting particular elite interests (Kehr, 1965; Puhle, 1966; Nipperdey, 1966). Outside the Socialist subculture everyone used an inflated nationalist rhetoric in the pursuit of particularist interests. Thus a pattern developed whereby different elites egged each other on to "outnationalize" each other. Eventually, nationalism in German hands turned into its opposite, a disregard for the nation's welfare as profound as that of any of its propaganda victims.

In different guises, pseudonational political integration occurred again and again during the Weimar and Nazi periods. It thus constituted a persistent characteristic of modern German life. The Weimar period experienced not only a burgeoning crisis literature of which Spengler's *Decline of the West* was a prominent example; it also experienced the practice of crisis politics, both among the declared opponents of democracy and its ostensible defenders. One of the prominent forms of disparaging democracy was Hitler's virulent attack on the system as one run by "fulfillment politicians," people in the Reich government who, instead of opposing the "shameful Versailles *Diktat*," did all they could to pay the reparations. In line with the style of extremist political forces, Communists and National Socialists adopted crisis politics, a deliberate campaign to ruin democracy. But ostensible moderates did not shy away from the practice of crisis politics either. All of these pursued different aims, and Lindenberg (1978:43–56) gave us very illuminating examples how the pursuit of political ideals could eventuate in the complete disregard of the human costs of such "idealism." After the electoral victory of the Socialists in 1928, for example, union leaders felt encouraged to present demands on "economic democracy," worker participation in company affairs. On the very next opportunity of collective bargaining, the northwestern German iron industry rose to the challenge. They rejected an arbitration decision of the Reich Minister of Labor and locked out over two hundred thousand workers. Both parties abided by the law. The concrete results of adding to unemployment and already spreading misery in the nation was of little concern to either. This is a very moderate example. Crisis politics in a similar vein could also be practiced on a much wider scale. The desire to get rid of the reparations payments, that most hated symbol of the Versailles *Diktat*, was strong enough in Brüning, Chancellor and a member of the Catholic Center Party, to encourage Hitler in heating up his campaign against fulfillment politics. "Free expression of opinion," after all, was procedurally correct behavior in a democracy. In his memoirs Brüning tells us about his foreign- and domestic-policy objectives. Proving to the Allied powers that reparations were economically impossible was the way he operationalized his commitment to destroy the *Diktat*. Domestically, he wanted to please Reichspräsident Hindenburg, a man he venerated and who longed for the restoration of the monarchy. Making Weimar democracy unworkable seemed to provide at least an opportunity to return to the good old days of monarchical constitutionalism. Whether the breakdown of democracy made the restoration of the monarchy likely, that seemed to be another question. It also appeared to be irrelevant for practical purposes. To Brüning, developments subsequent to the breakdown of the system were matters beyond his control. All the chancellorship permitted him to do was use the office to pave the way for an alternative. Toward these ends, he pursued a fulfillment policy in the most literal sense that a superseded Dawes Agreement still allowed. Rather than act on the spirit of the Young Agreement in force, he abided by prevailing law, but in a manner to destroy it. He made sure that all reparations one could possibly pay were in fact paid. That deprived Germany's export-dependent economy of as much foreign currency as possible. Further, he did absolutely nothing to stimulate the economy. This happened early in 1932, when the German economy was near death. Recall the unemployment and related statistics of the previous chapter. Remember, there were six million workers without a job. Know that more than half of them were family men. If you have never seen the human face of starvation, perhaps you are familiar with the art of Kaethe Kollwitz to imagine the reality behind such statistics: sunken cheeks, matchstick limbs, bulging, dull, and listless eyes; these were the portraits of hunger, of men, women, and children in rags, perhaps ten million in all. The fact of widespread starvation counted little in the pursuit of the dream to restore the monarchy.

Brüning succeeded. So, shortly afterward, did Hitler. The common denominator in their achievements was the ability to treat people as mere statistics in sociopolitical experiments. That ability was not an invention of the Nazis. It rested instead on a longer practice of the use of extremist nationalist propaganda. In that practice, which runs like a red thread from the fleet propagandists of the Kaiser's days to the ruins of 1945, nationalism among the German elites turned into a socially effective commitment to unbelief as a role requirement for anybody who wanted to become and stay a somebody. And the resulting cynicism destroyed the trust language of influence, so that those who heaved Hitler into national leadership for their divergent purposes could neither stop the development toward totalitarianism, nor a push for *Lebensraum*, utterly unreal in the grandness of its design.

In conclusion, let us consider the short history of the modern German nation-state from the point of view of functional-system theory. That theory defines the modern condition as one marked by the differentiation of culture, society, and personality (Bellah, 1964). Responsibility before God, before men, and obligation to the self can no longer be simply the same. Therefore, the resulting modern form of individualism does involve the partial obsolescence of social honor as Berger (1970) has so cogently argued. No self-conscious multiple-role player in modern industrial society has anything like the capacity to feel insulted as had traditional man. In preindustrial times most social roles were ascribed to people, leaving them little choice. A person's sense of self was little more than a modest bundle of social roles. Humans were walking pieces of social structure, psychologically. They were rather literal carriers of the social honor of their station in life, and little beyond it. That much of Berger's theory is helpful. But he goes beyond this more modest formulation to suggest that it is a universal condition of the lives of men and women in all modern societies to have no sense of social honor whatever. That describes modernity in its excessive form, one where the ethical life of man becomes perverted into rampant situational ethics, a social situation in which all intersubjectively binding obligations disappear from public life. I shall indeed argue that this happened among elites in German society. But this is not the inevitable fate of modern men and women everywhere. Neither is it what the functional-system model of modernity implies; and even in Germany the institutionalization of rampant situational ethics was not some historical necessity. Functional-system theory of modernity stresses differentiation, not dissociation. If a modern individualism were to eventuate in nothing but situation ethics, it would be impossible to speak of any advantages in the division of labor in society. All the advantages of functional specialization and role differentiation would be lost. One cannot even imagine any police apparatus that could substitute for the loss of personal accountability in public life. Differentiation and organized complexity in the model of modern society are one thing; dissociation and chaos in social conflicts in the reality of one particular case are another.

However separate the symbolic realms of responsibility to ultimate values, of social responsibility to secular norms, and of personal obligations in the private sphere of intimacy, a model of modernity must specify mechanisms of their articulation. Otherwise such speculation yields only a

Hobbesian nightmare. More, a theory must also specify concrete social institutions providing such articulation. Some societies—as, for example, the American—have institutions specializing in the management of morals that these different obligations related to each other. The U. S. Supreme Court can be thought of as an organization designed for the management of contingency among obligations to culture, society, and self. Such organizations provide no guarantee against the possible dissociation of legality from legitimacy (Winkelmann, 1952). Formal justice can come to negate substantive justice, the kind men and women can feel as right in their hearts. But over the long haul, having an institution such as the Supreme Court makes such a schizophrenia about legality and morality, as happened in Germany's legal exclusion of Jews from society and her rampant conquest policies, less likely. This permits one to conclude that differentiation has gone too far when it has flipped over into simple dissociation—when a commitment to the mutual dependency among the norms of culture, of social, and of personal life has been abandoned and, above all, when no socially effective call for such mutual relatedness arises anymore from any sector in society.

Just how far this had come to pass in German society can be illustrated with one quotation so revealing of why the resistance to Hitler failed. When approached for help in March 1943, and so, long after the mass murder carried out by the *Einsatzgruppen* had become a well-known reality in higher Army circles, Hammerstein opined: "Yes, had he only a division under his command, he would not hestiate to fetch this devil [Hitler] from the bowels of hell itself; but that was precisely the problem, those who could act because they had the means did not want to, and those who wanted, could not" (Hoffmann, 1970:344). The German generals who mostly disdained Hitler could not rebel because they could not mobilize each other. That would have required shared ultimate moral commitments. But the sharing of such commitments beyond the intimate spheres of personal friendship or kinship had long disappeared from German society. For the critical majority of these generals, whose historical predecessors had once been the proud bearers of the Prussian state, the execution of legal orders, even if involving the death of millions of unarmed civilians serving no visible institutional purpose, remained subsumable under understandable norms of simple military obedience; but a conspirator who dared a coup for the sake of saving lives could be stamped a traitor (Hoffmann, 1970:213). Nothing could illustrate better the complete collapse of the very capacity to feel and act with moral responsibility than this ability to subsume mass murder under the label of warfare.

In this evolution toward the total irrelevance of more ultimate moral values in social life the history of chaos in conflicts played the major role in two ways. First, conflict alliances are unstable. That makes for unpredictability in life. Second, attempts to convert the resources a given one-dimensional elite does control into others it lacks, meet with random success. Sometimes you win, sometimes you lose. And while there is no direct one-to-one relationship between the social position one holds and the psychological implications for one's sense of self, that does not mean either that there is no connection at all. Psychologically, a person in a one-dimensional elite position knows only one thing with certainty: Nothing has endurance. The interest alliance of one day may turn to interest enmity the next. As a member of a cartel of anxiety one cannot rely on others for useful feedback concerning the question of who one is. Others are not the basis of socially valid and binding social identities. Nothing, however, can be quite as socially alienating as the combination of a performance ethic with institutionalized uncertainty. Then who one is, can afford to be, and can become are questions that find answers only on the cognitive plane, one devoid of emotional commitments, and one that we associate with that political flexibility typical of the modern totalitarian party apparatchik. Under such conditions the personal sense of self becomes desocialized, at least insofar as it involves serious and stable emotional commitments. Who one is in this emotionally binding way becomes a matter of privatized identifications with abstract cultural forms, religious or secular. The self becomes so radically subjectivized that it ceases to operate as a resource for that double contingency of normal social life on which the model of symbolic interactionism insists as the indispensable underpinning of all predictability in human relations. It does not take much imagination to see that once a process of subjectivizing the self gets under way, it becomes soon enough a self-fulfilling prophecy in social life. Where man has shifted his sense of personal self onto some cultural plane, where what he experiences is beyond the forces of social control, eventually he becomes incapable of responding on the social plane to any offerings of more ultimate moral concerns with an inner-wordly relevance. For then, what matters ultimately has no relationship to what matters in the here and now to one's fellow human beings in the finitude of life. Society becomes a scene of moral irrelevance, and moral solidarity shrinks to the circles of friendship and kinship, even there becoming questionable. Without implying that Max Weber would have been a Nazi had he had the opportunity, let me use the life of that remarkable man a last time to illustrate how far unpredictability in Germany could go. Several biographers tell us that no one could predict where Weber would take his position on the major issues of his day (Mommsen, 1974a:453; 1971:27; Dronberger, 1971:300). After the Second World War, when the reality of the Holocaust had become known among the educated, Ilse Dronberger (1971:341) asked Marianne Weber directly how her husband would have reacted to National Socialism. The only answer she received was this: "Every human being is a secret."

At the beginning of this chapter I asserted that one should not treat history as fated necessity. Neither genocide nor national suicide, these twin features of interest in Germany's short visit to the history of modern nation-states, were necessary. Hence we have to ask what the most likely alternative to her unholy mixture of cynical *Realpolitik* and pretentious romanticism in political life could have been. We know of one type of political regime capable of granting political stability to societies deeply split in their values. That is consociational democracy (Lijphart, 1968, 1969; Steiner, 1974). The essential features of a consociational democracy are but two: an elite trained for joint collaboration against the centrifugal pressures in society, and grass-roots *apartheid* at the bottom of society, where the ethical strangers live in "negative integration" with each other. Now, given the value dissensus in German society as well as the pattern of negative integration among some subcultural communities I have mentioned, these would make some kind of consociational political regime, though not necessarily a democratic one, the relevant alternative. For example, genuine aristocrats, more authoritarian and self-assured than Germany's commercialized Junker souls with their corner-grocer mentality (Weber, 1917a), might have arranged the murder of Gestapo chiefs in 1934 when Generals von Schleicher and von Bredow fell victim to the Röhm purge. Perhaps more self-assured and really class and nationally conscious middle-class bourgeois in the higher civil service like Max Weber could have done the same. A sociologist must admit to his occupational dilemma. Individuals do count in history. Finding some plausible answer to the question why these individuals did not appear on the scene to alter the course of history can serve us in the identification of the more crucial sociological variables. Even though the known forms of consociational regimes are all democratic, some of their features prove instructive nonetheless.

First, consociationalism has emerged only in small countries without any reasonable basis for aspirations to world-power status. Germany was a mighty nation among her neighbors in Western Europe. Second, viable consociationalism demands that elites in society can tolerate inaction, doing nothing rather than compromising when they cannot agree on some policy. We shall have to find out whether the different value formulas extant in German society had too much instrumental activism as one common denominator to prevent the corresponding tolerance of sheer passivity that consociational elites require for their collaboration against the centrifugal forces in their societies (Obler, Steiner, and Dierickx, 1977). One can also use the concept of efficiency to describe this idea. In purely economic terms, consociational societies are notoriously inefficient (Gurr and McClelland, 1971; Fox, 1978). They do so many things in double or triple fashion, depending on the number of segregated subcultural communities they have. One finds in them, for example, a doubling of institutions along lines of religious affiliation. There can be Catholic universities and Protestant ones, Catholic science and a Protestant one, Catholic unions and Protestant ones, Catholic and Protestant TV and the arts more generally, Catholic and Protestant soccer, welfare services, and strictly proportionate appointments by religion to the civil service, from the humble postal clerk to the level of permanent Secretary of State. Of course, this is waste or inefficiency only from the perspective of more value-integrated societies like the Anglo-Saxon democracies. In consociational societies one regards these patterns as integrative investments. They double or triple the upward-mobility chances in society regardless of the costs to the underlying population. In doing so, they provide the elites with an interest stake in inefficiency, if you like. But since in Western Europe, at any rate, these societies are also more open ones, permitting more upward and downward mobility from generation to generation than the Anglo-Saxon democracies (Fox and Miller, 1966), they also provide the more aspiring among their nonelites with a stake in inefficiency, so-called. Germans, I suspect, were too achievement-oriented to permit the development of this pattern. Third, as evident in The Netherlands, Switzerland, and Austria, consociationalism started before industrialization really got under way. In Germany industrialization preceded national unification to a critical extent. Apparently then, consociationalism must develop before the masses become mobilizable on a national scale (Pride, 1970). So far as is known, the nonelites in a consociational regime must be highly authoritarian in their patterns of deference to their own leadership groups. Upstairs in society, elites need high autonomy and real independence from grass-roots pressures if they are to collaborate on what is possible in a value-cleavage-ridden society and, occasionally, do nothing, no matter how deep the need downstairs. In the Dutch case, as Lijphart (1968:162) notes, "Deference may be a too weak term to describe this [required] attitude to authority; perhaps one ought to speak of 'docility.' " In Germany, one suspects, there was not enough docility among the nonelites. In short, rather than suspecting too much authoritarianism and obedience in Germany, as has been done so often in searching for the causes of her failure to develop a democratic polity (for example, Dahrendorf, 1965; Sontheimer, 1962), understanding the German polity as a ruthless conquest state that undid itself requires us to ask the opposite question: Was there perhaps too little true respect for any authority?

My interpretation of the unique production of hell that German politics realized follows in the methodological footsteps of Weber. I use variables useful in the analysis of any societal process. The uniqueness of the outcome I seek to capture in a unique constellation of values of these variables. The important constellation in the German case seems to me to be made up of: (1) value dissensus in society in the context (2) of a prior history of domination by interest constellations; (3) a process of elite destratification in the course of modernization; (4) the loss of the ability to regulate conflicts in society; and (5) a rising tide of inflated nationalism, which led to the withdrawal of morality from public life, the inflation of influence to worthlessness, and the deflation of power to sheer coerciveness. It is time to turn to the evidence.

CHAPTER FOUR

Value Dissensus in "German" Society

Shared value-commitments are destructive of a *Volksgemeinschaft*.
Reinhard Höhn (1935:83)

Reinhard Höhn was a social-science professor and an SS leader. Even though sociology represents an extreme instance of the demise of social science after 1933 (Lepsius, 1979), that was a rare combination of roles one could play in the Third Reich. Therefore, one can hardly ascribe the character of consensual expert opinion to Höhn's National Socialist conception of the word *Volksgemeinschaft*. Under the swastika, far too few social scientists with a sociological perspective practiced their craft to permit that. Nonetheless, Höhn's meaning reflects anything but an idiosyncratic view. More important, his meaning of the term reflects a historical truth. And it is significant that in its political use the German, and not only the National Socialist, conception of the term *Volksgemeinschaft* was one that turned its usual or ordinary meaning upside down. In common parlance, as well as in sociological writing, the word *Gemeinschaft* denotes two things: a community of people integrated by commonly shared values and an organismic image of society as an entity that adjusts to changes in order to remain the same. Now, whatever the ubiquitous references to *Volksgemeinschaft* in Nazi propaganda may have meant to various groups in Germany, and that was a matter deliberately left ambiguous (Schoenbaum, 1967), living still and looking back we know what the term did not imply. Neither during the Third Reich nor before among the folkish movements that used the term did *Volksgemeinschaft* ever signal a commitment to those kinds of values that could have guided political action in Germany toward the construction and preservation of a stable national social order, one sufficient unto itself and existing peacefully in a niche within the European nation-state system. On the contrary,

113

the Nazi *Volksgemeinschaft* in action was a continuation, though a more radical one, of the striving for world-power status or "a place in the sun" that characterized the foreign-policy aspirations of Imperial Germany under the Kaiser. The primary aim of the First World War had been the construction of a *Mitteleuropa*, a sphere of influence where Germany would dominate. Then, planned annexations of territory were modest, and they were to serve strictly military-security aims in protecting that sphere (Fischer, 1967). The Nazi New Order, however, was to be a large empire stretching to the East, with direct political domination emanating from Berlin. And *one* important domestic factor that favored this continuous striving for political dominance in Europe was the fact that the German people never came to agree on the question of who was German. However offensive to common sense, Höhn's idea that a *Volksgemeinschaft* would be destroyed rather than constituted by value consensus among its members does describe a historical truth about Germany. And that truth is one not confined to the era of the Third Reich. As one recent observer said: "Germans do not now and never have shared symbols of solidarity capable of fusing all the Germans together into a single cultural or symbolic constitution." And further: "One distinguishing feature of the German ethnic community is always to be divided in binary fashion over the very principles and symbols of solidarity, and not merely to be fragmented in practice. This is apparently not an adventitious phenomenon but part of German culture—as opposed to French or English national culture, or for other reasons even Italian or Spanish" (Pletsch, 1979:341–45).

Pletsch (1979), it would appear, is quite correct in his conclusions about the distinctiveness of the Germans. It is only the observations that he used to arrive at them that seem to me somewhat dubious. Primarily interested in substantiating his assertion that the contemporary Germanies in East and West are two nations rather than one divided into two states, he used such data as prevailing citizenship and currency laws, party programs relating to the "national question," and official dictionary definitions of the term "nation." But for his conclusion his historical observations are the more important. And on this point, he locates the start of this distinctively German contentiousness about the question who is a German and who belongs into the politically organized community in the Reformation settlement. At that time it was a matter of religious affiliation. Then already, depending on a sovereign's response to Protestantism, *cuius regio, eius religio:* If the Lord turned to Protestantism that was your official religious and therefore your official state identity, and if not, Catholicism and another state identity remained your lot. From there he sees a ribbon stretching to the present day, where *cuius res publica, eius ideologia:* If you live in East Germany your national identity is prescribed as socialist, and if you live in the West your corresponding lot is liberal-capitalist (even though the latter does not permit as much prescription from the top). In between, as it were, Pletsch reminds us of the "smaller Germany solution" to modern nation-building in 1871, which excluded the ethnic Germans of Austria while making citizens of Poles who happened to live in Germany and who, as I mentioned earlier, had their own political organizations and sent their own representatives to the Reichstag.

Pletsch alerts us to the fact that there is something unique about the Germans. There was also something "unreal" about them. Let me elaborate his observations in two ways to bring this "unreality" into sharper focus.

First, German history was also one of political struggles about the questions of who belongs, who is to be included, and who is to be excluded. From the Reformation wars to the nineteenth-century cabinet wars leading to the "smaller German nation" of 1871 to the reach for empire in two World Wars, there runs a thread of continuity in which the force of arms created facts concerning the nature of collective identity. Always these facts were subsequently subjected to legitimation by the force of law. It is German experience, then, that matters of collective identity are matters imposed from above, by secular political forces "dominating" individuals, prescribing for them who belongs and who does not and, in consequence, prescribing for them what it meant to be German. Who belonged to the Germans and who did not and why had always been questions settled in a manner that had nothing to do with shared culture in the narrower sense of the term. Nor had these been questions settled in a fashion respecting individual inclinations or personal convictions. As a result, society, membership in it, and therefore national identity never attained that character of taken-for-grantedness one suspects to find among the British or the French.

Second, continuity in struggles over belonging did not only operate on the territorial plane. Domestically, there were similar struggles about the question of who was to be belong rightfully, yet to be included, or excluded, from political life. During the Second Empire (1871–1918) and ideologically, the Socialists remained a suspect "fatherlandless rabble" in the eyes of those in the upper and middle strata of society who upheld the monarchical constitution as defining what Germandom was to mean. During the Weimar period, the "republicans by reason only" *(Vernunftre-publikaner)* contended with the "republicans by heart" about the nature of German national identity. During the Third Reich, and suspended into an ocean of mere technicians, a minority in the Army fought a losing rear-guard battle in defense of common sense, contending with a party minority of "racial totalitarians by heart" about the collective identity of the New Order (for example, Thorwald, 1975).

The point of all this is a simple one. The German contentiousness about the question of who is a German *and* the matter in which that question had been addressed historically are directly related to both the main show (the suicidal double reach for empire in modern times) and the sideshow (Jewish genocide). The profound moral indifference with which the German elites approached the inclusion of foreigners into the empire, or the exclusion of others from it, rested on this long-standing historical experience with inclusion/exclusion struggles. That politics ruled on the question of who belongs and who does not was a matter of utter familiarity. Thus deporting the Jews was simply a particular version of an old story, as was the prospect of having to cope with the Flemish, Poles, or Ukrainians in some manner when the drive for empire had been completed. Never had more ultimate or moral beliefs been the decisive forces on the question of who belongs into the political community. That question had always been decided by interests—political and economic. And so, to the better educated and those with some historical conscious-ness in Germany, approaching that question from the perspective of morality was indicative of sentimentality or perhaps adolescent immatur-ity. Only sentimental fools or permanent adolescents would regard public life and events in it as having any direct moral meaning at all. But for "realists," or people who had grown up, politics was simply not the scene where one would take the Lutheran stance of "Here I stand, I cannot otherwise." Moral indifference to the exclusion of the German Jews from society, the first step to genocide, and moral indifference about the status of the conquered in the empire-to-be, a first step to national suicide in this repeated "*Drang nach Osten*," these were both matters deeply anchored in German political history. Only one qualification is necessary. It is a methodological one.

If political struggles and binary fissions over the very principles and symbols of solidarity were distinctive to German culture, thus leaving the question who was German forever open, that distinctiveness does not emerge from the kind of data considered by Pletsch. The Reformation settlement with its *cuius regio, eius religio* resolution was not an experience confined to German-speaking Europeans. When The Netherlands emerged from the breakup of the Spanish Empire, Dutch Calvinists disenfranchised their Catholic Dutch countrymen (Lijphart, 1968). In the wake of the First World War practically all the successor states to the Austro-Hungarian Empire had ethnics of their own kind across some border in a foreign nation and "foreign ethnics" within their own territories. By 1945 it was, in effect, the policy of the Allied powers that imposed the principle *cuius res publica, eius ideologia* on Czechs and Slovaks, a ruling reasserted by Russian tanks in Prague in 1968. Europe has too much of a common history in these matters to construct something distinctive in German culture from them. One must search for "enabling factors" that made it possible for Germans to construct from this more widespread and common historical experience their own distinctive culture trait: forever to be divided and to fight about symbols of solidarity and, eventually, to fight about them with that ruthlessness that manifested itself in National Socialism.

Reinhard Höhn's (1935) National Socialist conception of the word *Volksgemeinschaft* provides us with a clue as to the first of these "enabling factors." This upside-down meaning of the word points to value dissensus in German society. Germans, I shall contend in this chapter, never came to agree on fundamental societal values. The kind of values I have in mind here are commitments to value standards so general as to become constitutive of the structure of a total society, giving it, *when shared*, some distinctive character or national identity. This happens when such standards rest on "shared conceptions of the desirable type of society" respected by all or most its members (Parsons, 1968b:136). Let me emphasize by reiteration of ideas already presented in the previous chapter: The values I am addressing here are very general and abstract principles of evaluation. They organize hundreds of more specific normative beliefs by which we guide our conduct in family and factory, in the marketplace and at church. Men and women use such values to evaluate others and themselves, to present claims and defend the status quo, to reward for merit and dispense demerit, to express love or admiration that guides our conduct in emulation, and to utter hate or contempt that leads us into abhorrence of others. Innumerable are the social uses of values. But above all else, values are the primary tools with which we arm ourselves for conflict (Williams, 1979:26), whether nonviolent or violent, whether rule-governed and "civilized" or rule-disregarding and "barbarian." If one can demonstrate that there was no appreciable consensus on values of this order in German society, one generates data of more direct relevance to the moral indifference among the German people in general and among their elites in particular to the fate of the Jews, that sideshow, as well as to the fate of others in a conquest empire, the main show. Living in a society without shared values means living with ethical strangers. If you are used to that, the removal of some, even their removal to death, amounts to the disappearance of some "distant people," not people of your own kind with whom you are identified. Similarly, used to living with ethical strangers in the political community, for Germans changing the map of Europe by conquest was not something like a "rape of other people's ethical souls": for in the eyes of Germans and in their historical experience, only individuals and smaller subcultural groups, certainly not modern nations, were the carriers of values. The question is how to demonstrate this. Where does one find evidence on values in a historical period? How can one describe their nature? And how can one ascertain to what degree the Germans were not a people integrated by commonly shared values and so not really German? Let us see where to find the evidence and how one can answer these questions.

A Précis on Methods

Methodological considerations are nearly always exasperating. Many readers care more about results. However, if one is to understand results, some information how they were obtained is simply indispensable. That minimum of issues faced and decisions made I present here, leaving a more detailed account of all these methodological fine points to the Appendix.

What materials does one select to measure values in a total society before the advent of national sample surveys? Frequently in political studies one encounters methods that risk the danger of offensive circularity in reasoning. Values are abstracted from documents pertaining to political life, such as party programs, or speeches of political leaders; and political behavior is then "explained" in terms of the values so gained. Only if an investigator throws his net of observations on values very wide, covering, for example, the parties, the court system, the labor movement, academe, the writing of prominent intellectuals, and so on, as Dahrendorf (1965) did, does he avoid such circularity. My response to this problem was to opt for a narrow site of observation, but one as far removed from political life as possible. Using selection criteria proposed by Martel and McCall (1964), I used ethnographic-realist literature with a mass appeal as a source on the values of Germans. Ethnographic realism in a novel means that the people and places described strike the readership as a good account of the way people actually are, rather than as a reflection of the idiosyncratic or private view of the world of the author. The kind of novels I used were, then, the exact opposite of much of contemporary American literature, which does not even bother anymore about the boundary between private and public experience (Lasch, 1978:13–25). And literature with a mass appeal here means novels that attained undisputed best-seller status in a free market. All novels used were printed in tens and hundreds of thousands of copies, covering many repeated editions from the beginning of the unified modern German nation-state in 1871 to its demise seventy-four years later. None of the novels were ever "pushed" onto the public by any organization, such as the Gideon Society in America distributing the Bible, or the Nazi Party in Germany, which presented a copy of Hitler's *Mein Kampf* to every couple on the occasion of their marriage. The reason for not using literary material pushed by any organization is simple. Frequently, such literature is the most widely distributed and the least read.

Behind each copy of the novels I used stood at least one buyer who purchased it. If one makes the modest assumption that there was at least one reader for each buyer, one gains an extraordinary advantage. There is no need to worry about undersampling the readership of the nation here. With readers numbering in the hundreds of thousands, and a literature of enduring popularity throughout the lifetime of modern Germany (1871–1945), as indicated by the years in which reprint editions appeared on the market, use of such material "oversamples" the readership population to a phenomenal degree when compared with the sample size of contemporary national polls. But what about group bias in the readership? Were these novels perhaps read primarily by middle- rather than lower-class people, more by Protestants than Catholics, or Southerners than East Prussians? Today we know who smokes what brand of cigarette and reads what type of paperback. And while that type of consumer information simply does not exist for the novels used here, all the evidence that is available indicates that this literature was read by people from all walks of life and everywhere in the country. That evidence applies to a subsample of the thirty-one novels I selected. Numbering eleven, these novels were a quota sample of all those serialized in *Die Gartenlaube* over the years 1872 to 1900. *Die Gartenlaube* was Germany's equivalent of the late American *Saturday Evening Post*, a newsmagazine, devoted in part to "wholesome" entertainment. Further, it was one of the few, if not, indeed, the only newspaper with a genuine national distribution in Germany before the First World War. Therefore, it can serve as a medium of access to a nationwide readership. An analysis of letters to the authors of the novels and the editors of the magazine over many years did show that these novels were read by all the people, regardless of their creed, class, or regional residence (Zimmermann, 1963).

I was also interested in estimating regional variations in the values of the German people. Here I could exploit a fortunate fact. Germany had a distinctive tradition of regional literature in ethnographic realist fiction. Very prominent writers described people of their own kind, such as Bavarians, Rhinelanders, East Prussians, and so on. Again using only best sellers, the remaining twenty novels were selected with the aid of a standard source on this regional literature (Nadler, 1912–18).

While catching a national readership was thus a manageable task, the question of how representative my thirty-one novels are of all popular mass fiction consumed at the time remained open. To use statistical jargon, the "universe" of ethnographic realist German fiction with a mass appeal is unknown. Consequently, there is little point in using statistical tests of significance when trying to answer the question whether differences in values between such groups as Southerners and Prussians, or middle-class and lower-class people appearing in these novels are due to chance. All that is clear here is the fact that this is not an issue of numbers. Vast numbers of people read my thirty-one novels. Huge numbers found themselves and the others in their nation described therein. But since the representativeness of the sample of novels remains unknown, one has to live here with the following reasonable assumption: Given that this is ethnographic realist fiction, describing people how they really were, and given its indisputable popularity, it is unlikely that the sample misrepresents the universe. If the appeal of this type of literature does rest importantly on its realism (Martel and McCall, 1964; Colby, 1966), whatever the size of the universe, novels belonging to it ought to be homogeneous in the truth of their descriptive accounts. That fact diminished significantly the chance of picking unrepresentative and therefore misleading material. Mass appeal, then, is very important; that is why sales success, and not what a high-school teacher may regard as good-quality writing, served as the criterion of selecting novels.

One more comment on the problem of selecting the novels is necessary. Theoretically (Parsons, 1951; 1968b), the values of interest here ought to be regarded as the most stable features of any society. Because they are standards of evaluation, and very abstract ones at that, a great deal in society can change without necessarily bringing about change in such values. Of course, in the real world they may well have changed. And so the reader may well wonder why I did not inquire by covering also novels popular during the Weimar Republic and under the swastika. One reason has already been mentioned. It seemed imperative to avoid selecting material with any political sponsorship. That would have been very difficult for anything published during the Third Reich. While that does not exclude the fiction of the Weimar period from consideration, it simply is a safer procedure to stick with popularity of an enduring character. It assures one that nothing overtly political ever sponsored these novels in the market. Therefore, their mass appeal is real and not contrived. Beyond that, I lean for justification on an expert on German society and a sociologist who in his role as theorist is not at all shy in proclaiming his belief in the ubiquity of change in social life (Dahrendorf, 1959). Though implicitly, as may be natural for a man with such persuasions, Dahrendorf

(1965) argued for value stability in Germany throughout the modern period since 1871, conceding a *possibility* of value change only to the impact of the National Socialist movement.

Finally, using this type of fiction as a data base for values in society rests on one important assumption: Whatever reading a novel may mean to a reader, and that can cover many things, one of the ends served is instruction. The major characters in this type of fiction serve as models of identification and distantiation, telling the reader who he or she is and ought to be, what one ought not to be like, and who some clearly identified others are and how one ought to be like or unlike them. Such novels are often filled with blatant moral messages. They have heroes and villains. The former are models of identification, the latter models of distantiation. Content analysis of "good" and "bad" people in literature therefore can reveal the prevailing value standards that people ought to be devoted to and the values one should shun. It was also possible to classify the characters with sufficient reliability by social class, region, and urban or rural setting. The values coded for the "good guys" in these categories therefore yield information about variations in values among the German people accordingly. But while variations in values by region, class, and urban-rural context could be estimated, the one possibly critical division in German society these novels shed no light on was religion. References to religious belief and behavior proved too elusive to classify the characters as Catholic or Protestant, to say nothing of further divisions among the latter. Neither could one use a regional label as indexing religious denomination indirectly. With some exceptions, such as Upper Bavaria, where practically all were Catholic, the Germans of different denominations lived far too much cheek by jowl (Ravenstein, 1883) to use state boundaries, dialect regions, or any other geographic clue in the novels to determine a character's religious affiliation. Thus the data presented below permit no examination of possible value cleavages by religion.

The value orientations reflected in these novels were subjected to content analysis with the aid of a fifteen-item values questionnaire. The questions, deliberately general in format, covered a broad domain. They ranged from a character's "philosophy in life," "obligation to society," and "obligation to self," to "kind of intelligence valued" (see Appendix). Four different answers were provided for each question. The answers expressed a commitment to one, and only one, evaluation standard as follows: (1) social utilitarianism (universalism performance); (2) effectiveness in group performance (particularism performance); (3) group solidarity (particularism quality); and (4) an idealist commitment to explicit codes (universalism quality). Having read a novel, a coder filled out the questionnaire for its characters. Coding amounted to rank ordering the four evaluation standards provided for each question, from 1 or "most reflected" in that character to 4 or "least reflected."

To find out whether the answer categories did indeed measure the value standards they were supposed to indicate, I relied on the "informed-jury technique." Three colleagues familiar with this typology of value standards and its theoretical background (Parsons, 1953; 1961) served as validity coders for the questionnaire. After three revisions of dubious items among the answer categories, average agreement on concept validity among the three came to 89 percent, with a range from 83 percent to 93 percent. To find out whether the values questionnaire worked reliably, or whether in the hands of other coders it would produce the same distribution of values in these novels, a student of German literature was engaged to serve as a "reliability coder." A thirty-minute "crash course" on the concept values in the work of Kluckhohn and Parsons aside, this coder had no training in sociology whatever. The reliability sample covered most authors, and 13 novels with 62 main characters. The latter made up a 27 percent reliability sample of all 230 fictional characters in the study; and they also comprised a cross section of all by region, social class, urban and rural context, as well as men and women depicted in fiction. Coder-investigator agreement on rank 1 of the answers reflecting the value standard "most reflected" in that character's behavior proved insufficiently reliable. But agreement on the first two ranks came to 79 percent. That is why the study is based on thirty measured value orientations for each character (two answers reflecting the "most" and the "next most" important value standard broadcast by a character). The unit of analysis, however, is the number of mentions the four value standards received in coding this sample of German ethnographic realist fiction.

To conclude these comments on methodology, one should point out that such raw agreement rates between people who do the measuring in fact underreport the validity and reliability of the data generated. Why this is so is described in the Appendix. Let me note here only the practical implication. In considering the quantitative distribution of societal values below, any difference of 6 percentage points or more is one to be respected. That magnitude of differences in value orientations cannot be attributed to errors in measurement.

In turning to types of societal values measured and described in terms of "images of the good society" below, let me note that the questions in the coding instrument could be grouped to reflect orientations to four basic issues in social life: (1) the purpose of associating with others; (2) balancing the needs of individuals and those of social organizations, or the individual-group dilemma; (3) legitimating inequalities; and (4) legitimating change and stability in social relations.* These four issues provide convenient reference points in describing and contrasting the four types of value systems or "images of the good society" the study addresses.

Four Types of "Images of the Good Society"

I have used four types of value standards in order to go beyond an old and persistent tradition in sociological thought that focuses only on two: *Gemeinschaft* and *Gesellschaft* values. Using these terms, Levy (1964:247; 1979), for example, has repeatedly pointed out that all societies have both types of values, and that what varies is their relative predominance. But this dichotomy is scarcely enough even to approximate the diversity of norms that guide our conduct in different situations. Intuitively, such norms seem to be anchored in different values. In our market relations we put the emphasis on individualism, universalism, and performance, thus communicating the primary relevance of social utilitarianism. In our family lives we stress the interdependence between individual and group and owe each other loyalty on the basis of our membership rather than our daily achievements. *Gemeinschaft* values seem to be the cement of family life. In factory or office, in turn, we behave as if upholding corporatist values, and that means buckling under to the demands of organization, or collectivism rather than individualism. It also means loyalty to the place of employment, or particularism, but also having to earn our right to belong every day, or stressing performance. At church we relate as members of a "communion" (Schmalenbach, 1961), or as people who come together to share ultimate concerns. On that occasion, and in that setting, we acknowledge each other as creatures who search and care about meanings that transcend what we can understand rationally with common sense or the tools of science. And there we articulate, we share, and we recommit ourselves to the conviction that what we can grasp and manipulate in the here and now, or in the finitude of individual lives, can never be enough to make and keep us human. And so religious ties emphasize the quality of the human condition as anchored in purposes larger than man. Additionally, in Western religion, with its Judeo-Christian tradition, that means the primacy of universalism. It also implies an activist stance vis-à-vis the human condition or a conviction that what we believe must have some relevance to what we do, and that a nonconcern with explicit codes of ultimate meaning would make us less than human.

Each one of these just-mentioned common social settings is organized

---

*See Table A-2 in the Appendix: (1) combines question Nos. 9, 13, and 14; (2) is the sum of answers to question Nos. 2, 3, and 8; (3) that of question Nos. 10, 12, and 15; and (4) combines question Nos. 1, 5, and 11 for change and question Nos. 4, 6, and 7 for stability.

primarily around one value principle. Market relations express utilitarianism. In the family, *Gemeinschaft* solidarity is the organizing principle. In formal corporate organization effectiveness in cooperation ranks supreme. And in the religious life idealist commitments to explicit codes of ultimate significance organize our relations. This gives us a broader basis in asking the question of which values "predominate." Otherwise, one can stick with Levy's suggestion and treat predominance or the hierarchy of importance among these value principles as that which give distinctiveness to societal values and therefore to the collective identity of men and women in different countries. To elaborate, one can imagine an ideal-typical society so profoundly utilitarian in character that even a relationship of romantic love is experienced—in the last analysis, as it were—as an association for mutual advantage, utterly voluntary, with limited liability, contingent for its duration on payoffs realized by each partner, and in these ways "just like" a market relationship between some buyer and some seller. Similarly, one can imagine an ideal-type society so deeply structured by commitments to the principle of "effectiveness in cooperation above all" that even a couple in love tends to act as if on some military mission. That couple may be organized with precisions into shifting leader-follower relations, depending what "hostile" force must be faced outside. If it is the in-laws, the female may be the leader; if it is the boss, the male may take over. In that fashion, even the intimacy of family ties may be "just like" army relations between some general and his troops. Depending, then, which one of these four value principles one treats as "predominating" and therefore as giving all social relations one particular cast, one can generate four types of societal values, or images of the good society. That is one way to go beyond the old familiar contrast between *Gemeinschaft* and *Gesellschaft*. In describing these four types I shall focus on their differences with respect to: (1) the purpose of association; (2) the balancing of individual and social needs, or the individual-group dilemma; (3) the legitimation of inequality; and (4) the legitimation of social change and stability. And I shall label the descriptions accordingly.

In the *market model* of the good society (1), all forms of social organization rest on the presumption that people join groups because they have things to exchange with each other. The nature of man and society is basically utilitarian. Whatever the goals—love or work, pleasure or prayer—all forms of social life, and so society at large as well, are supposed to have the basic character of a voluntary association for mutual benefit. In principle, all social bonds are bonds of limited liability, where you have to earn your membership. One enters them with relative ease; but one should leave when better chances for self-actualization wink elsewhere. Basically, any partner is a partner in some achievement enterprise; and relative satisfaction with mutual usefulness makes people stick with each other. Given this stress on utilitarianism and voluntarism, there is also one on individualism. Therefore (2), the individual-group dilemma, or the question whether the needs of the individual or those of the group should yield when the two clash, is one resolved in favor of the individual. Ultimately, so these moral beliefs assert, all organization exists to serve the needs of individuals. A just social order can only be one in which the individual pursuit of happiness is given maximum scope. Further, in so profoundly utilitarian a society (3), the most general symbol of utility, money, in the form of the wages of work, serves as the most essential measure to rank the individual's worth to society. Wealth symbolizes success; poverty, failure; and life is essentially a struggle for differential usefulness, which pits all the "right-thinking and right-feeling" in competition against each other. The market model of the good society insists that all social games worth playing must have winners and losers. This active model of the good society (4) is also an open-ended vision, a society infinitely revisable, just as the highest obligation to the self is unlimited self-improvement. Consequently, an expectation for social change is built into the model. Only a dynamic society and one changing its features can be a good one. The status quo is always on the defensive and tolerable only when it rests on stalemated interests, and a stalemate not resolvable by following the utilitarian rule "the greatest good to the largest number." So much for the elementary features of the market model.

While the *corporatist society model* shares with the one just discussed the commitment to achievement, in one critical respect it is not just a different value formula but also one opposed to the market model. Rather than being individualist in character, the corporatist society model implies collectivism. Here all forms of social organization, (1), rest on the presumption of the social character of human nature. This value formula contrasts the transitory, weak, and paltry individual with the continuity, the strength, and the majesty of social organizations. This lends a touch of edification to all forms of organized social life, at least with respect to in-group relations. Whatever the nature of the group, self-actualization on the part of the individual means active service to a collectivity transcending one's own life. *Human* life itself, so this formula, *must* be the sublimation of individual desires for the sake of the collective, for only the latter has sufficient permanence to realize any moral meaning. Strengthening one's resoluteness and control of "selfish" impulses are therefore the highest obligations to the self; obedience to authority and unceasing faithfulness in cooperation are the highest obligations to society. As a Prussian saying put it, man exists only "to do his damned duty and live up to all obligations," a formulation in which the notions of damnation, duty, and obligations all carry equal weight. In this model, the individual-group dilemma, (2), demands the clear-cut subordination of the individual to the requirements of organization. Given the overriding concern with collective effectiveness, the allocation of prestige, (3), rests on perceived indispensability to collective welfare rather than just wealth. Rank position within an organization and association with that kind of organization occupying a strategic position for many others are the main considerations in allocating prestige. The public-service occupations, military and civilian, tend to be the most admired. They symbolize guardianship for "society incorporated," as it were. In the private sector, occupancy of a leading position in companies with large multiplier effects, productive of more jobs and goods elsewhere, gives you more prestige and "importance" than work with fewer multiplier effects. Mere money income cannot measure this. And so money alone tends to be treated with relative disdain. But power is what people are to strive for; and it is power, or differential capacity to effect the fate of the nation, that serves as the primary basis for prestige allocation. Because the corporatist model also celebrates the idea of an active society, (4), change is expected and the status quo is on the defensive. However, under the impact of collectivist values, the measure of success is society's standing in the pecking order of international stratification. Minimally one must maintain one's position there; maximally one must improve it. And that introduces a pervasive ambivalence into all orientations to social change. One can never know whether advocates of change present their claims out of "selfish" institutional interests or genuinely represent the national interest. Concretely, while the only legitimate way to argue for change is one studded with references to national interests, the best way to defend the status quo amounts to accusing the advocates of change of the pursuit of some "narrow selfish" institutional interest at the expense of national welfare. A charge of immoral intent puts the proponents for change on the defensive. And in an active society, this, then, shifts the onus of proof to a place where it should not be. As a result, the style of managing social change is characterized by bickering, suspicions, and frequently wild accusations. Yet nearly all institutional interests in society must jump into the fray because competing for scarce resources is the main way to prove one's commitments to serve the nation. Orientations to the problem of change therefore fluctuate between acceptance and rejection, often accompanied by a sense of creeping despair about one's imperfect society, one seemingly threatened by its own internal dynamics, which at the same time make up the very motor of a good society that succeeds in the world at large.

In the *Gemeinschaft* model the basic purpose of all forms of human bondage is the satisfaction of the human need to belong. With solidarity, or need for affiliation serving as the blueprint consideration in all social organization, (1), this model of the good society is a profoundly static one. The emphasis is on social harmony, not on growth. And so, to the activists who believe in the corporatist or the market model, the believers in *Gemeinschaft* always appear as slackers. The reverse perception is similarly unflattering. In the eyes of the beholder of *Gemeinschaft* ideals, the activists are careerists or status seekers of one variety or another. They are people whose constant busyness *must* turn them into one-dimensional success strivers, good at getting ahead occupationally, perhaps, but poor specimens of the human species in all other respects. But this is only the beginning of contrasts and oppositions. With social harmony as the overriding blueprint standard in all social life, (2), the *Gemeinschaft* model implies rejection of the resolutions to the individual-group dilemma in the other two models. Instead of the individualism of the market model or the collectivism of the corporatist one, here the stress is on interdependence between the needs of individuals and the requisites of social organization. *Gemeinschaft* man is quintessentially social. Instead of getting ahead, he is supposed to get along. The whole issue of some presumed tension between individuals and groups tends to be resented as a false alternative and the wrong question to ask about the human condition. In this organismic image of the good society all parts are as essential to the whole as the whole is to the parts. This also impacts on prestige allocation (3). Once again in contrast to the preceding models, conformity with stereo-typed role performance at all levels in society is the overriding considera-tion in the unequal distribution of esteem. What counts is that each do his best at his particular place in society. And higher eminence, or prestige in the narrower sense of the term, is allocated to the interstitial roles in society, such as the professions. The clergy, the law, medicine, and the teaching professions make up the influentials. They constitute society's institutionalized wisdom, the people who know better than anyone else what is in the best interest of all. Occupations in the people-processing business are the managers of society's excuse culture. Theirs is the endless task of smoothing over disappointments, of articulating and integrating individual desire and organizational requirements, of fitting parts to the whole and vice versa, and so of enabling the organism to live and function. With a harmonious balance among all social forces as the highest ideal, (4), it is the advocates for change who are put on the defensive. In principle, those who propose newfangled arrangements must make a case for them. The ideal of harmony suggests that they can do so best by arguing some need to reconstitute a specific disturbance in the social organism. Thus planned change can be legitimated on the basis of responding to an offended sense of distributive justice rather than appeals to notions of progress. Apart from having it more easy in general, the forces representing the status quo can calways wave the banner of vested rights. In contrast to vested interests, which proclaim a right to perform some service, vested rights assert entitlement to some privilege. They derive their legitimacy from tradition. And where tradition commands respect, the burden of proof for change is placed where "it really ought to be," namely on a demonstration that new conditions threaten inequities harmful to the maintenance of law and order. Thus, in this *Gemeinschaft* image of the good society, the different parts are supposed to fit together. Each should play its appropriate part, in its different role, to sustain the whole; for that is why parts differ in the first place. Only human weakness or foreign influences sometimes disarrange the parts, thereby upsetting the whole. When they do, such forces must be neutralized by reasserting everyone's good old rights.

Finally, in the *communion model* of the good society people associate with or dissociate from each other in the service of a direct realization of absolute moral concerns. Regardless of the nature of social relations, the realization of ultimate concerns is the overriding purpose of all social life. Therefore (1), social organization exists, as it were, to transform human and social nature and transform them in accordance with some ultimate cultural concerns. Once again (2), the resolution to the individual-group dilemma emphasizes interdependence rather than individualism or collectivism. However, both individuals and groups are supposed to be nothing but the instruments of some larger transcendental purpose, secular or sacred. Both man and his relations are to be but the clay of history, objects to be molded according to the imperatives of belief. Accordingly (3), the highest honors go to those who most clearly symbolize whatever the nature of ultimate concern happen to be fashionable. Superior man may be some bearded revolutionary of a distant time and place, a sensitive poet "dwelling in another realm," or some phalanx of the shirt-uniformed marching to the drum beats of a glorious future or past but out of a contemporary misery of hopelessness. Whosoever commands the skills of a superior presentation of sincerity to commitments, commands the symbols of prestige. Only perceived differences in ability to care about ultimate concerns legitimate inequality in society. Those who excel in the presentation of sincerity are the recognized top dogs, while men of practical affairs tend to be viewed with suspicion. Turning to the issues of change and stability (4), people who see themselves as the instruments of compelling ideals want nothing but change or else seek escape. Whichever, they claim a vision of perfection. And doing this out of a sense of righteous conviction permits them few if any issues of negotiation. To the pure idealist negotiation always smacks of compromise with' "what is right," something one must be wary of lest one's effort to believe falters. Focused on the insufficiency of the world, the status quo tends to be seen as corruption itself; and change can be opposed with legitimacy only by arguing with "yes, but" formulations in which one presents "tactical considerations" why some proposed change cannot be implemented right now, if idealist goals are to be realized at all.

Ideal-type descriptions of value formulas are deliberate simplifications. Their main purpose is to highlight contrasts. For ease of overview, Table IV-1 summarizes these contrasting features. Let me emphasize the idea of both contrast and opposition in these value formulas once more.

For the believer in the corporatist model, social relations must be edifying if they are to count as really human at all. They must serve purposes larger than the interest of the individuals comprising them. For after all, individuals die, but organizations persist. It is this conviction that man *must* dedicate himself to some transcendent purposes larger than himself and still concrete that gives all relations—from the smallest group of two to the largest, the nation—some altruistic and idealistic flavor. As a consequence, to corporatist man believers in the market model inevitably appear as selfish and materialist creatures, as people, then, who are simply too hedonistic to deserve respect. The reverse view is similarly uncharitable. In the eyes of a social utilitarian the very collectivism of corporatist people appears as "slavelike," "authoritarian," and somehow basically immature, describing people who just never manage to stand self-confidently on their own feet. Nonetheless, both of these images of the good society share one element: A good society is an active one. Precisely this dimension is absent from the *Gemeinschaft* model. And that is why *Gemeinschaft* believers appear to people of either of these two other persuasions as slackers. But *Gemeinschaft* believers in turn regard the former as people too arrogant to appreciate that being human has far more to do with coping with problems that have no technical, rational solutions and muddling through as best one can than with forcing solutions on dilemmas that cannot have any. The *Gemeinschaft* creature, for example, can tolerate bureaucracy only if it is also somewhat corrupt; for to be perfect, a bureaucracy would have to treat people as "things" or entities to be evaluated ruthlessly with the same yardstick and in heedless disregard of differences in the needs of individuals and their capacities. Finally, with their disdain of the socioeconomic order and its raw interests, people committed to the communion model must reject believers in all three of the other value formulas simply because they are not tuned in directly

Table IV-1 Four Ideal-type Conceptions of the "Good Society" and Their Main Components

Type of "Good Society"	Perceived main purpose of associating	Resolution to the individual-group dilemma	Basis of prestige allocation	Principal bases of legitimations of	
				Change	Stability
Market model	search for useful opportunities	individualism: the individual has "end-in-itself significance"; the group instrumental meaning	utility in society: wealth	interunit competition	competitive stalemate
Corporatist model	search for superior effectiveness	collectivism: the group has "end-in-self significance"; the individual instrumental meaning	service for society: power	corporate rivalry	vested interests
Gemeinschaft model	search for belonging	organicism: individual and group have equal "end-in-itself significance"	contribution to harmony	disturbed equity	vested rights
Communion model	search for moral fulfillment	moralism: individual and group have instrumental significance	symbolization of cultural ideal: virtue	demands of moral conviction	"tactical considerations"

enough with more ultimate concerns. And the moralist in turn deserves rejection as utopian in the eyes of these others.

So much for the theoretical idea of value formulas with built-in contrasts in commitments. Designing a questionnaire instrument that can reflect such contrasts was based on the assumption that the values of men and women cohere, forming systems of beliefs. Only systematically related beliefs can tell us that value differences in society are not experienced as just differences in opinion. If the moral beliefs people hold cohere into systems of belief, then the encounter of people with different beliefs is an encounter with ethical strangers. Now, the degree of inner coherence in values here is simply an empirical question. I measured inner coherence with Pearsons' Correlation Coefficients. Such coefficients tell us, for example, the degree to which a market-model "definition of the social situation" in the perception of the purpose of associating with others is related to finding a market-model definition for the individual-group dilemma, allocating prestige, and the legitimations of stability and change in social relations. Doing that separately for all four models of the good society and relying on data from the "good guys" in the novels yields forty such coefficients, ten nonredundant ones for each of the four images of the good society. The size of these coefficients ranged from a low of .30 to a high of .73. This means that anywhere between 9 percent and 53 percent of the societal values were directly associated with each other. Further, the communion model of the good society was the most internally coherent of the four. That makes good empirical sense. Explicit idealists tend to be thoughtful about their values. The *Gemeinschaft* model turned out to be the least internally coherent. Of the ten coefficients in the communion model, eight were .50 or larger. In the market and corporatist models the corresponding figures were six out of ten. However, only four of the ten coefficients in the *Gemeinschaft* model reached that size of .50 or larger. In considering these results, one should note that inner coherence here refers to something like holding logically consistent beliefs: If you are committed to one model of the good society in one problem area of social life—say, legitimating change—you will also adhere to the same values in another—say, legitimating the status quo. Outside the area of scientific beliefs, however, consistency in the beliefs people hold seems to be a rare phenomenon. Even so modest a level of internal consistency in values as indicated by these results has not been found often (Rokeach, 1960; 1979:142; Converse, 1964). All one can conclude is that the values measured here reflect relative value systems rather than unrelated societal values. But we certainly lack comparative data on values to settle the question whether one ought to be surprised or dismayed about their degree of inner coherence. Let it be noted only that this degree of inner coherence was not an artifact of treating the data in aggregate fashion. When internal coherence of images of the good society was ascertained separately for different regions and social classes in the novels, essentially the same degree of consistency was found.

What about value consensus? How much can one reasonably expect in a complex society with a vast division of labor? And how does one measure such consensus? Now, and to repeat, the value orientations ascertained here were deliberately formulated in so abstract a form that it ought to be possible to relate to one's employer, one's spouse, political leaders in some voting booth, or to one's medical doctor all in one value mode, say in a market model frame of mind. However, for both theoretical and measurement reasons this remains an unrealistic expectation. To date the distinction between general societal values and those values governing various institutional spheres in a differentiated society such as the economy, the family, the polity, and so on, has not attained sufficient clarity for clear-cut operationalization (Rokeach, 1979). Therefore, consensus on values in Germany, as in other modern societies more generally, should be a matter of agreement on some value hierarchy that identifies values of higher, intermediate, or lesser importance (Williams, 1979). Working with four images of the good society, as I do here, consensus is a function of two things. First, for whatever group in question—a region, a social class, a nation—a value hierarchy exists when some image "predominates" (by virtue of high relative frequencies in the group), and another or others are of "intermediate" and "subordinate" importance (by virtue of correspondingly lower relative frequencies in that group). This is just a measure of value consensus among the members of the group. Second, value consensus in the larger society is then a function of agreement on the same value hierarchy between the groups. If one finds a value hierarchy with some clearly "predominant" and "subordinate" images of the good society for all the Germans studied here, German society can be said to have been one integrated by common values; if not, it was a nation without an "ethical soul," at least in terms of *societal* values. Now, a condition of complete value dissensus, or of a total value chaos, can be specified here without any arbitrariness. With four types of values measured, total dissensus obtains when all four occur with equal frequency or in the form of a 25 percent random distribution. From the point of view of values, and given the restrictions on available data here, German society can be characterized as having been a genuine "mass society" with nothing but "atomized individuals" if one finds such a random distribution in value commitments (1) in the nation as a whole (all "good guys" pooled); (2) in all regions; (3) in all social classes; and (4) among all urban and rural people. Put differently, if nothing but random distributions in societal-value commitments emerge, no matter what group or subculture one considers, then groups with shared values were absent from Germany, and "each man was truly an island unto himself." In contrast, any deviation from a random distribution, or a 25 percent representation of all four images of the good society for some group signals a value hierarchy, and therefore some value consensus among the members of the group. The only decision needed is what percentage deviation from randomness in the distribution of societal images should be regarded as "significant" or large enough to assert that a value hierarchy has been found. The error of measurement, those 6 percentage points mentioned above, can serve as a benchmark here. Accordingly, finding some image of the good society represented to the extend of 31 percent or more of all the values measured for a group makes that image "predominant" for the group. An underrepresentation of 19 percent of less, on the other hand, turns an image into a "subordinate" one; and images with representations falling in between mark them as of intermediate importance for the group. But how much of a hierarchy may prevail beyond these just-defined benchmarks need not concern us. In comparing the value systems of groups, the question is whether they have the same or different hierarchies. If they have the former, they can be said to have shared common values; if not, value dissensus prevailed among them.

This completes consideration of those points necessary to understand how the societal values of the German people were measured here. Let us turn to the results.

Germany: A Nation without Shared Societal Values

With its nationwide distribution and a readership from all walks of life, the quota sample of novels from *Die Gartenlaube* was a very relevant source whence Germans could have learned what the modern nation was supposed to be like and what value commitments membership in that nation involved. Yet when analyzing this "national" sample of German realist fiction by "good" and "bad" characters separately, a genuine value chaos emerged for both. All four of the societal images occurred in roughly equal proportions. Among the "good" characters not one of the societal images figured as a predominant set of value commitments, and not one could be singled out as a subordinate commitment. The same was true for the distribution of values among the "bad" characters. The "Germans," so it seemed, could not agree on the shape of the desirable type of society to uphold and build; nor could they agree on an image of the undesirable type of society to avoid. Closer examination of the novels, however, revealed that they were not filled with descriptions of "Germans." Instead, one found there Bavarians, Prussians, Rhinelanders, and other regional folk. In its serialized fiction, *Die Gartenlaube* did not instruct its readership about models of the good or the bad Germany because there were no Germans in these accounts. In terms of societal values, then, the realist fiction of the only truly national newsmagazine before the First World War made no contribution to nation-building whatever.

With but few exceptions all the characters in the *Gartenlaube* novels could be classified by region and used for the assessment of value consensus across regions. Before turning to that effort, one may examine the values of all the "good" and all the "bad" people in these novels in order to see whether some lowest-common-denominator beliefs emerge as to models of the good and the bad society. The results of this search are displayed in Table IV-2. As can be seen, there was very little agreement about the nature of the desirable society. Among the "good" characters

Table IV-2   Models of the "Good" and the "Bad" Society in Germany
(Percentage of Societal Values Coded for "Good" and "Bad" Characters)

Societal values	Good	Bad
Market model	19	37
Corporatist model	28	32
Gemeinschaft model	28	20
Communion model	24	11
Sum percentage[a]	99	100
Number of values coded	(5,820)	(1,080)

[a]Errors in percentages due to rounding.

three of the four images of the good society occurred again in roughly equal proportions, and none of these three deviated sufficiently from a random distribution. Once again one finds relative value chaos. Only one, the market model, registered here as a "subordinate" set of commitments (19 percent representation). The major values of the market model are those of individual achievement, freedom of choice, the privilege of reaping the benefits from being a winner, and having to shoulder the burden of becoming a loser. They are, in short, the classic virtues of the capitalist society. The Germans agreed that these had to be subordinate values. But what they were to be subordinate to remained a matter of dissensus. However, as evident in the values coded for "bad" characters, there was some structure in beliefs about the nature of an undesirable society. Keeping in mind that this was a lowest-common-denominator type of agreement, most Germans, so it would appear, rejected a capitalist society with the state as servant of its dominant interests (market model, 37 percent, followed by the corporatist model, 32 percent, as predominant patterns). Beyond that it was only clear that a bad society would be one where explicit concerns with ideals ranked subordinate in the value hierarchy (communion model at 11 percent representation). Put differently, the message broadcast by bad characters in the novels was twofold. First, whatever the shape of the nation, it was not to be a capitalist society with the state as a servant of the winners in the competition of the marketplace. And second, with some agreement that the immoral amounted primarily to deficiency in observing explicit rules of decency, one does find this nugget: Whatever the shape of the good German society, a reverence for explicit rules of conduct, and so "a legalism above all else" was to be part of it.

Summarizing the findings on societal values to this point, one may conclude as follows: Since there was no hierarchy to cherish among the images of the good society, the German people as a whole shared few if any common values. What little they shared was an anti-image. Germany was *not* to be a liberal capitalist social order, the kind of social order where, to use contemporary American folk speech, "looking out for No. 1" was a right, winning a virtue, and being a loser the near-ultimate defeat. Beyond this negative agreement, however, a value chaos prevailed; on the national level Germany was a mass society. And, possibly aware of their profound differences, Germans emphasized a need for "idealism." "Bad" people were not just bad by virtue of their action, but by reason of their disregard for explicit rules of common decency. And so, by implication, whatever the shape of the good society (a matter on which there was no agreement), "doing right" or "going by the book" was absolutely essential if a chaos in commitments to the good society was not to eventuate into a chaos of conduct. This finding is in partial agreement with McClelland's (1964) study of middle-class boys in postwar West Germany. He, too, found that they were far more "idealistic" than their American counterparts. Disregarding the time periods here, the main difference is one of interpreting this "idealism." As will become clear in a moment, this was a kind of defensive idealism, one resting on consciousness about value differences in society. A first step toward understanding this "unholy mixture of idealism and realism" in German political life is the recognition that their much-commented-upon "idealism" was a reaction of anxiety, one resulting from appreciation that their nation was a mass society but one made up of more structured and opposed value communities at the regional level.

Germany: A Nation with
Regional Value Cleavages

If one were to take a map of Imperial Germany showing her internal political units, the regions covered by the ethnographic realist literature would appear as follows. Prussia covers the provinces of East and West Prussia, Brandenburg, and Pommerania. Even though the Rhineland was part of the Prussian state, it has been treated here as a separate region. What counts in examining value cleavages is not formal statehood, a matter subjected to considerable changes in the wake of the Napoleonic wars in Germany, but a distinctive regional identity in rough analogy to the concept of ethnic heritage typical in immigration countries like the United States. Germans thought of themselves as Bavarians, or Black Forest people, or Mecklenburgers, or Friesians, and so on. And it is this regional sense of identity that is of interest when raising questions about regional variations in societal values. The internal political boundaries of Imperial Germany by no means corresponded to such cultural regions. This was particularly glaring in the case of the Prussian state, a historical bureaucratic empire par excellence (Eisenstadt, 1963), and that means a polity that came to include people of very diverse regional traditions. The label "Prussia" for a region may therefore strike the reader as of questionable value. I have chosen it because of my interest in the values of the upper classes in German society. And among them, the figure of the Prussian officer was an utterly familiar landmark in the terrain of value orientations. A Prussian officer was thought of as the bearer of a distinctive ethos. That notion was manifest in everyday language conventions. I recall from my childhood days the saying: There are only three figures who have given structure to the culture of Western Europe—the Spanish *grande*, the English gentleman, and the Prussian officer. Whatever sense or nonsense may lurk beneath such a saying, here it can serve us well. In Germany, a Prussian was a reference point in the landscape of values. It will pay to find out what these values were. And since it was supposed to be a Prussian officer who crystallized these values best, it is fortunate that the geographic areas covered by the regional label "Prussia" here were precisely those from which the military and civil bureaucracy of the Prussian state recruited its higher officer corps until 1918 (von Preradovich, 1955). Though part of the Prussian state, that did not necessarily make a Prussian of the Rhinelander. Geographically, the region Rhineland here covers a rectangle between the cities of Trier and Kreuznach in the South, and Wesel and Hamm in the North. The Southwest covers the states of Baden and Wuerttemberg; and the South the state of Bavaria without its western exclave. Thus I can present data on the values of but four regions. And while this is by no means an adequate coverage of regional subcultures in Germany, it is one including the most important of the commonly recognized regional subcultures. Even today in West Germany, one contrasts those living north of the River Main with those south of it as different species of Germans; and both sides of that divide are represented in the data on regional value cleavages. All but a 10 percent minority of the fictional characters could be classified as belonging to one of the four regions. In contrast to the nation as a whole, definite value hierarchies were found in each region (see Table IV-3).

Starting with images of the good society, in Prussia the corporatist model was a predominant commitment, the market model a subordinate one, with the *Gemeinschaft* and the communion models ranking in between. A very different value hierarchy prevailed in the Rhineland. Here the market model was the predominant commitment, while the communion model was a subordinate set of values, and the corporatist and the

Table IV-3   Regional Cleavages in Models of the "Good" and the "Bad" Society in Germany (Percentage of Societal Values Coded for "Good" and "Bad" Characters)

Societal values	Prussia		Rhineland		Southwest		South	
	Good	Bad	Good	Bad	Good	Bad	Good	Bad
Market model	18	38	32	34	20	37	15	38
Corporatist model	36	30	26	27	19	35	27	37
Gemeinschaft model	25	25	23	24	34	17	32	- 8
Communion model	21	7	19	15	26	10	27	17
Sum percentage[a]	100	100	100	100	99	99	101	100
Number of Values Coded	(2,040)	(360)	(810)	(180)	(1,230)	(240)	(1,140)	(180)

[a]Errors in percentages due to rounding.

Gemeinschaft models ranked in between. Yet a third value hierarchy prevailed in the Southwest. There the *Gemeinschaft* model was the predominant set of value commitment, the corporatist model was in subordinate place, and the communion and the market models ranked in a position of secondary importance. Finally, a fourth distinctive value hierarchy characterized the South. Similar to the Southwest, the predominant model of the good society in the South was the *Gemeinschaft* model. However, in contrast to their neighbors in the Southwest, Southerners were committed to the market model as a subordinate set of values while assigning secondary importance to the values inherent in the corporatist and communion models.

In sum, regional value cleavages in German society were deep. Of the four regions considered here, Prussia and the Rhineland had completely different value hierarchies; their predominant and subordinate values differed. People below the River Main formed a distinctive group relative to Prussians and Rhinelanders in their joint predominant commitment to *Gemeinschaft* values. They shared predominant values, but in turn differed in their subordinate values, and therefore also their secondary-value commitments. Thus, with four regions one finds three deep cleavages separating the Prussians from the Rhinelanders and both of these from the people in the southern part of Germany. Within that southern part, though, people did share at least their predominant commitments; and so the values' cleavage separating Southerners from Southwesterners was considerably less severe.

Turning now to images of the bad society, two main points stand out in Table IV-3. First, there was only one region, the Rhineland, where the value orientations of good and bad characters were identical. Among the Rhenish, so it would appear, badness had nothing to do with wrong beliefs in values; badness only resulted from wrong action. Perhaps this is reasonable in light of their predominant value commitments. The social utilitarianism so deeply inherent in their predominant market model made badness a matter of conduct, and not one of belief. Second, in all other regions the values of the good and the bad people differed. And badness was *not* just a mirror image of goodness. On the contrary, the image of the bad society was a relatively shared one. In Prussia as well as the two southern regions badness was first of all a matter of commitment to the market model. But also, and only in the two southern regions, badness was a matter of commitment to the corporatist model as well. Since the corporatist model was the predominant commitment of the good Prussian, Prussianism figured as societal evil in the eyes of the Germans living below the River Main. Further, the bad society was one in which the communion model ranked in a subordinate position, either by itself as in Prussia, or sharing that subordinate position with the *Gemeinschaft* model, as in the Southwest and the South. Thus the structure of the bad society discovered for the nation as a whole in the previous table was not an artifact of some gross national-average fallacy. Rather, while the German people were deeply divided by region in their beliefs about the good society, they shared some beliefs on the nature of a bad one. With the exception of the Rhineland, it was German to disdain the market model. Found in three out of four regions, this disdain made the Rhinelander the real ethical stranger, perhaps even the moral outcast, in the nation because that general object of disdain was the good Rhinelander's predominant commitment. Seen from the perspective of the others, people in the Rhineland not only had the wrong values; worse yet, with their commitments to pragmatism, individualism, achievement, and competitiveness, they did not even seem to care about values. For being the only ones in the nation who did not differentiate good and bad in terms of values, they lacked a German characteristic: to be concerned with values. The very fact that in all other regions the good-bad contrast was one involving values and not just behavior tells us that Germans were highly conscious about value differences. Never forget: Values are constitutive of a people and their institutions. They make up individual and collective identities. Being highly conscious about identities and differences in who people are and feel they *must be* means you cannot ask the classic question of all bargaining: How much? In situations where only material interests clash, one can always ask "How much?" bargain accordingly, and find some compromise. But you do not bargain about identity. Where genuine ideal interests clash, it is not a question of "how much" which structures conflict relations but rather questions of what and who will carry the day. The political consequences of this widespread consciousness about value differences in the nation will occupy us in later chapters. At this point one might conclude that living with ethical strangers in the same society was a fact of life in Germany. It is also important to realize the depth of the regional cleavages in values. Looking at models of the good society once again, observe that the highest commitment of a good Prussian, the corporatist model, was the lowest one for a good Southwesterner; the highest commitment of the Rhinelander, the market model, was the lowest one for Prussians and Southerners; and the highest commitment of both groups in the southern regions, the *Gemeinschaft* model, was of but secondary import to Prussians and Rhinelanders. On a regional level, then, there were distinctive subcultures, they differed, and Germans were aware of it. Regionally, Germans were value strangers to each other. But that was not all. Germans were also divided in their value commitments by social class. Yet due to insufficient data, models of avoidance as evident in the values of bad characters must be omitted from further analysis.

Social Class and Societal Images

Investigating class variation in societal images presumes that class position of the characters can be measured. With novels only a rough estimate was possible. The novels contained information about education, occupation, aristocratic status, and lifestyle. At least one of these characteristics was described for each character. Education was used for only a small minority of characters, mostly unmarried females with tenuous or unknown occupational status. These amounted to less than 10 percent of all. For this small group, then, a grade-school level of education was used as an index of lower-class status, and some high-school experience as indicating middle-class position. All the minority cases were exhausted by these two criteria. For the majority of cases, occupation of the household head was used to measure class position. Dependent-manual-employment status—as a factory hand or as an agricultural worker—served as an indicator of lower-class status. Nonmanual employment indicated a middle-class position, as did self-employment in trade, crafts, and agriculture. Given the considerable prominence of aristocrats in many of the southern and the Prussian novels, nobility was used as the main index of an upper-class position. In these stories the nobles had a very tenuous and exceedingly variable relation to the world of work. Some managed their country estates; others just lived off them, letting a manager do the work. Some nobles were found in military careers, others in court positions, diplomacy, or private scholarship. Using aristocratic status for inclusion in the upper class provided a very clear criterion. But it could not be relied upon exclusively, since no aristocrats occurred in the Rhenish novels at all. Rather than leaving the Rhineland devoid of any upper classes, in this region lifestyle was used as an index of class position. Where the stories told of such matters as keeping a big house for purposes of representation and receptions, country houses, travel to spas or abroad, or simply direct descriptions of extraordinary wealth, these features served for classification of the characters as upper class. Though very impressionistic, it was the best that could be done. We know from other reports (Kohn-Bramstedt, 1937) that the *haute bourgeoisie* of the Rhine considered itself upper class even though they felt uncertain about it, since they comprised new-status claimants. Some, for example, did not mind considerable personal financial costs in order to prove their upper-class position. One way of doing it was voluntarily paying higher taxes in order to be able to vote with the first-class voters of the Prussian three-class suffrage system, which served as a social-status criterion in pre-World War I days (Zunkel, 1962:101). Thus attempts to remove the class suffrage by some also amounted to attempts to deprive some of the merely rich of a coveted prestige badge. This points out a bias in terminology here. The term "social class" refers to stratified inequalities in society such that the richer are also the carriers of higher prestige than the poorer, and the wealthy are also those with superior political clout in society than the low-income groups. As will be demonstrated below, there is evidence showing that

Germany had no upper *strata* in this sense. Therefore, the terms "class" or "stratum" are used here without prejudice as to status consistency in Germany. The difference between lower and middle class here was primarily one of income or wealth. But that between middle and upper class lacked a single common denominator in inequalities. In the Rhineland the upper class were those of extraordinary wealth. But in Prussia some of the upper class were wealthy while others were impoverished aristocratic officers. These two regions were perhaps the most pronounced in status inconsistency. But as reflected in fiction, status inconsistency was not absent from the Southwest and the South either. The term "class," then, refers more to claims to some overall differential standing in society than to genuine consensus as to what was up, what down. One other feature of classifying the characters by social class needs comment. As indicated with the reference to factory or agricultural labor for the lower class above, lack of data prevented me from examining the values of different classes separately by urban and rural residence. However, as will be seen below, so far as one can see, urban-rural differences in values in Germany were few and unimportant.

But while the ethnographic realist fiction may well have been quite realistic with respect to status inconsistency in German society, it was unrealistic in presenting an adequate picture of the distribution of social classes in society. The lower classes were underrepresented in the fictional population. Their presence varied from less than 10 percent in Prussia to about a third of the fiction population of the South. The middle class was more adequately represented in literature. Their presence varied from a low of 39 percent of all in the South to a high of about two thirds in the Rhineland. The upper classes were overrepresented. The range here extended from a low of about a fifth of the Rhenish population in the novels, over about a quarter of that among the two southern regions, to a high of 45 percent in Prussia. So the data on the lower classes below must be taken with a grain of salt. One reason for their underrepresentation in the literature may well be its entertainment character. Most likely, describing the lower-class milieux was a preoccupation of writers with some political purpose, of authors who had some ideological ax to grind; and that type of writing was deliberately not covered.

What then of the values of various social classes in Germany? Were there important differences, as another student of literature has claimed (Jones, 1959), and did the subculture of class bridge the regional cleavages? Table IV-4 provides some answers. Reading sideways, from left to right, permits one to ascertain whether the force of social class shaped values into some class milieu bridging regional differences. Reading

*Table IV-4   Regional and Class Cleavages in Models of the "Good" Society in Germany
(Percentage of Societal Values Coded for "Good" Characters[a])*

Societal values	Prussia	Rhineland	Southwest	South
	All			
Market model	18	32	20	15
Corporatist model	36	26	19	27
Gemeinschaft model	25	23	34	32
Communion model	21	19	26	27
Number of values coded	(2,040)	(810)	(1,230)	(1,140)
	Upper Class			
Market model	13	27	14	8
Corporatist model	39	27	22	33
Gemeinschaft model	25	26	30	25
Communion model	23	20	34	34
Number of values coded	(930)	(180)	(300)	(300)
	Middle Class			
Market model	23	31	22	18
Corporatist model	32	27	16	25
Gemeinschaft model	24	22	34	30
Communion model	20	20	27	27
Number of values coded	(1,020)	(510)	(660)	(450)
	Lower Class			
Market model	17	37	22	17
Corporatist model	28	25	24	24
Gemeinschaft model	35	27	38	38
Communion model	20	12	16	21
Number of values coded	(90)	(120)	(270)	(390)

[a]Errors in column percentages due to rounding.

down, from top to bottom under each regional heading, allows one to assess whether social classes differed in their role as carriers of a regional subculture, and if so, who such carriers were.

Considering the value hierarchies of the three social classes in Germany, a fairly unequivocal message emerges from the table. It is one of division at the top and commonalities at the bottom.

Of the upper classes in the four regions, one, the Rhenish, displayed no value hierarchy. But the predominant values of the remaining three all differed. The Prussian Junkers espoused the corporatist model as their most important commitment. The communion *and* the *Gemeinschaft* models were the predominant values of the southwestern upper class. In the South one finds another combination again. The southern upper class were the bearers of a societal ethos that stressed commitment to the communion *and* the corporatist models as the highest obligation. Once again with the exception of the Rhinelanders, the only shared value among the upper classes in Germany was an agreement that the market model had to be a subordinate commitment. In short, among the upper classes one finds three distinctive value hierarchies in four regions; and the fourth of the Rhinelanders was missing by default. The Rhenish upper class was, in terms of values, a mass.

The values of the middle classes in German society also differed too much from region to region to provide any unifying bridge across them. Here among the four regions one finds three distinctive and different middle-class milieux. The Prussian middle class was similar to the Prussian upper class in emphasizing the corporatist model as the most important of all societal values. The Rhenish middle class was the bearer of a societal ethos in which the market model reigned supreme. But the middle classes of the two southern regions both shared a predominant commitment to the *Gemeinschaft* model of the good society. There was a similar diversity in values among the middle classes with respect to models of the good society that ought to be subordinate in the hierarchy of values. The Prussian and Rhenish middle classes hardly managed to isolate a model as of clear-cut subordinate importance. Closest in this respect were their commitments to the communion model as of least importance. And the middle classes of the two southern regions differed on subordinate values. While the Southwesterners identified the corporatist model as of least importance, that rank position was filled by the market model in the value hierarchy of the middle class of the South. In sum, the middle class in Germany contributed little to value commonalities across the regional cleavage.

Only the lower class in Germany shared a value hierarchy to some notable extent, thus providing a value community that crosscut at least some regions. Considering predominant values, only the lower class of the Rhineland were outsiders. Like their middle-class regional peers, the Rhenish lower class was also a carrier of culture in which the market model ranked supreme. But the lower classes in Prussia, the Southwest, and the South all shared a predominant commitment to the *Gemeinschaft* model of good society. There was, however, more diversity on subordinate value commitments. On that point the Prussian and the southern lower classes isolated the market model as the least important of one's values. But the Rhenish and the southwestern lower classes placed the communion model into a subordinate position. The finding of a common lower-class culture is, therefore, limited to sharing a predominant commitment to *Gemainschaft* values in three of the four regions.

In sum, the force of social class to cement society in terms of shared values across regional cleavages was very weak in Germany. Among the upper and the middle classes the German people were divided in their value orientations from one region to another. Only the lower classes formed a somewhat common class milieu that crosscut the regional divisions. There was, then, a pattern of division at the top and the middle, and relative unity at the bottom.

And who among the social classes were the most distinctive carriers of these regional-value cultures? Among the Prussians the answer is the upper class. Prussianism meant a predominant commitment to the corporatist model, a placement of the values of the market model into a subordinate position, and the placement of the values of the remaining two into an intermediate position (see category "All" in Table IV-4). That particular hierarchy of values was more pronounced among Prussia's upper class than among her middle class. The Junkers were the bearers of the Prussian ethos. In contrast, in the Rhineland the upper class was not the carrier of Rhenish values. Here the lower and the middle classes, in that order, were the main carriers of Rhenish values. Observe that a Rhinelander was a creature with a predominant commitment to the market model, a subordinate commitment to the communion model, while the values of *Gemeinschaft* and corporatism ranked in between (see category "All" under Rhineland in Table IV-4). That particular value hierarchy was most developed among the lower class. Their value profile was more marked (market model at 37 percent; communion model at 12 percent) than the corresponding profile among the middle-class people (market model at 31 percent; communion model at 20 percent, only). And the Rhenish upper class had no value hierarchy. The main carrier of Rhenish values, then, was the lower class, hardly an auspicious group for the spread of market values in German society. The values of the market model are those of individualism, achievement, competitiveness, and getting ahead in the world. They are the quintessentially lower-middle-class virtues of the famed Protestant Ethic (Weber, 1904–5). Sociologists have regarded these values as typical for the modern age from the early days of the discipline to the present (Toennies, 1957; Inkeles and Smith, 1974). In Germany, however, these allegedly "modern" value orientations were the predominant values of only one region, the Rhineland; and even there, the carriers of this "modern ethos" were the lower class primarily and the middle class only secondarily.

In the Southwest the value hierarchy was one in which *Gemeinschaft* values ranked supreme, the corporatist model was in a subordinate position, and the remaining two were of secondary importance (see category "All" under Southwest in Table IV-4). The main carrier of this southwestern societal ethos was the middle class. Upper-class people in that region were deviants. They had a simultaneous commitment to the *Gemeinschaft and* the communion models as predominant values, and they ranked the market rather than the corporatist model in a subordinate position. With the Southwestern lower class having a value hierarchy different in turn and more like the German lower class in general, social classes tended to fragment the regional-value subculture of the Southwest.

In the South the upper class was similarly deviant in value orientations from the middle- and lower-class Southerners. Note, to start with, that southern values in general were quite similar to the main version of lower-class culture in Germany. The southern value hierarchy involved a predominant commitment to *Gemeinschaft*, a subordinate ranking of the market model, with the corporatist and communion models ranked in between (see category "All" under South in Table IV-4). But the value hierarchy of the southern upper class involved a simultaneous commitment to the communion *and* the corporatist models (jointly making up two thirds of all values coded), a secondary commitment to *Gemeinschaft*, with the market model also ranking in subordinate position. Hence the upper-class deviance in value orientations amounted to a reversal of predominant and secondary-value orientations relative to the other classes in South. The carriers of the southern-value culture were the lower and the middle classes, in that order. The main difference in the carrier role of a regional ethos between these two was the greater stress on *Gemeinschaft* values among the lower than the middle classes. Having deviant values, the southern upper class contributed to regional fragmentation in values in that area. But sharing a common value hierarchy, the southern lower and middle classes "integrated" the South with the lower class in Germany on the one hand and segregated the South as a whole the more firmly from the rest of Germany on the other.

In sum, this analysis of societal values by region and social class in Germany reveals more fissures or cleavages than shared values. Only one class bridged the regional cleavages, and that one was the lower class. Three of the four regional upper classes had different value hierarchies, and the remaining one, the Rhenish upper class, was more a mass in terms of values because they shared no commitment to a hierarchy in values. Thus, in terms of values, Germany was a house divided at the top. The situation among the middle classes was similar. There, too, one finds more differences than shared value commitments in both the predominant and subordinate values of the good society. The German middle class reduced the fourfold regional diversity in images of the good society to only three. The value hierarchy of the Prussian middle class differed from that of their class peers in the Rhineland, and both in turn differed from the middle classes in the two southern regions who, in turn, shared more common values. And so Germany was also a house divided at the middle range of social inequalities.

Finally, the role of the main carrier of regional subcultures in societal values was quite unevenly distributed among the various classes. Only in Prussia was the upper class the main bearer of the Prussian ethos. Sharing with them a predominant commitment to corporatism allowed the Prussian middle class to participate in that role. If the higher-ups in the society are the more consequential, the relative sharing of a common value hierarchy between Prussia's upper and middle classes contributed to cementing that region against all others in Germany. No such role of so contributing to intraregional solidarity can be attributed to the other three upper classes. They contributed to further within-region fragmentation in value orientations. This was especially evident in the fact that the upper classes of the Southwest and the South had value hierarchies different from their respective middle and lower classes. These upper classes were deviants in the eyes of the lower orders in society. Given their superior endowment with the scarce and unequally distributed resources in society, their deviance in value orientations from the rest of the population probably contributed to cynicism. If the top dogs have the wrong values and you, sitting somewhere below, know it, you may safely conclude two things: First, being on top has nothing whatever to do with any effective claims about morally deserving the advantages; second, getting there may well take many-splendored efforts but a genuine resocialization into commitment to any particular value hierarchy *in order to legitimate* superior status is not among them. Put differently, a demonstration that three of four upper classes in German society had values different from the people below them, and remembering that this was the case in a society with high ethical consciousness, is evidence that the elites in German society lacked legitimacy. The only exception in this respect were the Prussians, precisely, those who had been in the vanguard of national unification in the nineteenth century and those whose middle and upper classes became the dominant political forces in Imperial Germany, a position that was significantly altered only with the arrival of Hitler. And that means that in Germany not shared legitimacy beliefs but interests were the bases of domination. A society where the top dogs lack legitimacy tends to be one ruled by "interest constellations" (Weber, 1922:941). What counts for political stability is satisfaction of the material interests of strategically placed groups and governmental effectiveness, not belief in values. An ineffectual government is one that deserves to be swept away because it fails to earn the right to rule every day; and it does not matter much to most whether you switch from constitutional monarchy to democracy, or from democracy to dictatorship, because no form of regime can find any substantial footing in the values of a people so diverse and so divided as the German were.

The German people were certainly divided by region and by social class. But were there also value cleavages between the city and the countryside? Let us see.

Urban-Rural Differences in Societal Images

The plot settings in the stories easily permitted a threefold classification of the characters. Where a setting was exclusively in the city, the characters were classified as urbanites; where the story played exclusively in the countryside, they were classified as rural. Some stories, of course, involved shifting scenes. Here the characters were classified as "mixed." To illustrate, this last category could refer to migratory factory laborers who kept their families in a village while working in the city, or to upper-class households who maintained two residences. On this basis, 50 percent of all characters turned out rural, 31 percent urban, and 10 percent mixed, a distribution telling us that this kind of entertainment literature had not yet caught up with the growing urbanization of society. It should be noted that the urban condition was not confined to big metropolitan centers in this classification. Rather, "urban" included any *Stadt* milieu, ranging from the small residential capital to the big metropolis of Berlin. As to regional distributions, the southern material turned out nearly exclusively rural. With this exception there was sufficient variation to examine possible urban-rural cleavages in the values of the Germans separately by region. However, potentially these data remain "contaminated" by social class, just as the preceding class analysis of values remained possibly contaminated by urban-rural differences. Too few cases is of course the reason.

With this cautionary note, Table IV-5 presents the results of the inquiry of urban-rural differences in values. Reading from left to right can tell us whether some particular ecological setting—the urban, the mixed, or the rural—helped bridge the regional cleavages in values. Reading down from top to bottom can tell us whether the ecological setting reinforced or fragmented regional subcultures.

One glance at the rural portion of Table IV-5 attests to the absence of any general peasant culture bridging the regional-value cleavages in Germany. The values of the rural folk in four regions displayed no less

Table IV-5   Urban-Rural Cleavages in Models of the "Good" Society in Germany
(Percentage of Societal Values Coded for "Good" Characters[a])

Societal values	Prussia	Rhineland	Southwest	South
		Urban		
Market model	21	32	20	—
Corporatist model	33	23	24	—
Gemeinschaft model	25	21	29	—
Communion model	20	24	27	—
Number of values coded	(660)	(360)	(360)	(30)
		Mixed		
Market model	17	—	10	—
Corporatist model	37	—	13	—
Gemeinschaft model	27	—	34	—
Communion model	19	—	42	—
Number of values coded	(420)	(30)	(120)	(0)
		Rural		
Market model	16	33	22	15
Corporatist model	38	29	18	27
Gemeinschaft model	25	26	37	32
Communion model	22	12	23	26
Number of values coded	(960)	(420)	(750)	(1,110)

[a]Errors in percentages due to rounding.

than four distinctive hierarchies. A comparison with the category "All" in Table IV-4 shows that each parallels exactly the regional-value hierarchies. The rural folk in Germany did not cement society either. By and large this can be attributed to the underrepresentation of the lower class in the data generally, and a proper mixture of the middle and upper classes in the rural portion.

Turning to the urban folk now, where there is at least information covering three regions, did the city bidge the regional differences? Once again the answer seems negative. The city folk in three regions were divided in their value hierarchies three ways, almost. In Prussia the corporatist model was again the predominant set of values, while the city people of the Rhineland placed the market model at the top of their commitments. The urban population of the Southwest, however, scarcely had a hierarchy in their value commitments. They were more an urban mass. Thus in two of three regions the predominant values of the city folk were again identical with those of their regions (see category "All" in Table IV-4). But the city people also displayed less of a value hierarchy. Note that in the Rhineland and in Prussia one finds only one of the images of the good society in a predominant position but none "making it" to a subordinate one. Rather than attributing this to some "homogenizing" impact of an urban way of life, though, it probably reflects more a class effect. Among the urban population of Prussia and the Southwest, the latter an urban mass in terms of values, over one half were upper class, about a third middle, and the rest were lower class. And Table IV-4 tells us that in Prussia the upper classes were more the bearers of the Prussian ethos than the middle classes. Further, that table tells us that the upper classes in the Southwest were deviants from the prevalent values of their region. The weaker hierarchy in the values of the city folk therefore reflects class differences. The same is true for the Rhenish urban population. Here one found only upper- and middle-class people in the cities as described in novels. And still, the Rhenish value formula with the market model in predominance emerged. Recall (from Table IV-4), the Rhenish upper class was an upper mass; and the lower classes there were the main bearers of the regional culture. The absence of any subordinate image in the weak value hierarchy of the urban Rhenish people can, therefore, be attributed to the mixture of middle and upper classes represented in the cities.

The very fact that the regional value hierarchies remained the decisive ones to this point in the analysis of urban and rural effects tells us that the preceding class analysis of values was not much contaminated by urban-rural differences.

With very few data in the "mixed" residential setting, the message can be brief. Here also, similarity in residence pattern failed to bridge the regional cleavage. In two regions, one finds again two contrasting and different value hierarchies. The Prussians in this milieu reflect more Prussian values, the Southwesterners those of the upper class in the Southwest, a matter directly attributable to their class character: In the Southwest all people with dual residences were upper class.

Since the differences in values between the rural and the urban folk in Germany were small and reflected more the mixture of social classes than the impact of some urban or rural way of life, these data cannot be used to answer the question of whether perhaps the people in the countryside were the main bearers of a region's culture. That is, of course, what men and women with nostalgic proclivities for the good old days always suspected. But while the information in Table IV-5 at first glance may confirm such suspicions, let me emphasize: That is more appearance than reality.

As the preceding analysis has shown, Germany was a country with enormous value diversity. This was not just a matter of the minds and hearts of men and women. It had consequences. One of these was the country's communications system. And a brief demonstration that Germany had no cultural center, never developed a nationwide professional press, and had an intellectual establishment celebrating diversity as a cultural asset may conclude this survey of value orientations.

Many modern societies have not only a political center, their capital, they also have a cultural one. A cultural center puts its stamp on the ebb and flow of current conventional wisdom. At least for the more educated in society, such a center can provide direction and a measure of unity, if not in opinion, then still in areas of concern and standards of judgment. Values may often be espoused in the form of mere lip service. But if appeals to values cover the same evaluation standards and emanate from the same source, such a center can reassert the validity of standards nonetheless. Britain has her London. France, culturally speaking, is Paris. Germany hardly ever developed a comparable city. Culturally, she was always a multicentered entity with no one center gaining national significance and acknowledged supremacy. During the nineteenth and well into the present century, Munich and Dresden were the homes of painters, Leipzig and Stuttgart the centers of the publishers. Cologne and Frankfurt were the cities whence came the more important newspapers. A legacy of Germany's many dukes and princes emulating the splendor of *le Roi Soleil* on a small scale before unification, geographic cultural pluralism remained her feature afterward. The picture was the same for the seats of higher learning. No top universities comparable to Oxford and Cambridge or the Americn Ivy League could be found. Overall eminence in scientific or philosophic achievement did not vary appreciably among the universities of Heidelberg, Marburg, Berlin, Jena, Tübingen, Leipzig, or Halle. Engineering science organized in separate institutions added to diversity. In the creative arts Berlin achieved some prominence during the 1920s but only for a short time, its leadership being challenged by Munich. Even the Nazis, who succeeded more than any previous regime in liberating Germans from particularist bondage, celebrated their liturgical commitment rites in the South while wielding power from the North. They declared Munich the "City of the Movement," supplied it with shrines to hold its "heart," but allocated its "brain" to Berlin.

Similarly, no national press, professional, nonpartisan, and, therefore, authoritative like *The Times* in Britain or the *New York Times* in America ever emerged in Germany. Prior to 1933 one of the few newspapers with a nationwide readership was the *Gartenlaube*, a weekly more devoted to "wholesome" entertainment than political news. Other papers with more than a local distribution were consumed by specialized audiences. As Roepke (1946) observed for the pre-Weimar years, everyone in Germany swore by his habitual paper, his *Leibblatt*. And so one learned of the opinions of other people only the caricature offered by one's own partisan press. The pattern of a manifold partisan press as the main sources of news in society changed but little during the Weimar Republic (Lowie, 1945). In terms of the printed mass media, Germany's modern communications contributed to segregation rather than providing for national integration. When, finally, well after the assumption to power of the totalitarians, the Nazis' main newspaper, the *Völkische Beobachter*, and their ubiquitous radio commentator, Fritsche, did manage to penetrate the last corner of the *Reich*, both were the servants of the Ministry of Propaganda. As a consequence, among the educated, both soon lost credibility, and they were replaced in fact by a foreign authority, the BBC, as a more reliable source of news during the war (Boberach, 1965).

Further, the country's modern communications system was not the only organization of value dissensus. The intellectuals made their own and distinctive contribution to value pluralism. During the nineteenth century, their orientation to the diversity of the Germans was ambivalent. On the one hand, they fought diversity as "backward particularisms"; on the other, they praised it as an expression of cultural richness (Lowie, 1945). Gradually, the celebration won out. They developed a simple ideological message: Cultural diversity of a people means quality and constitutes the wellspring of development and progress; cultural homogenization signals stifling stagnation and, eventually, cultural decline. Such views celebrating the virtues of value pluralism were pervasive enough to influence educational policy. Under the Kaiser, the Prussian Minister of Culture, for example, rejected the introduction of uniform school readers, giving avoidance of "stifling uniformity" as the main reason (*Protokolle,* 1897:2,280–83). The intellectuals' commitment to cultural and value pluralism in German society was only partially interrupted by a short-lived minority of Germany's professoriat before the First World War. Including such luminaries as Treitschke, Delbrück, and Max Weber, they preached a gospel of value integration with an ideology of nationalism (Williams, 1966; Ringer, 1969). While some of this group became associated with the Weimar regime, any genuine unifying influence was severely challenged through the influence of a Keyserling and an Oswald Spengler, who spread the message of cultural doom, mysticism, and its characteristic mixture of cultural xenophobia and xenophilia. Division among intellectuals was also characteristic of the Nazi era, when the SS intellectuals had nothing but contempt for the movement's official philosopher, Rosenberg (Höhne, 1967:183–209). A preference for diversity of sorts found its last and perhaps somewhat comic expression in Rosenberg's love of many uniforms. To this lonely philosopher of Nazism such variety symbolized the wealth of ideas (Rosenberg, 1964).

Summary and Conclusion

The salient facts of this chapter can be summarized under four points. First, in terms of societal values Germany as a whole was a mass society. Second, the German people made up a conglomerate of regional cultures with different and opposed value systems. Third, neither the value systems of various social classes nor those of urbanites or rural folk bridged the regional cleavages to any important extent. Only one, the lower class, provided a value milieu cross-cutting at least some of the regions. In contrast, the values of the upper classes were quite different, signaling division at the top of society. Moreover, the value commitments of three of the four regional upper classes that could be studied were deviant in the eyes of the lower orders in society. And the values of the fourth, the Prussian upper class who had been decisive in the making of modern Germany as a nation, were anathema to most people in other regions of the country. Fourth, and last, as evident in a discovery of different values among the good and bad people in fiction, in the absence of a cultural center and with intellectuals celebrating cultural diversity as a national asset, Germany was not only a country without "Germans," hers was a people highly conscious of value dissensus in society.

And what of the political implications? What light does the fact of value dissensus in society shed on that level of moral indifference among the German elites that permitted the pursuit of Empire to the point of national suicide and mass genocide?

To begin with, a demonstration of as much value dissensus as prevailed in Germany is *one* way of asserting that the modern "German" state had remained a curious kind of "historical empire" (Eisenstadt, 1963). This "German" empire was a modernized version of an ancient form of governance. Instead of "underlying masses" uninvolved with the affairs of the state (Deutsch, 1953), it had politically mobilized masses. Instead of clinging to traditional legitimacy beliefs of authority, the idea of rational legality was developed to a point of pure "decisionism" where the law lacked any sacred dimensions resting on shared beliefs.

Among the educated in society, a combination of division in values among elites, acknowledgment of value differences, and illegitimacy in the eyes of nonelites implied no less than a *de facto* commitment to "domination by virtue of interest constellations" (Weber, 1922:943) rather than authoritative rule resting on shared legitimacy beliefs or common convictions about who owes obedience to whom, for what, and why. And that in turn provides the foundation for an apparently reasonable pursuit of empire as an alternative to nation-building in modern times. Put differently, celebrating unrestrained value pluralism permits modern man to pursue imperial aspirations because a committed value pluralist negates the idea of citizenship as a moral community. Instead, such a person is convinced that modernity means the inevitable, the necessary, and the irreversible destruction of any direct connection between personal and lower-level group identities, on the one hand, and the more encompassing political ones, on the other.

During her short visit onto the stage of modern nations, Germany reached for empire twice. The moral insensitivity to other peoples' national identities that such endeavor entails was one anchored in the domestic political experience of her more educated groups. In terms of broader societal values, they had no national identity; they knew it; and they proceeded to try to turn into some modern virtue what was but a historical defect. They became the political practitioners of modern man's central moral temptation: The belief that man makes himself, that all reality is but a social-reality construction, unrestrained by history. If you are committed to the idea that neither personal nor group identities below the nation have much to do with the form and size of the polity in which you live, then you may conclude that demands for such direct connections reflect little more than the nostalgia of peasant souls. And, being modern and "realistic," you know that the peasant ways of life are doomed anyway, and you may proceed to behave accordingly. Convinced that the public sphere in modern life must be devoid of the possibility to realize any substantive ethics directly because it must be a "bureaucratic cage," and so an amoral sphere (Weber, 1915), you may commit yourself to *decisionism*, a totally secularized understanding of law serving nothing but the interests of men in their short-run lives, as they unfold and change. You believe that modern law can be made and unmade or changed, unrestrained by any traditional or "sacred" fetters. As a consequence, the authority of the state comes to rest entirely on procedural legality. Then "domination by interest constellations" becomes the overriding reality; and forms of governance, whether monarchy or democracy, totalitarianism or authoritarianism, and their ideologies are mere window dressing. That is a way of saying that state authority ceases to depend on legitimacy or shared secular convictions among concrete human beings as to what is or can be right, and what is or must be indisputably and unarguably wrong if humans are to remain humans. A finding of as much value dissensus as prevailed in Germany is evidence that Germans lacked a shared secular morality. In such conditions everything does indeed become possible as long as you observe procedural niceties. The latter apply only to the jurisdiction of the law, not beyond the boundaries of the state. Being already used to living with strangers within the bounds of the law, what happens to strangers beyond them mobilizes even less concern.

The fate of strangers remains some statistical event; and what you hear or even see about it registers with as much impact on the heart as any series of numbers.

But professed beliefs about the modern condition, its value pluralism, and some necessarily amoral character of the public sphere were not as unambiguous and free of ambivalence as I have just described them. That Britain, France, or the United States had some "mainstream" in their societal values and so could credibly claim some shared national identity, with a morally compelling character, whatever their internal diversity, was known in Germany. And the more educated could construct a sense of uniqueness out of this contrast, one that emphasized action, leaving the outcome to the future. If it was German to struggle forever about the question of what was German, and who was to be included or excluded, as Pletsch (1979) has argued, then this "German" cultural trait rested on value dissensus in German society and the attendant appreciated fact that the question of a national identity was still an open one. Consequently, political ambitions were not constrained from any such quarter as shared societal legitimacy beliefs. If a national identity were a universal feature of modern society, Germans believed they could leave their options open. That could be a topic to worry about "after the war," and in the meantime you could convince yourself that "dynamic social change" (that pervasive sociological piece of contemporary ideology) characterizes any modern social order. You could see virtue where timid souls saw a Hobbesian specter and assert, like Reinhard Höhn (1935), that sharing values would undermine a dynamic *Volksgemeinschaft*.

Germans, I have argued, were used to living with ethical strangers in their modern polity. More an empire than a nation-state, one generation had lived there under three political regimes. Twice they had reached to enlarge their empire. The second time around, the attempt gained nationally suicidal proportions eventuating in mass genocide of other people. The elites in Germany, so my contention, could not stop this conquest extremism. When risk-taking amounts to the abandonment of common sense, the most relevant resource for regaining it is shared values. And the elites in Germany shared no values. One may doubt that there is any direct general relationship between the stupidity that nations are capable of and the forms of government they have. Nonetheless, democratic regimes may be the slower or the more conservative ones when it comes to losing one's head. They have freedom of the press and institutionalized respect for political dissent. More opportunities to learn and relearn just who proclaims what as the national interest, therefore, exist in them than in dictatorships. That is why the "German problem" has so often been studied in terms of explaining the failure of developing a stable democracy (for example, Dahrendorf, 1965). Such an approach implies that a democratic Germany would have been one without imperial aspirations and without the capacity for mass genocide. Not subscribing to this view just so directly, one may yet examine what light a finding of deep value dissensus in Germany sheds on this question: Why no development toward democracy there?

The relationship between value orientations and type of political rules remains anything but well understood. Nonetheless, the available knowledge points to some direct connection between supremacy of the market model in a country's value hierarchy and *competitive* liberal democracy (Lipset, 1960; Almond and Verba, 1963). That is why Dahrendorf (1965) examined the values of the Germans in his analysis. If my results on this point have advantages compared with his, they lie in the replicability, the simplicity, and the brevity of the message. The market model of the good society in Germany was admitted only as a subordinate commitment on the part of most Germans. As a predominant set of values, that model was despised by most. The Rhenish were the single exception. In short, the distribution of societal values in Germany was not one just unfavorable to the development of this type of Anglo-Saxon democracy; the values of the German people at large opposed such development.

But quantitative data on values and social-class analysis have another advantage. The resultant findings can suggest also why the alternative to this competitive model of democracy, the *consociational* form (Lijphart, 1968; 1969; Steiner, 1974) did not emerge in Germany either. Designed to account for political stability in societies shot through with value dissensus, the consociational model of democracy postulates segregation at the bottom and unity at the top of society as a precondition for stable rule. The former prevents the politicization of value differences in society. The latter, in the form of specific elite norms that compel leaders to work for solidarity in and against all centrifugal forces of society, operates to depoliticize what value conflicts may rise to the top. In terms of getting things done, consociational democracies appear to be relatively inefficient (Gurr and McClelland, 1971). They need more time and other resources for integrative investments that prevent the outbreak of unmanageable conflicts. Tolerance of inefficiency, or comparative ineffectualness, in the formation and execution of national policies, is, then, another requisite for consociationalism. And of the four types of values used in this chapter, *Gemeinschaft* values support such tolerance of ineffectualness the most. But in Germany, as has been seen, there prevailed relative value unity at the bottom and much more value dissensus at the top of society, the reverse of the historical conditions that led to consociationalism in The Netherlands (Lijphart, 1968). And while *Gemeinschaft* values were predominant at the bottom of society and in the two southern regions, such predominance characterized only one of the four regional upper classes and only one half of the regional middle classes. Thus, not only was the patterning of values such as to make the breakout of value conflicts more likely at the top than at the bottom, but also the values of the Germans were too activist in nature to generate sufficient tolerance of ineffectualness, a feature required for successful consociationalism.

But no amount of value dissensus can suffice to explain that level of moral indifference that reigned among the upper reaches of Germany on her march to national suicide and mass genocide. So extreme a form of moral indifference can develop only among very peculiar elites. Let us see what consequences value dissensus had in regard to elite formation in German society.

CHAPTER FIVE

One-dimensional National Elites: Impressions from the Pages of Social History

Prologue

The previous chapter presented evidence that Germany was composed of different value communities. A "nation" in name only, the country was deeply split into regional subcultures with quite different value hierarchies. Important also was the finding that the upper classes of various regions did not share common values. Drawing on the best evidence at hand—and that, admittedly, is impressionistic—this chapter examines the impact of such value diversity on change in the nature of the country's elites. I have argued in Chapter III that a society with high value dissensus should be one where modernization eventuates in the development of de-stratified national elites. Put in a nutshell, the argument can be stated in two parts. First, everywhere modernization entails the emergence of new social figures, men who excel at some new skill such as the industrial entrepreneur or manager, the technical expert with certified special knowledge, the politician with a mass appeal. To begin with, such "new men" control only one of society's scarce resources, the one directly related to new skills of management. For example, as the new creators of wealth, industrialists emerge as the newly rich; but they are not thereby automatically carriers of high prestige in society. The politician excelling at the new skill of mass mobilization emerges as the newly powerful; but that in itself guarantees neither income nor high prestige. Second, assuming that humans everywhere strive for status consistency, other things being equal, the probability for success in that endeavor ought to be a function of consensus on societal values. Where the population shares commitments to the same image of the good society, the carriers of new

157

skills can claim to make a specialized but nonetheless commonly valued contribution to building the modern society. But under conditions of value dissensus the object of modern society is itself in dispute. Commonly valued contributions to building the good society do not exist. Then claims to entitlement to more diffuse rewards fall on deaf ears, as it were. The newly rich may remain the merely rich; the newly powerful, the merely powerful; and the newly prestigious may be saddled with a fate of remaining the merely prestigious. Such elites can be called one-dimensional by virtue of control over only one rather than several of society's scarce and unequally distributed resources.

Scattered, and mostly impressionistic, evidence suggests that modernization in Germany did eventuate in the rise of such one-dimensional elites at the national level. The fact that I am dealing with national elites in this respect deserves emphasis. In regard to societal values, Germany was a genuine mass society only at the national level. Therefore, it should be only, or at least primarily, national elites that show the character of one-dimensionality. Also, the evidence from the pages of social history cover only national elites. Thus *nothing* in the story to unfold below should be read to imply *general* elite de-stratification at regional and local community levels as well. Indeed, because there was more value consensus at the regional level, one would not expect a development toward one-dimensional elites there. My interest focuses entirely on Germany and the fate of that "nation." Now, the evidence to be reviewed below does show that Germany's national elites had been only very tenuously linked throughout the modern period. The rich in the country had very little in common with the highly educated. Prestige was nearly monopolized by the military officer corps, a group that in turn shared little with the top people in Germany's economy or the recognized top dogs in her cultural life, the professoriat.

Let me add a comment clarifying how my approach to the study of elites differs from the more conventional forms. The classic questions pursued in the sociological study of elites have been *whether* modern societies do have a coherent elite, one with social homogeneity, uniform in their commitment to shared values, in contact with each other, and therefore capable of acting in concert to realize their common interests; and if so, *who* these might be (for example, Putnam, 1976:107). Not too long ago methodological considerations dominated the discussion of these two questions. If you followed a reputational procedure (for example, Hunter, 1959), one involving asking people in high positions, "Who runs this show?" invariably so, it seemed, you would generate information pointing to the existence of a unified elite, one in charge of all important affairs. On the other hand, if you used Dahl's (1958; 1961) "issue approach," where one selects issue areas such as education, medical care, or economic problems and then inquires who are the initiators, the contestants, and more generally the participants in the policy process, invariably (so it seemed again) you would generate findings showing a pluralist elite structure with quite different people playing the role of "influentials," depending on the issue area (for example, Rose, 1967). Theoretically, the latter approach implied that a modern complex society can have only functional elites with relevant technical expertise and knowledge; modernity implied the necessary and inevitable doom of an "upper establishment" made up of generalists (Keller, 1963). Meanwhile, some ways out of the methodological impasse have been found by combining the reputational and issue approaches and by enlarging the scope of inquiry to cover the relations among political parties, legislative assemblies, the executive branch of government, and the higher civil service. Thanks to such developments, one can reasonably assert: A modern society can have an integrated national elite. The United States is a case in point (Moore, 1979). But the centralization of power varies impressively among modern societies and, apparently, rather independently of the nature of the political regime. For example, the centralization of power in Britain, a competitive democracy, is far closer to that of the Soviet Union in the post-Stalin era than that of the United States, another competitive democracy, and the political offspring of good old England at that (Gilison, 1972). Whatever the varied approaches and the advance in knowledge here, such studies share a common characteristic. This is the assumption that the question of a coherent national elite in modern society is one pertaining to the commonality in outlook and the sharing of interests and values among the incumbents of elite positions in various institutional sectors of society. Rarely if ever is the question raised whether such incumbents in elite positions have the means to act in concert. Put differently, by definition, as it were, the incumbent of an elite position is deemed to have the ability to affect the action of nonelites. That ability is the meaning of the term "elite." And while one may not wish to quibble with that meaning in general, it still pays to inquire more closely just what resources various elites do command. My contention is that the one-dimensional elites in German society did not command resources of a sufficiently generalized nature to act in concert, no matter what their desires in this respect may have been.

An examination of this contention requires the use of four kinds of unequally distributed resources in society. One can get four by making a distinction concerning the last of Max Weber's (1922:926–40) famous triad of wealth, power, and social honor. The last can be divided into prestige on the one hand and cultural honor on the other. Following in part usage in research on occupational ranking (Inkeles and Rossi, 1965), prestige here refers to imputed differential importance to society. However, I add a qualification, answering this question: Important for what? The attributed importance is one pertaining to the resolution of conflict. Prestige, as used here, is deference accorded to someone, or to an institution or its representative, on the basis of an attributed superior ability to contribute to conflict resolution in society. On the one hand, prestige is a reward rendered for such presumed contributions to conflict resolution. On the other hand, someone in a prestigious position can speak with a special language of enhanced persuasive powers, influence (Parsons, 1963a), which is a facility for managing solidarity. In this just-mentioned sense, advice from a prestigious source exacts compliance because people believe that the "influential" knows better what is in their own best interest in getting along with others than they do themselves.

Cultural honor, in contrast, is more general. It consists in attributed differential moral worth and moral expertise. On the one hand, cultural honor is a reward rendered for perceived examplary moral understanding and conduct; on the other hand, it is also a facility used for the management of moral beliefs (Parsons, 1968b). In the latter sense the value rhetoric coming from some recognized source of moral expertise—a bishop, for example—commands respect because it constitutes an "official" message concerning the recipients' good standing in the moral community. If he fails to heed the call, he may find himself excluded from some company of decent people; if he does shape up, he may enjoy a sense of righteousness.

In regard to power, except for confining it to the governmental sphere with an eye on policy consequences, rather than also covering power relations in a family, I follow Weber's (1922:926) usage: Power is the ability of some to realize their own will through others, regardless of the motives of the latter. Additionally, let me note: Power is legitimate primarily, if not exclusively, if it is perceived as a facility to coordinate cooperation in pursuit of some common goal. Whatever a leader's personal inclinations here—and of course he may pursue power for its own sake—the acknowledged rewards for leadership that followers may grant are rarely wielding power itself. The pursuit of power as a pure reward is usually attributed to the "power-hungry," "authoritarian characters," or other kinds of bad people. Acceptable rewards for leadership tend to be prestige, cultural honor, perhaps even wealth. One of the main reasons for this is easily discerned. Whereas money, that classic language of the marketplace, is a medium of inducement that always presupposes some measure of voluntary consent in striking a mutually acceptable bargain, the language of power symbolizes negative sanctions—bearing down with the law on the other person, or threatening him with a gun (Parsons, 1963b). The more power is legitimate, or the more obedience to authority eventuates into automatized discipline, the less aware is the compliant party of implied negative sanctions (Weber, 1922:946). On the other hand, the more brittle the authority or the less legitimate power is, the more does the language of power evoke the specter of violence.

The point in covering this familiar conceptual terrain with so many words is a simple one. In societies highly integrated by shared values these four resources are themselves patterned into an order. Some are regarded as of more value than others. More important yet, highly value-integrated societies, or subsectors in them whose members share common value commitments, tend to have regulatory norms specifying under which conditions and on what terms people may exchange one scarce resource for another (Eisenstadt, 1971). However, relative value consensus *is* the most critical precondition for strata formation at all levels of social inequalities. With such norms regulating legitimate exchange patterns, new elites have a chance to acquire a multidimensional status that is respected by others. In that way they come to control generalized resources. But in a society as shot through with value dissensus as Germany, that was an improbable outcome. Let me turn now to what social historians can tell us about it.

Germany: A Society with One-dimensional National Elites

The evidence on the relations among the elites can be conveniently organized by considering three groups in turn. These are the academic and administrative, the military, and the industrial elites. The objective is to gain an impression as to how much of a given resource any one of these commanded relative to all the others including the political elite, defined narrowly as incumbents of executive positions at the national center. The relative standing of the political elite proper can then be left to emerge as a result of comparative elimination of alternatives.

Germany had a very distinctive feature, the presence of a noneconomic upper-middle class. Their views on politics, economics, and socioeconomic change differed from those of the Junkers and the commercial and industrial classes (Ringer, 1967). This assessment of nineteenth-century German society continues with a description of what my terminology would define as a group of the merely cultivated—namely, a cultural elite possessing extraordinary amounts of cultural honor but little else. A university education was a uniform prerequisite of belonging to it. Occupationally, most members of this elite were civil servants of one variety or another. Professors and lecturers, the clergy, secondary-school teachers, higher bureaucrats in government, and judges made up the bulk of this group. Numerically a minority were the members of the free professions, and artists.

Accentuating the significance of higher education, all of these, irrespective of their occupation, could call themselves *Akademiker*—that is, people pedigreed with higher learning. Except for those in the free professions, and a minute minority of professors with very high enrollments, all had to manage on a rather modest income. In 1915 a study of higher civil servants found that two thirds had an income between 4,000 and 8,000 marks annually, while the vast majority of Germans enjoyed an income of about 3,000 marks per year just before World War I (Bechtel, 1956:360). However, at this time a yearly income of 60,000 marks among the managers and owners of private industry was not unusual. Such a discrepancy between the private businessman and the higher civil servant had not existed earlier. In 1848, for example, leaving private industry to serve the state at a higher level still proved a financial gain even for men who had been very successful in business. Yet 67 years later, about one fifth of Prussia's higher civil servants earned less than 4,000 marks a year, while a manager often made 15 times as much (Most, 1915:194, 204). The change in the economic position of higher civil servants was apparently very rapid. Already in 1855 Prussia had 25,000 taxpayers whose income exceeded that of a "government councilor" *(Regierungsrat);* by 1913 200,000 taxpayers had a higher income than such an official. Relative impoverization also affected His Majesty's Minister of State. In 1885 there were only 537 taxpayers reporting an income higher than that of a minister; by 1913, however, with over 21,000 in that income category, the minister had long lost his standing among the upper 10,000 in income. Furthermore, it could also be demonstrated that 30 years in service would enable a higher *Beamte* (civil servant) with 3 or 4 children to double his income. But these years would also saddle him with a net loss of 20,000 marks even if he lived as frugally as possible within the limits befitting his station (Most, 1915:190, 193). Many members of academe also found themselves in genteel poverty. At the end of the nineteenth century, university *Privatdozenten* either received no salary at all, or a very modest stipend, equal to that of primary-school teachers—namely, 1,500 marks per year. A higher rank category somewhat analogous to associate professor made as much as secondary-school teachers, with a salary of 5,000 marks per year. Full professors had a fantastic salary range from 6,000 to 40,000 marks, depending on enrollments. In 1900 their average annual income in Prussia was 12,000 marks (Ringer, 1969:37–38, 54).

Thus teachers and scholars, priests and artists, civil and military officers were already "underpaid" before World War I. They could not live according to a style appropriate to their station. This group also suffered the most during the postwar inflation that wiped out their property, monetized as it was. If a higher official managed to get by because he had married "outside"—say, a dowry-equipped daugher of the entrepreneurial middle class—her savings literally disappeared. In 1913 12 percent of the personal income in the nation still derived from capital sources, but by 1925 this portion had shrunk to 2 percent. Personal income from capital sources hardly ever regained even half its significance until 1931, when that proportion came to just under 6 percent (Bechtel, 1953:386). The income loss sustained by higher officialdom was apparently particularly severe. In 1913 a higher official had still earned seven times as much as an unskilled laborer. By 1922 a higher official made only twice as much. Furthermore, while farm wages rose, total blue-collar well-being became more secure, and big-business income increased considerably during the Third Reich, the relative poverty of the higher civil servant remained unchanged. In 1939, a *Regierungsrat* in the Finance Ministry with 2 children had a yearly income of 5,660 marks, which, given the expense of a style of life befitting his station, left him with a net annual deficit of nearly 10 percent. During the period 1934 to 1939, the number of businessmen with 25,000 marks or over, on the other hand, had increased more than any other income group in the business sector (Ringer, 1969:64; Schoenbaum, 1967:149, 220).

But while the income of the highly educated "melted away, their status remained high for a long time" (Ringer, 1969:63). Being an *Akademiker* proved of considerable advantage on the marriage market. "A maiden who married an official despite his lack of wealth could hope to die a *Frau Geheimrat*" (Eyck, 1962:67). Similarly, "the proud wife of an impoverished university instructor was still a *Frau Doktor*, and this meant something" (Ringer, 1967:127). According to the historian, it meant prestige. Three factors, however, suggest that it was not prestige in my sense of the term. Instead, officials were the bearers of cultural honor. First, very few people went to a university. Indeed, few attended secondary or high schools. In 1900, the ratio of elementary- to secondary-school enrollment was more than 30 to 1. Furthermore, for every 10,000 in the population only 1½ passed the Grade 13 final high-school exam *(Abitur)*, which entitled one to enter university. And of these again, 83 percent actually attended university (Ringer, 1969:39).

A university education was therefore an attribute of a very small minority. In addition, the educational system showed a near complete separation of popular and practical from "higher" and therefore "cultural" education. The realm of higher education did not penetrate into the primary schools, for example, as primary teachers were trained at special teachers' colleges, institutions not connected with the universities. Also the organization of technical training was not only outside the universities but also very specialized. There were *Hochschulen* for engineering *(Technische Hochschulen)*, separate academies for garden architects, for agriculturalists, and for foresters. Second, not only university attendance but even secondary schooling in a *Gymnasium* was restricted to a tiny minority. The critical barriers to admission here were those of status as well as money (Ringer, 1967:128, 132–33). Thus a good majority of specialists and technicians, those most crucial in the industrialization of society, were not *Akademiker*. Third and most important, the German ideal of higher education prescribed that *Bildung* should affect the whole person, not "just the intellect." Undoubtedly this conception promoted another—namely, the idea of the true human being as a cultivated one. The earlier "arrangement" between the Church and the absolutist states, which had brought about the benevolent political neutrality of the former, contributed its share to the meaning of being cultivated. That covered quasireligious, primarily aesthetic and philosophical interests, and so matters relatively divorced from political, social, and practical issues (Sauer, 1966:417). Given these conditions, as well as *Akademiker* status rather than occupation as a criterion of membership among the higher educated, one might conclude that they constituted a cultural elite. It was a very specialized elite, one accorded higher wisdom in questions affecting the universal human condition rather than mundane social conditions or politics.

For Germany's political development during the nineteenth century and for the Prussian state until 1918, the significant feature was the discrimination against the most educated in the franchise. With relatively low income, the majority of this group was barred from equality in voting even on the local level, where the property franchise had been introduced in the post-Napoleonic reform era. Also, since the principle of the welfare state had already been recognized in the Prussian constitution of 1789, the demand for equalizing the suffrage remained a narrow issue. One could not argue that the state should recognize social rights. It was then a highly educated but economically weak group of prominent people who called for the equalization of political rights. And the only weapon available to them was appeal to public opinion and morals. But in a territory with a high diversity in values such an appeal remained inherently weak. As a result, attempts to place the university-educated one class higher in voting than their income permitted failed as late as 1910. Counting little in matters of wealth and political rights, they probably placed the accent on inner virtues and a certain degree of other-worldliness in the realm of ideas in order to compensate partially for their status inconsistency in this world (Koselleck, 1966; Ringer, 1969:46).

The relative economic deprivation of this group hardly ever changed. If anything, inflation during the Weimar period worsened their position by wiping out savings and turning fixed pensions into empty paper claims. It is therefore probably correct to estimate that the relation between cultural honor and wealth stayed moderately negative throughout the whole of the modern period: The more you had of one, the less you had of the other.

Keeping in mind that all these estimates of relative status-incongruence are confined to the elites rather than applicable to the population in general, what can be said about the relation between cultural honor and prestige? It seems fairly clear that higher civil servants, as well as the free professions, these bearers of cultural honor, ranked definitely below the military officer corps in terms of prestige. Impressionistic evidence on this point is abundant. Two illustrations might suffice. First, for any middle-class son in Germany, becoming a reserve officer in the armed forces was as self-evident a requirement of middle-class life as going to college is for an American middle-class son (Kehr, 1965:55). Second, one reason why a good portion of the Prussian urban liberal bourgeoisie gave priority to national unification, rather than franchise equalization, during the nine-teenth century was a clear recognition of "the inevitable supremacy of the military in the Prussian state." As they saw it, the unusual military burden on Prussian society derived historically from Prussia's scattered territories, as well as from her historical role in supplying defense forces for the smaller German principalities. Unification would spread that burden and therefore "rebalance" the distribution of imputed social importance. This logic could lead to the demand to support a phenotypi-cal *Obrigkeitsstaat* as the only instrument of unification in order to alter it ultimately through its very success (Winkler, 1968). Also, there can be little question that the military's eminent position in terms of imputed importance to society lasted until the end of the Kaiser's rule in 1918 (Ritter, 1965: II, 117–31).

At least two important aspects of Weimar political life suggest, however, that the Army's prestige did not suffer as much as one might expect after a lost war and a change of regime. On the one hand, there was the relative success of the "stab-in-the-back legend." Though fed by diverse sources, the legend served to protect the prestige of the military institution. On the other hand, the very fact that military circles could supply the relatively plebeian Nazis with an effective measure of social acceptance also attests to the continuing prestige of the former (Berghahn, 1966:129, 214, 245–55). With the armed forces restricted to one hundred thousand men, a result of the Versailles peace treaty, the Weimar

Republic frustrated a lot of status aspirations in the German middle classes. Moreover, three facts suggest that the superior prestige of the military officer corps in German society did not suffer much under Hitler either. To begin with, the decision not to build a brown-shirt militia officially maintained the Army's position as the sole instrument of force. Though completely under civilian domination, one could still make a career in the Army without membership in the party. As an Army officer, you had entered a world where the Nazi Party could not touch you. Apart from the world of business, the armed forces made up the only sphere where that was possible. Second, eventually, the combat SS grew to a size where it could constitute a real challenge to the military as the monopoly bearer of arms for the nation. But SS soldiers took their Army colleagues and superiors rather than the SS hierarchy as the authoritative reference group (Stein, 1966). Finally, the fact of the war itself undoubtedly was the most significant force in maintaining the dominant prestige position of the military. In short, all the indications are that—excepting perhaps the few prosperous years of the Weimar Republic—the military outranked the top civil service in prestige throughout the modern period to the very end of the Third Reich. The higher civil servants, and the professioriat in particular, were the pre-eminent bearers of cultural honor in Germany, while the military, and the generals in particular, held a near-monopoly over prestige (Mommsen, 1966; Schweitzer, 1964).

Regarding the question whether the civil service had political power, either in terms of being considered in policymaking or directly formulating policies, any adequate answer would call for a decisionmaking study. Nevertheless, something can be said even in the absence of such data. One can provide two estimates. One involves scanning the whole period and trying to come up with some overall judgment in regard to changes in the political significance of the top civil service. The other considers some given point in time, where one answers the question whether top civil servants as a social group, or a minority of these, were more than instruments of the executive.

In Prussia the clearest case involving the top civil servants as the major politicians occurred during a period lasting from the post-Napoleonic reform era to about 1848. During that time Prussia was ruled by "bureaucratic parliamentarism," a system of consultation among officials at several levels of government and involving outside expert counsel as well. Operating somewhat like a university seminar with *Bekehrung durch Belehrung* (conversion by teaching), this was a time when the administrative apparatus had replaced the monarch and the legislative (Koselleck, 1966). Subsequently in Germany this form of rule appeared only once and in connection with the design of the Weimar constitution. Under Bismarck the top civil servants were, in effect, mere instruments of the politician both in external and in internal affairs. This passive role was only dramatically reversed when the relationship between Chancellor and Emperor turned to one of conflict between Bismarck and the young William II. Given the monarchical constitution, any tension between Emperor and Chancellor had to transform the top civil service into a pivotal political force. If they sided with the monarch, they would automatically support a trend toward personal rule; if they sided with the Chancellor, they would support the trend toward parliamentarization of the regime. Bismarck's departure then led to the period of imperial personal rule (Röhl, 1967a). The position of the civil-service elite in that conflict had been decisive in retarding parliamentarization. By 1899 personal rule had gone so far as to reduce the ministers to "confused lackeys carrying out the orders of the All-Highest," leaving the Kaiser as the only one who knew what and why things happened (Röhl, 1967b:267). Judging by the same source, around 1900 some twenty men determined the internal and foreign policies of the Empire. Among these the Kaiser, with his military, naval, and court advisers played the major role, the seven Prussian ministers and the six Reich state secretaries the minor one.

Relative to the period of personal rule, the political significance of the civil service as a corporate group increased again during the Weimar period, though more in internal than in external affairs. With the national government characterized by high cabinet instability, the Prussian administration became an important governmental source for Germany (Jacob, 1963:66–107). Relative to Weimar, in turn, the political significance of the civil service under Hitler declined again. According to Mommsen (1966:119–21), the party's initial attempt to absorb the bureaucracy failed. Characterized by a standoff, the relation between party and administration probably turned to an advantage of the regime as the bureaucracy gave some stability to the political system. But the higher bureaucrats increasingly lost any capacity to influence policymaking. Eventually, the practice of subjecting the commands of political authority to normative-legal control before implementation practically disappeared. Such a practice was of course in principle unreconcilable with totalitarian rule. Its decline may therefore be used as an index of the effective subordination of the civil-service bureaucracy to the politician.

Thus over time the relation between cultural honor and political power was quite varied; and because of regime changes with their attendant uncertainties that relationship was often quite ambiguous. It seems to me dubious to designate the "mandarin aristocracy of cultivation" in the higher civil service as Germany's "ruling class" even for the days of the Kaiser, as Ringer (1969:3–9, 120–23) has done.

Considering the relation between cultural honor and political power at given points in time cannot alter that picture either. The main reason was Germany's mode of governance in regard to the relation between top bureaucrats at the center and the officials in the field (Jacob, 1963). Despite checks from legislative assemblies at the county level *(Kreistage)*, and in Prussia at the provincial level as well *(Provinciallandtage)*, there was a certain amount of fusion between executive and legislative functions at lower levels of government. Whether in the form of executive orders or legislation, the institutions at the center always produced *general* policy directives, but seldom instructions about means. Implementing a policy in many fields was the responsibility of the *Landrat*, the county administrator, who enjoyed considerable discretion. As he decided on the question "how," it was he whose actions affected the population. The Weimar Republic maintained these conditions to a large extent, and the Nazis boosted the position of administrators by attempting to diminish legal restraints on their actions. This meant that there was no clear-cut *de facto* relation between civil-service rank and political power. Specialists in the Ministries of Finance, Agriculture, and the like, even at high levels, were often dependent on lower-ranking officials in the Ministry of Interior, which supervised the general field administration where policy was implemented. Sometimes these higher-level specialists had even less political power than the realtively lowly *Landrat*. Under the Nazis with their institutionalized disorder, some *Gauleiter* ruled like autocrats in their domain, while others exercised little if any state authority (Peterson, 1969). One should also keep in mind the great mixture of occupations in the cultural elite with its members in the judiciary, the Churches, the educational realm, and the free professions. Such wide-ranging occupations tell us that a good portion even of the higher civil servants never actively participated in policymaking at the national level. Furthermore, policymakers there often did not take the group as a whole into consideration when formulating policies. Thus indirect political influence was also not an attribute of the group as a whole.

Evidence on the relative social isolation of the cultural elite from other elites in society will be presented below. Keeping in mind that they were isolated, what then can be concluded concerning the political consequences of this particular one-dimensional elite? Concentrating on its center, the professoriat, three inferences can be tentatively offered. First, through an explicit commitment to an ideology of partial modernization, these "mandarins" significantly contributed to the legitimation of monarchical constitutionalism in the Kaiser's days and undermined that of Weimar democracy. Second, they also helped in the development of uninstitutionalized political conflicts in German society. Third, their "idealistic conceptions" of the role of the intellectual in society also contributed to depriving the political process in Germany of an input of imagination and to some degree even of functional expertise.

Though divided into a majority of "orthodox idealists" and a minority of "realists" or "modernists," Germany's professoriat before the First World War uniformly rejected the modernity of the English model. In their minds and hearts, hatred of England and pursuit of empire were related commitment concerns (Kehr, 1965:149–75). Their perception of an all-pervasive social utilitarianism with its "typically individualist Anglo-Saxon bent" in Western democracies generally led them to develop the ideal of a "cultural state" as a self-conscious alternative goal of modernization. Such a state was to guarantee the survival of a rich and varied cultural life and an all-pervasive ethical consciousness into the modern age. Both groups were quite in agreement that the individualist utilitarianism of the West would have to lead to the victory of the masses. And that, so they believed, would eventually degrade man to the status of a smart animal, one cognitively better equipped than others, to be sure, but an animal, and so a creature alive only to satisfy hedonistic interests, nonetheless. The only difference between these two factions was that the minority of "modernists," mostly in the social sciences, saw this development as more or less inevitable, one that could be slowed down at best but not fundamentally altered. The orthodox majority, on the other hand, saw itself as the savior of man from this horrible fate (Ringer, 1969:128–99). In part, taking such a position also amounted to an attempt to defend and advance one's interests as a social group. Advocating a "cultural state" *above* particular interests in society meant that they as spokesmen for the whole were also seeking political power. In this view, the legitimacy of a regime was not to derive from the right of kings, nor from the people—for that would mean voting, democracy and inevitable mobocracy—but from its cultural content and its service to the spiritual needs of the nation instead. As Ringer (1969:11) put it polemically, for the professoriat, "the state lives neither for the ruler nor the ruled as a whole, it lives for and through the men of culture and their learning." In practice, however, a kind of "arrangement" existed between the cultural elite in academe and the political elite in the ministerial bureaucracy, quite similar to the "arrangements" between Church and state, and between state and the bourgeois elite of wealth to be mentioned below; this one amounted to a grant of legitimacy to the regime in return for insuring minimal civil liberties, a legal state, and more important, the provisioning of support for higher education without insistence on immediately practical returns to any one group in society. Put into a short formula, the professoriat rendered legitimacy to the monarchy by celebrating the Hegelian state and Germany's cultural mission in the world in return for an undisturbed pursuit of scholarly interests financed and protected by the state.

Aware of the value diversity in Germany, and even committed to it as something worthy of preservation, the professoriat propagated the ideal of "inner cultivation" as a substitute for a national identity. In order to compensate for the essential *Ersatz* nature of such a collective identity, the professoriat then erected the mandarin symbols of "higher integration" by propagating Germany's cultural mission to the world in external affairs as a substitute for a "state without a purpose" internally. In the context of an appreciated value diversity within the nation, the state could not be used overtly to transform society toward some model of the good society. In that place the mandarins projected perceived Western trends toward mass society through democracy into their own country, made themselves the league of defense against this "terrible modern drift," and provided the state with a universal purpose for mankind: maintaining the ideal of cultivation in the context of growing technology and organizational achievements in the war. As one of them expressed it: "We want to defeat England, not to imitate her. Her example shows all too clearly where it leads when a state follows commercial and industrial interests exclusively. The belief in the intellectual and spiritual *(geistige)* world, in the life of the whole which transcends the existence of the individual, the belief, which awoke in all of us during the early days of August 1914, must never more die out" (Ringer, 1969:186–87).

The basic assumptions of mandarin politics were that it was possible and desirable to keep the political process free of the language of economic and class interests. Formulating these ideas in great detail and making them available for others in the main constituted their contribution to the noninstitutionalization of political conflicts in Germany. Whether as spokesmen of naval interests or Pan-German romanticism, whether as producers of a dichotomous imagery of hero and trader cultures or as celebrants of the integrative rites of the "spirit of August 1914," the professoriat taught the use of extreme nationalism and "higher ideals" in general as tools for the advancement of particularist political interest (Ringer, 1969:134–40, 182–85). An inevitable victim of this sort of agitation on the part of the core of Germany's bearers of cultural honor was the peace movement. As Chickering (1975) has shown, nowhere else in Europe did disarmament interests proceed with as much caution— always presenting themselves as hard-minded realists rather than as soft-hearted utopians—and nowhere did they meet with as much conde-scending disdain as in Germany.

But the mandarin style of agitation became the general model for the Wilhelminian era as well as during later regimes. As a result, society was deprived of a mechanism to distinguish particular from national interests. And no identifiable groups, indisputably ruling and therefore truly accountable for the fate of the nation, emerged. In Germany's political language the haunted national interest had become everybody's business.

During the Weimar period a minority among the mandarins became *Vernunftrepublikaner*. Actually yearning for a return of the monarchichal system, a wish that they deemed unrealistic, they emphasized a distinc-tion between the form and the content of a polity. In this view, all that mattered was the content, and a factual cultural state could be preserved even under full democracy in a republican form, provided elites would act accordingly. But even this group remained conditional democrats, willing to grant legitimacy to Weimar only if it supported culture. On the other hand, the majority of the orthodox viewed the Republic as the culmina-tion and embodiment of national decadence. For them the cultural state had been lost, and crass material interests dominated public life. They regarded the Republic as so corrupt that nothing less than a "spiritual revolution" would do to save the nation (Ringer, 1969:200–26).

One consequence of such radicalism was a widespread alienation of intellectuals from practical politics. Weimar's intellectuals, in and outside the university, on the right and on the left, came to share one character-istic. This was a commitment to the "primacy of the spiritual in politics" and a similar commitment to a thorough politicization of the intellectual life. Instead of making the intellectual resources of the country available for political problem solving, this led only to the production of utopian myths and increased political agitation. The imagery of "fate," "blood," and the communitarian organismic ideal of society, so prevalent on the right, invited nothing but rejection on the left, which in turn trumpeted its anarcholibertarian and individualist creed. Yet as they were alike in their fundamentalist moralizing, they could respect each other as genuine idealists, a matter that only contributed to their mutual isolation from practical politics. In 1925, for example, one of the most prominent leftist journals, *Die Weltbühne*, went so far as to publish an explicit call for noncooperation of the nation's intelligentsia in national affairs. Emphasiz-ing that reality demands compromise and the inconceivability of exercis-ing any authority without committing some injustice, the writer urged total withdrawal for the sake of spiritual purity (Enselling, 1962:130–40). How far this call was actually heeded cannot be examined here. But politicians in the established parties ceased to take seriously any of the intellectuals' battles, seeing in them nothing more than possibly useful propaganda material.

A second consequence of radicalizing the political discourse was a near complete dichotomization of the public media in the Republic. A journalist could either belong to the Ullstein group on the left or Hugenberg's media empire on the right. A wish to belong to some moderate group in the middle nearly condemned him to unemployment or else demanded forgoing any participation in the national press, and writing for some obscure small paper instead (Gay, 1968:133–35).

Last, while the professoriat itself remained monarchical-conservative in the main, their call for a spiritual revolution to save the nation led their students to the one group that offered a new revolution—namely, the Nazis. The professors had stimulated them to a national alternative. The NS call "Germany Awake" came to fill the activated imagination with hope. As a result, the Nazis had captured the German Student Association by 1931 (Ringer, 1969:250, 436).

Thomas Mann remarked somewhere that the ideal-typical German was a university professor, a general of the Army, and a person with a "von" in front of the last name, thus signaling a claim to nobility as well. Unless the tale of social history to this point and its continuation below are simply utterly mistaken, so wrong as to be beyond redemption, that ideal was never realized at the top of German society. Let me now turn to the military officer corps, trying to make a case that they were a national elite of the merely prestigious.

During the seventeenth century, the Prussian Junkers constituted a general "establishment" commanding uniformly high amounts of all four social resources here considered. Their first loss involved political power. The modernizing monarchs of the eighteenth century needed to obtain their compliance in centralizing political power, and they succeeded in "making an arrangement" with their recalcitrant nobles. This involved the transformation of communal into private property, with the Junkers' earlier feudal rights and obligations becoming a right in land as a capitalist resource. The Junkers in turn yielded political rights that had been theirs as an estate. As a social group the nobility also became the main recruitment base for the military officer corps as well as a monopoly supplier of horses for the Prussian Army. Thus the Prussian monarchy succeeded in transforming a politically powerful social stratum into political underlings (Kehr, 1966). The ascribed connection between noble rank and social and economic privileges was further eroded by the Prussian reformers during the early nineteenth century. Making land mobile on the market and attaching patrimonial rights to property rather than to noble status contributed to the embourgeoisement of the Junkers. Henceforth they were to combine claims to special status rights with pure class interest. During the first three decades of Germany's Second Empire the estate owners lost their police powers, their own representative body, and at least in principle their tax-exempt status as land owners. Many also lost their lands to wealthy commoners. In 1885 only 32 percent of the land in the seven eastern provinces was still owned by aristocrats. One third of even the larger estates with twenty-four hundred acres or more had become the property of commoners. Yet although their operating practices as land managers or businessmen in agriculture differed little from the rationality of contract in commerce and industry, by the middle of the nineteenth century, *embourgeoisement* did stop short of investments in ventures other than land until 1918. Apparently a member of a military caste could not become "a trader" without endangering the caste character and thus losing a claim to superior social status. This, however, meant losing economic superiority consonant with prestige as soon as industrialization had created a managerial bourgeoisie. As to the remaining political impotence for the Junkers as a group, the Prussian reformers had pushed them into a position of opposition to the center from which they never wholly recovered. While the Junkers predominated in the Prussian field administration until the end of the Weimar Republic, they did not predominate in the central Berlin bureaucracies, the seat of basic policy-making. Here commoners predominated; and while they were frequently ennobled as a reward for faithful service, this was an achieved aristocratic status *(Erwerbsadel)* definitely second in prestige loading (Rosenberg, 1966; Koselleck, 1966:67; Jacob, 1963:96–97; Röhl, 1967b). While the old aristocratic families receded far more from the scene of politics in the Austro-Hungarian Empire than did the Junkers in Prussia (von Preradovich, 1955), the latter's predominance at the lower levels of government at best obstructed but did not alter the trend toward the emergence of a group of the merely prestigious.

For it was in the armed forces where the aristocrats of Prussia and of Germany generally found their lasting place. In 1920 one half of all generals, close to a third of all general staff officers, and one fifth of all captains were aristocrats. Yet aristocrats made up a mere 0.14 percent of the population. Also, due to the reduction of the military in the wake of the Versailles peace treaty, on the one hand, and the influence of the presidency of old Field Marshall von Hindenburg in the Weimar Republic on the other, that dominant presence of the aristocracy in the Army had somewhat increased by 1932 (Müller, 1970[?]:68). Modestly educated as a rule, the higher officer corps were excluded from the cultural honor elite. Modestly paid and with shrinking incomes from their land holdings, they were definitely poor in comparison with the merely rich in industry. And with changing fortunes in the role of the higher officer corps as political influentials, politics did not make any significant contribution to their status re-equilibration either.

If the higher military officer corps were to be credited as the politically powerful, it should have been for their role in foreign policymaking. But in that field their fortunes varied greatly. The politics of the high command until the end of the Weimar Republic and that of Tirpitz' naval propaganda machine under the Kaiser before broadly suggest a zero correlation between prestige and power. Sometimes the bearers of prestige could translate that resource into power; at other times and more often, the majority of the higher officer corps could not. But a definite abdication from political power in foreign relations came only with Hitler's civilian domination of the military (Craig, 1964; Carsten, 1966).

As to the development of a one-dimensional elite of wealth, the key lies in the fact that the Prussian monarchy succeeded a second time in transforming a potentially powerful social group into political underlings. This time it was the entrepreneurial, managerial, and financial bourgeoisie during the nineteenth century. By a combination of state socialism and private capitalism, the monarchical system became a good place for the conduct of business. Rather than relying too heavily on taxes, which called forth pressures for parliamentarization of the regime and suffrage equalization, the Prussian modernizing state financed its greater needs by state-owned enterprises and loans from private capital markets (Kehr, 1965:56). Rather than push for democracy, the German bourgeoisie preferred to make money off these circles, who had an interest in preserving the monarchical system. That preservation directly depended on the cooperation of the bourgeoisie. For many years prior to 1918, on the average, commoners and the newly ennobled made up about three quarters of all in the Prussian House of Representatives, a bourgeois representation about twice the size of that of both Houses of Parliament in Britain half a century earlier (Moore, 1966:36–37).

The pursuit of economic profit rather than that of power in terms of the equalization of the suffrage remained a stable pattern among Germany's bourgeoisie. You could always make deals either directly with the political executive branch of government or through the manipulation of administrative law. A few examples may do. Prussia financed the war of 1866 against Austria by a sale of a state-owned railway line; during the Weimar Republic Prussia's "red czar" consolidated state-owned enterprises, a policy that among other aims circumvented the Reich finance-equalization plan of the Republic (Winkler, 1968). Whether supportive of the National Liberals' monarchical allegiance, organized in the German People's Party during Weimar, or marginally represented in the "Chief of SS Circle of Friends" during the Third Reich, the economically important acted as an interest-specific pressure group oriented only to the maximization of business chances. They never came to constitute an institutionalized political force that could be held accountable. Given an unstable iron-and-rye coalition, which found no genuine continuation after 1918, it seems as though power and wealth remained essentially segregated throughout the modern period. Let me draw on some quantitative evidence to shore up this contention. For the period stretching from the last quarter of the nineteenth century to the first decade of the twentieth century, it seems fair to assume that only the really wealthy among the entrepreneurs sat in Parliament. After all, one had to have quite some surplus income to afford it. And during that period, and in contrast to the comparative representation of commoners in the legislatures mentioned above, Germany's entrepreneurs were significantly less represented in the Reichstag and the Prussian House of Representatives than were those of Britain in their House of Commons. For many years the German figures were between one half and one third of those prevailing in Britain (Zunkel, 1962:189; Ringer, 1969; 45; Guttsman, 1963:79–97).

Not surprisingly, the merely wealthy were most socially isolated during the first part of the nineteenth century in Germany. At that time they did not even strive for status congruence; but when they tried it later on, they failed. During the earlier period, for example, the Rhenish-Westphalian entrepreneurs had no contact with the much poorer academically trained officials (Zunkel, 1962:74–95). These entrepreneurs also maintained ties to members of the free professions only if these had proved their worth to society by attaining considerable wealth. The economic elite in general considered intellectuals as interesting only to the useless *(Nichtstuer)* in society. Furthermore, anti-aristocratic and antimilitary in orientation, the merely wealthy resented the "Prussian arrogance" of the civil and military elites in their region. Income and prestige cleavages were thus superimposed onto the regional cleavage. Highly endogamous within their own group, the merely wealthy not only closed their ranks vis-à-vis those below them, they also regarded marriage to members of other elite groups as equally "inappropriate" *(nichtstandesgemaess)*. After 1850 this group began to fight for generalized status recognition. They acquired country estates, engaged in the ritual of the hunt, purchased a first-class vote by paying higher taxes than were necessary, and encouraged their sons to acquire the reserve-officer patent in a "good regiment." Other symbols of intended generalized status, such as the title Commercial Councilor and orders of merit for the fatherland, were avidly sought as well. As Zunkel (1962:99–127, 118) put it, "Whereas the Frenchman desired the order of the *Legion d'Honneur*, the Englishman yearned for the M.P. after his name, the German wanted the title Commercial Councilor." The fact that the symbol of hoped-for generalized prestige in the German case was in fact recognition for a specialized contribution—namely, one in economics—adequately expressed the difficulty the Germans met; for these attempts to become a generalized stratum of the higher-ups in society remained only marginally successful even in the Rheinland, though they succeeded there somewhat better than elsewhere. There was no marriage into the aristocracy; a few managed to have their daughters accepted by the newly ennobled *(Briefadel)*. The highest order a businessman could ever hope for was the Red Eagle Order Fourth Class, a decoration that a civil or military bureaucrat could obtain by mere seniority. Social contact with the cultivated also remained marginal because the sons of the wealthy did not ever develop any genuine commitment to the ideals and rigors that "higher learning" demanded. In Germany as a whole, and in Prussia in particular, the distinctions between the professional officer and the Sunday soldier, between inherited and acquired landed-estate ownership, and between genuine and "merely achieved" noble status remained viable (Zunkel, 1962:128). Since the wealthy as a group lacked a university education, one might conclude that Germany had an elite of the merely wealthy in addition to her one-dimensional elites of social prestige and cultural honor.

As in the case of the civil service and the military caste, the relation to power was essentially ambiguous for the wealthy as well. At times their single-minded pursuit of business chances had profound political consequences; at other times the very lack of institutionalization of the connection amounted to political neutrality. The direct deals with the governmental executive in Prussia retarded franchise reform as well as parliamentarization of the Prussian state. Deals with the unions at the close of World War I significantly contributed to negative integration of the working-class movement. The support of *Erfüllungspolitik*—when that meant the gain of international credit standing—and the subsequent shift against reparations and support of the "national opposition" to the Weimar regime—when that seemed more profitable—were strategies with a profound impact on German political life. They prevented the emergence of a unified liberal party. They also contributed to the dissolution of the last great coalition of Weimar before Brüning's era of rule by presidential decree, when the prevalence of business orthodoxy in unemployment policy alienated the Socialists. Intermittent in temporal terms, contradictory in effect, and brought about more by influential individuals than by organized business as a whole, it would seem that wealth lacked any systematic association with political power as well.

Restricting the term "power elite" to cabinet officers including chief executives at the national level, and confining the evidence on elite stratification to direct relationships between any two social résources, the relation between political power and the remaining three resources has been exhausted above. Political power showed a zero correlation of stable ambiguity to wealth, prestige, and cultural honor. Indeed, it would not be difficult to show that Germany's three political regimes had cabinet members who were highly educated as well as those with little more than primary schooling. For example, Bismarck, Rathenau, and Goebbels were the former; Caprivi, Ebert, and Hitler were among the latter. Also, at the start of their terms of office, one found there the rich, Rathenau, Cuno, and Goering; and the poor, Caprivi, Scheidemann, and Hitler. Some, like Bismarck and Stresemann, commanded great personal prestige; others, such as Brüning and Seldte, little. Some, finally, commanded some personal charisma, as did Bismarck and Hitler; others wielded practically no moral authority, as, for example, Bülow and von Papen. No doubt such examples could be given from almost any Western government. The point here is structural. Germany's one-dimensional national elites made such patterns of relative status deprivation typical for the incumbents of high political offices. When a general assumed executive functions as President, War Minister, or *éminence grise*, he came characteristically from a group high in prestige but poor economically. When a civil servant assumed executive roles, he again came from an economically marginal group that could, however, claim superior cultivation to anyone else. And when a businessman rose to political prominence, then he usually came from a group lacking in social prestige. Last, when a party politician rose to executive position, his background could be as wide as the total societal spectrum.

Let me summarize this picture of the gradual dissolution of elite stratification in German society as it emerged to this point in the narrative. Then let us take a look at some quantitative evidence that also indicates that modern Germany had no "ruling class" worthy of the name.

The state-Church "arrangements" under the absolutist regimes of the eighteenth-century helped to produce a one-dimensional cultural elite. In return for economic security through taxation, the Church had granted the absolutist monarchs a benevolent political neutrality. Engaging in standardized Sunday services for the masses, and refraining from involvement with issues of the day, the Church lost the allegiance of the educated minorities, who turned to the spheres of philosophy and aesthetics in search for meaning in life. This cultural and quasisecular elite in turn came to an "arrangement" with the state. They would grant legitimacy to the state in return for assured tax support for higher learning and a minimal meddling with the content of cultural pursuits. Declaring a university education as the *sine qua non* for belonging to the cultural elite succeeded. But attempts to raise the qualification of higher learning to the level of an attribute of generalized standing in society failed. Rejected as useless theoretical eggheads by the entrepreneurs and managers of a rapidly developing industry during the nineteenth century, the cultural elite remained isolated from that of wealth. But these newly rich came to constitute an elite of the merely wealthy, because they too made a kind of "arrangement" with the political elite. Scared by the Red menace, the wealthy were willing to grant legitimacy to any political regime that guaranteed a favorable business climate. Prussia's modernizing monarchs or their bureaucratic dictators, however, had also succeeded in "making a deal" with Prussian Junkerdom. In guaranteeing private-property rights first, and later a differential claim to predominate in the nation's military elite, the Prussian Junker officer gradually developed into a bearer of mere prestige. For Wilhelminian Germany this left some tenuous bond between political power and social prestige, though one probably more relevant in foreign than in domestic affairs. While neither money nor "learning" *(Bildung)* could be used reliably to gain access to the national executive, a higher military rank was still of some use in this respect.

While the professoriat in the main clearly supported the monarchy and provided indispensable legitimation, one can argue a similarly tenuous bond between cultural honor and political power. That connection was indirect, operating through fidelity to the Imperial Crown on the part of the higher civil servants who had absorbed the ideal of the cultural state when at the university. But losing the First World War, the reduction of the armed forces during Weimar, and the symbol "democracy," interpreted as the arrival of the mass age and the end of mandarin security, loosened the remaining tie between cultural honor and political power. From the perspective of the ivory tower, Weimar had only three recognizable elites: an economic one that prospered, a political one that managed to limp along, and a cultural one that suffered and seemed doomed to elimination. Furthermore, the fortunes of the former two were seen as subject to sudden and unanticipated change (Ringer, 1969:246). But in view of the very success of the military to bestow respectability on the Nazi *ex plebes*, that perspective remains too narrow. The military had retained its superior claim to prestige. When the Nazis arrived on the scene, the system of stratification among the German elites was already so fragile that little was left to be destroyed. All the Nazis had to do was to dethrone the vestiges of the traditional bearers of cultural honor, and do that in the most radical fashion possible; for then, what everyone had suspected all along would become official: Modern society recognizes only the functionary at the top; his control over resources is job-related and therefore strictly confined; as he has only a one-function resource to command, that one function is his sole responsibility; and the idea of personal moral responsibility for the country as a whole at the top of society is as outdated as the memory of a countrywide establishment. And on this point the Nazis succeeded brilliantly. Calling for a "spiritual revolution to save the nation," the mandarins in academe had prepared the ground for their own displacement. Resplendent in a variety of party uniforms, the higher party functionary, the new labor leader, the Hitler Youth commander, and the higher SS leader now proclaimed to incarnate the new morality of an "awakened Germany." Youth believed them, but no one else. And the cultivated mandarins in the educational realm, the judiciary, and the civil service lost their traditional claim to superior moral insight. But it was not only the academic youth that had become tired of seeing in higher learning the most important aspect of Germany's alleged alternative to modernity. That aspect, the notion of a cultural state, had never been of any help to the lower middle class, who felt increasingly threatened in its lifestyle by big corporations and big unions (Lebovics, 1969). And so the Nazis succeeded in discrediting the older symbols of cultural honor. But given the inflationary use of symbols in the propaganda of totalitarian rule, they were far more successful in destruction than in establishing any genuine trust in the new symbols of a dynamic *Volksgemeinschaft*.

The NS regime built its legitimacy finally on the personal epiphany of the *Führer* rather than on a relatively well-structured ideology. That demanded of each organization in the private and the public sectors of society to invoke legitimacy for their actions in terms of executing the *Führer's* will. Formally, this amounted to the monopolization of moral authority by the charismatic leader. Factually, it meant the removal of any concretely present source of moral authority in society. The reasons were practical as well as system-inherent. No single leader could settle the myriad of policy disputes among multiple competing agencies and interest groups. And settling such issues in authoritative fashion would have introduced an element of ideological legitimacy. But an organized ideology, a sacred text, was something Hitler abhorred. He feared ideological beliefs as constraints on his freedom of action (Nyomarkay, 1967). His preference for a contentless charisma of action (Nolte, 1965:402–54) perfectly matched the deep value dissensus among the Germans.

According to these impressions from the pages of history it seems as though the dissociation among the elites in German society became progressively more severe as one moves from the nineteenth century to the midtwentieth century. Some very limited quantitative evidence bearing on the elites of Weimar Germany and the Third Reich supports this interpretation.

Zapf (1966) was able to determine the social characteristics of approximately 250 members of 14 elite groups in 1925, and in 1940, and in 1955 for West Germany. The social characteristics were age, percent of Southerners in the group, social status of the father, and educational status of the elite member. All the data could be ordered into four equidistant levels. This made it possible to construct two simple indices of heterogeneity. When an elite is composed of the incumbents of more than one position, such as the Minister of Culture, other cabinet ministers, party leaders, leaders in Parliament, and chief executives of the *Länder*, which for this discussion together constitute the political elite, the total number of levels that separates each of these groups from each other was expressed as a percentage of the total number of possible levels that could separate all. This index measures internal or intragroup heterogeneity. In comparing different elites with each other the same procedure was employed, but the actual number of levels that separated all the components of the two groups was now expressed as percent of the total possible number of levels under the assumption of complete intergroup polarization. This index measures intergroup heterogeneity.* Both indicators permit us to compare intra-elite with interelite heterogeneity over time. One can estimate, therefore, whether the social distance within and between elites increased or decreased. The results are reported in Table V-1.

As to the internal composition of the elites, the political, as has been pointed out above, consists of leaders in government, party, and the legislature. The "foreign-relations elite" here denotes ambassadors and generals. Combining these two was possible because generals and ambas-

---

*The indices of heterogeneity were computed in several steps. First, Zapf's table on p. 198 concerning the West German elites was reconstructed omitting the two new criteria of resistance to the Nazis and religious affiliation by using the base data provided on pp. 193–94. Second, similar tables were constructed for the years 1940 and 1925. Third, maximum internal heterogeneity was arithmetically determined in terms of the number of levels that separate various groups that compose an elite. With four equidistant levels, the maximum distance on a given scale is 3. Since there are four scales,—that is, age, percent of southern origin, social status of father, and educational level of elite member—two groups can be separate by 12 distances. Three groups can be maximally apart by 24 distances, four groups by 48, five by 72, six by 108, and seven groups by 144. Fourth, maximum interelite heterogeneity under the assumption of total polarization among each of the component parts of any two elites compared was then set at 12 x (number of groups in elite 1) x (number groups in elite 2). The index of intra-elite heterogeneity within a given elite was then the actual distances found as percent of the maximum possible. Interelite heterogeneity was the actual distance between each of the components of the two elites compared, expressed as percent of the maximum possible. Cf. Wolfgang Zapf, *Wandlunger der deutschen Elite.* München: R. Piper Verlag, 1966, pp. 192–98.

Table V-1 Dissociation among the German Elites, 1925–55: Percentage of Intra- (figures in parentheses) and Interelite Heterogeneity in Age, Education, Region, and Social-class Origin

1925

	Pol.	F.R.	Ad.	Econ.	Cult.	Labor	Avg.
Pol.	(55)	31	34	27	34	55	36
F.R.		(42)	33	29	37	54	37
Ad.			(42)	33	33	79	37
Econ.				(8)	29	54	34
Cult.					(58)	62	39
Labor						(—)	61

1940

	Pol.	F.R.	Ad.	Econ.	Cult.	Labor	Avg.
Pol.	(47)	52	53	43	37	45	46
F.R.		(50)	29	29	42	67	44
Ad.			(25)	25	33	71	42
Econ.				(33)	33	67	39
Cult.					(42)	62	41
Labor						(—)	62

1955

	Pol.	F.R.	Ad.	Econ.	Cult.	Labor	Avg.
Pol.	(28)	32	22	30	35	62	36
F.R.		(25)	29	12	37	54	33
Ad.			(17)	33	33	67	37
Econ.				(0)	33	67	34
Cult.					(67)	54	41
Labor						(—)	61

Increase/Decrease in social distance among elites

	1925–40	1940–55	1925–55
Increases	8	2	6
Decreases	4	9	4
Stable	3	4	5
Number of elites compared	15	15	15

Pol. = political elite
F.R. = foreign-relations elite
Ad.   = administrative elite
Econ. = economic elite
Cult. = cultural elite
Labor = top union leaders/NS Labor Front
Avg. = average percentage of heterogeneity among elites

sadors in Germany differed significantly on only one dimension—namely, education. The ambassadors were uniformly high in educational qualifications; the generals uniformly low (Zapf, 1966:194). The administrative elite consists of top bureaucrats in the judicial system and Secretaries of State in the major ministries. The economic elite includes top managers and leaders of business associations. The "cultural elite" consists of newspaper editors and Church leaders, and the labor elite of top union leaders and NS Labor Front officials. Thus an index of internal heterogeneity could be computed for all elites except the last.

For our purposes the most important results are indicated in the lower right-hand corner of the table. Here I listed the number of increases in the interelite heterogeneity indices as noted in the three matrixes for the years 1925, 1940, and West Germany's 1955. This shows at one glance that interelite dissociation increased from Weimar to the Third Reich. Of the fifteen comparisons over half—namely, eight—showed a greater distance in 1940 than they had during the Weimar period. Moving from the Third Reich to the West German remainder in 1955, on the other hand, shows a counter trend: greater homogenization among the elites. Nine of the fifteen interelite indicators decreased. Essentially the same result emerges in terms of the average distance separating any one of the elites from all the others. Excepting the labor elite, which was the most isolated from all the other ones in all three years, the average social distance among the Weimar elites ranged from 34 percent to 39 percent of total polarization. In the Third Reich the respective range extended from 39 percent to 46 percent, while the West German postwar elites roughly returned to the condition prevailing during the Weimar Republic.

The change in intra-elite heterogeneity did not follow the same pattern, moving toward greater homogenization instead. From Weimar to the Third Reich only two elites increased in the diversity of their social characteristics: the foreign-relations elite and the economic elite. All the others decreased. Excepting the cultural elite, this trend toward greater internal social similarity of the elites continued to 1955 in West Germany, only in a more pronounced manner. The West German "half nation" by and large had elites who were relatively homogeneous in their internal composition. But of the five cases where internal heterogeneity could be calculated, the averages of interelite heterogeneity exceeded the intra-elite measure in four. The distances among the elites were larger than that which separated the members within a given elite. Though arrived at by different means, this finding led Zapf to conclude that West Germany had no "establishment" (Zapf, 1966:199). I concur because an interelite heterogeneity of 33 percent or more signals that the elites were separated by four levels or more on four scales where the maximum distance was three levels on each. As the distance between the elites was larger during the Third Reich, and just as large during the Weimar period, one can also conclude that the German nation had no establishment earlier. What differed in the earlier national situations was that the elites within themselves were far more heterogeneous than in the later western part of the divided nation. As one goes back in time, therefore, the members of a given elite shared a formal position status but little in social characteristics. While such a relative lack of distinct social boundaries would favor exchange of personnel among elites, actual crossovers have apparently been rather rare in Germany not only after World War II but earlier as well (Zapf, 1966:188–90). Of course, similarity and dissimilarity in social characteristics do not tell us anything about actual cooperation or conflict about national policies among the elites. At best they tell us something about one source for "defining situations" in similar or dissimilar ways. To the extent that any two groups share in social characteristics they might also see social events in similar terms. And this extent was low in the Third Reich as well as during the Weimar Republic.

Thus impressionistic as well as some quantified evidence indicate that elite stratification in modern Germany was fairly low and apparently became progressively lower until the nation expired.

Conclusion

And what have we learned to this point about the moral indifference among Germany's elites? Essentially two facts have emerged. The previous chapter has shown that the upper classes in Germany were divided in their values, and in some regions, they even had values opposed in their hierarchy of organization to those of the middle and lower classes in society. It follows that the top of society lacked legitimacy. Upper classes, of course, are not identical with national elites. Still, most of the latter were recruited from the former. The labor leaders were the only certain exception to this rule. After the introduction of democracy in 1918 and with the entry of mass politics, some of the chief executives of government also came from the middle or bottom of society. Nonetheless, for the majority of the national elites discussed in this chapter, upper- or upper-middle-class origin remains a fact, and therefore their legitimacy deficit in the eyes of others in society can be assumed. Now, as just demonstrated, they remained one-dimensional elites. Thus they also lacked in generalized resources. Germany's elites, then, suffered from a double deficit—one in legitimacy, the other in broader resources. And so they had a double reason to form a "cartel of anxiety," and not only after the end of the nation-state in 1945, as Dahrendorf (1965:297) has asserted, but also throughout the short lifetime of modern Germany as a unified country.

Such are the conditions that turn elites into segregated corps of pure functionaries, men who take an interest only in their narrow institutional affairs and maintain absolute political neutrality in regard to everything else. Perhaps one can take the Reichswehr, Weimar's shrunken hundred-thousand-man army, as symptomatic in this regard. While they did look out, as best they could, for their own interests, the idea of political neutrality became the professional soldier's ideology. The Weimar Republic manifested this idea in very practical legal terms. A professional soldier had neither the active nor the passive franchise; you could not run for public office, nor could you participate in voting, unless you resigned your commission first (Müller, 1970 [?]:72). The official idea here was simple and clear: The Army was supposed to be *nothing but* an instrument of the state and never, as an institution, contribute to the policy content of the state. Others (Müller, 1969; O'Neil, 1966) have analyzed the Reichswehr's ideology of political neutrality using documents that reflect the beliefs of the generals. My contribution here is social structural, and more general. Deprived of legitimacy *and* of generalized resources, each of the one-dimensional elites in Germany could ideologize the functional neutrality of the technical expert because none deserved trust in terms of shared values and none controlled generalized resources that make it possible to speak the language of trust with responsibility. And knowing it, one could respond by throwing the idea of a sense of comprehensive moral responsibility for society as a whole into the dustbin of history and stake one's brittle pride on being a technical expert.

All this does not deny the possible relevance of striving for status consistency, even among so systematically a set of the relatively status deprived as Germany's one-dimensional elites. If one sticks to the assumption that striving for status consistency is a human universal, a finding of one-dimensional elites alerts one to the expectation that these ought to have been quite active ones, each attempting to secure something of that scarce resource held almost monopolistically by another. And while de-stratified inequalities in society ought to make for unregulated social conflicts, as I have argued in Chapter III, that does not mean that such struggles have no focus at all. Let me return, therefore, briefly to the use of correlational metaphors to describe the nature of elite de-stratification in Germany. With four scarce resources under consideration here, the total number of bilateral relations between any two is six. Consequently, one can redescribe the whole discussion about one-dimensional elites in German society by stating which scarce resource was related in what way to another at the elite level of Germany throughout most of her history, certainly since 1918. As a summary device, the metaphor of correlations reveals the following picture:

Resources			*Correlations*
political power	and	prestige	= zero
political power	and	wealth	= zero
political power	and	cultural honor	= zero
prestige	and	cultural honor	= negative
prestige	and	wealth	= negative
wealth	and	cultural honor	= negative

Recall that participation in policymaking at the national center was intermittent for the merely prestigious, the merely wealthy, and the main bearers of cultural honor. Sometimes each had enormous impact on policymaking; at other times each was an abject bystander to events entirely beyond its own control. Here I have simply described that condition in terms of zero correlations, signaling accidental, or random relations, between political power, on the one hand, and the three other resources on the other. Similarly, because the higher officer corps of the military was always modestly educated in comparison with *Akademiker* in the higher civil service and always poorer than top managers in private sectors of the economy, prestige was negatively correlated with cultural honor and wealth at the elite level of the country. Finally, since the wealthy were definitely undereducated in comparison to the *Akademiker* in the civil service in general, one finds also a negative correlation between wealth and cultural honor. Observe, nothing changed here. Using correlations is merely a different mode of describing the situation.

But this way of looking at history is revealing. Note that in the table picture above there is no elite stratification (absence of positive correlations). Still, there was some "structure." Next to three random relations, one does find three negative correlations. Assuming that people who have plenty of one resource will try to use it to acquire what they do not have, such a correlational picture tells us how they might have gone about it. Correlations tell us which conversions of one resource into another some reasonable actor could have tried, and which he would avoid. Negative correlations signal an invitation not to try a conversion. You know that the two resources do not go together with each other; indeed, the more of one some people have, the less they have of the other. If such a negative correlation is an appreciated reality of social life, a reasonable man would not try to convert what he has for what he lacks, because chances are he will lose in the bargain. He might be left with less of the one resource he does have than he had before. Relative to patterns of negative correlations, though, zero correlations are an invitation to try some conversion.

Certainly, that is still quite a gamble. You know that some who tried in the past succeeded, while others failed. You know also that your gain, if realized, may not last long. Nonetheless, if you are striving for status consistency at all in a situation of nothing but negative *and* zero correlations, trying your luck in the area of zero correlations is the only thing you can do. Consequently, this correlational picture above tells us that there was but one royal road to status consistency. That road led over political power. Trying to convert wealth, prestige, or cultural honor into political power gave you at least some chance for success, while trying any other conversion was doomed to failure. One should expect, therefore, that the absence of stratification at the elite level not only led to ever more anomic social-conflict patterns, as has been argued in Chapter III, but that political mobilization in society at large assumed ever more militant forms as well.

If a search for power was the only reasonable thing that one-dimensional elites could try, they would have to struggle in truly Hobbesian proportions. Eventually, all would have to speak the language of power in a highly inflated propagandistic way, each claiming that its perception of the haunted national interest was just as valid as that of any other. Let us see whether the patterning of conflicts became increasingly less ordered and more militant as one moves from the beginning of modern Germany in 1871 to her demise as a unified country in 1945.

CHAPTER SIX

State and Society in Wilhelminian Germany: The Birth of Mass Politics

Prologue

In my student days during the early 1960s Leni Riefenstahl's movie *Triumph of the Will* was a staple of the American campus movie fare. Depicting a Nuremberg Nazi Party rally, you could get the idea that the National Socialists invented the mobilization of the masses to nationalist fervor. You might also receive the impression to seek the essence of National Socialism in the search for community. For that movie was a masterful blending of political and religious symbolism. Both impressions, however, would be quite erroneous. The practice of mass politics antedated Hitler. And the heedless pursuit of empire, that main show, reflected the pursuit of power among de-stratified elites. Divided in values, lacking in legitimacy and, as one-dimensional elites deprived of command over more generalized resources, the German elites came to perceive the public sphere as an amoral one and the state as a pure instrumental power association, an entity inherently serving the interests of some at the necessary cost of the interests of others. "Realpolitiker" of such persuasions are very good at unleashing sociopolitical conflicts. But deprived of both shared beliefs and the concentration of resources, they are also very poor at regulating conflicts. The self-destructive nationalism of German society was the resultant of a three-factor constellation: value dissensus, de-stratified national elites, and a socially structured inability to regulate conflicts. Such a society can easily mobilize for war, but it lacks self-steering capacity to conduct war with any semblance of rationality.

In this chapter I confine myself to Wilhelminian Germany and focus on three elements of the country's political life: (1) a preference for a strong state, or national output center which, while celebrated in Hegelian terms, was in fact used as an instrument for the defense and advance of separate lifestyle interests; (2) a weak party and parliamentary input system serving particularist interests; and (3) conflicts pitting separate political value communities *(Gesinnungsgemeinschaften)* against each other. However, rather than dwelling again on the history of political ideas in their highbrow or lowbrow forms (Stern, 1965; Mosse, 1964; 1975), my focus is on the imperial constitution, on patterns of the national vote as a measure of the fragile legitimacy of the regime, and on the activities of some of the most important pressure-group propaganda organizations before the First World War. Regarding the latter I shall use the Agricultural Association as an ideal-typical illustrative case. All this serves *not* to shed doubt on the fact that the new mass politics was a "nationalization of the masses" (Mosse, 1975), but only to demonstrate that behind the many-splendored rhetoric of the day stood massive material and status interests eventuating in orientations that were the antithesis of a caring concern for the welfare of the nation.

The Second Empire:
Selected Aspects of the Constitution

The constitution reflected the "desire for strong government" in the way it defined the power jurisdiction of the offices of Emperor, of Chancellor, and of the Federal Council, and their mutual relationships. The Emperor as chief of the executive, the civil bureaucracy, and the armed forces practically symbolized the sovereign. While the constitution defined the Federal Council as the depository of sovereignty, it remained so obscure as never to attain this position in the eyes of the people (Huber, 1963:809). In effect, imperial Germany was a single-chamber political system, for the Federal Council constituted a delegates' congress of the member states. The delegates were not elected parliamentarians charged with policymaking independent of their constitutents and in accordance with their conscience, but rather representatives appointed by the state governments and bound to their instructions. The Council's jurisdiction included the initiation of legislation, participation in budgetmaking, all foreign treaties, and the declaration of war. Concerning the last item, the powers vested in the Council exceeded those of the Reichstag. Thus the Council was a full partner in legislation. However, the originally intended function of the Council was not the promotion of national legislation, but rather the blocking of any that might be inimical to the interests of the member states. The members of the Council—mostly civil servants— were to form a kind of watchdog veto committee. Although the Chancellor—usually in personal union with the Prussian Chief Minister *(Ministerpraesident)*—controlled the seventeen votes of the Prussian state on the Council, that was less than a third of all votes. Thus the Council had an absolute veto over any legislation proposed by government. In practice, the Council rarely used this power. Avoiding the role of "obstructing unity," the Council mostly managed to present itself as a united front of experts who brought the form of Reichs legislation into line with the state constitutions without ever altering the content of federal law. What little prestige the Council had has been attributed to this detached and neutral policy (Huber, 1963:850).

This limited role of the Council contrasted sharply with the office of Emperor and Chancellor. Emperorship in personal union with the Prussian monarchy was hereditary, accountable to none, and inviolable. These three elements could be used for the exercise of dictatorial powers. Characteristically, the German constitution lacked a catalogue of basic rights; inclusion of a rights catalogue in the constitution had been proposed by some liberals, debated in the Reichstag, and rejected by a vote of 223 to 59 (Huber, 1963:758). These rights had already been left out of the earlier constitution of the North German Federation on the grounds that such a catalogue would violate the federal principle, as such rights were already part of the state constitutions. This rationale reflects the prevalence of particularisms and clearly was only one reason. It would have been quite easy to devise a rights catalogue general enough to include all the basic states' rights by subsumption.

One might suspect, therefore, that there was another reason. The principle of the supremacy of any federal law over states' law suggests that this other reason was political rationality—that is, a desire not to limit political action that might become necessary for the preservation of the empire by some inviolable rights of individuals. In the history of Western constitutionalism, the basic rights—freedom of person, of expression, of association, etc.—have provided the ultimate basis of the polity. They specified not only some of the reasons for political association, they also provided an essential component of the legitimation of political authority. Jointly, such rights set some limits to the range of political action possible. They were products of value fundamentalism and in a sense partook of the sacred. Whether or not such rights were subject to change through constitutional amendment—and this varies from case to case—the public message of such rights was to set limits to the claims of the territorial collectivity vis-à-vis its constituent parts. At the same time, this was also a message that set limits to what was to be subject to rational deliberation and therefore to uncertainty. In the German constitution, the only item falling into the category of "things untouchable," however, was the

Emperor serving as a symbol of the unity of the nation. As that unity was not to be impeached, the Emperor had to be inviolable and accounta-no one.

The most important function of the Emperor—in effect the very pivot of his role—was the appointment and dismissal of the Chancellor, for practically all the Emperor's other political duties were tied to the consent of the Chancellor; with written Chancellor consent, the Emperor was to (1) participate in policy setting with the Chancellor, (2) call, adjourn, and dismiss the Federal Council, and with the additional consent of the latter dismiss the Reichstag. Further, the Emperor was to conduct foreign policy, and with the additional consent of the Federal Council, declare war. Only the Emperor's command authority over the armed forces was outside the Chancellor's countersignatory power. Formally, administrative authority over the armed forces, insofar as it dealt with questions of size, equipment, and salaries, was shared with the Reichstag, which had to vote the requisite funds. But in practice, personnel policy of the military was beyond the reach of parliamentary scrutiny (Kehr, 1965:78; Röhl, 1967a:272). Thus while the Emperor remained formally unaccountable, in the main he could act only with the consent of the Chancellor. The countersignatory powers of the latter covered every conceivable act of His Majesty, including speeches and letters to relatives if these were members of reigning houses. As the Emperor would not appoint a Chancellor totally unacceptable to the Reichstag, since this would simply stop lawmaking, the Emperor's real power rested with dismissing a Chancellor whose policies or style he disliked, and calling elections.

In fact, excepting some intermittent periods of personal rule by William II, it was the Chancellor who governed most of the time (Huber, 1963:822). The Chancellor had a double responsibility: one vis-à-vis the Emperor, whose approval he needed to remain in office; another vis-à-vis the Reichstag, whose support he needed to put policy into practice. He was also responsible for all government departments for whose actions he had to answer to Parliament. Yet two points need emphasis lest the erroneous impression of a dictatorial chancellorship emerges. First, the Chancellor's actual power was quite contingent on his getting along with the Prussian ministers. Prussia covered two thirds of the empire; therefore imperial policy was very much contingent on Prussian governmental support. Any Chancellor who was to be an active leader needed to command considerable influence to retain that support. The usual practice of double-office incumbency involving personal union in the offices of Chancellor and Prussian Chief Minister was by no means sufficient to control the Prussian ministries, a fact that became painfully obvious to Caprivi (Röhl, 1967a:85). In fact, particularisms were so strong that the system actually needed as influential a leader as Bismarck to work at all smoothly. Second, the formal lodging of sovereignty in the Federal Council always gave a Chancellor the option to deny that any real center existed at all. Without a Reich cabinet and in a federation where the states exchanged ambassadors with each other, it could and rarely did happen that a Reichstag did not face any executive at all but, as Röhl (1967a:21) put it, "a nebulous, anonymous, faceless body fading away when attacked."

When the Chancellor had to answer to the Reichstag, this was a very restricted ministerial responsibility whose only enforcement means were bad publicity. The Reichstag lacked an effective no-confidence vote. All it could do was to subject the executive to severe public criticism and stop his salary. The latter measure of censure was never practiced (Huber, 1963:893). Parliament therefore could not itself determine the composition of the executive; neither could Parliament exert any direct control over the conduct of foreign affairs. Military alliances, any treaties that did not affect existing federal or state law, and the declaration of war remained outside parliamentary control. The executive could not by itself declare war but needed the consent of the Federal Council. This, however, was not a parliamentary institution. The Reichstag could only block the long-range effectiveness of the executive by refusing to grant funds. In the short run, all the Reichstag could do was mobilize public opinion. It is important to note, therefore, that the constitution itself provided the first factor for politics through mass agitation that proved destructive of the empire, since no effective ways existed to integrate conflicting mobilized interests. In practice this constitutional arrangement rather effectively insulated national policymaking from party responsibility. But it did not protect the executive against populist pressures. The ambivalence about legitimate sources for political innovation appears most evident in the relative powers of the legislative and the executive. Hardly anywhere else did theory and practice diverge as much. The written constitution allocated the right to initiate legislation to the Federal Council and Parliament, not to the imperial executive. This meant that the member governments as well as the representatives of the people were defined as legitimate originators of change, but the federal executive was not. In fact, however, the executive's right to propose legislation had been accepted as "in accordance with the spirit of the constitution" after a very short time (Huber, 1963:857). This constitutional change without amendment resulted most directly from the conservative forces in the Prussian state Parliament. In terms of the written constitutional requirements, the Chancellor could have proposed legislation to the Federal Council in his role as Chief Minister of Prussia. Yet in this capacity he was accountable to the Prussian Parliament, which, with a conservative majority securely based on the three-class suffrage system, could block modernizing proposals inimical to traditional interests. In order to emancipate the federal executive from a dependence on Prussia, Bismarck and the Federal Council succeeded in establishing the right of the Chancellor to propose federal legislation to the Council. This constitutional change was a result of the desire to circumvent particularist interests that interfered with what was regarded as national interest. And the consequent development of executive initiation in the legislative field rapidly turned the written constitution on its head by making the federal executive the most important initiator of change.

The social security legislation of the empire, involving compulsory health, accident, and old-age insurances, was prepared by the Reichs bureaucracy and submitted by the Chancellor. So was the legislation concerning unions, collective bargaining, and the setting up of arbitration procedures in labor disputes. The social security legislation had been passed in the 1880s and the labor legislation during World War I. Other examples of federal legislation dealing with preventive medicine for man and beast and with finance reforms could be cited. These modernizing reforms originated with the Reichs bureaucracy, a corporate estate of experts based on education, and specialist *Tüchtigkeit* (proficiency), which developed an explicit ethic of state service and neutrality vis-à-vis societal interest groups (Huber, 1963:976–68).

Another index of the tendency to maximize executive power can be seen in the then current constitutional interpretation concerning the resolution of intralegislative conflicts in budgetmaking. The constitution demanded that a budget be passed each year. It also required the executive to spend expenditures as voted by the Federal Council and the Reichstag. But the constitution was silent on what was to happen if the Council and the Parliament failed to agree on a budget. While this circumstance never actually occurred, constitutional thought at the time demanded that the Emperor declare an operating budget by emergency decree and subject it to post-factum legislative ratification in the succeeding session. The idea was that government must carry on regardless of a stalemate of conflicting interests (Huber, 1963:956).

A third index of the demand for high executive power may be seen in the unconstitutional manner in which the German Army was created and maintained. According to the constitution, Germany was to have a federal Army composed of the contingents of the armed forces of the states. As such, the armed forces would have been under full imperial command only during wartime. In fact, the imperial Army was created *praeter constitutionem* through bilateral treaties between the Prussian and other state governments. With some minor exceptions concerning officer appointments in the case of Bavaria, this transformed all state armies into one unified imperial Army, continuously under the command authority of the Emperor.

The relation between federal and state laws may serve as a final index for the preference for "strong government" or the dominance of the executive branch. Unlike the United States, Germany had no national Supreme Court specializing in constitutional issues. Whatever judicial control there was in this area had been assigned to the Federal Council. But while the original purpose of that institution was the protection of the rights of member states, it hardly ever altered federal laws infringing on states' rights. Instead, prevalent constitutional thought and practice at the time interpreted the supremacy of federal over state law as calling for change in the latter in case of incompatibility (Huber, 1963:956–68). Constitutional practice therefore moved in a direction favoring the unitary state at the cost of the confederation. I shall indicate in the next chapter that the same trend prevailed during the Weimar Republic.

Germans favored a "strong government." This found expression in relative dominance of the executive over the other branches. There were at least three areas in which no immediately effective parliamentary control existed. These concerned the makeup of the national executive (the Chancellor), the conduct of foreign policy, and the command authority over the armed forces. In all three the essence of the monarchical principle had been preserved. In these areas the Emperor was not just a figurehead who "reigned" but an actual participant in rule. And because of the absence of immediately effective parliamentary controls, one might designate that regime as authoritarian. But that feature was actually less a straightforward function of its design. It was more a consequence of societal values that emphasized activism, on the one hand, and entailed a high appreciation of value diversity, on the other. In imperial Germany no law could be created without Reichstag assent. And that meant that no particular national administration could act against a united parliamentary opposition for more than two sessions. But the high value dissensus in society made such a united opposition in Parliament a very unlikely event. And while the constitutional rules of the game certainly permitted the gradual transformation of the regime into a fully democratic one by the simple device of stopping all legislation until a Chancellor and cabinet truly serving at the pleasure of a Reichstag majority would emerge, the German parties in Parliament hardly ever formed stable coalitions in support of or opposition to a government with sufficient resolve to bring this about. As a result, imperial Germany was ruled by the management of shifting party coalitions in Parliament, coalitions whose party composition shifted from issue to issue. That mode of governance is "rule by interest constellations." And this style of political rule corresponded far better to a society as deeply divided in values as Germany than any type of rule based on substantive legitimation beliefs. It has been usual to view imperial Germany as a Junker-dominated *Obrigkeitsstaat* where preindustrial elites fought a losing rear-guard battle against the forces of modernization (Wehler, 1973). Let us turn briefly to voting data to see what light they can shed on this question: Premodern authoritarian polity, or domination by virtue of interest constellations?

Voting and System Support

The hypothesis that imperial Germany was ruled by interest constellations yields three propositions regarding the voting patterns before the First World War. First, support for the regime should show a long-term declining trend as one moves from the founding of modern Germany in 1871 to the eve of the war. The reason is charmingly simple. Rule by interest constellation rests on interest satisfaction. The rulers have to earn the right to rule every day. Therefore, the regime gets used up over time, just like a towel in a bathroom becomes smelly with repeated use. And so on the national level electoral support for pro- and antisystem parties should display a long-term secular decline for the former rather than fluctuations reflecting the varying fortunes of economic growth or foreign-policy concerns. Second, when looking at regional variations in regime support, Prussia should be the place where regime support falters first. Rather than shoring up the polity, the Prussians should turn out the most dissatisfied of all Germans. In Prussia, as shown earlier, the predominant value commitments were those of the corporatist society; and this was true among both the upper and the middle classes. And it is these corporatist values above all others that call for an active government that earns its pay every day. Now, the reader familiar with the German political scene may protest. He may recall that the Prussian state had a three-class suffrage system. While the franchise for the national vote, the Reichstag elections, had been equalized, the franchise for the Prussian state elections was one where the votes were weighted by income. This amounted to a partial disenfranchisement of the lower-income groups in Prussian state elections. And so, rather than reflecting anything about the impact of Prussian values with their insistence on earning one's right to rule every day, a greater disaffection from the imperial polity as reflected in Prussian Reichstag votes might be seen as a kind of protest vote against the political inequality so blatantly preserved in the Prussian three-class suffrage system. However, this alternative "protest-vote hypothesis" would call for the same rate of decline in regime support in the Rhineland as in Prussia; for being part of the Prussian state, the lower-income groups in the Rhineland were just as much disenfranchised in the state elections as the less well off elsewhere in the Prussian state. Third and last, if the imperial polity was a premodern authoritarian regime, the level of support it enjoyed should have been greater in rural than in urban-industrial regions of the country. In sum, the hypothesis of "domination by virtue of interest constellations" calls for three patterns in the Reichstag votes: (1) a secular decline in regime support on the national level; (2) Prussians leading all others in Germany in withdrawing regime support; and (3) small urban rural differences in regime support. Still, votes are a very fragile base of information concerning such issues.

From a motivational perspective, a vote, like love, is a many-splendored thing. Casting one's vote for the same party or candidate may result from many and conflicting interests and desires. That is why, at best, aggregate voting statistics provide only a crude indicator of regime support. Nonetheless, the Reichstag elections provide the best available mirror of the people's choice. The Reichstag suffrage was equal, universal male, and secret. But it had one source of inequality that gave greater weight to rural than to urban votes. The constituency boundaries had been set in such a way that one Reichstags seat was available for one hundred thousand inhabitants on the basis of the 1864 population census. Subsequently these boundaries were not revised, and urbanization and industrialization brought about an urban-rural imbalance such as one finds in many countries. But that imbalance affected those parties ostensibly supporting the monarchical system as well as those opposing it. The Socialists and Left Liberals, for example, clearly stood for change of the regime, while the Catholic Center Party and the National Liberals clearly favored its preservation. In the 1912 election, to take one year toward the end of the period where my hypothesis calls for maximum withdrawal of regime support, the National Liberals, the Socialists, and the Left Liberals all experienced parliamentary underrepresentation due to this urban-rural imbalance. That underrepresentation amounted to 29, 25, and 26 percent, respectively. The Catholic Center Party and the Poles, on the other hand, gained parliamentary overrepresentation by about 33 and 29 percent, respectively (Gabler, 1934:6–8). I shall have to rely on the distribution of Reichstags seats when answering the question whether the imperial polity enjoyed greater support in the countryside than in the cities. Therefore, it is important to note that the rural-urban imbalance in the votes did not systematically favor or disfavor opponents and supporters of the regime when treated in aggregate fashion. This imbalance did not only punish the

Table VI-1 Reichstag Voting, 1871–1912: Percentage of the Prosystem, the Antisystem, and "Other" Votes[a]

Year	Prussia			Rhineland			Southwest			South			Nation		
	Pro	Anti	Oth.	Pro	Anti	Oth.	Pro	Anti	Oth.	Pro	Anti	Oth.	Pro	Anti	Oth.
1871	77	15	8	87	7	6	90	7	3	59	10	30	71	19	10
1874	76	16	8	92	7	0	88	12	0	88	6	4	74	18	10
1877	73	20	6	92	7	0	87	13	0	86	14	0	71	20	9
1878	76	19	5	95	5	0	84	16	0	90	9	0	74	18	8
1881	59	37	5	89	10	0	77	23	0	81	18	1	60	31	9
1884	58	37	5	87	12	0	78	22	0	83	17	0	62	29	9
1887	65	32	3	89	9	2	84	16	0	83	17	0	67	24	9
1890	50	46	4	78	20	2	68	32	0	74	26	0	54	38	8
1893	50	42	6	82	17	2	61	36	3	60	27	14	51	37	12
1898	45	46	9	77	19	4	61	35	4	53	25	22	47	38	15
1903	44	48	8	75	23	3	59	35	6	60	26	15	47	41	12
1907	43	46	10	74	21	4	53	40	8	61	29	10	47	40	13
1912	38	53	9	68	28	4	54	43	3	52	40	8	42	47	11

[a]Prosystem votes = Conservatives, National Liberals and allied groups, and the Catholic Centrists; Antisystem votes = all Left Liberals and Socialists; "Other" = mostly particularists and splinter parties: Poles, Guelphs, Alsatians, etc. The national prosystem vote is a more conservative estimate than the regional estimates, since in the latter the votes for the Peasant League (*Bund der Landwirte*) and allied groups were counted as conservative votes. The Southern antisystem vote is probably underestimated since the electoral district of Munich was not included in the figures. The regional estimates derive from a compilation of the party vote by electoral district by Dr. W. Schulte of the University of Mannheim. His generosity in supplying the data is gratefully acknowledged. The regional labels correspond to areas used in the study of values above.

Sources: For the national vote: H. Gabler, "Die Entwicklung der deutschen Parteien auf landschaftlicher Grundlage von 1871–1912", inaugural dissertation, Friedrich-Wilhelms Universität, Berlin, 1934, p. 6; H. Rehms, *Deutschlands Politische Parteien*. Jena: G. Fischer Verlag, 1912, pp. 85–86; for the regional vote, 1871–81: *Statistik des Deutschen Reichs*, 1. Reihe, Bd. 14, S. V, 1–154; Bd. 8, S. II, 73–111; Bd. 37, S. VI, 1–86; Bd. 53, S. III, 1–50; 1884–90: *Monatshefte zur Statistik des Deutschen Reichs*, Jg. 1885, S. I, 105–47; Jg. 1887, S. IV, 1–43; Jg. 1890, S. IV, 23–00; 1893–1907: *Vierteljahresbefte zur Statistik des Deutschen Reichs*, Jg. 1893, S. IV, 1–55; Jg. 1898, Erg. II to III, Jg. 1899, Erg. II to I; Jg. 1903, Erg. II to IV; Jg. 1904, Erg. II to I; Jg. 1907, Erg. II to I, H to III, and H to IV; 1912: *Statistik des Deutschen Reichs*, Bd. 250, H 1–3.

parties favoring parliamentarism, as the Left Liberals and the Socialists; it also adversely affected the National Liberal supporters of monarchism.

With these qualifications in mind, one can use the distribution of Reichstag votes as a rough indicator of the level of popular support of the imperial regime. It is quite easy to divide the German parties into those supporting the constitution and those demanding full democratization of the polity. Their programs and the nature of their electoral campaigns leave little doubt on this point. The supporters of the monarchical system were the Conservatives, the National-Liberals, and the Catholic Centrists, at least since 1898; the outspoken advocates of full parliamentarization, on the other hand, were the Left Liberals and the Socialists (Röhl, 1967a:204, 250–51). In Table VI-1 I have called the former "pro-system" parties and the latter "antisystem" parties. It is further possible to represent the party votes by regions, such that this analysis of the votes parallels that of societal values in Germany.

Table VI-1 presents three findings. All of them support the contention that imperial Germany was ruled by interest constellations. First, note that one finds a secular decline in system support in the nation as a whole. The antisystem votes rises from just under one fifth in 1871 to just under one half by 1912 (see "Nation"). The prosystem vote shows a corresponding decline from just under three quarters to just under one half. Also, over the course of these thirteen Reichstag elections the rise of antisystem sentiment was a fairly gradual phenomenon. There were only two interelectoral periods when the antisystem vote jumped by 10 percent or more: in 1881 and in 1890. Second, in each election, the size of the antisystem vote in Prussia was larger than that of the other three regions. Further, the growth rate of the Prussian antisystem vote outstripped that of the other regions. Antisystem sentiment had already passed the one-third mark in Prussia by 1881. In the Southwest that occurred in 1890; in the South only by 1912, while the Rhenish never turned that much against the empire. Third and last, a comparison of the antisystem vote in Prussia and the Rhineland completely contradicts the "protest-vote hypothesis." Considered on a regional basis, the imperial polity received its highest level of support from the Rhinelanders. From the election in 1874 to that in 1912 the prosystem vote of the Rhinelanders was larger than that of any other region in the nation, and it was especially and consistently larger than the corresponding Prussian vote. Now, the lower-income groups in the Rhineland were just as much relatively disenfranchised in Prussian Landtag elections as those labeled Prussians in the table. But over two thirds of the Rhenish retained allegiance to the empire until the last election in 1912, while Prussia was the only region in

Table VI-2 *Industrial and Agricultural Constituencies and Their Reichstag Representation in 1907*[a]

	Industrial urban	Industrial rural	All industrial	Agricultural	Total
1 Conservatives and National Liberals	35	47	82	57	139
2 Catholic Center	35	32	67	46	113
3 Liberal	27	14	41	09	50
4 Socialist	47	04	51	—	51
5 Other	09	15	24	20	44
					(397)
1–2 Status-quo parties:	70	79	149	103	252
3–4 Liberal and Socialists:	74	18	92	09	101

[a]Adapted from H. Gabler, "Die Entwicklung der deutschen Parteien auf landschaftlicher Grundlage von 1871–1912," Inaugural Dissertation, Friedrich-Wilhelms Universität, Berlin, 1934, p. 16.

the nation where a majority of the electorate had turned against the empire by that time.

And what about urban-rural differences in regime support? Can it be said that the imperial polity was a Junker-dominated authoritarian regime, supported by peasant allegiance and grudgingly tolerated by a disaffected industrial and urban population? So far as one can see from Reichstag mandates, the answer is no. Available for only 1907, Table VI-2 shows quite clearly that the status-quo parties outranked the antisystem parties in "all industrial" regions quite significantly. Even in the "industrial urban" regions the antisystem parties gained just a tiny plurality of four seats over the status-quo parties. Of course, antisystem sentiment in the empire was higher in the modernized portions of the country; indeed, it was practically absent from the countryside. Nonetheless, as clearly shown in Table VI-2, the view of the imperial polity as an outdated regime supported by the forces of tradition and opposed by those of modernization finds little support in available voting data.

In the absence of survey data where the people tell a pollster why they vote the way they do, what one can learn from analyzing voting statistics remains precarious. Keeping that limitation in mind, what has been learned here points to rule by interest constellation. The most important factor in that interpretation was the fact that the Prussians were the spearhead in withdrawing support from the imperial polity. I shall show in the next chapter that the Prussians also forged ahead of others in withdrawing support from Weimar democracy. To the Prussians symbols of legitimacy did not matter much; what mattered was regime effectiveness. And while electoral returns reflect this political culture orientation better for Prussians than for anyone else, it was a dominant trait in German political culture at large. Germans always lived in segregated political communities, in one great "negative integration" with each other rather than as a "nationalized community." This emerges clearly from an analysis of Reichstag election returns by party from 1871 well into the Weimar Republic until about 1928. Throughout this period one finds extraordinary stability in electoral support for four parties, or better, groups of parties: the Conservatives, the Liberals, the Catholic Centrists, and the Socialists (Lepsius, 1966a). Controlling for slowly rising voting participation rates as well as population growth over this period, it turns out that these parties lived with each other in a kind of peaceful coexistence like the separate denominations of the Christian Church that had lost their missionary ardor. No party made significant inroads on the electoral turf of another. All integrated their segregated clienteles or political customers around different key issues, which also served, in turn, to preserve party loyalty. The Conservatives had formed a following around the conflict between monarchical loyalty and democratization. The Catholic Centrists had formed their political community around the issue of education in the struggle between Church and state. The Liberals, professed champions of democratic equality, rallied their supporters against the "reactionary forces" of conservatism on the one hand, and the specter of the dictatorship of the proletariat on the other. And the only political force that grew significantly with the industrialization of the economy were the Socialists. But even they were able to organize only about one half of the industrial proletariat in Wilhelminian Germany (Lepsius, 1966a). Now, because this fourfold party system was so stable in Germany, one can generalize the "negative integration" thesis developed for the Socialists (Fraenkel, 1958; Roth, 1963) and apply that metaphor to all four political communities in Germany. Whatever their "sound-and-fury rhetoric," all four of these political milieux lived so peaceably with each other because parties in Germany served primarily to protect some way of life from encroachment by others. For forwarding demands to the national center, though, Germans used organizations other than parties.

This essentially defensive and culturally protective role of the German party system also emerges from a study of their organizational forms. Nipperdey (1961) concluded that the parties before 1918 were vehicles for pronouncements on *Weltanschauungen* more so than instruments deployed to bring about change in society. Excepting the Socialists, their organization was highly decentralized and characterized by an antiquated, dilettante leadership of honoratiores. The parties were characterized by an incapacity to produce effective leadership, powerlessness, absence of responsibility, and low prestige among the population. Instead of developing realistic policies, they only "quarreled" with government. In cases where there was a mass organization, the latter sometimes was auxiliary to, sometimes dominating the party. But in general the mass organization was always relatively independent of the party and therefore yielding a pattern quite different from that of Communist parties and their front organizations in the recent history of Eastern Europe. The Socialists of prewar Germany were supported by the unions, but the latter also changed the party toward taking more accommodating and "realistic" policy positions (Roth, 1963). In the case of the Conservatives, the Agriculturalists *(Bund der Landwirte)* practically owned the Conservative Party for many years (Puhle, 1966). Similarly, the Catholic *Volksverein* was always more than a mere appendage to the Center Party (Ritter, 1954). These mass organizations were the mobilizers of the people.

It might be said that this extraparty source for mobilization kept the masses neutralized vis-à-vis the party more than vis-à-vis the national polity. If so, it probably had a double effect. On the one hand, the noninvolvement with parties permitted considerable degrees of party-leadership autonomy in the absence of charismatic party leaders. On the other hand, it supported the idea that parties should not touch the national center "hovering above" societal diversity. While Nipperdey (1961) sees this as a result of the primitive organizational structure of the parties, at least two reasons shed some doubt on this view. First, if the parties were to be seen as incompetent organizationally, as Nipperdey describes, it remains a bit of a puzzle why such perceived incompetence never eroded party loyalty and recruitment. Second, the mass-based propaganda organizations were not characterized by primitive organization. Why would the Germans organize effectively for propaganda but not for the parties? The mass organizations were also ostensibly political, though they belonged to the "save the nation" or "save the Church" variety, emphasizing universal instead of narrow partisan and social diversity. If by "quarreling" one means defense of *vested rights*, one may conclude that "parties that only quarreled with government" were precisely the kind of political parties that Germans, apprehensive about their value differences, preferred. On the other hand, for making government do what *vested interests* demanded, the leading cadres used mass and propaganda organizations. Far better than parties where the voting procedure would force the recognition of value differences, such organizations could claim to address some ostensible national interest. Beyond the reach of votes in a recurrent way, reliance on mass and propaganda organizations allowed one to pursue one's objectives without accountability. And given the insecure national unity, such a political division of labor seemed the "appropriate thing" to do.

On the Emergence of Mass Politics

Structurally, the imperial polity was a "top-heavy" one. In terms of bureaucratization the executive was far more developed than the weak parties and Parliament. But this combination yields but limited validity to the image of the polity as an authoritarian state where the monarchy, the higher civil and military bureaucrats, and an alleged Junker caste "hovered above" divided social forces dominating the parties. The parties aside, little else was dominated by the top. Even Wilhelminian Germany had no united ruling class, self-confident about shared interests, and in control of what issues could become public and which were kept out of the political domain. The history of mass and propaganda organizations provides ample evidence on this point.

By the latter half of the nineteenth century, Germany was not a traditional communal society anymore. Especially around the turn of the century, associations of many kinds grew by leaps and bounds. From the singing club to the nationally organized special-interest association, there was no dearth of opportunities for joining. The old adage "three Germans, a club" carried considerable reality. Insofar as sheer affiliation with intermediary organizations can serve as an index of integration (Kornhauser, 1959), the lot of Germans was not that of the isolated, atomized mass man. But they were integrated into a plurality of warring groups. In the absence of a comprehensive survey of all nationwide organizations, one can gain only a glimpse of this apparent plethora. In seventeen pages of his study on the Agrarian League, Puhle (1966:143–59) mentions about thirty other organizations; and that number by no means covered all. Some of these organizations were very large; others were small. Among the former was the Navy League, reporting a membership of 1 million in 1906. The Catholic *Volksverein* had 800,000 members in 1914; the Agrarian League reported 330,000 for that year, while memberships in excess of 100,000 could also be found among the National Antisocialist League and the German Nationalist Office Trainees Association (Puhle, 1966:150, 37). Of intermediate size with membership in the tens of thousands were the Association for Germanism in the East *(Verein zur Förderung des Deutschtums in den Ostmarken)*, the National Security League, the German School Association, and the Pan-German League. Among these, the Pan-Germans were the smallest. In 1912 they had a membership of 17,000 organized in 239 locals a year later. The largest was the Germanism Association, which recorded a membership of 52,000 in 1909. All of these were patriotic organizations. Their membership and leadership were predominantly middle ·class. Among the Pan-Germans, two thirds or more of the officers of local branches were teachers, businessmen, or officials. The same held true for the leaders at the district level; and in 1906 and 1914, 57 percent and 62 percent, respectively, of the total membership belonged to these three occupations. The Pan-Germans published a weekly and an annual handbook, but subscriptions to the former remained below 9,000. Their propaganda impact was therefore relatively small. Income and expenditures of this organization grew from 22,000 marks in 1894 to just over 100,000 marks in 1907. They also managed to send between 15 and 34 of their members to the Reichstag, with most of these (61 percent) belonging to the National Liberals or the Reichspartei, and the remainder to the Conservatives and two small middle-class parties. The Anti-Semites, on the other hand, belonged among the smaller groups, with a membership in the lower hundreds. In contrast, with a membership of 1 million, the Navy League is instructive. In 1906 its paper, *Die Flotte*, sold 300,000 copies. During the same year one of Germany's two mass parties, the Socialists, reported a membership of only 385,000. The local press apart, the national paper of the SPD, *Vorwaerts*, only had a circulation of 52,000. In short, several of the voluntary organizations were considerably larger than most of the parties; some of the voluntary organizations dwarfed even the largest political parties (Wertheimer, 1924:58–77, 121–36; Röhl, 1967a:255; Kruck, 1954).

Looking at the organizations listed by Puhle reveals three interesting characteristics. Imperial Germany had organized Anti-Semites and organized Anti-Anti-Semites, Agrarians and Anti-Agrarians, a Socialist Party and an Anti-Socialist League, Industrialists *(CVdI)* and Anti-Industrialists *(BdI)*, with the former representing heavy industry and the latter secondary industry; and a Navy League as well as a kind of Anti-Navy League *(Freie Vereinigung für Flottenvorträge)* (Kehr, 1965:142–43; Nipperdey, 1966). First, then, there was some tendency for each nationally organized special interest to spawn its relatively issue-specific counterorganization. Second, about one fifth of the organizational labels encountered in the study by Puhle included the term *Bund*. While occurring only in a minority of cases, it still reveals an interesting feature of these intermediary organizations. To varying degrees most of them constituted ideological associations. Whether the ostensible objective was the advancement of an economic interest, as in the case of the industrialists, or of a pure and direct *Weltanschauung*, as in the case of the Pan-Germans, expressive symbolism played an important role in most cases. The pursuit of material interests was typically accompanied by pronouncement of lofty ideals, and one was promised salvation from alienation. Third, these organizations are very difficult to classify in functional terms. They acted like a party in mobilizing public support for national policy. But they also acted like a typical pressure group, not only because they operated in the legislative chambers, but primarily because they enjoyed electoral immunity. As one did not normally vote for them, one could not hold them accountable for the consequences of their agitation and influence peddling. Failure in attaining societal objectives could be blamed on the executive alone. Finally, these organizations also acted like value movements or near-totalitarian parties in that they engaged in mobilization from the top down and made extensive use of direct value appeals. Keeping in mind this triple characteristic of the use of value appeals, electoral unaccountability, and mobilization from the top, one might designate them as agitprop pressures. The Navy League provides the best example. Officially created to "have a centralized mass movement at the Kaiser's disposal at all times," it actually became as much an arm of the Navy Command, industrial interests, and the Pan-Germans (Röhl, 1967a:245–55). In addition, diverse interests often banded together in a kind of ideological holding company. The Cartel of Achievement Estates *(Kartell der Schaffenden Starnde)*, for example, was a national propaganda collective of the Agrarians, the Industrialists, and a conglomerate of militant middle class groups themselves organized in the National Middle Estates Association *(Reichs-deutsche Mittelstandsvereinigung)* (Puhle, 1966:161–63). Thus if the essence of mass politics lies in the mass mobilization of diverse interests in the absence of institutionalized mechanisms to aggregate and integrate them, then Germany's agitprop pressures signaled its emergence already during the empire.

The agitprop pressures provided for their members a mild kind of involvement with liturgical association. Compared to the national liberation festivals earlier in the century, these liturgical forms of the Second Reich lacked spontaneity (Mosse, 1975:93). They were engineered from above, providing spectacles for an audience. Nonetheless, whether he read his paper or pamphlets, attended mass meetings or "lectures," the member received assurance concerning an interpretation of society. He learned that whatever ailed the world had one and only one correct explanation, and he also "experienced" that there were thousands like him, who believed as he did. For those outside the tightly integrated subcultural *communities* of the Socialists and the Catholics, however, such assurance on beliefs and the maintenance of hope were all the benefits derived. Beyond that the individual still had to face the world of daily routines on his own. For the oligarchic elites, on the other hand, agitprop pressures provided employment, avenues for status advancement, and honoraria. For the functionaries there was employment and the chance to gain political prominence; for professors (frequently hired as experts), a side income and the lure of fame; for the sponsors behind the scenes, a chance to steer legislation to one's advantage.

Unfortunately, no exhaustive study of Germany's propaganda organizations seems to exist. An impression of how they probably worked can be gained, therefore, only from individual cases. The agrarians and the industrialists would seem to be the most suitable. The following account primarily draws on Puhle's (1966) study of the agrarians *(Bund der Landwirte)*.

During the nineteenth century the development of railroad and steamship transportation changed Germany from a grain exporter to a grain importer. For the East Elbian Junkers this meant unstable prices, foreign competition, and a general decline in economic security. Just how serious the situation was is reflected in the change of ownership among the eastern big estates. Between 1835 and 1885 about 87 percent of these had changed ownership, often at very reduced prices. By the end of the period only about 13 percent of the estates were still in the hands of Prussia's "old families." The prospect of losing their way of life led the Junkers to abandon their endorsement of the free-trade gospel and embrace protectionism instead. It also led them to discard their engagement in multiple and uncoordinated farmers' associations and their merely informal lobbying in the Reichstag, and to seek centralized organization and public-opinion management instead (Puhle, 1966:17–29; Kehr, 1965:84–85). Lobby activity had proved an insufficient instrument. Their alliance with the industrialists, their partners in the unstable iron-and-rye coalition in the Free Economic Bloc of the Reichstag dating from 1868, had already once become dependent on Bismarck's intervention and had gained them only limited advantages. To them the famous coalition appeared as an uneven alliance in which the industrialists gained much more than they themselves. The coalition really broke down in the 1890s, when Caprivi actually lowered already ineffective grain import tariffs by one third in order to facilitate industrial exports (Böhme, 1966:535, 561–64). They therefore looked for more effective ways to protect their interests, which above all meant gaining independence from such unreliable partners as the industrialists and the executive.

Bismarck's use of public opinion in his handling of the *Kulturkampf* and the anti-Socialist laws had already pointed to an unmined source of power: populist pressure. They could take a further cue from the Association of Iron Manufacturers, which in 1878 demonstrated what was to become Germany's new politics. Instead of acting as a classic lobby, this group had mobilized public opinion and directed it against the executive (Böhme, 1966:388). This skeleton of a tactic the Junkers perfected into the agitprop pressure technique by adding five elements: (1) centralized nationwide organization for propaganda; (2) infiltration of government bureaucracy at various levels; (3) pressure on Parliament as well as on the executive; (4) infiltration of one political party to the point of acquisition; and (5) the financing of election campaigns for the candidates of many parties in exchange for legislative support.

The Agrarian League was founded in 1893. Membership, growing from 100,000 in the 1890s to 300,000 by 1914, was composed of less than 1 percent of great estate owners *(Grossgrundbesitzer)*, 75 percent of medium and small farmers, and about 20 percent of artisans in towns and cities. During the first three years the East Elbians predominated in the membership; later the majority came from the western regions. The organization's membership therefore crosscut three cleavages: class, region, and urban-rural. This feature provided the basis for the development of a radical middle-class nationalist ideology (Puhle, 1966:37–38; 101–3).

Concerning organizational structure, the agrarians featured a presidium composed of a 3-man board, a civil-service staff with pension rights of 353 officials and 407 full-time employees without job-tenure rights. As to the presidium members, 2 were from East Elbia, 1 was an aristocrat, 1 a professor of history, and 2 were landowners. Serving on the board was a full-time occupation. There were no factional conflicts before 1914. It should be emphasized that the staff listed excludes blue- and white-collar employees in chemical plants, fertilizer firms, agricultural-machine companies, and purchase and sales cooperatives operated by the agrarians as well. The staff listed is only that of the propaganda apparat, including a publishing house, 5 newspapers (1 of which appeared twice daily), and 25 periodicals. This propaganda empire had its headquarters in Berlin and engaged in nationwide media and election campaigns. The organization maintained election managers in 250 electoral districts. The vast majority of these were in Prussia; just over one half of the managers were large estate owners, and about 30 percent were also aristocrats. Concerning stratification, the only point of interest here was the fact that the high aristocracy and the really rich owners did not participate in the affairs of the organization. It was one created for the defense of the status-threatened (Puhle, 1966:41–68).

With respect to money, annual membership fees for the period 1894–1902 averaged about 500,000 marks. The operating budget in 1907 was just 1 million marks (Kehr, 1965:131; Puhle, 1966:46). This was still rather modest compared to the financial muscle of the Navy League or the industrialists. The former's voluntary contributions in some years came to nearly 500,000 marks. The latter spent an estimated 3 million to 4 million marks on the 1912 national election alone (Kehr, 1965:144; Nipperdey, 1966:378). Since such statistics do not differentiate between ordinary membership fees and donations from wealthy supporters, it is difficult to estimate how much worth the mass membership attached to the liturgical services rendered. Kehr (1965:144) concluded for the Navy League that membership fees probably outranked individual grand gestures of the wealthy many times, at least for the years 1901–3. Still the agrarians could pay a 10 percent dividend on publishing investments in 1910, suggesting that the mass clientele spent considerable sums on the printed media (Puhle, 1966:49–55). All one can say with some certainty is that there were millions of Germans who deemed it worth their time and effort to support a variety of organizations supplying them with beliefs about society and some hope to translate ideals into practice.

If one takes the existence of a serious competitor as a standard, the agrarians had become the only effective political representative of the German farmer by 1909. In Prussia, including the Rhineland, the organization's functionaries had infiltrated the Chambers of Agriculture

(Landwirtschaftskammern), where they served provincial governments in an advisory capacity. In the Prussian East they had also penetrated into regional government and into another agitprop pressure, the *Ostmarkenverein*. These groups collaborated in importing cheap Polish migrant farm labor. Ideologically the agrarians cooperated with the Anti-Socialist League, the German Students' Association, and above all with the Pan-Germans, who served as an ideological holding company providing many agitprop pressures with "spiritual weapons." The agrarians' relations to the Navy League and the colonial interests were coolly neutral, while the Anti-Semites, Naumann's *"National-Soziale"* (patriotic social reformers), and the Socialists were their declared enemies (Puhle, 1966:143–51).

More important for their efficacy, however, were research and information services supplied to Reichstag deputies. They could fill a desperately felt need there because the early imperial legislature was quite unprepared to handle technical problems. In the 1879 tariff debates, for example, the M.P.'s had no clue as to the consequences of the proposals they were to decide (Nipperdey, 1966:373). Finally, concerning electoral efforts, the agrarians used a three-pronged attack: (1) They put up their own functionaries for office in the Reichstag and the Prussian landtag. (2) They ran their members as candidates of the two conservative parties. (3) They offered electoral-campaign aid to the candidates of all other parties save two, the Socialists and the Left Liberals. In all this the agrarians succeeded brilliantly. In the 1898 Reichstag election nearly one quarter of the elected M.P.'s were members of the Agrarian League. During subsequent years to 1912, between one fifth and over a third of the Reichstag deputies were either members of the agrarians or had been elected with the aid of the organization and so were obligated to support its program. As to political parties, the agrarians practically owned the German Conservative Party's parliamentary section in the Prussian Landtag and commandeered the allegiance of one half of the M.P.'s of the Free Conservatives as well (Puhle, 1966:168–70).

Opinion seems to be divided as to what this electoral success augured with respect to controlling legislative votes in the House. While there remains little doubt of the agrarians' influence in the Prussian legislature, the Reichstag story seems less clear. They did, of course, maneuver themselves into appropriate committees, exerted pressure on the House leadership, traded favors, and in general acted in the style of contemporary parliamentary operators. Nevertheless, Nipperdey (1966:374) granted all pressure groups only limited success, feeling that they were successful only if they did not meet with strong opposition—for example, on issues like the liquor tax and tobacco excises, but not on "the big issues." Puhle's (1966:202, 243) findings on the agrarians agree in part but also show that the threat of withdrawing future campaign support proved an effective control on legislative votes. Given many pressure groups of the traditional kind and many agitprop pressures, and the fact that such organizations as the agrarians, the Navy League, and the industrialists were either the largest or the most wealthy, the truth lies probably somewhere in between.

For present purposes the general level of success in legislative action is not important. What matters is that agitprop pressures led to a legislative development that, once set in motion, could not be stopped and inevitably led Wihelminian Germany into unmanageable foreign relations. Beginning in 1897 and extending at least to 1902, the agrarians consistently voted for fleet-construction bills sponsored by industrialists and the Navy League. In exchange the other side voted for tariffs restricting grain imports (Puhle, 1966:141; Kehr, 1965:166). This simultaneously alienated England and Russia pushed Germany into diplomatic isolation and doomed her attempt to change the balance of power in Europe. Rather than seeing in this the mere coincidence of partially conflicting class interests leading to the use of foreign policy as a permanent instrument of class warfare (Kehr, 1965:165), it was more likely the natural outflow of the emergence of systematic mass politics in a polity with weak integrative institutions.

What agitprop pressures did was to supply a systemic aspect to practices of infiltrating the executive branches and arousing and manipulating public opinion that had already existed before. A few examples may be in order. In 1876 sections of the provincial administration in the West *(Regierung Düsseldorf)* had become spokesmen for the industrialists. The formation of eight pressure groups in the Reichstag specializing in tariffs had led the industrialists to deploy a strategy of information saturation. They flooded the executive (Reichskanzleramt), other provincial and regional governments, and the Reichstag deputies with expert reports. These practices were but an inflated continuation of the quasiparliamentary bureaucracy of the pre-1848 Prussian style of government by seminar. Now, however, with many more participants and mobilized mass sentiment, this technique failed to work. Spectacular PR shows in the form of national congresses attended by hundreds of industrialists, many professors, and the press had been launched in 1877, 1878, and 1893. Sometimes these advocated tariffs, sometimes Army expansion. Using the press to intimidate executive rivals in the ministerial bureaucracy had been used by insiders—for example, Posadowski—as well as by the grand old man in and out of office, one of the more spectacular of Bismarck's instances being the publication that Germany's secret defense alliance with Russia had not been renewed (Böhme, 1966:426–59, 485; Röhl, 1967a:111, 155, 207). Formal organization systematized these multipronged efforts to get one's way. With multiple agitprop pressures, however, this was also the beginning of the systematization of systemlessness in Germany's political inputs.

On the day-to-day operative level one key to understanding the growth of systemlessness in political demands resides in a monarchical system that made the executive branch the most important immediate initiator of legislation. Once an agitprop pressure had made the executive respond, success in the national Parliament was nearly guaranteed, for agitprop pressures transformed particularist issues into vital national interests that no one could oppose. Just as a vote against Bismarck had signaled a vote against the empire, so after his dismissal, a vote against the government increasingly became one against the nation. One's position on tariff legislation and the fleet-construction program had become an index of one's national loyalty (Böhme, 1966:474–572; Nipperdey, 1966:372). To a fateful degree this made the practitioners of mass politics the long-run victims of their own techniques. The agrarians, for example, seldom succeeded in stopping a Reichstag legislative drive for some ostensible national interest no matter how much inimical to their interests. Their only recourse was the use of state jurisdiction. Only from their safe bailiwick, the Prussian assembly, could they stop measures they did not like (Puhle, 1966:241).

Germany's new politics had been introduced by Bismarck. But while his tremendous personal prestige allowed him to remain master over the ambitions he mobilized, his followers lacked that capacity (Böhme, 1966:419; Röhl, 1967a:50–55). The Wilhelminian polity had the façade of a beautifully orchestrated concert, where Bülow made *Weltpolitik*, Miquel specialized in coalition-building and support mobilization, and Tirpitz built the grand fleet. The reality, however, was an ever-increasing level of noise where each of many agitprop pressures treated society and polity as nothing but an opportunity setting for its interests. For the Navy command, Germany's foreign policy, her government, her constitution, and her domestic political conflicts were all to be adapted to the needs of fleet construction. More or less the same held for the Army, the Junkers, and the export and import interests. No one shied away from creating conflicts in order to advance his particular interests. All claimed to be dedicated to the nation. To swamp the public realm with nationalist messages in order to gain a competitive advantage for resource mobilization against others was the universal practice. Navy propaganda, for example, was spread through fifteen hundred newspapers. A willing professoriat, including some of Germany's most illustrious names such as

Delbrück, Schmoller, and Max Weber, was deployed to fight the propaganda battle at innumerable public lectures and in print. The anti-Navy League employed their own professors. The Colonial Association sponsored hundreds of "academic talks," and printed and distributed hundreds of thousands of pamphlets celebrating the theme of the world-historical role of sea power. This indeed was mass mobilization of political support in the grand style (Röhl, 1967a:168, 253–55). And under its cloak the most diverse of interests could be pursued. Three more illustrations may suffice to establish the very likely arrival of mass politics during the empire. The first concerns the relation between the Junkers and the industrialists; the second the spiraling of fleet and Army budgets partially resulting from that relation; and the last the pattern of war-aims debates.

To the agrarians the industrialists symbolized "modern society," a model of the good society that was anathema to traditional Junkerdom, which rejected "Westernization." To be sure, unlike the Left Liberals, the economic bourgeoisie only wanted to be "like England" in terms of her economic standing in the world. But for the Junkers, these were hardly more than academic distinctions. What is more, the industrialists used an argument to support fleet construction that constituted a double challenge to the Junkers. A fleet was indispensable, so it was argued, in order to enable Germany to break a possible food blockade by external enemies. Dependent on food imports, Germany would be lost without a fleet in such an emergency. This not only challenged the traditional supremacy of the Army in the defense establishment, it also diametrically countered the Junker claim for agricultural autarchy, which constituted the only chance to save their way of life in German society. Politically, if anything, the Junkers found Russian autocracy far more to their liking than any democratic Western forms. Yet the Junkers engineered a policy to shut off grain from Russia and turn her into an enemy. At the same time the Rhenish rich, more favorably disposed to England, pursued a fleet policy that alienated the English. Operating with the slogan "power and national independence are more important than wealth," the compromise meant the pursuit of wealth and opposed societal ideals at the expense of national security. The industrialists took England as their model, rejected Russian autocratic backwardness, but alienated the very society they considered exemplary. The Junkers acted in a similar fashion to Russia. During the last prewar decade this self-created encirclement by hostile powers and the self-generated internal conflicts became paired with a fatalistic acceptance of the inevitability of war. Fleet and Army budgets spiraled in mutually reinforcing fashion. Even though after 1902 the General Staff was opposed to further expansion of the Army on the grounds that too many "unreliable elements" were already wearing the uniform, a Reichstag fueled by agitprop pressures to grant money for anything ostensibly in the national interest kept the pressure on. Army expansion could be slowed down but it could not be stopped. The sage Bismarck had warned that Germany would be lost in any two-front encounter, but the country sailed precisely toward it. Moltke and Schlieffen erroneously believed that no capitalist economy could sustain prolonged warfare. Consequently they planned for blitz campaigns, but only in the West (Kehr, 1965:94–110; Böhme, 1966:450; Fischer, 1967:35–37, 86, 95).

Internal diversity was also mirrored in the war-aims debates. The industrial interests propagated the vision of a *Mitteleuropa*, a European economic community under German leadership, and the direct annexations of raw-material bases in Belgium and in the Don, Lvov, and Caucasus areas in the East. For colonial interests the war was fought to acquire a *Mittelafrika* belt. The Navy command insisted on the annexation of the Belgian coastline as a defense line against Britain. The *Ostmarkenverein* and allied *völkische* groups wanted a Polish frontier strip to repatriate Germans from Russia and expatriate Poles toward the East. For them, therefore, the war was fought to gain more *Lebensraum*. For the professoriat the war was to establish "the German spirit" and *Kultur* as a determining force for world history. For the German ruling houses the war was to rebalance the domestic political map, abolishing Prussian predominance in the empire. Toward that end, Bavaria's Crown Prince Ruprecht demanded the annexation of Holland for and the inclusion of Alsace-Lorraine into the Bavarian state. The Socialists' major newspaper, *Vorwaerts*, was telling the working class that they fought for the liberation of the Poles from the Czarist yoke (Fischer, 1967:101–17, 155–81, 239). For the Army the war was fought to improve Germany's future defensive posture, which meant acquisition of forts in the West, and a strategically advantageous frontier strip in the East. The specifics of these demands varied over time. But their general thrust toward conquest and the diversity of rationales and ideals involved remained constant. War-aims and internal politics were completely interlocked, making a mockery of the proverbial "state hovering above societal interests." By 1917 the monarchical groups insisted on a Hindenburg annexationist peace lest the inability of the system to reward the returning soldiers drive them into revolution. The antimonarchical forces insisted on a Scheidemann nonannexationist peace, and the conflict between the two drove Bethmann Holweg out of office. Here, then, the idea "what is good for one's own vested interests is good for the fatherland" had become the general maxim of action for multiple agitprop pressures. What was good for the Army, the Junkers, export, heavy industry, the colonial office, *Ostmarken* dreamers, the House of Wittelsbach, and *Kultur*, was also supposed to be good for the fatherland.

Veritably, the Germans were riding a tiger of mobilized aspirations they themselves could no longer control in the service of their own interests. Ethical strangers to each other, theirs was but a pretense of nationalism, one used as a cloak to treat political opponents with that statistical detachment that marks the believer in the bureaucratic cage of modernity.

Toward an Explanation of the Emergence of the Politics of Agitprop Pressures

While a more comprehensive theoretical interpretation of a practice of mass politics developed to the point of the abandonment of common sense will be presented in the last chapter, some of the ingredients of that theory can be provided best at this point. In explaining the emergence of agitprop pressures it seems useful to distinguish proximate from more distant factors. Among the former the more important would seem to be: (1) a continuing insecurity about national cohesion; (2) the absence of a unified ruling stratum; and (3) a severely inflated nationalist propaganda undermining the credibility of political leadership. Among the latter, Germany's value "system," with its pervasive heterogeneity and its dichotomization of the public-private domain, seems the most crucial.

Turning to the first, threats to national union were still felt in Wilhelminian Germany. Röhl (1967a:32, 80–81), for example, reports two instances where imperial court circles expected secession. In 1886 Philip Eulenburg, one of the most influential of the Emperor's advisers, expected a secessionist coup by anti-Prussian aristocrats in Bavaria. He feared that these enemies of the empire were aided by the Pope and "other foreigners." Such fears were widespread again in Prussian Government circles in 1892, when they were fueled by a turnover in personnel in the reigning Catholic houses of Austria and Bavaria. That such fears were more than the products of overanxious souls is illustrated by an explicit threat to leave Germany issued by the King of Wuerttemberg as late as 1912.

Concerning the power-elite problem, the single most important factor was the constitutional provision for a monarch who reigned and ruled. Regardless of how pervasive or intermittent, of how independent or "puppetlike" Wilhelm II's "personal rule" was, contrary to the Japanese Emperor, the German head of state could not be insulated against partisan politics. He was embroiled in politics, and the authority of his office suffered in direct proportion to the attempts of various groups either to find his support, or to blame their defeats on his meddling. With the bureaucracy having become the scene of partisan politics and an "engaged" Emperor, there was no institution strong enough to integrate conflicting interests all claiming to be supported by a mobilized public.

Another factor underlying the absence of a unified power elite was the corrupted Junker spirit. The agrarians and their ideological collaborators, the Pan-Germans and allied *völkische* elements, used a middle-class ideology that preached a warfare against class warfare. To traditional Junkerdom this was a class-alien outlook, suggesting that the Junkers were ready to speak a language of radical discontinuity from their traditional outlook. Thus Germany was not only characterized by sections of a "feudalized" middle class who had "lost their class honor" (Bramsted, 1964:191–236; Zorn, 1966); equally important was the "broken moral spine" of Prussia's elite have-beens. According to Born (1966:278), "under Frederick William IV Prussian conservatism was still a *Weltanschauung* (loyalty to the King was unproblematic), under Bismarck it was still a value tradition, but under Caprivi it became a mere interest position."

But this cannot be read as a simple time series from one state of reduced complexity to another—that is, from "loyalty to the King as natural as daylight," to "a mere value tradition," to "a mere interest group." In fact, the Junkers never became a mere interest group before 1945, which brought the official end of Prussia as a political entity and of the Junkers as a social group. The key to the Junkers' response to modernization was a severe emotional bitterness. These self-conceived pillars of the state saw themselves unjustly treated. They never sought predominance in wealth. They were even willing to accept economic privations if that had been a necessity for the health of the state, and one they could understand. But since they could not see why a costly fleet should be constructed to guarantee food supplies from abroad, which meant favoring the Rhenish plutocracy at the expense of their own role as the nation's food supplier and the primary pillars of the Prussian state, they reacted with deep resentment. In responding to the challenge from the merely rich, they tried to reconcile the unreconcilable and proceeded to fight a state that they had been brought up to serve. In this process they ended up calling for agricultural state socialism while supporting massive state subsidies for private profits in fleet construction in exchange for tariff stop-gaps in their declining economic fortunes (Puhle, 1966:32–53, 230). Relying on propaganda organization, allying themselves with questionable literati and ideologues, with the lower-middle class, and those especially adept in the presentation of verbose sincerity, they ended up in a web of lies and became dependent on precisely those strata they had been taught to despise. They could not even convincingly adopt a strategy of maintaining loyalty to the monarch and opposition to his government because constitutional theory and practice calling for an active monarch prevented it. Their alienation from central government had started in 1815, when the bureaucracy had interfered with their way of life by making real-estate property mobile (Koselleck, 1966). Just how contradictory their ideals and their action had become after one hundred years of an unwanted opposition role can be seen in the fact that these advocates of monarchical rule supported moves to spread the Communist revolution into Russia, Persia, India, Egypt, South Africa, and Eire, as a way to win in the First World War (Fischer, 1967:84, 120–52). A century of status threats and value conflicts had turned this erstwhile proud pillar of the Prussian monarchy into protofascists for whom belief and action, principle and tactics had become completely dissociated.

A third among the proximate factors was the inflation of nationalism. The nationalist groups sang the song of sectional and institutional material interests as well as the realization of different models of the good social order. The Socialists, on the other hand, preached the theme of class conflict and the future classless society in their papers, but they had actually made it quite clear that they would fight for the fatherland with as much loyalty as any bourgeois. They had announced their patriotism and renounced the general strike as early as 1905, repeated their position in the Reichstag in 1907, and reiterated it at party congresses in 1907, 1910, and 1911 (Groh, 1966). They also voted for war budgets and credits without a murmur until 1917, when internal factionalism (USPD) and a change in the fortunes of war made unproblematic patriotism rather problematic (Fischer, 1967:328). Yet the message output of agitprop pressures had been so massive that neither specific statements nor action altered one's views about others. The stereotypes of "Junker," "monopoly capitalist," "leftist-bourgeois," and "unpatriotic Socialist" had become fixed reference points of orientation. They had become the signposts of a definition of society that called for the ruthless pursuit of one's own interests and ideals against perceived multiple other moral strangers. And agitprop pressure politics had become the universal means. Somewhat like an inflationary economic mentality, the Germans had developed an inflationary political mentality—that is, a set of orientations that refused to recognize any intrinsic limits to power solutions.

Turning to the more distant factors, Germany's internal diversity at the value level not only transformed several old-established leading strata into one-dimensional elites, it also made them fear a loss of integrity through actual nation-building. Living among moral strangers, one had to be on guard lest "they take over" and create a society inimical to one's own cherished way of life. At the beginning this problem was particularly felt in Prussia. Her conservatives feared and resented the concessions made to the South. Giving sovereignty to the Federal Council led Prussian Conservatives to fear that Bismarck was ruining the Prussian state. The National Liberals concentrated in the West and the South of the nation still wanted a unitary state with an executive under parliamentary control. The Catholics resented Protestant predominance in economy and polity. The Socialists constituted a threat to self-proclaimed patriots, antiparliamentarians, and *"völkische"* groups (Röhl, 1967a:17–18). With increasing industrialization Socialist strength continued to expand, and the ideals of a liberal-bourgeois society gained ground. During the eighties it became apparent to the Conservative forces that the preservation of the monarchical system could not be guaranteed through an alliance with the National Liberals. Thus the Puttkammer era brought some realignment with the symbols of Christianity and a state engaged in a fused class-and-value conflict against the proletarian threat and its allied intellectual liberals. By the nineties a kind of triple alliance emerged that included the economic bourgeoisie, the military, and the civil bureaucracy. Oriented against the Socialists and the principled democrats, this alignment meant much more than simple class conflict. In fact, Bismarck's policy to forge an alliance of property against the poor had failed just as his attempt to let economic integration "spill over" into political integration (Kehr, 1965:67, 113; Rosenberg, 1931:37). For the Junkers any genuine alliance with Rhenish plutocracy would have implied adapting oneself to a much-maligned "commercial spirit." That would have constituted a loss of integrity. In 1891 the government's legislative program sailed through the Reichstag with rare Socialist support. The right, however, was upset about success "at such a price," while the left became impatient about rewards for their collaboration. Principles always played an extraordinary role. When a Prussian minister proposed to resign because the Landtag's opposition condemned him to inaction, Emperor and Chancellor persuaded him to stay for the sake of principle. During the nineties court circles saw the dilemma quite clearly. If you ruled moderately like Caprivi, the inevitable result would be the republic; but if you remained Prussian, the inevitable result would be the breakup of Germany, for Southerners would never accept the Prussian style. As the Emperor's Easter Message of 1917 with its vague promise of some change in Prussia's class suffrage and the ensuing protest in the Prussian upper chamber showed, these conflicts were never solved (Röhl, 1967a:76, 150, 192; Fischer, 1967:34).

Among the distant factors the single most important one, however, was value diversity and the resultant orientation to the political sphere as an inherently amoral one. This related directly to the emergence of mass politics by creating a demand for liturgical services among the population and an opportunity to exploit that demand among elites. By defining religious involvement solely as the achievement of "other-worldly in- sight," and the "this-worldly" social sphere as one of mere interests outside the realm of ultimate significance, modernizing social change created a huge demand for secular explanations. Such demands can be far better satisfied in societies where the leading groups share values than in a case like the German, where consciousness about value differences had led the educated to believe in the inevitable privatization of moral commit- ments in the modern world. In the former, like the United States, it remains a reasonable idea to suggest that a modern secular moral culture can be as binding on men and women capable of reason as the religious morality of an earlier day dictated it (Lidz, 1979). But to the one- dimensional elites of Wilhelminian Germany that proposition would have been sheer sentimentality. Let me elaborate briefly.

Everywhere modernizing change creates demands for special mecha- nisms to reduce moral complexity. The primary reason for this lies in the spreading belief that the social world is man's creation. Such a belief generates several sources of uncertainty. Three are of special relevance. The very realization that the extant social order constitutes man's creation makes that creation morally problematical. There is not just the usual gap between the real and the ideal; value commitments themselves become problematical. As Taviss (1968) pointed out, ideals become rather proble- matical when they shift from the realm of the unattainable to the realm of the realizable. Before that shift, men can maintain commitments to a variety of ideals with minimally reflected priority. But after, given the idea that one can never realize "everything," conscious priority decision- making is called for. Thus modernity makes morals themselves proble- matical. Also, if society is created by man, it can be different tomorrow. Therefore, second, the future becomes a source of uncertainty. Finally, position in society, our place in the division of labor, becomes a source of uncertainty. For if *homo faber* is the creator of his world, then participating in that creation in different ways very likely leads him to view it from different vantage points. Thus, third, the presence of others doing different work becomes a source of uncertainty. With uncertainty grow- ing, the demand to reduce it also grows. And where religion leaves a void, secular beliefs are likely to fill it.

For Wilhelminian Germans man's capacity to change the world had been a recent and very impressive experience. Theirs was a brand-new industrial society, and one that worked. Theirs was a brand-new modern unified nation-state, if one still insecure about national identity. And it had been power that had wrought these changes; and power, so it seemed, was *the* universal mechanism of complexity reduction. "Revolution from the top," and ultimately one powerful man, Bismarck, had created the nation. The new economy had been created by powerful personalities, Krupp "and people like that." Germany's Army had been victorious thanks to powerful men such as Moltke and Schlieffen. Indeed, with the right talent at the right place, nothing seemed impossible, if you had but the power. And so there was a demand to know what had happened, what was happening, and what was going to happen. Contrary to America, where the early state-Church separation had created a social structure suffused with universalist religious commitments, as de Tocqueville (1954:46) observed, the state-Church "arrangement" in Germany had left society a thoroughly secularized realm. Action in that realm was governed only by the universal service norms of *Tüchtigkeit* and *Sachlichkeit*, these classic virtues of the bureaucratic employee. Effectiveness in cooperation was the only "value" Germans could share; and that meant they were able to take a "strong nation" as much for granted as a self-evident common good as the gospel of economic growth in our contemporary world and one just waning now from its ruling position in conventional wisdom. In Wilhelminian Germany the idea "the more power the better" was as unproblematical moral as the notion "the more wealth the better." Investing power had come to be governed by standards of effectiveness, just like a prudent man invests money according to tenets of profitability. These matters were not supposed to have any direct religious or moral significance. But for active men having learned such an orientation does not signify the absence for a need of assurance that one is doing right. Liturgical services rendered by agitprop pressures provided that assurance. For Germany's one-dimensional elites, in industry and commerce, Army and Navy, academia, and the press, the demand for such assurance provided a golden opportunity to mobilize public sentiment for the pursuit of interests. Aware of living in a society of moral strangers, and dedicated to a secular outlook that shunned "sentimentalizing" all this-worldly activity, they could use ideological appeals in a purely instrumental fashion. Aware as well of a still fragile national unity, they "knew" what would legitimate demands: nationalism. Grasping on agitprop to pursue their interests, these oligarchs in Army, Navy, the *Hansabund*, the Pan-Germans, the agrarians, and the industrialists all *presumed* that "father state" would somehow integrate conflicting demands. At any rate, they did not care to make that their business. Thus the politics of agitprop pressures developed: first, because value dissensus invited it; second, because the constitution permitted it; and third, because the status insecurity inherent in one-dimensional elites fueled it.

The moral indifference of Germany's elites was, so I postulate, an outcome of value dissensus and elite-destratification. In this chapter this has been manifest in the pursuit of self-regarding policies, which led the country into a war constellation from which there was no escape. Nonetheless, the details through which such indifference became operative remain important, for it is in the details rather than the abstractions in which one can see history. Three of these details have been singled out for attention simply because they figured so prominently in the main show, the drive for empire. The first was a preference for "strong government." When opportunities arose to move in the direction of a more unitary state these were exploited in Germany's Second Reich. This led to distortions in Bismarck's federal structure. In the main, the gap between constitutional theory and practice was always closed by shifting the initiative in the policy process to the executive branch of national government, thus emasculating the theoretical sovereign, the Federal Council. Representative institutions, on the other hand, whether in the form of the party system or the Parliament, remained the weaker parts.

Corresponding to this, the patterning of the Reichstag votes revealed that Wilhelminian Germany was ruled by interest constellations. These data showed an impressive stability of electoral support for four major groups of parties, on the one hand, and a gradual withdrawal of regime legitimacy in which Prussia took the lead, on the other. The former pattern suggests that parties functioned primarily as organizations defending segregated political subcultures from interference and encroachment by each other. This eventuated in a pattern of negative integration in the country as a whole, and so resulted in the gradual erosion of legitimacy of the polity. Looking at electoral returns from urban-industrial and rural areas also indicated that the *Kaiserreich* was hardly experienced by the electorate as a premodern traditional polity. The considerable support the Wilhelminian polity received from the modernized sections of the country constitutes independent evidence for the assertion that domination by interest constellation characterized the Second Reich.

But while the parties remained by and large ineffectual, both by constitutional design and by party strategies in Parliament, which simply never forced the issue of parliamentarization, the Wilhelminian polity was one suspended into a very active society. Little wonder then that other organizations filled the gap and provided opportunities for participation in political life. These involved patterns of mass mobilization, patterns undertaken both by the national executive and by outside groups. In each case, though, ostensibly national goals served merely as masks for particular interests. The first pattern is illustrated by Bismarck's famous ploys of using the *Kulturkampf* and the anti-Socialist legislation for his own purposes. Wilhelm II's search for plebiscitary support, his attempt during the nineties to become the "*soziale Kaiser*," as well as his famous utterance of knowing no parties, only Germans, before the outbreak of the war fall into the same category. Yet what had been a serious matter for Disraeli—namely, an earnest desire to mobilize the marginal classes for the state—had in German hands turned into a mere tactic. One of the reasons here was that the latecomers to nation-building and industrialism stylized the problem of modernity, putting it "on a higher level," seeking not to copy the West but to find a superior form (Kofler, 1966:587–90). In fact, this "superior form" meant agitprop pressure politics, an approach eagerly grasped by many groups, feeling real or imagined threats or seeking new opportunities. The use of systematic organization for propaganda, lobbying, and infiltration of executive agencies coupled with an identical language of nationalist commitments were admirably effective means for the ruthless pursuit of particularist interests. But while individual groups profited for a while, the nation was driven on a foreign-policy course that led to war and defeat. The net effects of agitprop pressure politics were: (1) the politicization of everyday life; (2) the transformation of politics into detailed interest issues; and (3) the steady erosion of the capacity of the parties (Nipperdey, 1966:386) and the executive to integrate conflicting demands into more realistic national goals. The rampant nationalism provided only the most general of directions, a grandiose search "for a place in the sun." Characterizing Germany's entry into the First World War as an "original example of faulty brinkmanship" (Geiss, 1966) remains a very appropriate formulation.

None of these three features—the preference for a unitary state, domination by interest constellation, and agitprop mobilization of the masses—can be directly attributed to the authoritarian nature of the Wilhelminian polity. All three characterized the politics of the Weimar Republic as well, only in more intensified form.

CHAPTER SEVEN

Weimar and After: The Politics of Ideological Militancy

The German people are quite fair;
Each only claims his fitting share.
By "fitting" though, one understands,
What fits one's and one's cronies hands,
Everything else is too complex,
For such simple, honest intellects.

Goethe
(in Zahme Xemien)

Prologue

World War I apparently intensified Germany's two main political-action characteristics. Both the reduction of politics to the opportunistic pursuit of particular interests and the simultaneous search for some order-creating and order-maintaining center became more frantic. A study of the shifting tactical alliances among labor, industry, and Army during the war concluded that an ever-increasing practice of formal rationality among these groups led to a decrease in society's substantive rationality. The more vigorously the different parts of the nation pursued their own aims rationally, the less rational became Germany's pursuit of national goals (Feldman, 1966:519–33). Pressured from multiple sources and partly penetrated by outsiders, neither the executive nor the bureaucracy, neither the Army nor the Reichstag had been able to provide effective leadership for a nation at war. Rather than uniting the elites of various sectors in society, the war proved a divisive force, presenting new opportunities and a sense of increased urgency for status consistency and the struggle about the nature of the good society among a people so deeply

220

divided in their values and so conscious about that division. The pursuit of the war in conjunction with important disagreements about its aims, disagreements openly displayed in fierce public debates that everyone could see, had so delegitimated the Wilhelminian polity that "neither hand grenades nor machine guns destroyed imperial Germany, but rather a lack of faith in its own right to exist" (Eyck, 1963:II:173). After Auschwitz that verdict would apply to more than the political system; it would encompass the German nation-state; for while the elites during the First World War still cared about war aims that one could grasp in common-sense terms even though their very inability to come to any consensus turned their behavior into a contentless search for power, the latter had become the ruling principle of action among the various leadership circles under the Nazis to the point where historians have to study Hitler's philosophical and architectural interests to discover anything about his aims (Aigner, 1978; Thies, 1978). As in the First World War, so in the Second World War: The search for empire was importantly fueled by the striving for status consistency among one-dimensional elites whose relative status deprivation made them boundlessly self-assertive.

Weimar democracy was but an interlude in this story because a change in political regime remains far too weak a force to bring about more value consensus and consequent chances for re-stratification at the top of society. In fact, a lost war, the Versailles *Diktat*, and the very symbol of democracy with its legitimation of societal dissensus all combined to exacerbate rather than to attenuate Germany's structurally based aspirations for empire in which the concrete questions about the organizationally possible simply disappeared from the horizon of relevant concerns as did any caring concern with the fate of the concrete human beings involved.

The Versailles Treaty, perceived by many Germans as a national disgrace, burdened the new regime with the taint of impotence, while underwriting the war-guilt clause saddled it with a deeply felt moral humiliation. As Eyck (1962:I:126) put it, exaggerating only a little, "99 percent of the Germans believed they had been duped by the armistice." Also, the new regime, democracy, signaled that now numbers were really to count. For Germany's diverse segregated value communities, this amounted to an invitation to realize their disparate conceptions of the good society by intensified efforts at support mobilization. For the ultraleft Spartacus League, the new situation offered an opportunity to accomplish the dictatorship of the proletariat. For the majority Socialists, the trade unions, and the democrats, it meant a chance to bring the liberal society into being. They felt strongly enough about it to use the Army to crush the revolutionary left (Eyck, 1963:I:50–53, 1979; Halpern, 1965:188).

Beyond these two groups Germany had lukewarm adherents of democracy as well as those who yearned for the reintroduction of the monarchy. There were the republicans "of reason" rather than "of heart"; genuine monarchists, as among the supporters of Kahr in the South; and nationalist opponents to a democratic Germany, as among the Northern *Stahlhelm* and Hugenberg forces. An overtly antirepublican message was already broadcast in 1919 by a convention of the Pan-Germans (Turner, 1963; Halpern, 1965:191, 235, 269; Waite, 1952:266–81; Berghahn, 1966:6; Eyck, 1963:I:142).

Both the lack of legitimacy of the regime and the heightened but unintegrated political activities persisted. The first was reflected in the continuing pattern of revolution from above, the second in cabinet instability. While the end of World War I brought rebellion to Germany, there was no real revolution. The parliamentarization of the regime was initiated by the Emperor in response to Army pressure. The Emperor's abdication was authorized by himself and announced by his last Chancellor, Prince Max of Baden. Hindenburg, who had been instrumental in closing out the monarchy, had to conceal that fact forever after from the public and as much as possible from himself (Eyck, 1963:I:142–49; Reinhardt, 1962: 642–43). Hitler assumed executive authority with the aid of the President of the republic and could maintain himself initially only because that aid permitted him to draw on three sources of legitimacy simultaneously. These were: (1) rational-legal, through presidential appointment and coalition formation with the Conservatives; (2) traditional, through the conduct of ceremonies at the Potsdam garrison church and later at Hindenburg's funeral, ceremonies that symbolized the fusion of Wilhelminian with Nazi Germany; and finally (3) charismatic, through the conduct of liturgical rites at party conventions (Lepsius, 1968). Commitments to the "good society" were so fractionated in Germany that there was never sufficient thrust for a revolution from below. It seems likely that the Weimar regime could be established in the first place primarily because of the threat of foreign occupation; in its absence the later Nazi regime had to draw on diverse sources of legitimacy.

"Democracy," however, symbolized the opening up of new opportunities. It signaled the disappearance of the "authoritarian state" hovering above societal divisions, and a new freedom to attempt to translate one's vision into reality. A simple measure of political stability suggests the change. Comparing Chancellor turnover during the Empire with cabinet turnover during Weimar shows the following: The forty-eight-year-old Wilhelminian polity had eight Chancellors. The fourteen-year-old Republic had twenty cabinets. The average lifetime of an administration was therefore six years under the Kaiser and eight months under democracy

(Eyck, 1963:Appendices; Huber, 1966:III:159–60). In fact, Weimar compared quite well to the ill-famed French Fourth Republic, where average cabinet duration was about seven months (Macridis, 1963:139). Finally, if the use of plenipotentiaries by the *Führer*, the overlap of functions among the agencies of government and party, as well as the constant jurisdictional disputes among the many Nazi organizations can be seen as a totalitarian regime's "functional equivalent" to cabinet turnover, then political instability was rampant under the Nazis as well (Höhne, 1967).

To Germany's segregated value communities, "democracy" had meant that more could be gained *and* lost in the republic than under the *Kaiser;* for now the society was to be more "open" and government more responsive to the people. Almost the same, however, can be said for the regime change from Weimar to the Third Reich. Except for Jews, those identified as leaders of the political left during Weimar, and those contemplating a direct challenge to the *Führer*, the very dynamics of totalitarian politics and the absence of a rigid ideology created a virtually limitless range of opportunities for the advancement of any conceivable interest and cause (Schoenbaum, 1967).

With nonaggregable societal ideals and revolution from above, the change of regime from the empire to Weimar amounted to very little change in Germany's basic political pattern. Intense political mobilization continued, and so did society's inability to attain officially proclaimed objectives. Opposed fronts frustrated each other's ideals, lost legitimacy in the eyes of their constituents because of their ineffectualness, and so contributed to disillusionment with the regime itself. This chapter illustrates how the nationally suicidal nature of German political life was reflected in Weimar's constitutional history, the waning support for the regime, and the role of the militant organizations.

Some Aspects of the Weimar Constitution

A constitution can be examined as a statement of intent embodying the vision of the good society on the part of its formulators as well as their idea of a polity appropriate for it. The constitution makes an interesting document for our purposes for three reasons. First, it was fashioned by self-conscious democrats of socialist and bourgeois leanings amid the ruins of the defeated imperial order. As a contemporary put it: "They [the formulators] could be adjudged worthy of the greatest admiration if the historical background is remembered against which they worked—a picture . . . made up of defeat and humiliation, disappointment, starvation, revolution, and on top of it all, the despair generated by a peace treaty impossible of fulfillment" (Oppenheimer, 1923:4). Second, the constitution was never abrogated until 1945 because it lent itself to the legal introduction of totalitarianism, a result hardly anticipated by its creators. Third, both the negotiations concerning the original draft and the subsequent history of constitutional reform attempts illustrate clearly the divergent views prevalent in Germany.

Reflecting the desire for "strong government," the intent was to create a far more unitary state than the Wilhelminian polity had been. This was evident in a number of provisions. The relation between the federation and its seventeen *Länder*, as the former states were now called, was subject to the formal principle that federal law "breaks" state law (Article 13). Second, though the constitution remained silent on the details of tax collection and administration, with the exception of customs duties (Articles 6 and 134), an implementation law made these matters federal to the near-total exclusion of the states. The federation also took over such revenue-producing enterprises as the railways, and the postal and telegraph services. Third, the office of President, filled by direct popular ballot, was given more powers than had been allocated to the Emperor. The President could dissolve the national Parliament (the Reichstag) without the consent of the Upper chamber (Reichsrat) which had been necessary before. He could initiate a popular referendum against decisions of the Reichstag, and Article 48 gave him the authority to rule by emergency decree, using the Army to enforce his decisions, and suspending seven of the fundamental rights. These covered the inviolability of person, home, and property; the secrecy of the mail; and the freedom of movement, association, and the press (Huber, 1966:III:130–36, 145–48; Oppenheimer, 1923:29–30, 43). While dependent on Reichstag consent for such dictatorial powers, this safeguard was reduced by the fact that the President could dissolve the Reichstag at will and govern alone for sixty days before its re-election (Reinhardt, 1962:649). The number of times he could dissolve Parliament was not limited either. A kind of hypothetical limitation existed in the prohibition of more than one dissolution of the House for "the same reason." Yet the President gave the reasons, and whether he used the same twice could not be challenged with the force of legal consequence (Huber, 1966:III:160). Most important for rule by presidential decree was the constellation of political forces in Germany. Neither a Reichsrat if split by *Länder* particularisms, nor a multiparty system if productive of unstable House coalitions, nor a Chancellor dependent on an improbable majority House support could effectively oppose the President (Schulz, 1963:211). Article 48 then created more than an *Ersatz Kaiser;* it also created a potential dictator. The hopeful search for a power "above" divisive social forces had been firmly anchored in the constitution.

Moreover, rule by presidential decree was not the only constitutional provision for the abrogation of the separation of legislative and executive functions. Legislative tasks, principally assigned to Parliament, could be delegated by that body to the executive in the form of "enabling laws." The only limitation put on this source of dictatorship was the requirement that such laws had to serve "specific purposes" and that such delegation had to be specifically limited in time. Until 1923 seven such enabling laws were used. One authorized the executive to negotiate the armistice, three to transform the economy from war to peace conditions, one to ward off foreign encroachment on the monetary system, and two were general enabling laws to deal with the 1923 economic crisis. For the remainder of the republic, enabling laws were not used, resource being made to rule by presidential decree instead. In 1933, however, a Reichstag majority supportive of the Hitler-Papen cabinet "enabled" the transition of the regime. Hitler continued to draw on this legal source of legitimacy by three extensions. Only the last, in 1943, broke with formal legality by the failure to specify a time limit (Huber, 1966:III:185–88, 604). Thus while the constitution embodied the principle of differentiating legislative and executive functions, it also contained a considerable instrumentarium to fuse these functions "when the nation's interest seemed to call for it."

But fusion of legislative and executive tasks was not confined to the top level of government. This legacy of absolutism was permanently enshrined at lower levels as well. Here too this was not an emergency provision, but normal instead. At the provincial, district, and county levels of the Prussian administration, the agents of the *Land* government were engaged in executive, legislative, and frequently also judicial tasks. Excepting the provincial level of government, which the other *Länder* did not have, the situation was quite similar outside Prussia. The *Landrat* (county administrator) illustrates this fusion. He was a general-purpose administrator, supervising the police, conducting local elections, collecting taxes and statistics. His police functions were the most important because all regulations *(Verordnungen)* carrying the force of law were issued as police decrees. Implementing general directives in the area of mining, construction, factory legislation, public health, crime, forestry, land tenure, turnover, and income taxes involved issuing police decrees in the form of prohibitions. Thus the county administrator, an official of the Ministry of Interior, had a sort of legislative role. Though he had no direct authority over specialists—for example, the field agents of other ministries such as finance, Agriculture, and so on—they depended on the *Landrat*. Only he could facilitate their work. For example, if a veterinarian needed a quarantine ordinance, the *Landrat* had to issue a corresponding decree (Jacob, 1963). To avoid misunderstanding, I am not suggesting that the

county administrator had dictatorial powers. He was subjected to coun-
tervailing forces of representative institutions at provincial and county
levels *(Provinziallandtage, Kreistage)*, for example. I am merely pointing out
the central role of the national Ministry of Interior in the governance of
Germany, a role ever enhanced in importance as one moves from the
Kaiser's days to the end of the nation under Hitler.

Executive and judicial functions were also fused in Germany's administrative courts. Designed to curb and control administrative abuse, these
courts included civil servants in the role of judges, often the very officials
whose conduct had caused the complaint. Nevertheless, over time these
courts had developed a body of case law limiting administrative discretion
(Jacob, 1963:51–53). The Weimar constitution also provided for the fusion
of legislative and judicial functions in the national constitutional court
(Staatsgerichtshof). This court was to adjudicate conflicts between the
Länder, between one of them and the federal government, and between
national legislative and executive agencies. Membership on this bench,
however, included the litigants—that is, members of Parliament and the
Reichsrat (Huber, 1966:III:193). At the lower county level the Republic
did not alter the fused executive and legislative role of the county
administrator. If anything his use of rule by police decree was
strengthened, though his dependence on political parties in the county
council and county committee also increased. And while the Nazis simply
abrogated administrative courts at lower levels to free their agents from
judicial fetters, a genuinely independent court system did not develop in
Germany until after the division of the country, when it appeared in
contemporary West Germany (Jacob, 1963:100–5, 216, 176).

The desire for "strong government" and Germany's diverse values were
reflected in the constitution's rights catalogue, its provisions for amendments, and the composition of the Federal Council (Reichsrat).

If one important aspect of democracy lies in granting respect to
individual rights and protection to minorities, the rights catalogue, its
volume notwithstanding, in fact guaranteed very little to anyone. There
were hardly any safeguards against the use of political means to alter such
rights. Covering fifty-seven articles, organized in five sections dealing
with fundamental rights of the individual, social life, religion, education,
and economic conditions, the constitution was full of promise and short on
any real guarantees. Placing the collective interest squarely above individual desires was not only explicitly enshrined in Article 163, it also was
reflected in the absence of a genuine *habeas corpus* guarantee. The principle
of the "inviolability of person" in fact amounted to no more than an
instruction to the executive arm to explain to an arrested person on whose
initiative and why he had been deprived of liberty and to acknowledge his

protest. Omitting seven explicit specifications of duties from the rights catalogue, twenty-two, or 44 percent of the remaining rights, were in fact delimited by such formulas as "subject to legislation," or "within the limits of existing laws." Of the seventeen sections dealing with individual rights, eleven, or nearly 65 percent, were so delimited. For example, freedom of movement including emigration, was "guaranteed, subject to legislation." This meant that a law of 1919 enabled local authority to bar anyone from settling in a community because of a shortage of housing, and that a set of federal laws passed in 1919 prevented any well-to-do person from emigrating and staying well-to-do (Huber, 1966:III:145–54; Oppenheimer, 1923:192). Such provisions do more than illustrate the tension-ridden relation between legitimacy and legality, a characteristic of all modern societies. They show that in Germany legality had attained relative supremacy. The Germans had pushed that "faith in procedure," on which Max Weber's category of rational-legal authority rests, to a point where legitimacy interests ultimately could succeed only by extraprocedural means. Collective rights, especially if forcefully advanced, could count more on being guaranteed. But the guarantee of basic individual rights that found no agitprop spokesmen was necessarily always a precarious matter in a society as pluralist in values as this, and one that had carried the rational legalization of authority that far.

On the other hand, the rights catalogue was a genuine reflection of the diversity of often conflicting ideals. The polity was to protect the institutions of marriage and the family, to "guarantee" the preservation of the independent middle strata in agriculture, the crafts, and commerce, as well as the right to unionize and the principle of parity between employers and employees in settling wage and working conditions. It was to "guarantee" property, but also to enforce cartelization of private industries, and the rights of unions to participate in management "if the welfare of the nation so required." The principle of a uniform school system was established, but parochial schooling was guaranteed as well for those who demanded it. There were no fewer explicit provisions for the use of government to interfere with social stratification. The constitution covered such items as prohibition of private preparatory schooling, expropriation of large estates for agricultural settlements, socialization of industry, and protection and support of the interests of the working class as well as those of the "old" middleclass, many of which were quite contradictory (Huber, 1966:III:150–53). The egalitarian ideals of the Socialists figured here as prominently as the desire for status differentials of the bourgeoisie; a stratificational view of society with its emphasis on the desirability of equilibrated status sets was as much represented as the compensatory nonstratificational view.

Very little was really guaranteed, and nothing was defined as "untouchable" by political process. With Germany's diversity in values it was apparently difficult to guarantee anything with firmness. Any one such unshakable principle was bound to constitute an encroachment on someone else's most cherished principle. But sharing a commitment to the amoral public sphere, "subject to law" meant that nearly everything could be done to manipulate society. Not only did the constitution explicitly bid farewell to a laissez-faire conception in economics, there were also very few barriers to amendments. Except for a two-thirds quorum requirement in Parliament (Reichstag), constitutional amendments did not differ from ordinary legislative acts. No separate approval by state legislatures was required. Furthermore, depending on size, the *Länder* were unequally represented in the Reichsrat. The only change relative to imperial Germany was a *clausula antiborrusica*, specifying that no land could be represented by more than two fifths of all the votes. Half the Prussian votes were therefore not directly controlled by the Prussian Government, but by their provincial governments instead (Oppenheimer, 1923; Huber, 1966:III:163, 140).

In sum, as a statement of intent concerning the desirable social and political order, the constitution displayed the following characteristics. The nature of the social order to be constructed was not to be prejudged; neither was that of the polity. Essential commitments included only the maintenance of a formal nation-state, internal order within it, and a desire for "strong government." Indeterminacy as to content and "open-endedness" as to the territorial boundaries characterized the rest. As to the form social development might take, a socialist society was as much a possibility of the future as a corporatist one that would protect the integrity of segregated cultural communities. Neither the leveling of social inequalities nor their preservation and perhaps further intensification by political means was precluded. The nature of the regime was not fixed either. At the national level the only "untouchable principles" were full parliamentarization and proportionally representative electoral laws. While the latter was made mandatory also for the *Länder* constitutions, government dependence on parliamentary support was not a requisite for *Länder* "democracy." This facilitated the later emergence of "caretaker governments" in the states, a development that further delegitimated an already inoperative democratic regime. At the national level liberal democracy was as much a possible future as right- or left-wing populist dictatorship. Last, territorial open-endedness was formally recognized. The German-populated parts of Austria "belonged" to the Reich, if not in full governmental practice, then at least in principle. The constitution therefore provided a source of internal legitimacy for Hitler's later *Anschluss* (Huber, 1966:III:204, 135–55, 189–93).

While empty of nonambiguous content, the government was not to be a regulator of "marginal affairs" (Gellner, 1967); instead it was to be an active force in social development. Though a federal system, the intended sovereign was the Reichstag. The constitution had intended to assist all trends toward a unitary state and hinder all federalizing trends. Not only did the design for federal tax collection transform the *Länder* into grant-in-aid dependencies of the federal government, a finance equalization law of 1922 further accentuated central controls. This law called for the automatic redistribution of finances whereby the richer *Länder* had to support the poorer without being given a corresponding differential weight in policymaking. The net intent, representation without taxation, was to weaken rather than strengthen *Länder* particularism. The richer states were to be treated as equal with the poorer; the latter made more dependent on federal largesse. According to design, the only important functions left to the states were the regulation of local self-government, agriculture, and forestry, excepting labor law in these areas, housing, land settlement, Church affairs, education, and the fine arts. Again, however, the constitution "guaranteed" all these *Länder* functions "subject to federal legislative change" (Schulz, 1963:205; Dietrich, 1966:252; Oppenheimer, 1923:24, 34, 37).

But the gap between principle and practice remained wide. Separated by different ideals, those supporting the unitary state idea failed to translate it into real life. Equally separated by different ideals, the opponents of the principle of federal supremacy failed to bring about legislative change also. These differences were evident during the drafting of the constitution as well as during the subsequent history of constitutional reform. No one regarded the constitution or any aspect of it as a "sacred cow." Every group expected every other to try and manipulate it for its own advantage. Just how instrumental an orientation to the constitution prevailed can be gleaned from the political rights granted to civil servants. Civil servants should have full political rights, because "all parties attempt to change the constitution" (Schulz, 1963:209). Regarding the constitution as an instrument for practical interests in society was a view prevalent among Germany's professors of constitutional law as well. A study of the writings of the most influential of these experts concluded that only one among forty-nine took a clearly antidemocratic stance. The vast majority, however, could be described as "nondemocratic" strict logical constructionists. They were nondemocratic in the sense that they did not regard the law as the embodiment of any value principles but rather as arrangements. Kelsen was perhaps most explicit on this point. He not only suggested that the structure of government need not symbolize any societal value commitments, but also defined genuine value relativism as the very basis of a democracy (Schad, 1963:51). These legal theorists were *Vernunftrepublikaner*. They accepted the constitution, first because the *Kaiserreich* had demonstrably failed, and second, because nothing better existed as yet. They were also largely in agreement that no legal order could "determine" what constitutes the good society, nor adjudicate what constitutes differential contributions to some societal goal. These orientations permitted the use of democratic means for the pursuit of non- or even antidemocratic goals. The test was merely whether action followed legal requirements, not whether it "violated" the spirit of the constitution. Given a conflicted and a very marginal "spirit," that was perhaps inevitable. The Weimar constitution gives you the impression that the call of the national anthem "Germany, Germany above all" had been translated into the centralization of power, while any concerns with legitimacy beliefs had been effectively replaced with a commitment to "legality above all."

If value diversity in society was a more indirect influence on these developments of a constitution "without direction," what were some of the more immediate factors that translated these conceptions into the script? Probably the most important single factor here was the involvement of civil servants in the drafting of the constitution and the subsequent reform attempts. This group was responsible for a relatively widespread concern with unity in form rather than content, and a preference for legal-technical accuracy rather than logical coherence in the principles espoused. Of the 129 participants at the 1919 constitutional conference, conducted under the auspices of the Reich Ministry of Interior, 84 were higher civil servants of the Reich and *Länder* bureaucracies, 5 were military officers, and only 35 (or just over a quarter) were party politicans. This body then constituted an assembly of the *ancien régime* in Germany, a composition hardly promising for a really new start in the republic. Although this body was rather elite in composition, its members did not feel constrained from constantly appealing to the general public and voicing their profound disagreements as to what and whom a unitary state should serve. The continuing conflict involved bureaucrats in the public and private sectors who used juridical arguments and "diplomacy," sending "ambassadors" to each other. The form was reminiscent of relations between sovereign states (Schulz, 1963:124, 486). These negotiations illustrate well how the specification of a goal immediately encountered opposition, and how a principle once emptied of a specifiable content could be supported by different groups for nearly opposite reasons.

To the "principled democrat" Preuss, the original drafter of the constitution, a unitary state was to serve two ends; building democracy from the bottom up through self-government, and removing the Prussian "reactionary" threat once and for all by carving up the Prussian state. Antimonarchical sentiment as well as anti-Prussianism were clear motives. One of the Reichstag Socialists supporting this position formulated the reason succinctly: "Prussia gained its position by the sword; that sword has been broken. If Germany is to live, Prussia in its present form must die" (Schulz, 1963:137). The proposal to carve up Prussia encountered the opposition of the Prussian Socialists, however. In a Landtag session of 1919, they declared their willingness to dissolve Prussia *provided* other states would follow suit, a goal specification of the unitary-state issue that aroused the expected protest in the South (Schulz, 1963:244–48, 494). Henceforth, abolishing the Prussian state was an achievement reserved for the Nazis. The Catholic Center Party supported the unitary-state conception in the hope of preserving the state's neutrality in education. While they had feared a radical national Parliament under the empire, they now expected the worst from socialist-infested *Länder* Parliaments. The Bavarians, principally opposed to a unitary state, which they saw as a threat to their way of life and still genuine monarchical attachment to the House of Wittelsbach, came to agree to a unitary design because they saw in a "strong President" the best guarantor for *Länder* rights as well as a counterforce to a secessionist move in their Palatinate exclave. To the representatives of the Southwest a unitary state signaled increased Prussian domination. This had to be opposed if their working democracy was to be protected. The Prussian Socialists had succeeded in equating the dissolution of Prussia with the abrogation of federalism in the justified expectation that this would defeat both. Since the Prussian state was dominated by the Socialists, more opposition from industrialists emerged. The southern federalist forces could link up with Rhenish industrialists opposing the unitary-state idea. For the latter a unitary state signaled the victory of socialism (Schulz, 1963:171, 190, 194, 201). A final "resolution" of these conflicts in the form of a principle unitary by design but not in practice gained acceptance at the conference with the appeal to nationalism. The argument that Prussia had to be maintained lest the Reich fall apart brought the issue to a temporary solution. The final version of the constitution was accepted against the votes of the Radical Socialists (USPD), the Nationalists (DNVP), the People's Party (DVP), and a few Bavarian delegates (Schulz, 1963:165, 171). Thus the early and later anti-Weimar forces had already emerged in 1919.

The pattern of conflict in which no issue was definitely settled also continued later. The cleavages in the constitutional reform attempts were ideological, territorial, and class-based. None showed sufficient superimposition to facilitate a strong enough alliance to move the constitutional problem either in a federal or a unitary direction.

For the Bavarians the guiding maxim was: Whatever serves the interests of Bavaria and its independence serves the interest of the nation. They first opposed Weimar by illegal means, then learned that the regime was a better protector for their way of life than any visible alternative and came to defend the regime by legal means to the very end. Among the Socialists in the Reichstag a similar orientation prevailed, only with a rather different content. Whether the issue was the introduction of centrally administered progressive taxation—which to them signaled a step in the direction of "socializing society"—or strengthening the Reich bureaucracy to penetrate the resistant *Länder*, the Socialists in the Reichstag acted according to this maxim: Whatever serves the advancement of socialism serves the nation (Schulz, 1963:454–59, 592, 219, 326). For the Prussian Socialists, on the other hand, Prussia was the overriding concern. They now "commanded" the Prussian state apparatus, an asset that they sought to preserve and enlarge wherever possible. This meant, first, strong government through administration from the top down; second, acquiring more territory wherever possible; and third, trying to fuse the Prussian and Reich governments again on the imperial pattern, if and only insofar as that served the welfare of the Prussian state (Schulz, 1963: 239, 258, 326). "Whatever serves the development of liberal democracy from the bottom up serves the nation" became the guiding principle for the Liberals (DDP). They regarded *Länder* particularisms as sources of reactionary sentiment and therefore advocated their abolition (Schulz, 1963:327, 478). "Whatever serves the interest of business serves the nation" was the maxim of Germany's big-business interests represented in the People's Party. While they had argued against a unitary state in 1919, they changed their tune as reparations payments proved to be essential for foreign credits. They came to embrace a unitary state granting maximum freedom for private enterprise as the ideal. Big business did not confine their efforts to directing "their" party and mobilizing the public. They pressured the Reich's executive directly by an alliance with the Allies' reparations agent. The latter's interest in insuring reparations regardless of Germany's internal political constellation came to coincide with that of big business interested in *Erfüllungspolitik* as the best road toward maintaining credit-worthiness and regaining a competitive position in the international market. This meant now, above all, an executive strong enough to resist anti-*Erfüllung* political forces at home (Schulz, 1963:300, 576). For the Nationalists (DNVP), who made reform their principle vehicle for mobilizing support against *Erfüllung*, anything was desirable that weakened parliamentary institutions. For these groups, a unitary state was the ideal if it could serve as a beginning of Germany's national rebirth. They acted on purely ideological grounds. For the Catholic Center Party the most relevant issue was always the school question. Whichever form of government promised freedom for Catholic teaching was welcome. Supporters of the unitary-state solution to about 1920, they later vacillated to such an extent that no clear position emerged again. For the Reich ministries, particularly those of Economics and Finance, the guiding principle was institutional enhancement. Consequently they were antifederalist and supported any plans that promised to enhance the rationality of administration, regardless of what was to be administered. Principally because of these different reasons, no stable coalition among these various groups ever emerged. As a result, constitutional reform remained a verbal battle, a fight about "Germany's soul," involving shifting alliances and mutually cumulating frustrations rather than any resolution (Schluz, 1963:477–85, 608). That pattern, however, was characteristic of Germany's party system as well.

Some Aspects of the Party System and Regime Support

In considering the instability of Weimar, both at the national and regional levels, some of the heavy burdens the young republic carried have to be kept in mind. By and large these burdens helped to fan Germany's inherent dynamic divisiveness rather than to create it. These burdens served in the fashion of clothes hangers. One could fasten mobilized commitments to diverse images of the good society onto them. Put differently, the effect of these burdens was more symbolic than real, but therefore productive of more real consequences. The most important of these burdens were: (1) territorial losses involving about 13 percent of the former Reich; (2) the "theft of the colonies"; (3) the abolition of conscription (enshrined in the constitution); and (4) above all, the war-guilt clause, when most believed "perfidious Albion" to have been the instigator of the war, and the concrete acceptance of the guilt clause in the form of reparations to be paid until 1988 (Eyck, 1963:I:109–126; II:180–90; Halpern, 1965:386; Horkenbach, 1930:I:365). The reparations issue illustrates the symbolic nature of the burdens best. Governed by standards of realism and oriented to ability to pay, the negotiations about the reparations bill dragged on for years, coming to a final settlement only in 1930. For many years Germans were reminded of their national shame.

The final settlement, about 110 billion Reichsmarks, was not only less than earlier demands, but also was well within the national capacity to pay. Germany was in a position to advance a loan of 3 billion Reichsmarks to France in 1926. Germany could also afford to spend about 667 million Reichsmarks per year on armaments during 1925–27. Hitler was able to boost the annual armament expenditure to 10 billion Reichsmarks during 1934–39 (Eyck, 1963:I:306; II:75, 143–49). Thus what hurt was having to pay for what appeared to be the questionable sins of the fathers to the third generation. The high figures on armament expenditures should buttress this symbolic interpretation, despite the fact that the republic suffered nearly continuously from economic difficulties.

In addition to economic problems, particularly during the inflation of 1923, and continuously high unemployment (Halpern, 1965:264; Bennecke, 1968:154–72), the republic suffered serious secessionist threats until 1923–24. These threats arose in the Rhineland, the Palatinate, and Bavaria. Supported by the French, three parties in the Rhineland agitated for independence from the Reich. Separatist *Putsche* occurred in seven major cities, and one large trust corporation "recognized" the separatist government by paying taxes to it. In addition, the Rhenish separatist moves coincided with a "separate from Prussia" movement supported by industrialists, bankers, and prominent leaders of the Rhenish Centrists. Leftist coups succeeded in Saxony and Thuringia, while Bavaria's monarchist *Putsch* successfully defied the federal government. The army proved a dependable instrument in suppressing Leftist rebellion but failed to act against the southern monarchists and the earlier Kapp rightist *Putsch* in Berlin. Charging discrimination, the Socialists left Stresemann's second cabinet. During 1924 the federal authority had become so weak that even the judiciary rebelled. The High Court had ruled to revalue debts in order to protect creditors from losses through inflation. When the Reichstag attempted to legislate a general revaluation margin, the High Court intervened, expressing "displeasure" with interference in the judges' discretion and prevented a general regulation (Schulz, 1963:314–17; Eyck, 1963:I:147–51, 241–47, 271–89; Halpern, 1965:275). While these overt challenges to the national center declined in later years, the continuing viability of the underlying dynamic dissensus in German society became manifest in the relations among the political parties.

Until about 1928 Germany's four-column party system remained fairly well intact, though subject to gradual erosion and factionalization. One factor in political instability was undoubtedly factionalism within the Catholic and Socialist parties. Among the former, a Bavarian branch separated over the issue of federalism and states' rights. Among the latter, the Radical Socialists had already split off during the war. When they later rejoined the majority Socialists in 1922, their voters turned to the Communists (Neumann, 1965:47). Similarly, the failure to consolidate the two principal liberal middle-class parties also contributed its share to instability. But as the cases of Norway and The Netherlands show, neither a multiparty system, nor a proportionate electoral law by themselves spell instability (Eckstein, 1966; Lijphart, 1968). More important in the German case was a continuing electoral practice of "negative integration," whereby the parties remained oriented to their traditional clienteles and refrained from "raiding each other's support bases." But in Parliament they engaged in shifting tactical alliances for short-term opportunistic advantage. The reasons for cabinet dissolution clearly demonstrate the point. Of the twenty cabinet turnovers, only five occurred because of defeat at the polls or because of a parliamentary vote of no confidence. Nearly three quarters of the cabinets fell because the partners in coalition were tired of it. Any one or several expected better opportunities for their interests in a governmental realigment. Additional evidence bearing on the same point can be found in the reasons for the dissolution of Parliament. With a four-year legislative term Weimar could have had five Parliaments until 1933. Instead there were eight, and all were dissolved prematurely. Six dissolutions occurred due to conflict between government and Parliament, including two where Parliament was too divided to form a government. One Parliament was dissolved because of an impending vote of no confidence, another because a popular referendum called for the support of Hitler. No Parliament was ever dissolved because the administration could not raise sufficient parliamentary support for a specific policy and turned to the people for support. The closest Weimar ever came to letting the people judge involved three dissolutions where the issues were Parliament's refusal to extend fairly general enabling acts or a similarly general rule by presidential decree. Mostly Parliaments were dissolved because the parties in coalition could not maintain sufficient unity within their own ranks (Huber, 1966:III:159–62; Bracher, 1955:34).

In making and breaking coalitions, the parties came to act in a fashion similar to pressure groups, only with this important difference: Because they were parties and frequently involved in government formation, they destroyed a national center against which to act. With rapid cabinet turnover no real executive in terms of a national decision center existed. That center "disappeared," as it were, behind a confusing smoke screen of a triple fusion in political functions. These covered executive, legislative, and support-mobilization functions. "Government," parties, and legislature became one, and who was responsible for what became mysterious. These fusions were only partially offset with rule by presidential decree, for the latter was contingent on parliamentary support. Having destroyed an identifiable center, the parties turned on each other in a pattern of conflict relations where one frequently changed one's partners in coalition in a constant search for the best possible deal under changing circumstances. In so doing the party system lost the capacity to fight any issue through to some visible degree of resolution. Confusion, mutual frustration, and increasingly ineffectual government were the outcomes.

Futhermore, nearly all the major parties frequently participated in cabinets. Thus most became associated in the public eye with responsibility for ineffectual government. The Center Party had been a member of all eighteen cabinets before the last Brüning administration, ending in June 1932. The Democrats (DDP) had participated in sixteen; the People's Party in ten; the Bavarian Centrists in nine; and the Socialists in eight. The successor to the Conservatives under the *Kaiser*, the German Nationalists (DNVP), on the other hand, had participated only twice. Thus only the right, the extreme right, and the extreme left had not become tainted with the blame for ineffectual government (Huber, 1966:III:614–15). With most of the parties involved in an ineffectual polity, they and the regime gradually lost legitimacy. This process is shown in Table VII-1, which lists the pro- and antisystem vote for the nation throughout the republic and regionally since 1924.

Keeping in mind how imperfect an estimate of legitimacy aggregate voting data are, the calculation of the overt antisystem vote in this table is conservative. The German Nationalists have been included continuously because they formed themselves self-consciously "in opposition to the 1918 revolution" and had voted against the constitution in 1919. Even though they declared a principled opposition to Weimar only in 1928, their propaganda had been anti-Weimar most of the time (Neumann, 1965:61–71). The People's Party has been included only intermittently. Since they voted against adoption of the constitution in 1919, their popular votes during that year were counted as antisystem. Yet despite their party platform of 1920, which was clearly monarchical, antirevolutionary, and anti-Weimar, their leader Stresemann, a *Vernunftrepublikaner*, gained national eminence in his six-year conduct of foreign policy. Since this role was given wide press coverage and did make him the archenemy of the "national opposition," the vote for the People's Party was counted as pro-Weimar from 1920 until his death in 1929 (Turner, 1963:261; Halpern, 1965:199). The Bavarian Centrists were overtly anti-Weimar only until 1924, a period during which they collaborated with the similarly monarchical but anti-Prussian protesters in Hannover. Subsequently the Bavarian Centrists made their peace with Weimar (Schulz, 1963:332, 592). Since the swing came in 1924, the May vote was counted as antisystem, the December vote of that and subsequent elections as a

Table VII-1 Reichstag Voting, 1919–33: Percentage of the Prosystem, the Antisystem, and "Other" Votes[a]

Year	Prussia			Rhineland			Southwest			South			Nation		
	Pro	Anti	Oth.	Pro	Anti	Oth.	Pro	Anti	Oth.	Pro	Anti	Oth.	Pro	Anti	Oth.
1919													76	22	1
1920													58	40	2
1924 May													49	46	5
1924 Dec.	51	43	6	70	25	5	66	19	14	61	26	13	60	34	6
1928	53	38	9	65	23	11	65	17	19	60	21	19	59	30	11
1930	38	52	10	47	40	12	50	31	19	54	26	20	43	50	7
1932 July	33	66	2	46	51	3	43	49	8	51	43	5	38	60	1
1932 Nov.	31	67	1	45	52	3	41	51	8	50	44	6	36	62	2
1933 Mar.	27	72	1	41	57	1	36	58	5	44	53	3	33	66	0

[a]Prosystem Vote = Socialists (SPD), Centrists (Z), Democrats (DDP); People's Party (DVP), 1920–28, and Bavarian Centrists (BVP), Dec. 1924–1933. Antisystem Vote = German Nationalists (DNVP) and allied splinters (Kons. VP, Christl. soz. VD, Landbund, Landvolkpartei), Nazis (NSDAP), Radical Socialists, and Communists (USPD-KPD); Bavarian Centrists and Guelphs (BVP-Dt. hann. Landesp.), 1920–May 1924. "Other" = Guelphs (Dt. hann. Landesp.), 1919, 1928–33, Peasants (Bauernp.), Economic Party (W), and other splinters.

The regional vote for the elections of May 1924 and before have been omitted because of changes in the electoral districts. The regions have been delimited to coincide with the data of the value analysis and the imperial votes. Prussia here comprises electoral districts 1 through 10; the Rhineland, electoral districts 17, 18, and 20 through 23; the Southwest, districts 31 and 32; and the South, districts 24, 25, and 26.

Sources: On the national vote: Ernst R. Huber, Dokumente zur Deutschen Verfassungsgeschichte. Stuttgart: W. Kohlhammer Verlag, 1966, pp. 606–7; on the regional vote: Wilhelm Dittmann, Das Politische Deutschland vor Hitler. Zürich: Europa Verlag, 1945.

pro-Weimar vote. After December 1924 the Guelph protesters were also counted as "Other."

Comparing the level of national support for the Weimar regime with that for the *Kaiserreich* before ("Nation" in Tables VI-1 and VII-1), three characteristics stand out from the figures. First, while both regimes faced significant antisystem sentiment throughout their duration, this was higher during the republic. The lowest antisystem vote recorded for the Wilhelminian polity was about 18 percent in 1874 and 1878. The corresponding Weimar figure was 22 percent, in 1919. Second, while the opposition to the imperial regime showed a gradual but relatively steady rise, the antisystem vote of the republic seemed somewhat more responsive to economic conditions. Antisystem sentiment declined during the financially more stable period 1925–28. Third, while the proregime forces retained a relative majority for nearly forty years under the Kaiser, the republic lost majority support after eleven years, in 1930.

Two further differences between the two political regimes, not visible from the figures, were also important, however. The quality of the antisystem sentiment had changed. The opposition to the Wilhelminian polity had been basically civil, a term simply inapplicable to the virulent hatred and contempt spewed at the republic and its "November criminals" in countless editorials and speeches by the right. Second, the antiregime forces under the *Kaiser* had one element in common, at least during later periods: They desired parliamentarization primarily, not necessarily abolition of the monarchy. At the end of the war even the Socialist leader Scheidemann tried to save the throne of the Hohenzollern (Reinhardt, 1962:643). Among the major countercontestants of the democratic republic, no such common element was to be found anymore. At least three contradictory counterideals were prevalent: the dictatorship of the proletariat, the desire to return to a monarchical-authoritarian regime, and the Nazi hope for a New Order. Thus relative to the Wilhelminian polity, opposition to the republic was stronger numerically, more intense emotionally, and more diverse in the counterideals propagated. The republic never enjoyed traditional legitimacy. Furthermore, despite the grass-roots emphasis built into the constitution with its several possibilities for launching a popular referendum, the constitution had never been submitted for ratification to the people directly (Oppenheimer, 1923:157). This suggests that chances for passage had been slim in 1919.

The rapid decline of system support as indexed by voting data, and the extraordinary government instability as indexed by cabinet turnover would seem to support Eckstein's (1961) theory of regime stability. According to this view, democracy could find no social roots in Germany because authority relations throughout the wider society were too authoritarian. One implication of this theory is that Prussians should have been in the lead among the antidemocratic forces of German society because historically the predominance of the army, the prestige of the officer corps and, indeed, the hierarchy of values all combined to make Prussia more of an authoritarian society than other regions. And one glace at Table VII-1 would seem to confirm these speculations. As indexed by votes, Prussians were the first to abandon Weimar democracy, and they abandoned the republic the most. But if one takes a longer historical perspective the Eckstein thesis breaks down, for another of its implications is that Prussians should have been the most supportive of the Wilhelminian polity. Yet the contrary was the case. The alternative perspective suggested here is that consciousness about value differences in German society produced an appreciation for domination by interest constellations and therefore a propensity to withdraw support from any form of government that failed to earn its right to rule. And instead of any Prussian proclivity for authoritarian forms of rule, this tendency was most developed in Prussia. The historical continuity in the regional distribution of the antisystem vote from the days of the *Kaiser* to and throughout Weimar democracy yields supportive evidence on this point. Let me elaborate.

In Germany before the First World War casting a vote for the Socialist or the Left Liberal parties was your main tool to vote against the system. The former vote had much to do with the transformation of Germany's artisans into an industrial working class. And that clashed with religion. Protestants found it easier to become supporters of the Socialists than Catholics did. Nonetheless, region exerted a greater influence on voting. The sources listed in Table VI-1 make this rather clear. They tell us that the Socialist vote in Prussia grew from 2 percent in 1871 to 39 percent in 1912. The corresponding figures for the Rhineland were 5 percent and 24 percent, respectively; those for the southwest, 3 percent and 30 percent, respectively; and those for the south, 2 percent and 27 percent, respectively. But while Prussia was more Protestant than the other three regions, the religious differences were far too small to account for most of the regional contrasts in joining up with the Socialists. Furthermore, support for the Left Liberal democratic opponents of the Wilhelminian polity also forged ahead in Prussia. In 1871 12 percent of the East Elbian Prussian votes went to the Left Liberals. By 1912, 14 percent did. And here too the respective figures in the other regions were lower. The corresponding percentages in the Rhineland were 1 percent and 4 percent, respectively; those in the southwest, 6 percent and 13 percent, respectively; and those in the South were 9 percent and 12 percent, respectively. Thus one learns that the level of Left Liberal opposition to "the authoritarian" Wilhelminian polity was higher and consistently higher in Prussia than elsewhere.

While abandonment of the imperial polity required a Socialist or Left Liberal democratic vote primarily, abandoning Weimar democracy required shifting one's vote from these parties and voting for the Radical Socialists (USPD), the Communists, or the Nazis. And once again, the Prussians were in the lead. Again the antisystem vote was consistently highest in Prussia and lowest in the South (Table VII-1). A clear rank order in the time needed for the antisystem vote to reach absolute majority was present too. In Prussia this happened in 1930; in the Rhineland it occurred in the first 1932 election, in the Southwest in the second 1932 election, and in the Deep South only in the March 1933 election. In fact, the Weimar Coalition (Center, Democrats, and Socialists) retained a majority in only five of the thirty-five electoral districts in the first 1932 national election. Three of these were in the Rhineland, and two in the South. Similar patterns existed in state elections. While the Weimar coalition lost the majority in the Prussian Landtag elections of 1932, the respective houses of Bavaria and Wuerttemberg were still controlled by a pro-Weimar majority (Bennecke, 1962:183, 192; Huber, 1966:610–11). To return to the Reichstag vote in Table VII-1 once more, if one takes the economically more stable year of 1928 as a departure date and the last free election of November 1932 as a terminal date, Prussia lost 42 percent of its pro-Weimar vote over this period. The corresponding figures for the Rhineland, the Southwest, and the South were 31 percent, 36 percent, and 18 percent, respectively. Clearly, abandonment of the republic was primarily a Prussian and least of all a southern phenomenon.

Let us recall two facts mentioned in Chapter II. The ideal-typical Nazi voter was a Protestant, middle-class, small-town person. And, in the nation as a whole, there was a near-perfect positive correlation between the rise in unemployment and the Nazi vote. Considering these facts suggests that Protestants insisted more on performance than Catholics did; and since Weimar democracy clearly did not deliver, Protestants should have withdrawn their support at a faster rate than Catholics. As evident in Table VII-2, this was only partly true. Part A of the table tells us that Catholics came to the defense of democracy in only two of the three regions that could be examined. They did so in Prussia and in the South. In the Southwest, in contrast, the anti-Weimar vote of Catholics was higher than that of Protestants in five of six elections examined here. What is more, when one considers ranges and means in religious differences and compares them with the corresponding figures for regional differences in Part B of the table, the Prussian spearhead in withdrawing system support from the regime becomes very noticeable again. The religious differences

Table VII-2 The Anti-Weimar Vote by Religion and Region (Percentage of the Antisystem Reichstag Vote)

Electoral district number	Dec. 1924	1928	1930	July 1932	Nov. 1932	Mar. 1933	Range	Mean
A. Religious Differences								
Prussia								
8 90% Prot.	34	30	39	63	63	70		
9 88% Cath.	35	31	43	53	52	60		
Difference: Prot.-Cath.:	-01	-01	-04	10	11	10	-01 to 11	4.2
Southwest								
31 68% Prot.	21	15	26	46	47	57		
32 58% Cath.	17	18	37	52	54	60		
Difference: Prot.-Cath.:	04	-03	-11	-06	-07	-03	-11 to 04	-4.3
South								
26 30% + Prot.	35	30	29	51	52	56		
24 74% + Cath.	23	17	26	40	41	53		
Difference: Prot.-Cath.:	12	13	03	11	11	03	03 to 13	8.8
B. Regional Differences								
Prussia (1)	43	38	52	66	67	72		
Rhineland (2)	25	23	40	51	52	57		
Southwest (3)	19	17	31	49	51	58		
South (4)	26	21	26	43	44	53		
Differences:								
(1)-(2):	18	15	12	15	15	15	12 to 18	15.0
(1)-(3):	24	21	21	17	16	14	14 to 24	18.8
(1)-(4):	17	17	26	15	23	19	17 to 26	20.8

Sources: For the religious composition of the population, *Statistisches Jahrbuch für das Deutsche Reich*, 1937, p. 18; Theodor Kraus, et al. (eds.), *Atlas des Östlichen Mitteleuropa*, Bielefeld: Velhagen & Klasing (n.d.), p. 32; for the votes see the sources in Table VII-1.

in the antisystem vote average under 9 percent; the regional differences between Prussia and the other three regions were much larger, averaging between 15 percent and 21 percent. Note also that these are not misleading averages. For practical purposes, the range in percentage-point differences attributable to religious affiliation was always lower than that attributable to region.

In short, insofar as available data can tell, region was always the more critical variable in delegitimating the polity in Germany than religion was, regardless of whether one deals with the collapse of the imperial regime or that of Weimar democracy. Even though voting for the Nazi Party was only one way to vote against democracy at the time, what about the regional distribution of the Nazi vote? Gaining 33 percent of the nation's ballots in the last free election of November 1932, the Nazis gained the most in East Elbian Prussia (36 percent), followed by southwestern support (30 percent); next came the Southerners, with 28 percent casting their ballots for Hitler; but the Rhineland, where the Communists gained the most from dissatisfaction with a nonworking democracy, voted the least for the Nazi Party (23 percent) (computed from Dittmann, 1945).

However, voter dissatisfaction with ineffectual government did not translate itself directly into government instability on a regional or a state level. Throughout most of the Weimar period the Prussian state had been run by the Socialists. They collapsed not in response to Hitler, but vis-à-vis a coup from above engineered by a conservative, von Papen. In view of Binion's (1976) psychological argument that Hitler's mentality fitted that of all Germans hand 'in glove, understanding how and why the Prussian state government gave up its life toward the end of Weimar democracy is very important. It will be seen that this had nothing whatever to do with any shared psychological propensities between Adolf Hitler and the people. Keeping in mind that Prussia made up about two thirds of Germany both in population and in geographic area, only an analysis sensitive to regional differences can help our understanding.

As already mentioned, the Weimar Republic had twenty cabinets at the level of national government. Cabinet instability was the mark of German democracy throughout its thirteen years of life. The twenty national administrations enjoyed an average lifetime of eight months. Weimar Germany had twelve Chancellors, and they came from four parties. The longest time any one of them was Chancellor was three years. In Prussia herself the situation was quite different. Not counting the two-day administration of Marx, Prussia had only six cabinets with an average lifetime of twenty-eight months. Further, the Prussian state had only three chief executives, and they were recruited from only two parties. One of them "ruled" Prussia for twelve years. Compared to the Reich,

Prussia was like a Rock of Gibraltar in government stability during the Weimar regime. Also, Bavaria was much more stable than the nation. Bavaria had eight state cabinets with an average lifetime of nineteen months. All of her four chief executives were recruited from one party, if one excludes the early instability before March 1920. And one of these chief executives "ruled" Bavaria for almost nine years (Huber, 1966:III:612–19; Schwend, 1954:569–71).

Bavaria's earlier instability probably reflected more a concern with protecting its way of life than widespread genuine monarchical convictions. Nevertheless, the South made two contributions that proved very important for later Nazi success at the national level. One of these involved the bestowal of respectability on the Nazis by association with the preindustrial elites of the empire. This laid the foundation for Hitler's later capacity to draw on traditional legitimacy. The other contribution was that Bavaria granted protection to the private armies of the political right during the early years of the republic. In the early twenties the Nazis not only enjoyed an inflated numerical image in the press, one that they cultivated quite self-consciously, they also enjoyed an inflated image of respectability, one they cultivated no less assiduously. Reports on SA maneuvers, detailing thousands and hundreds of thousands of participants in the fields of Bavaria, were often vastly exaggerated, since usually more than one half the participants belonged to nationalist militias, such as Bavaria's Home Guard, rather than to the SA or to the Nazi Party. Parades with banner and song had been a normal feature of German associational life, applying in equal measure to gardening clubs, sports, and singing associations, as well as to political groups. What favored the Nazis was that while the little clubs could hope to be reviewed by members of local elites, the joint parades with the Home Guard brought out the dignitaries of Kahr's monarchical regime, including generals and Crown Prince Ruprecht of Wittelsbach. Thus the Nazis seemed far more important both in numbers and in elite support than they actually were (Berghahn, 1966:58–59).

That the South should give birth to the Nazi movement and later spurn it was hardly an accident. The "blood-and-soil mysticism"—that is, the more atavistic explicitly antimodern components of Nazi ideology could be born out of a commitment to defensive traditionalism (Swanson, 1967:247). However, if Schoenbaum's (1967:xxii) formula of the Nazi movement as an "antibourgeois revolution against industrial society by bourgeois and industrial means" can be interpreted as an antimodernist revolt with modern means and mostly modern consequences (Dahrendorf, 1965:431–48), then the later lack of enthusiasm in the South also makes sense; for once the Southerners detected the modern aspects of totalitarian politics, particularly the total disregard for established custom, they lost enchantment with the movement in direct proportion to that discovery.

The Prussian state, on the other hand, showed almost a reversed pattern with an early and firm establishment of democracy and a later sudden collapse vis-à-vis von Papen's doubtful legal takeover. Here the majority Socialists, acting in alliance with the Army, suppressed the left radicals early in the regime. Subsequently, a stable Weimar Coalition retained a Landtag majority until 1932. Keeping in mind that Prussia with the Rhineland included covered the most economically developed part of Germany makes the contrast of Prussian stability to the instability at the national level even more remarkable. Suffering the most from economic dislocation, democracy in the Prussian state was the most stable. Essential in unraveling this Prussian political puzzle is the recognition that Prussia's democracy was one more in form than in content. Particularly conspicuous was the absence of grass-roots populist "participatory" components of democracy. Indeed, it may not be an undue exaggeration to suggest that stable democracy here was in part due to non- if not antidemocratic elements in Prussia's political culture and values. Reduced to a short formula, it seems as though the hallowed Prussian discipline maintained democracy; but it also made democracy equally susceptible to antidemocratic forces if the assault was carried out by legal means.

Prussian values restricted the legitimacy of political change to a source "from above"—namely, top leadership. Revolution from above fitted this requirement. The *Kaiser*'s formal abdication, its announcement by the imperial Chancellor, and its acceptance by the Army command undoubtedly helped the transition to democracy in the first place. It was a legal transition. Parliamentarism had entered the stage in a proper way. If the Socialists had a majority, then that was a consequence of the new rules of the game, and it was the Prussian's duty to carry on. While new contenders for political power were principally denied legitimacy in Prussia, the term "contenders for power" was always applied to groups operating outside the official political system, whatever the latter's normative content. In the early years of the republic the most notable of such contenders were the radical Left Socialists and the Communists; and these were crushed by force. And while the Army proved an unrealiable instrument to crush the rightist extremists in the Kapp *Putsch*, the simple refusal to cooperate with these illegal usurpers on the part of the higher civil service in Berlin brought this episode to a speedy close. Being illegal, a proper Prussian higher official could not grant them money, regardless of where his sympathies might lie (Eyck, 1963, Vol. I:151). The Prussian values of duty and discipline also helped greatly in the Prussian Socialists' decision to place law and order above experimentation and to consolidate and secure the state, which they now "owned," rather than to seek any immediate translation of ideological demands into practice.

Emphasizing the formal nature of Prussian democracy, one observer concluded: ". . . no one would want to declare that Prussia was governed more democratically, socialistically, or even less centralistically than any other *Land*" (Schulz, 1963:610). Under the "Red Czar" Braun, who held the Prime Minister's portfolio for twelve years, Prussian social democracy was Prussian first, democratic mainly in form and law, and socialist hardly at all. It was scarcely an accident that the prewar right-wing revisionists of the Socialist Party were concentrated in the Prussian Government. Being Prussian meant under "socialism" what it had always meant: placing the state's interest above any other, pursuing it with vigor, and keeping every other internal interest as much as possible in line with *raison d'état*. Social democracy here had a thoroughly Prussian face. The civil service was largely kept intact, even though it was certainly known that its sympathies, particularly in the field administrative branch, were with the monarchy rather than with the republic. But the civil service had always been the backbone of the Prussian state. The preservation of the latter demanded the retention of the former, especially since the Army had been reduced. Even rule by police decree in the field, the traditional Prussian method of administration-*cum*-legislation, was strengthened (Schulz, 1963:236; Jacob, 1963:96–105). Second, the unions were bureaucratically run "from the top down" and with iron discipline. The same applied to the Socialist Party in the cabinet, the state Parliament, and the field. Third, socialism meant augmenting the state's income independently of taxation as much as possible, as had always been the Prussian custom. The Socialist government consolidated the state's mining enterprises, organized the Prussian electrical companies, and thus succeeded in offsetting revenue losses incurred through the federal interstate finance equalization plan (Dietrich, 1966:252–53).

The essential continuation of traditional Prussian policy is best illustrated in the history of constitutional reform (Schulz, 1963:305–18, 492–587). Here Braun's instructions to the Prussian Ministry of State were worthy of Prussia's monarchs. To seek the enlargement of Prussia in any form and to oppose diminution of her territories or any other assets in whatever shape were guiding principles. Just how much this Socialist acted in the spirit of the House of Hohenzollern can be gleaned from a speech delivered in 1921: "Prussia's historic mission has been to act in the interest of the Reich; and the Prussian people will seek the predominance that is their due *regardless of the constitutional prescriptions*. It would be a misfortune not only for Prussia but for the Reich as well, if those who strive for her dissolution out of an aversion against the 'old Prussia' were to succeed" (Schulz, 1963:308–9; emphasis supplied). Committed to regaining Prussia's hegemony in Germany and centralist bureaucracy, all attempts at social reform, welfare politics, and demands for more self-government at the local and provincial levels in East Prussia and in the Rhineland were stifled. Furthermore, Braun sensed, probably accurately, that the confluence of "democracy and the deep divisiveness among the Germans" in the Reichstag not only constituted a threat to German unity but to Prussia as well. From this perspective, keeping the Prussian state functioning constituted for him the only road to preserve the nation. Reliable governmental functioning in Prussia, the largest part of Germany, would actually mean having one functioning government in the country. But what seemed possible in Prussia, democracy in form rather than content, did not seem feasible at the national level. Braun did not actively seek nor support attempts to return to the Bismarck pattern of combining the Reich offices of Chancellor and the Minister of the Interior with their respective Prussian counterparts in personal union. This pattern resurfaced only briefly during 1928–30, when Severing headed the Department of Internal Affairs in Prussia and in the Reich. Moreover, Braun, wary of tying his coalition to an uncertain Reichstag condition, actually favored a weak Reich Government with the Socialists in opposition. That augered to him a situation where the Socialist Party could not be blamed for ineffectual government at the national level, while the nation's "real power" actually rested with the Prussian Government. In leaving the Prussian higher bureaucrats undisturbed, and in maintaining good relations with the Army command and the industrial interests in the Rhineland, with a simultaneous guarantee of educational autonomy to the Catholics, Prussia's republican boss kept intact the one principle on which the Prussian polity had always rested: satisfying the interests of powerful oligarchies while preserving autonomy from them as much as possible in all matters not immediately their concern. In maintaining strict cabinet discipline vis-à-vis the Prussian House, firm cabinet autonomy vis-à-vis the parties forming the Weimar coalition, and an equally strict discipline within each of the coalition House parties to shield his administration from parliamentary attack, Prussia's socialist "Czar" also maintained another principle of traditional Prussian politics: keeping aloft the appearance of executive monopoly over the initiative in all phases of the governmental process.

Parliamentarization of the Prussian regime demanded only two additions for preserving the old style of governance in all essentials. The function of representing the Prussian state to the Reich had to be allocated to an appointive office to insure Prussian executive control. Braun made sure that only officials of the Prussian Ministry of State performed this role. The other necessary addition concerned a mechanism to maintain a stable Landtag support to keep the coalition legally legitimate. That, however, could not be insured. The Prussian Republic rested as much on purely formal rational-legal legitimacy as had the Prussian monarchy most of the time. Prussians voted because that had become their duty as citizens. But this did not transform them into "republicans of heart." Once the votes officially withdrew legitimacy from the Prussian Weimar coalition, neither the control of the police, nor that of the unions, neither possession of a considerable left militia of the republic, nor Braun's basic commitment to preserve the Prussian state enabled the "Red Czar" to prevent the takeover of the state by the Reich in 1932. When von Papen's administration took over Prussia, it did not enjoy the support of the people. That was a well-known fact. von Papen, however, had acted under a presidential emergency decree. And appeal to the law in the form of a suit in the Reich Court was the only defense that a leadership that had remained Prussian and administrative at heart was capable of (Huber, 1966:III:506–36; Dietrich, 1966:255). Prussian democracy had been a stable one because it was democratic in form only, but Prussian in essence. The form vanished in true Prussian style as a result of compliance with a simple order from supervening rational-legal authority. In the style of its life as well as its death, Prussian republicanism had remained an expression of the Prussian ethos.

The imperial polity, as I observed earlier, had suffered from a reversal between principle and practice in politics that drove Wilhelminian Germany into a two-front war. Prior to World War I the spokesmen of an alleged national interest, the Junkers and the industrialists, had in fact acted on class interest. The compromise of these intrinsically opposed interests had alienated Russia and England. The Socialists, however, those much-maligned "infidels of the fatherland," had come to act as patriots while before they had preached the gospel of Marxist enlightenment. This reversal between the principles enunciated and the action sustained also characterized the republic.

Of the considerable foreign-policy successes the Weimar politicians scored, there was but one that found the approval of the "national opposition" of the right. This was the Rapallo treaty with the Soviet Union in 1922. With no territorial alterations and the renunciation of any compensation claims for war damage, this treaty showed that the "war-guilt lie" and its consequences could be defeated. Yet anything short of total victory in this area earned one the unremitting hate of the right. Stresemann's considerable achievements in bringing Germany back into the Western community of nations as a respected member was consistently greeted with charges of a sellout of national interest. World War I had involved 30 nations, 65 million men in arms, 8 million dead, nearly 25 million wounded, and an estimated total cost of about 180 billion dollars (Reinhardt, 1962:644). For Germany, accepting the Versailles Treaty, regardless of the circumstances, had meant accepting responsibility. Therefore, the governments' ability to reach a final settlement of about 110 billion reichsmarks amounted to a reduction to less than a quarter of the total burden under prevailing rates of exchange. But the nationalists opposed the Dawes and Young plans with vehemence (Halpern, 1965:293, 386). Similarly, the Locarno agreement in 1925 should have warmed a patriotic heart. It brought no less than a guarantee of Germany's western frontiers, freedom from Western interference in settling her borders in the East, where she had lost territory, and admission to the League of Nations as a leading power. But the nationalists decried these achievements as treasonable *Erfüllung* of the Versailles *Diktat*.

The Socialists, on the other hand, consistently supported the foreign policy of the leader of the party of business interests, and often the bourgeois administration in the bargain. In external affairs they always put national over class interests. They even collaborated with their outspoken class enemy, big business, as represented in the People's Party to fight inflation. They went so far as to grant these people an enabling act insisting only on the inviolability of their own "sacred cow," the eight-hour day. When a bourgeois-rightist coalition government moved against the eight-hour day, the Socialists found their opposition hampered by their desire to support the government's foreign policy (Halpern, 1965:150, 203–361). Sacrificing class interest, however, had not earned the Socialists any appreciation among the right. By 1930, with their patience exhausted, the Socialists refused a reduction in unemployment compensation, which pre-Keynesian economic orthodoxy dictated. As one of them put it, they were no longer willing "to put some imaginary national interest before the proletariat's class interest" (Eyck, 1963:II:110). And it remains an irony of history that the last democratically legitimated Weimar administration should fall because the Socialists for once brought principle in line with practice (Eyck, 1963:II:244–50).

In explaining this phenomenon of a reversal in principle and practice on the part of the parties at the national level, the already referred to triple fusion of executive, legislative, and support mobilization functions constituted one factor. To this should be added on further fusion. Most parties in Germany did not act as parts of a nation who saw their role in relation to the whole. Instead, they acted as the direct political arm of distinct social communities. They were the direct instruments of diverse social forces and did not transform particularist interests into universally valid national social problems (Neumann, 1965:25–27). The parties acted as though a national center existed rather than accepting it as one of their tasks to create one. This, in turn, created the impression as if all were in permanent opposition, an impression much exploited by the national opposition. When considered in terms of their ideological slogans, most parties were failures vis-à-vis their special clienteles. One of the few exceptions would seem to have been the Catholics' educational ideals. The Center Party succeeded in preventing the introduction of a uniform secular school system, an unconstitutional success at that (Eyck, 1963:II:150–51). Publicly identified as failures, the party system as a whole lost credibility, and Weimar democracy lost legitimacy. But while multiple structural fusions can account somewhat for the outcome, they cannot explain why the German party system remained underdeveloped in the first place.

Here the prevalent value dissensus suggests "institutionalized insincerity in the public realm" as one answer. Extreme diversity in societal ideals in the context of a widely shared conception of an amoral public sphere deprived the national society of any genuinely "sacred" aspect while supplying the leaders of the segregated subcultural communities with a highly instrumental orientation to the role of ideals in public life. Put differently, in such a society the law had no "spirit," it only had a letter to be observed. Society was not an object of moral respect; it was an entity to be manipulated. Living among a multiplicity of moral strangers, one had to observe the letter of the law lest the association into a nation disintegrate. But to feel bound by some "spirit of the law" not only made no sense, since such a spirit was nonexistent, it also seemed to be irresponsible, since the potential development of such a spirit in the future demanded a ruthless pursuit of the advancement of one's ideals and interests in the present, lest the future be shaped by others to the detriment of one's own integrity. This dilemma supplied German political life with its deceptive veneer of idealism beneath which hid a ruthless opportunism. In order to maintain the loyalty of one's own constituents, one constantly had to espouse some cause. In order to recruit new entrants into the political system, one could present one's cause according to effectiveness criteria alone. In a society where a profound value dissensus dictated the practice of domination by interest constellation but one coupled with high levels of political mobilization, such a competitive support process eventually must give the edge to new political movements, regardless of what kind of regime is involved. The basic reason is that the main participants in the political system suffer more from its legitimacy loss than the outsiders. In Wilhelminian Germany the insiders were the monarchical parties; during Weimar they were the democratic forces.

The idea of an amoral public sphere facilitated both the temporary alliance among moral strangers and the misrepresentation of one's own ideals to new groups in order to attract them to one's colors. Thus the People's Party, representative of big-business interests, for example, could collaborate with the Democrats and the Socialists in supporting the payment of war reparations under inflationary conditions when this was good for business early in the regime. The People's Party could also form an alliance with the national opposition later when that promised to retard the drift toward a more egalitarian welfare state not regarded as "good for business." The Socialist community, on the other hand, could develop a left militia that espoused militarism, nationalism, and an advocacy of a Greater Germany (*Anschluss* of Austria) in order to attract youth who seemed to respond to this imagery more favorably than to the orthodox Marxist gospel. To the core members of the Socialist subculture, one could argue that the left militia was after all not the party (Rohe, 1966:51–55, 104, 250). The net effect of this instrumental play with the ideological concerns of men and women was further to erode what little class character the Germany party system had. Even the one class party, that of the working class, became less so. It has been estimated that the nonworking-class vote of the Socialists increased from about 25 percent before World War I to about 40 percent by 1930. Similarly, the successors to the prewar upper-class Conservatives, the Nationalists (DNVP), increased their support among the newly impoverished middle class (Neumann, 1965:32–34, 61). But the discrepancy between "theory" and practice hurt the Socialists, who participated in Weimar far more than the Nationalists, who largely refrained from collaboration with the regime. From 1919 to the election of November 1932, the Socialists lost 46 percent of their vote, the Nationalists only 15 percent (Huber, 1966:III:606–7).

Weimar democracy had led the Socialists to an elite position among the German parties. While theirs was a predominance in terms of the size of electoral support and therefore one "deserved" according to the tenets of the democratic rules of the game, they were nonetheless seen as having politically profited from the fact that the country had lost the war. Democracy, and with that their predominant position, had fallen into their lap by virtue of the collapse of the Wilhelminian polity, one attributable to a lack of faith in its own right to exist. And the democratic republic had become a reality without any important contribution on the part of the Socialists. To the party oligarchs of these once-discriminated-against sons of imperial Germany, formal patriotism now proved more urgent than revolutionary change; for preservation of the nation seemed a prerequisite to its transformation. For this reason, as well as their own version of a commitment to a strong nation, reconstituting the sovereignty of the country in a real sense of being masters in one's own house became their first order of business. In contrast to other countires, Germany had financed the First World War through inflation rather than by taxation. That was perhaps the best indicator of the fact of rule by interest constellation under the *Kaiser* as well as her fragile national unity at the mass level of society. And for the new democratic republic this meant a huge public debt (Eyck, 1963:I:131). Given the conventional wisdom of economic thought of a time when Keynes had yet to make his way, the only hope lay in the reduction of reparations payments and the reconstruction of an economy that deserved trust in the eyes of the capitalist West, the only source of credit for German business. And so, now also instrumentally oriented to matters of ideology, the Socialist leadership tried to convince the party's fundamentalist believers in socialism that economic recovery and genuine sovereignty had to be the priorities of the responsible Socialist. "Socialism now" was simply out of the question.

For the nationalist reactionary groups, particularly the Prussian conservative strata, the situation was almost reversed. Weimar meant that they had lost not only the war, but a state as well. The new system was so alien to their traditions in its appearance that they felt nothing but hate for it. They had also been doubly implicated in the creation of the system. As self-conceived pillars of the Second Reich, the lost war was most directly their responsibility; and the Army, the sole arm of their tenuous elite position in German society at large, had brought about the abdication of the Emperor. Hence the expiration of the monarchy rested on their shoulders primarily. Further, be it recalled, beyond these immediate needs to deny such realities, opposition to Berlin had been a long-standing tradition among the East Elbian landed upper class. Now, for once, one could oppose central government in a fashion unrestrained by loyalty to King and fatherland. Without a King of Prussia and an Emperor of Germany ostensibly representing a national community, the haunted fatherland stood exposed as having been some dream. Now that dream had vanished; neither King nor fatherland existed any longer, and one could act with nothing but alleged political realism. Just how far this alienation could go is illustrated in a 1932 campaign speech by Hitler in Pommerania, one of the Junker strongholds of the country. Out to mobilize support, Hitler here placed the New Order squarely above the fatherland in its extant form by denying Weimar Germany his SA and SS troops to defend the eastern borders against feared Polish incursions (Eyck, 1963:II:364). For these self-conceived professional patriots and loyal Prussians, the potential loss of further territory was apparently nothing compared with the urgency to reclaim their state from its internal enemies. As always for this group, sheer class interest coincided with their vision of the good society, for just during that time the Weimar regime had given new impetus to "colonizing the East"—that is, advocating the settlement of an agricultural yeoman class in East Elbia. Denouncing the plan as "agrarian Bolshevism" (Eyck, 1963:II:380–81), the Prussian upper-class opposition to Weimar could combine a lofty idealism with healthy economic self-interest, once again at the expense of national interest.

According to Bracher (1955:47) the ultimate reason for the failure of Weimar democracy is to be seen in "the confluence of an apolitical orientation with an apolitical veneration of power." Let me fill the term "apolitical" with some content. Living in a formal nation-state populated with many groups who remained moral strangers to each other, the apolitical orientations among the Germans largely amounted to an inordinate insensitivity to the convictions and ideals of others. Segregated into isolated subcultures, one could treat outsiders somewhat like traditional men treated actual foreigners, as creatures not quite belonging to the same species. This effectively interfered with the aggregation and integration of interests but not with political mobilization on a massive scale; for an orientation to an amoral public sphere fostered a conception of power as merely another societal resource, like wealth. This unproblematical orientation to power, under the slogan "the more, the better, " was quite disproportionate to the inability to compromise and the resulting primitivity of an undifferentiated political structure. On the level of political culture it was German to be ambivalent about legitimate sources of political change, to be fearful about new contenders for political power, ambivalent about partisan strife, and desirous of "strong government." Germany, so it seems, succumbed to the Nazis because their image conformed to the conflicted elements of this political culture the best. The Nazis operated on the principle of formal legality, yet claimed to be revolutionaries; they were new contenders for political power, but also pretended to be nothing but a modern version of what had been Prussia's glory; they were for unity, but also offered a corporatist societal image; they were against partisan strife, but offered undreamed-of opportunities for its practice; and they offered a "strong government" but one where even the most directly opposed interests were to be satisfied. Above all, they did little to specify the future in any concrete way and offered an escape from a painful present.

For Germany's one-dimensional elites it was these features in their very contrariness that made the Nazis an acceptable alternative. They seemed to promise a more dynamic form of domination by interest constellation than the country had ever known. Therefore, they also heralded truly unprecedented opportunities in the struggle for status congruence, for "becoming somebody again." If there was any symbolic fit at the level of sociopsychological drives between Adolf Hitler and the Germans, that had nothing to do with racism and far less to do with resentments about the war just lost than has been claimed (Binion, 1976). But there was a fit nonetheless, if not one between Hitler and the people at large, then one between that dynamo of a political drummer and the relatively status-deprived elites in Germany. By social origin Hitler was lower middle class (Fest, 1973:29–44). He therefore came from a classic group of relatively status-deprived in industrial society, the white-collar salariat in the public and private sectors of economic life (Mills, 1951). These are people with claims to respectability and prestige that typically outrun income. And while the reaction to inconsistency of status does depend on the nature of the dimensions involved, when these are both achieved, such as a claim to prestige based on education but unrewarded in income, then the patterns of frustrated "one-upmanship" do lead to a common fate of stress, of resentment, and of anger in public interactions (Lenski, 1966:86–88; Kriesberg, 1979:264–65). Often such anger may remain quite muted. Potentially, however, the status-inconsistent are always the active ones in society. However lowly of origin, Hitler had made it. He was a classic parvenu, and a political one at that. To the elites in German society whose historical position directed them toward a search for "power above all" in order to overcome status inconsistency, such a political parvenu could symbolize inspiration. The "glove that fits the hand" symbolic fit pertained to a common fate of status inconsistency, and one that could be overcome, or so it seemed, but not to anti-Semitism, racial mysticism, or any ideologism.

If so, one would also expect an increase in the extent and intensity of extraparliamentary political organizations and their activities. Relative to Wilhelminian Germany, this apparently happened in the Weimar democracy.

Organizing for Propaganda and Force: A Note on the Weimar Militias

Just as with democracy, demobilization after the war remained more formal than real. With a reduction of the official Army to 100,000 men, many of the soldiers—officers and rank alike—could not be absorbed into the civilian labor force of an economy weakened by inflation and depression. Furthermore, the republic's official Army seemed insufficient to deal with problems of internal violence and external threat to the borders in the East during the early years. Thus for both economic and political reasons, the private armies of the Free Corps movement enjoyed public toleration and occasional deployment by the offical government. A study of forty such freebooter corps, probably representative of most, described their members as Fascists. They had no political program and were proud of it. They loved "action," pure and simple; they were anti-Semitic but in that only tools of other interests; they were not uniformly anti-Communist, but they were people who had definitely lost all remnants of a genuine loyalty to monarchy after the failure of the Kapp *Putsch* in 1920. Outlawed thereafter, some found their way back into the official Army, others joined Hitler's SA, and yet others kept their organizations alive behind the front of legitimate business establishments in trucking, road construction, detective agencies, or agricultural communes financed by East Elbia's estate owners. This "vanguard of Nazism" was also financed by big business. For example, one of their murder victims, Rathenau, had also been one of their more prominent supporters, to the tune of 5 million dollars. One tentative estimate put their strength at 200,000. They produced a daily newspaper, a newsmagazine, a political-anthropological monthly, and distributed 7 million pieces of propaganda in a single year alone. By 1931 their youth work involved close to 500,000 youngsters (Waite, 1952:182–220, 266–76). The Free Corps served the republic in eastern border regions, but they also supported the rebellious Kahr regime in Bavaria. Though financed by the federal government at times, they actually deprived it of a monopoly of force, at least until 1923 (Schulz, 1963:357). Except for the states of Saxony and Thuringia, the freebooters were everywhere under the control of the right-wing political groups. The freebooters constituted a support of Weimar democracy only when the suppression of leftist radicalism was at stake.

However, the freebooters were merely an early special case of a more general phenomenon during these years: the growth of militias. During the Weimar regime no less than 22 rightist and 7 leftist militias were outlawed for various periods of time. Mostly this meant only that they carried on their activities in clandestine fashion (Huber, 1966:III: 269–70). The pattern of organization and counterorganization already familiar from Wilhelminian days also came to characterize the militias. On the right the most important were the Soldiers' League *(Stahlhelm)*, and Hitlers Storm Troopers (SA). On the Left the Socialists formed a leftist militia, the Banner Black-Red-Gold, hereafter referred to as the Banner.

Founded in 1918, the Soldiers' League attempted to use the camaraderie of the trenches as a general template for the molding of civilian social life.

Egalitarian in outlook at first, this group was quite supportive of the republican regime during the early years. Yet the group's basic experience, the war, permitted them to conceive of politics as only a continuation of war by other means. Acting as a reserve army, deployed as auxiliary riot police, and involved in the Ruhr rebellion as well as in Hitler's Munich *Putsch*, the League split into three factions by 1922. One of these, mostly situated in Bavaria, was nationalist, monarchist, and federalist; another took Mussolini's success as their model; a third simply became a special police for Kahr's Bavarian regime. The traditional Prussian-Bavarian enmity also affected the League, pitting a northern faction, who selected the Banner, Jews, and the Catholic Church as their enemies, against a southern branch, who defended the Catholic Church and regionalism. Though never an official policy, anti-Semitism became an increasing practice, leading the Jewish members to leave the organization to form their own (Berghahn, 1966:13–75). Antidemocratic sentiments also gained ground, emerging into an official declaration of war on the Weimar Republic by 1928. The national convention of that year announced the new policy in unambiguous language: "We hate the present form of the German state with all our hearts because it denies to us the hope of freeing our enslaved fatherland. It denies us any opportunity to cleanse the German people from the war-guilt lie, and works against the gain of necessary living space in Eastern Europe. . . . We oppose the political system that regulates this state as well as all those who support it with their never-ending compromises" (Eyck, 1963:II:167). Numerically the League was an impressive force. In 1925 they had a membership of 260,000, which grew to 327,000 by 1931. They were capable of massing between 100,000 and 200,000 men for conventions or demonstrations in any one city. In 1925 their monthly regular income was about 60,000 Reichsmarks. They maintained a daily newspaper with a circulation of 200,000, a monthly, and acquired the well-known conservative *Kreuzzeitung* in 1931 (Berghahn, 1966:85–237). But their major objective, the unification of all nationalist forces to overthrow the system, failed principally because of a severe split over the adequate means. The question of whether one should overcome the system "from the inside" with the help of President Hindenburg, or from the outside with the help of Hitler, was never settled. More generally, leadership was also a problem. Spanning across the regions in German society, not class-specific in membership, and lacking both a developed ideology and charismatic leaders, the League constituted a conglomerate of militant discontent rather than an organization capable of generating genuine consensus concerning the nature of the new order they strove for. They were united in their hostility against the present regime, but remained

disunited concerning the content of its alternative. The pervasive disagreements over the means were little more than reflections of the
disagreements over the ends pursued.

In this respect the League was rather similar to its major opponent, the
Banner. This nationwide defense corps of the republic was more united
against the specter of several rightist and the Communist alternatives than
on the question of what extant democracy should mean. The organization
was founded in 1924 with the explicit purpose of defeating the forces of
the nationalist opposition. The task was to save democracy, pure and
simple, and not to reason why or what democracy might be. The
Socialists had their own interpretation about the antirepublican wing of
the Free Corps and the Soldiers' League. According to this view, these
groups had turned against Weimar because they felt discarded by it.
Having saved the republic from the Communist threat during the early
years, the republic had dismissed its saviors. Such an interpretation
demanded that one had to organize for the defense of the republic by
copying the means of the attacker, since only that would prove that the
republic rewarded real patriotism. This meant using the symbols of
nationalism and militarism, and using force, and so the deployment of
antidemocratic means. It meant more yet. As the enemies of the republic
derived their support from all quarters of society, the Banner too strove to
create an impression of representing the republican elements of all strata
and regions, even though the organization in fact was the creature of the
Socialist community (Rohe, 1966:27–72). Reaching a membership of 3½
million, the Banner was undoubtedly the largest political organization of
the nonparty variety in Germany. Even when considered only in terms of
its activist core of a million men, the Banner still outranked the army 10
times. Financed by the Socialists, the Reichswehr, wealthy individuals,
and Jewish organizations, the Banner had an annual operating budget of
10 million to 12 million Reichsmarks (Rohe, 1966:73–77). The centralized,
hierarchical nature of the Banner's organization, with its military-tech-
nical branch composed of officers and ranks and youth camps, was in all
essentials like the organization of its opponents, the League, the SA, and
the Communist Soldiers' League (*Rotfrontkämpferbund*). The one distinguishing characteristic vis-à-vis the Nazi Storm Troopers was a colle-
giate top. The Banner was run by a committee, not a *Führer*. In all other
respects, however, the Banner, with its uniforms, parades, demonstrations, mass rallies, military exercises, and the use of violence, gave the
League good reason to complain that the left militia had stolen its very
own form. In maintaining rifle clubs and conducting shooting competitions, in financing a rifle factory in Austria and engaging in violence that

brought court sentences to 3,000 members by 1932, in developing a leadership cult in 1931 and in the use of intensive propaganda activities on a nationwide front, the Banner too had come to take the soldier as the central model of political man. During one month of street fighting in 1932, for example, the Banner shared 99 dead with its opponents; a later casualty list enumerated 64 dead for the Banner, 42 for the Nazis, 5 for the Soldiers' League, and 3 for the Communists (Rohe, 1966:114–207, 342, 425). Though the leadership of the Banner never became a victim of its own propaganda and activities, the *Gemeinschaft* ideology of the trenches and the militaristic style of action caused considerable confusion at home and abroad, where the Banner was sometimes seen as a branch of the Pan-Germans (Rohe, 1966:126–42, 234).

Intent on transforming "republicans by reason" to "republicans by heart" whatever the cost, the Banner even tried to outdo its nationalist opponents in nationalist ideology. In addition to copying their rightist opponents in style, the Banner was also explicitly for the Great-German solution, which had failed in 1871. They decried the Prussian Junkers as antinationalists, alleging that they had sold out on the Austrian Germans for the sake of selfish interests. The Banner tried to identify itself with the "true Prussian tradition," that of the reformers, which had allegedly lost out in 1848. In 1926 the Banner sent formations to Vienna, where they staged the largest *Anschluss* demonstration of the Weimar Republic. Excessively nationalist, charging the monarchical right with unpatriotic sentiment and factual treason to the nation's interest, while copying their methods, the Banner achieved little more than deepening the right-left cleavage in German society (Rohe, 1966:205, 227–44).

But that deepening cleavage did not enhance the solidarity within either camp. Similar to the Soldiers' League's failure to unite the forces of the right, the Banner proclaimed to stand above parties but failed to achieve any solidarity among the republican forces. Almost 90 percent of the members of the Banner were also either members of the Socialist Party or its sympathizers. The leadership of the Banner derived nearly entirely from the socialist subculture; only the leading cadres of the technical-military branch were new men. Though it published its own two newspapers, few saw the Banner as anything more than a paramilitary arm of the Socialists. Furthermore, organizational involvement in the Banner did not prove to be an advantage for Socialist or other leftist politicians. Its nationalism and military stance caused factionalism within the Socialist Party, the Banner, the unions, and between the unions and the party. Committed pacifists objected to the military stance, fundmen-talist socialists to the nationalist propaganda, liberals to the *Gemeinschaft* myth, committed proletarians to the absence of class consciousness, and party bureaucrats objected to the sheer fact of a competing organizational apparatus (Rohe, 1966:266–342).

In response to the apparition of a Hugenberg-Hitler alliance in the 1931 Harzburg Front, the left formed its counterfront. This was the Iron Front, composed of the Banner, the national federation of labor, and the Socialist Party. A Professor Tschachotin, erstwhile student of Pavlov, was engaged as an expert in psychological terror to weld the republican forces together and confuse the opposition. Though not as factionalized and basically conflict-laden as the Harzburg Front, the Iron Front was quite as ineffectual. Neither concerted action in counterviolence, nor a general strike were seriously planned. Threats uttered in these directions were made conditional on Hitler's "doing something unconstitutional." But Hitler did not oblige, and after his legal assumption of executive power, the Banner literally vanished overnight, with many of its members seeking admission into the Soldiers' League, which in turn sought refuge in the SA, and few receiving admission in either (Rohe, 1966:386–487).

The one of the three big militias that was to be "victorious" was in fact the smallest. Founded in 1922, the SA grew from a small band of tough guys to a force of about 800 in Bavaria by the end of the year. One year later, at the time of Hitler's *Putsch*, the SA had an estimated strength of 1,560 men, but in their military maneuvers they were neither under the command of Hitler, nor exclusively at the call of Röhm, but under the control of the Army instead. After the *Putsch*, starting anew, the SA, now on its own, grew to a strength of 15,000 men by 1927. By 1929 an additional 5,000 had been added, and recruitment from the unemployed doubled the membership to 30,000 by 1930. Two years later, a Prussian police survey put the SA's strength at 225,000 men at the beginning of 1932. And on January 30, 1933, Hitler's feast of assumption, total SA strength was put at 300,000 (Bennecke, 1962:30–42, 78, 105).

In sheer manpower these three militias outnumbered the Army by about 16 to 1. But the numerical strength on the right did not augur well for its success. While an Army study in 1932 "officially determined" that the Army lacked sufficient monopoly of force to guarantee the constitution against the Nazis and the Communists (Huber, 1966:III:561–63), this probably reflected far more a lack of will to fight for the republic than an accurate assessment of the actual strength of contending forces on both sides of the right-left cleavage. The Harzburg Front meeting, which was to ally the Soldiers' League with the SA, had been so conflictful that it lacked even in propaganda effect. Berghahn (1966:185–86) tells us that the meeting was marred by near-violence. Hitler refused to salute the parading Soldiers' League and stayed away from dinner with their leaders. SA and League members came to blows about which flag to fly from the convention hotel, with the SA sponsoring the swastika and the League the imperial colors. Thus, even if one were to grant authenticity to that alliance, the combined strength of the right amounted to a force of only 600,000. Similarly, if one discounts considerable portions of the Iron Front as unreliable forces and takes only the activist core of the Banner directly into consideration, then the organized paramilitary of the Republican forces with a million still outnumbered the right by a ratio of about 10 to 6. Adding the Army to the Republican side and the Communists to the opposing one hardly would have tipped the balance in favor of the organized opponents of Weimar. On the contrary, the republican forces were far superior numerically.

Neither superiority in terror nor in propaganda contributed to Hitler's success. In both terms his were the weakest forces. Concerning propaganda impact, the Nazis had 5 dailies and 26 weeklies in 1929. By 1931 they had been able to increase their printed output to 12 dailies and 33 weeklies (Bennecke, 1968:29). But the Socialists fielded 203 newspapers with a combined circulation of 1.3 million copies in 1929. Even in 1932, with 135 newspapers, their press impact was far larger than that of the Nazis (Koszyk, 1966:37, 43). The Nazis might have "outmet" all others, as Allen (1965:294–95) put it, offering liturgical ceremonies of hope more frequently, consistently, and fervently to more people than any other political organization. However, since they gained votes quite disproportionate to their local presence, particularly in East Elbia (Bennecke, 1968:30), they succeeded in harnessing an essentially contentless protest vote, rather than endorsement of Nazism in any of its varieties. In view of the above, Eyck's judgment concerning the fall of the empire would seem to apply to Weimar as well. As with the first, the second German national regime fell essentially because of a lack of faith in its own right to exist.

Conclusion

Like the Wilhelminian polity, democracy in Germany fell because the underlying reality of politics was a continuation of domination by interest constellations. As too few among the critical elites had been genuinely committed monarchists to save the throne, far too few during the Weimar Republic had ever moved from the status of "republicans by reason" to that of "republicans by heart." Only the end of democracy came faster and by more spectacular means. That was attributable to more spectacular domestic failure in coping with the economic distress of the Western world at the time that registered in the United States as the Great Depression while manifesting itself in Germany as runaway inflation.

Important remains the fact that all the patriotism displayed by the Socialists remained in vain. However superior in resources regarding numbers mobilized, and ideas spread in their newspapers, and related efforts, the ostensible defenders of democracy succumbed to inferior forces because they shared with them one critical feature: an orientation to the state as a mere instrument for the advancement of particular interests in society, and one that only fools hankering to some romanticized past would ever confuse with a genuine community of people by virtue of shared beliefs in unalterable moral principles. Just like the Wilhelminian polity, Weimar democracy was characterized by a continuing inability for consensus formation. But while the agitprop organizations under the *Kaiser* had operated mainly with the spoken and the printed word, political mobilization in the republic in addition increasingly involved bodies and fists. Politics of the street, of the stadium, and of field maneuvers with thousands and hundreds of thousands on the march became standard features.

Men living at or below the subsistence level spent a considerable portion of what little they had on political activities. Estimates indicate that it took about 15 years for the man on the dole to die. In the early 1930s, for example, a man with a family of 4 children received 15.80 marks in unemployment benefits. Of such a meager allowance one dedicated Communist regularly spent 2.30 marks per week, or 14.6 percent of his total weekly income, for the party. There must have been many such cases, however, for it was not too different in other political organizations. Most of the little men in the SA had to defray the expenses for food, transport, and uniforms out of their own pocket. They received financial support from the organization for out-of-town activities only (Bennecke, 1962:141, 168, 204–6). Thus there were probably millions of poor people in Germany who spent far more than the biblical tithe in the service of their political cause. Such a finding does not augur well for the metaphor of the Germans as traditional subjects, noninvolved and passively oriented to an *Obrigkeitsstaat*. The image of a mobilized populace of political activists seems closer to the truth.

Though efforts intensified and multiplied, the positive concrete ends pursued by various groups were not realized. Next to a constantly deteriorating economy this failure in goal attainment applied to groups as well as to society. Weimar society was not closer to socialism at its end than at the beginning. It was not a more liberal society either, if by that one means above all a willingness to accept the inevitability of social and political conflicts and a consequent commitment to their institutionalization by peaceful regulation. A return to a monarchical, more authoritarian state with minimal popular participation seemed as far off in the 1930s as it had before, and the Communist utopia, though growing in electoral terms, remained the ideal of an increasingly isolated minority. The attempts at constitutional reform remained stalemated as well. Excepting the Southerners, most groups here aimed at a unitary state, though for quite different reasons. Even in terms of actual administrative unification the republic did not proceed much beyond what it had already attained in 1919. In 1927 the Reich Unemployment Insurance Authority was added to the Reich Finance Administration. Next to the postal and railway administrations these two were the only Reich bureaucracies with a field staff. The *Länder* continued to administer all other national policies under their own auspices, and very likely without any really increased responsiveness to the national center (Jacob, 1963:73–95). With a decline in the legitimacy of the political system came a decline in support of those political forces that had been associated most directly with the symbol of democracy. Support went instead to outsiders and opponents of the regime. Only the negation of the Weimar polity itself succeeded, and not in terms that signaled consensus on an alternative. Ultimately, victory was to go to those who only vaguely knew what they did not want.

Political mobilization rose to unprecedented levels. Fragmentation of the political forces on the right and on the left was one result of mobilization. Deepening cleavages between the two camps and within each on both sides was another. Inflation of political messages to the point of near-perfect confusion was a third. Neither the People's Party, the Nationalists, nor the Nazis on the right could form a viable coalition, nor was this possible on the left. In fact, the continuing *embourgeoisement* of the Socialists and their willingness to copy the nationalist-militarist style of their rightist opponents cost the party more support on the left than what it gained from the middle and the right (Hunt, 1964:142–48). Furthermore, the activities of the Banner contributed to the formation of additional splinter parties on the left (Rohe, 1966:386; Hunt, 1964: 233–36). The resulting multiplication of divisions and the decline of crosscutting cleavages can hardly be accounted for in terms of economic distress alone. Multiple value-cleavages in connection with a near-completely instrumental orientation to ideals when pronounced for public consumption, were the more important factors.

When the Banner and the later Iron Front tried to overtake the right ideologically on the right, the republican forces simply lost credibility among the general public as well as among their own adherents. When members of the Soldiers' League and the SA came close to physical violence concerning whether the imperial colors or the swastika standard should decorate the major hotel of the Harzburg Front convention, then this too was an adequate expression of the division on the right. For the nation the sporadic and inauthentic Harzburg Front became a crucial analogue to the earlier iron-and-rye coalition. It was again an alliance of ideological strangers united momentarily on short-run interests, defeating the Republic while being deeply divided on long-run goals—that is, on what German society should be like. Instead of an alliance between Junkerdom and industrial interest, the Harzburg Front was more one between the Junkers and the Nazi *ex plebes*. It symbolized the apparent association between the social prestige of the Old Germany and what paraded as the new virtues of the Third Reich. Hindenburg was a member of the Soldiers' League, and the League marched with the SA at Harzburg. Hindenburg was also a Junker. Moreover, the convention was graced by the attendance of General Seeckt, a Prussian Crown Prince, and other luminaries of Prussia-Germany. The prestige representatives of an old order here bestowed respect on the advocates of a new one. In addition to rational legality and a charismatic leader, which the Nazis brought along on their own, this gave them an indispensable third source of political legitimacy without which they could not succeed: traditional authority. That endorsement, moreover, could not be withdrawn easily again, lest the highest prestige group of the older order was to reveal in public a terrible truth which it had to hide even from itself: that men who proclaimed to be the incarnation of the Prussian ethos of self-abnegating service to the state, had, by unsuccessful adaptation to modernity, in fact ended up as the opposite of their official identity—a class seeking to maximize its advantages regardless of the consequences for the nation. A few individuals of this older prestige group "found themselves" later and managed to die in the only way adequate to their tradition—namely, by opposing the Nazis (Schramm, 1964). For the status group as such and for the nation, however, that inauthentic association between the symbols of the Old and the New Germany became the proverbial moving finger that writes and having writ, moves on. And in light of the General Staff's ineffectual opposition to Hilter's early pursuit of *Lebensraum* before the fall of France (O'Neill, 1966), a slightly altered version of the remainder of these immortal lines applies as well: Nor all their piety nor wit could change a single line, nor all their "fears" wash out a word of it.

CHAPTER EIGHT

The Nazi New Order:
Institutionalized Disorder

The *Weltanschauung* propagated under National Socialism was a glove tailor-made to unleash the barely contained social forces inherent in Germany's social structure with its deep value cleavages, on the one hand, and its one-dimensional national elites, on the other; for in such a context of appreciated value pluralism with its concomitant privatization of morals, these elites all could come to pursue a similar position-determined interest. Unidimensional in their resource base, all could strive for the resources they lacked. And conquest of a continental empire in Eastern Europe "promised" a most alluring start in the competition for a more generalized social status, the acquisition of power. If the essence of economic modernity is the production of wealth in abstract form—not wealth tied to any particular good or service or any particular mode of production or any particular market, but wealth, period, in whatever form—Germany's modern history can be read as an overweening reach for political modernity, the unconstrained pursuit of power, period, in whatever form. "Power over nature," so we are told, "is something men can share. Power over men is something for which men must compete" (Deutsch, 1970:25). Now, striving for status resources is striving for some form or other of power over men. While the German elites did that at home, the major advantage that the pursuit of empire yielded was simple and twofold. It provided space for power opportunities where one could avoid a direct clash with established groups at home, and it provided all with a conveniently stretchable legitimation formula, getting on with the war effort. All that was neccessary was a *Weltanschauung*, and one at once progressive in providing an utterly unsentimental perspective on the relation between the individual and society, and reactionary in promising

263

to shatter all vestiges of bourgeois respectability in the pursuit of individual success.

The fierce, if not ruthless, striving for generalized status that a suitable *Weltanschauung* could unleash is not so difficult to envisage. Consider the merely wealthy man, a German *Schlotbaron*. His was "the power" to command impressive liquid resources, fixed assets, and large bureaucratic organizations in the economy. But for all that wealth and its associated claim to super competence in matters economic, the rewards of prestige commensurate with so much wealth remained beyond his grasp. Next to a general of the Army, the institution exercising a relative monopoly claim over prestige, he was a nothing. The general, in turn, was not much better off. For all the splendor of the uniform he could wear, for all the glances of admiration and envy that he, the walking symbolic depository of the Prussian tradition, could attract—and these were considerable, for the figure of the soldier is the fiduciary of trust in the functioning and permanence of the political entity in any *de facto* empire, whatever the name of the polity—he knew all too well that his was the fate of a relative pauper. Or consider the merely virtuous man, the German mandarin. Professor of physics, of history, or of geopolitics, whatever the discipline, the university professor was the walking depository of value-relevant knowledge about the human condition in changing times. For all his weighty knowledge, for all the adulation pouring forth from less-honed minds, he could never escape the experience that chance governed the implementation of his function, providing a think tank for the nation.

To suggest that following Hitler's pursuit of *Lebensraum* in the East yielded more attractive opportunities for the striving toward generalized status for Germany's one-dimensional elites than just slugging it out at home may strike one as absurd today. How can one designate going to war against most of the industrialized world as some path of lesser resistance here? But such common-sense rebellion is burdened by the wisdom of hindsight and some notions we have today about an inexorable drive to endless war toward domination of the whole world, and eventual self-destruction, notions we *now* ascribe to Nazi totalitarianism. In 1939, or indeed before the defeat at Stalingrad, such perspectives were not apparent to Germany's one-dimensional elites. For example, Hitler had no interest whatever in the conquest of the British Empire. It just so happened that Britain refused to play the role he assigned to her in his plan for Germany's ascendancy to world-power status (Aigner, 1978). That, as we know, did not deter the German elites from following Hitler's pursuit of *Lebensraum* in the East *before* gaining some settlement of the war in the West. Also, ever since the sage Bismarck and his famous reinsurance treaty with Russia, a two-front war had been the haunting specter of all with foreign-policy concerns in Germany. And so, if one assumes that people generally, and elites especially, experience their national identity through identification with a particular political framework, some living constitution articulating the relations between the individual and the state and among the major institutions in society, unleashing the dogs of war on the East without resolution of the war in the West remains an instance of a brazen abandonment of common-sense self-interest. But with the removal of the assumption, you also remove the object of self-interest and self-preservation, that identity-conferring character of social institutions. Then some of the apparent mystery disappears. Accustomed to rule by interest constellation, none of the modern political regimes in Germany have ever acquired a collective identity role in the eyes of the elites. And the German elites could elaborate their historical experience into an ideological outlook on the modern condition of man. That outlook proclaimed that all our public lives are governed by the single standard of occupational success, and success in the here and now, within the grasp of mortal finite man, the individual. Where there is no identification with institutions outlasting the short lifespan of individuals, assertions of permanent national interests become nothing but the expression of self-serving group interests. What is more, believing that references to larger institutional interests are mere propaganda advanced by careerists out to succeed and advance themselves does not lack all empirical truth when it comes to the much-belabored term "national interest." Modernity means change. The median lifespan of political regimes in the last century was impressively short, ranging between nine and twenty years (Gurr, 1974:1,493). If one discounts such exceptions as the United States, Britain, Sweden, and Switzerland, one can assert: "In past recorded history, the political system under which most persons in most places lived was older than the individual. It is only in our time that most of the world's adults over thirty are older than their political regimes" (Deutsch, 1970:73).

If modernity means change, you can come to believe that what was right yesterday may well be wrong today. It would appear to follow that modernity means moral uncertainty. One response to this situation has been noted. In America it is a creeping tendency to confuse the moral with the legal (Maguire, 1975). Given the exceptional durability of the United States constitution and the near veneration it seems to enjoy, such confusions may well articulate morality with legality. More generally, though, modernity would seem to imply reliance on legality as a substitute for public morality. Direct moral sentiment has as its proper place only the intimate circles of friendship and kinship. Outside these spheres you argue with what is legal and what is possible, seeking a tenuous foothold in empirical truth as a guide to making behavior right. And that is a socially structured slippery slope that can seduce many otherwise reasonable men and women to slide down to *de facto* moral indifference in their public behavior. In Germany we are confronting a case of one-dimensional elites. By definition they suffer insecurity in the right to rule; by definition also, they are prone to seek to attain more generalized status resources. Unconstrained by shared values, they could embark on a course that comes natural to such elites, the course of power accumulation through empire-building. Some protest against the acquisition of Poles, Czechs, Russians, and so forth in the New Order inspired by a nationalist morality had to lack credibility. Such a man appeared a dreamer, a sentimental fool hankering after an ideal, and one that lacked all basis in the empirical realm. That civic-text ideal was that men and women ought to identify personally with their state and nation. Historical reality, with its profound level of political instability, however, designated such a notion a pipe dream, just as much a private fantasy and as inconsequential in the everyday realm of *Realpolitik* as Heinrich Himmler's actual charismatic leader-figure, Henry the Lion (Fraenkel and Manvell, 1965). But neither could the man inclined to resistance rely on law. For warfare, slave-labor recruitment, population resettlements—in short, nearly the whole array of human suffering and death—were all perfectly legal. Only the death factories themselves were ostensibly illegal. And, as well shall see in a moment, that lent itself to some interference in their operation.

For understanding the nature of modern sin, the withdrawal of moral concerns from public roles in our lives, however, it is important to keep organized mass murder in perspective. That point, one already made in Chapter II, bears repeating here. Killing the Jews and other "useless" humanity was a mere sideshow for practically all Germans who came into contact with the Holocaust Kingdom. But pursuit of empire was their main show. One should not succumb here to the temptation to assign a legitimation function to a polity that needed practically none. Nothing could be more erroneous than the belief that racism, making Europe *"judenrein,"* was a necessary legitimation commitment by which the German leadership circles hoped to earn their anticipated top-dog position in the New Order of National Socialism. False comfort lies on that road to apprehending the Holocaust. Racism was a central element in Hitler's own world view, one he shared with a very small circle of associates from the days of struggle for power before 1933. But "Germany's war against the Jews" was a mere sideshow of the war for *Lebensraum*, and none of the principal figures who ran the sideshow—whether Himmler or Heydrich, Eichmann or Höss, Pohl or Gluecks—were people who bothered with ideology. Two facts should not recede from our minds here. First, the imperialist war-aims Germany pursued in both World Wars were practically identical (Fischer, 1967; Bengtson, 1962). Second, the critical people on which any industrial order depends for its accomplishments are not street bullies but bureaucratic functionaries, the products of a middle-class upbringing. Those of Germany's middle-class sons who survived the pursuit of empire under the imperial flag dedicated themselves to the same ends under the swastika. On neither occasion did their pursuit of world-power status *require* legitimation in the form of anti-Semitism. On the first occasion that propaganda trumpet was conspicuous by its absence. If the same people can pursue the same ends, first without any political racism, then with it, the burden of proof about the relevance of anti-Semitism in Germany's short-lived national existence and the havoc she wrought in Europe clearly shifts to those who wish to make a case for it. Rather than assigning a legitimation function to the Nazi *Weltanschauung*, its important role has to be seen in unleashing the enormous social dynamics inherent in Germany's social structure; for if there was an essential difference between the *Kaiser*'s polity and the Third Reich's, that was evident in the greater political mobilization and the evident radicalism with which the pursuit of empire was conducted the second time.

A society as deeply divided in values as Germany, as modern in its major institutions of economic, scientific, and political life, and one saddled with one-dimensional national elites in relentless competition for generalized status with each other can be likened to a bursting bottle of champagne where a defective cork cannot withstand the pressure from inside. That cork was the Nazi *Weltanschauung*, and it played a double role. On the one hand, it served as the defective cork releasing the dynamics of a social structure that combined value dissensus with de-stratification of the elites; on the other, it also provided a channel for the energies to flow in one direction: conquest of an empire in the East.

The Nazi *Weltanschauung* played this double role because it was both a mentality and an ideology. Drawing this distinction has led Juan Linz (1964) to argue that mentalities characterize authoritarian regimes, while ideologies prevail in totalitarian ones. But in Nazi Germany one finds both. Ideologies are more or less elaborated systems of thought, often in written form. They are not only explanations of social conditions but also instructions as to what to do about them. Mentalities are more vague sets of symbols; they provide noncodified ways of reacting to situations in that they are ways of feeling and thinking, but ways always more emotional than rational. Historically, ideologies are usually found among the revolutionary forces, the forces of society that clamor for change.

Mentalities are usually found among established groups like the military and the civil service, to whom change will mean a new political task-master. In the nineteenth-century continental European context, mentalities were often made up of nationalism, xenophobia, and an "antipolitics outlook." The latter was a disdain of those games of party politics that make dissensus and conflicts in society visible, treat such conflicts as natural, and seek solutions by bargaining. To the military or civil-servant bearer of a mentality here, such bargaining appears as haggling. This reaction is simply an aversion against the intrusion of the behavioral patterns of the marketplace into the political process, an intrusion that these groups experience as demeaning. Before the open democratization of political life, the military and higher civil service were the bearers of the realm. Associated with the monarchy, they symbolized and represented the political center. And that position as the state-bearing groups was more or less an unchallenged one. All the perks of office such as tenure, judicial control exercised by peers, and old-age pensions, however much they had been won in struggles between staff and monarch, eventually emerged as rights of an estate in society. But this lasted only as long as these state-bearing groups could claim to represent the center. Democratization of political life transforms all such cherished rights into mere pork-barrel advantages. Today, for example, the plutocrats among the retired in industrialized countries are the ex-civil servants of the central government. Their pension replacement rates of prior earnings top those of all others in society (Kaim-Caudle, 1973:37). But we tend to see this as an unfair advantage; for government service to us today is just one form of employment much like others. It no longer has the aura of center representation it once enjoyed in historical empire societies. A mentality, then, is the reaction of groups to whom political modernization in terms of democratization means status threat. In Germany this phenomenon was unusually severe because of the de-stratification among national elites during the nineteenth century. Here it was not only the higher officer corps, civil and military, but also the economic and cultural elites, one-dimensional elites all, who suffered from a sense of status insecurity. That turned them into creatures of a reactionary mentality. To them Nazi slogans were invitations for attempting status equilibration. Theirs was a reaction, always more emotional than rational, but nonetheless a consistent one to see in "Germany Awake," the "leadership principle," and *"Lebensraum"* mere opportunities to add prestige to power or vice versa, to marry wealth with prestige or vice versa, or to amalgamate power to the position of a mere bearer of cultural honor or vice versa. In short, the symbols of National Socialism were characterized by a division of labor. To the elites in society Nazi "ideology" was primarily a mentality.

Hitler's well-known contempt for Rosenberg's *Myth of the Twentieth Century*, the one serious attempt of turning Nazi thought into an ideology, as well as Hitler's utter disregard for the party program, permitted treatment of the Nazi slogans as a mentality (Fest, 1973).

To Hitler himself the *Weltanschauung* was both a mentality and an ideology. Some of his beliefs he adhered to with that fanatical zeal and conviction we attribute to charismatic figures; others served as mere means for his ability to believe. And that division of labor is critical in the thesis of moral indifference at issue here. Anti-Semitism served him as a means to believe with fanatical consistency in his social Darwinist philosophy of history (Fest, 1973). The *"Drang nach Lebensraum"* was for Hitler an ideology, a set of ironclad commitments, to which he adhered from the beginning of his political career to the very end; for he was indeed convinced that all of human history was a ceaseless struggle for supremacy among peoples or races, a distinction he never bothered much about intellectually. That ability of his to believe in such a ceaseless struggle—not of classes, the Marxian version, but of peoples—reassured him in his self-conception as a missionary figure in the history of the German "people," and so of his historical right to absolute personal rule in Germany's foreign-policy objectives. Killing Jews and Gypsies, the mentally defective, and other "useless bits of humanity" such as POWs no longer able to work were means of reassurance that he could believe with real consistency while most others in his surroundings and the world at large were weak, basically incapable of any real commitments. Behind Treblinka, Chelmno, Maijdanek, Sobibor, and Auschwitz-Birkenau stood nothing but Hitler's own self-legitimation needs as the man who took his "people" on a mission for *Lebensraum*.

And to grasp how vast the indifference to the suffering of concrete human beings, and yet how real the passion Hitler could attach to mere abstractions, a good beginning can be made with the meaning of the term the "German people." That concept had no content that common sense can grasp. Nonetheless, for Hitler it was the vehicle through which to realize what history as a Darwinian struggle among peoples "dictated." For the one-dimensional elites, on the other hand, the *Diktat* of history and the "people" were mere conveniences for the search of a more generalized status. While it is hazardous to quote Adolf Hitler when asserting anything more generally about the Germans, his conception of the "German people" is an exception; for Germans never thought about themselves in institutional terms, and neither did Hitler about his people. Let me draw on the writing of a German "nationalist" to describe this disemboweled notion of the people. That notion was a sociological myth. It was a conception of a people utterly devoid of any institutional framework, or of rules of the social game describing patterns of rights and obligations that set "our people" apart from others. For a people as used to rule by interest constellation as the Germans, such a disemboweled notion provided a container for those who still had such needs to pour in whatever content they wished. But it also facilitated taking an ideological stance against all ideologies—indeed, against the very idea of man as a creature dependent on shared beliefs. "A state is to a people," so said the German "nationalist" (Deutsch, 1970:73), "as a suit of cloth is to a man. Just as a healthy man will wear out many suits in his lifetime, a people," he thought, should survive many states and political regimes. Hitler's notion of the German people was just like that, only more explicit yet. Let us listen to his voice (Fest, 1973:1,027):

A man said to me once: "Listen, if you do that, Germany will perish within six weeks." I said: "What do you mean by that?" "Germany will collapse." I said: "What do you mean by that?" "Then Germany ceases to exist." I answered: "A long time ago the German people survived the wars with the Romans. The German people survived the great migration of peoples. Later, the German people survived the great conflicts of the early and later Middle Ages. Then the German people survived the religious wars of more recent times. The German people survived the Thirty Years' War. The German people survived the Napoleonic wars, the wars of national liberation. It even survived the World War and revolution—it will survive me too."

If you stop to think here for a moment, and therefore do something that a person enraptured by a mentality does not do, you discover immediately that the German people is nothing or everything that ever breathed and lived over thousands of years covering forms of social organization that have nothing in common except a geographical space, and that one too conveniently vague. Clearly, these "Germans" never shared a language. They were heathens of various kinds, as well as Christians, and so they shared no religion. They were members of tribes with an economic base ranging all the way from hunting and gathering modes of production to industrialism, and a "people" politically organized in forms ranging all the way from primitive tribal democracy to contemporary complex political regimes. Such a conception of one's people was admirably suited to marry the rhetoric of nationalism with the hard interests of imperialism. And given the social dynamics inherent in a social structure that combined value dissensus with elite de-stratification, one brief glance at the National Socialist *Weltanschauung* should suffice to grasp why that marriage was more than a brief honeymoon.

If one asks what was the Nazi *Weltanschauung*, historians agree by now on one simple answer: Hitler's emotions and "philosophy of history." And crucial for its effectiveness were the foreign-policy aspirations that fit the earlier reach for "a place in the sun" (Fischer, 1967; Michalka, 1978). Let me rely on Broszat (1970) primarily to sketch the answer. He and Hildebrand (1978:180–81) treat elite de-stratification (dissociation between political power and economic leadership, in their terminology) as one direct cause of the acceptance the Nazi leaders found in the higher circles of German society. And it was the Nazis' "either-or radicalism," their forthright assertion to go forth and win all or to perish that appealed to one-dimensional elites equipped with a political mentality. Hildebrand (1978:180) makes this point by quoting from a speech of Göring to industrialists. That speech had the simple message: Don't calculate profit margins now; if we win, you will gain enough; otherwise we all perish.

Concentrated in Hitler himself, the Nazi *Weltanschauung* can be boiled down into three elements that cover all that was ever stable in his orientation set. The first was an emotion of hate. "Ideologically" crystallized into fanatical anti-Semitism and anti-Bolshevism, this emotion sustained his ability to believe in his mission to win *Lebensraum* in the East, the second element. The third, serving as the container of the former two, was his social Darwinist philosophy of history as a ceaseless struggle among peoples. This had a direct "moral lesson." Only the outcome, victory or ruin, decided who deserved to survive or to perish. It was therefore a waste of time to assign moral significance to any particular institutional framework. Since Hitler was the success seeker par excellence *and* a person who despised all fixed programs on principle, it was his personal need to believe in himself, or if you prefer, the internal legitimation needs of the Nazi polity on the smallest scale conceivable, which "needed" Treblinka. Though he never paid much attention to it, the death factory in operation sustained Hitler's self-confidence. That in turn permitted the chaos that was the domestic rule of Nazism, and his personal rule in foreign policy, which all those who competed for generalized status resources could use to their advantage. Everyone could "soldier" and by doing that accumulate resources and stave off the day of reckoning as to who would be the losers. There is no evidence that the *Endlösung* was planned but there is ample evidence in both Hitler's books that the pursuit of *Lebensraum* was planned. That plan attracted Germany's one-dimensional elites, and they needed Hitler as the integrative figure to turn an industrial social order into a social movement on the march.

But National Socialism also used the term *Gleichschaltung*, relay switching to coordinate all social forces under top directives. This term can lead to a profound misconception of Nazi Germany as an internally disciplined society, where Hitler pushed the buttons and everyone else danced according to the desired tune. But reliable discipline is always routinized discipline; and routinized discipline is possible only as product of institutional rules. Precisely that had to be avoided if society's forces were to be truly unleashed. The idea of *Gleichschaltung* is easy to grasp. It was to amount to the imposition of Nazi Party control on every conceivable formal organization in society, from a dog breeders' club to professional associations (Peterson, 1969). Yet it is important to understand that this Nazi Party control remained a farce because the party resembled more a series of baronetcies than a monolithic organization. An actual monolith would have meant the embourgeoisement of Germany's social forces. But with the decline of party hierarchs as the publicly most dominant political forces and the rise of the SS to prominence, domestic political chaos became the deep structural characteristic of the Nazi polity: a hidden but effective reality under a cloak of hierarchy (Höhne, 1967). *Gleichschaltung* effectively served to deprive the forces of social diversity and institutional conflicts between party and SS, SS and Army, and economy and the state of a mechanism of conflict resolution. All could claim to be the instruments of the *Führer*'s will, if only they "relay-switched" themselves into the movement. And only that together with the complete abandonment of domestic policy intentions, which had once mobilized the threatened old middle class in society to support the Nazis in their rise to power, made possible the pursuit of *Lebensraum;* for nothing less than the exact opposite of the earlier "restaurative" claims, not "antimodernity" but modernizing Germany along the lines of Western industrial societies more generally, provided the means for the war effort (Schoenbaum, 1967; Dahrendorf, 1965).

Perhaps the best short way to substantiate that Nazi rule in Germany was in continuity with the earlier patterns of rule by interest constellation is to present an outline of two aspects of Germany's conflict-ridden political life during that period. First, the prevalence of intra- and interorganizational conflicts reflects quite adequately the twin aspects of the heightened mobilization of the population at large. Second, the question of how mobilization spawned countermobilization can be examined on the basis of policy specifications that followed a law familiar by now: Whosoever succeeded in specifying a goal would also invite opposition and/ jurisdictional competitions over its implementation.

Intra- and Interorganizational Conflicts

In the area of civil administration, *Gleichschaltung* meant the nationalization of all the states' administrative bureaucracies. Placing all bureaucrats under direct Reich control, including personnel policy, was the main hierarchical control. The Nazis did conduct a political purge among the civil servants. Yet it remained a modest one. Conditioned to fidelity to "legality above all" by a history of rule by interest constellation, the civil-service corps rendered obedience to the new master as soon as orders followed proper procedure. For example, the Nazis did dismiss nearly all higher officials of Prussia's field administration (Jacob, 1963:128–32). But there were too few competent officials who were also genuine National Socialists. And the party was not prepared to place political convictions above competence in filling positions. As a result, the total number of personnel replacements remained relatively small. A professional civil-service law of 1933 enabled the regime to fire civil servants for political, economic, and administrative reasons. Though total figures seem unavailable to date, examples suggest that the Nazis replaced fewer officials than Weimar's "saving dictator," Erzberger. In Prussia about 12 percent of the civil servants were dismissed for political reasons. Another 15 percent were either demoted or pensioned off for reasons of economy or rationalizing the administration. The dismissal rates in the other states were apparently much lower. In Hamburg, for example, only 3 percent of the officials were affected by the law at all. In the Reich Ministry of Finance nearly 27 percent were affected, but only 3 percent fell victim to the political ax. The largest number of dismissals occurred in the Unemployment Insurance Authority, which had been a bailiwick of the Socialist Party. Here 3,160 employees were released (Mommsen, 1966:39, 54–57). However, in 1923 alone the Weimar regime dismissed 327,000 officials, reducing the staff of several federal ministries by nearly half and effecting a net reduction in national civil-service employment of 23 percent (Schulz, 1963:I:529).

The Nazis could not even staff the upper echelons by their own men since they lacked a sufficient number of qualified persons (Mommsen, 1966:107). In fact, within the national boundaries of 1933 the old civil service remained quite successful in warding off party encroachment. A genuine Nazi bureaucracy only developed in the occupied eastern territories. Joint appointments to state and party offices, party supervision of state officials, and usurpation of governmental administrative tasks by party organizations constituted other mechanisms to attempt insuring responsiveness of the administrative machinery to the new polity. Still, the textbook ideal, whereby the party was to decide on ends and the bureaucracy obediently wielded the means, was very imperfectly realized. The Third Reich probably insured some greater responsiveness than earlier regimes. Nonetheless, relative to its own official ambitions, the results remained woefully inadequate. The major reason was not resistance on the part of the old civil service, though. It was rather a lack of unity within the party, and an inability to control its own functionaries. Joint party-state appointments, though rare, mostly led the official concerned to identify with the government bureaucracy and lose his political zeal. Direct supervision of state officials by party functionaries worked only sporadically, depending on the accident of personalities involved. Usurpation of governmental tasks by party offices led to incessant conflicts and confusion (Mommsen, 1966:108–21; Jacob, 1963:132–51).

Furthermore, where the ideal of party supremacy was realized, it did not result in greater centralization and increased effectiveness in implementing policies devised at the top. For contrary to the image, the party was not a monolith but rather a conglomerate of different interests and personalities hanging together in name only. In Bavaria, whenever a *Gauleiter* (regional leader of the party) was effective in asserting his will over the administrative bureaucracy in his area, he was usually equally successful in maintaining his autonomy from central party officials in Berlin. Thus *Gauleiter* satrapies rather than centralized party control were the results (Peterson, 1969:149–223). Given the southern penchant for independence from the national center, the resistance to centralization was probably stronger there than elsewhere. But even if the other *Gauleiter* were merely half as concerned with their authority as their Bavarian colleagues, this still meant that the apparently *gleichgeschaltete* regime had in fact sustained a wholly unplanned increase in the number of "states." Weimar still had seventeen *Länder*. The Nazis decreed their disappearance by passing a national *Gleichschaltung* law. But they also learned soon that social reality cannot be simply legislated out of existence. In fact, reality changed in a direction opposite to the one intended. With forty party regions *(Gaue)* headed by party chiefs *(Gauleiter)* who tended to act in the manner of medieval fief lords, Nazi Germany had acquired close to forty states, if not in name, then often in fact of administrative decentralization (Espe, 1934:Appendix); for these *Gauleiter* by and large became more independent of Berlin than the state Parliaments of the republic had been. The party chiefs even revived a custom prevalent during the *Kaiser*'s days: They sent their own "representatives" to Berlin. Thus the legally nonexisting "states" in fact maintained a kind of ambassadorial representation in the capital. Furthermore, in Bavaria the party regional chiefs acted in their own interest first, as Bavarians second, and as "good National Socialists" last. Peterson (1969:18–66, 77, 97–133, 228) detailed at least twenty-three conflicts of an intra- and interinstitutional nature between the *Gau* and other party and governmental offices on the one hand, and the *Gau* and higher party offices at the Reich level. Some of these lasted several years, few ever reached any degree of recognizable solution, and many involved several party and administrative units at different levels, with shifting alliances among them. In most of these conflicts the overriding concern of the regional party chief was to maintain his independence.

Hitler's personal aversion against decisionmaking apparently increased over time. It "evolved," as it were, from rare but "set meetings with set officials" to "chance meetings with chance officials," and finally to "no meetings and not even written orders" (Peterson, 1969:15). That this was just an accident of personal idiosyncracy, moreover, seems rather doubtful. More likely it derived from an astute appreciation of how one could combine rule by interest constellation with the dynamics of a social movement forging East, for this style of leadership involved a structural preference for disorder at home. Interinstitutional, interorganizational, and interpersonal conflicts and competitions were encouraged. Attempts to delineate clear lines of authority and responsibility were discouraged, as were traditional jurisdictions of offices. Whether planned or not, the results were threefold. First, at home no institution and organization could cumulate a reliable power base for its operations. Second, the leaders of most institutions and organizations constantly had to exert all their energies if they were interested in maintaining and expanding their control over resources and maintaining their political relevance. Third, domestic policy implementation for the system as a whole suffered severely.

Unorganized conflict characterized intraparty factionalism before the war (Nyomarkay, 1967). Hitler's response to these struggles was to avoid any confrontation as long as possible. Only an anticipated direct challenge to his leadership would move him to respond to the constant calls "to settle issues." And when he did, he responded in a manner that settled few issues but reasserted and reinvigorated allegiance to his personal leadership by different factions that remained in conflict. As a result, no clear policy for the transformation of society ever emerged. Hitler succeeded in "disengaging" his party leaders from effectively dealing with the political issues and "re-engaged" them into a relation of personal fealty (Orlow, 1969). This pattern developed before the assumption of power and during the early years of consolidating it; but it did not change later either, at least not fundamentally.

Unorganized intra- and interinstitutional conflicts also characterized the foreign and domestic labor programs during the war and the application of war controls on the economy. Here the principal opponents were the Reich Ministries of Economics, Armament, and Labor, the German Labor Front, Göring's Four-year-plan Office, and the office of Plenipotentiary General for the Utilization of Labor. Despite the recruitment and deployment of over five million foreign workers and rising levels of output in the economy during the war, the conflicts and confusion of responsibility here too effectively interfered with the attainment of officially proclaimed goals. A resultant of conflicts among the Army, the party, the SS, and a propaganda that defined many recruits as subhuman, recruitment by force in the East significantly contributed to the armed resistance against the German occupier. Domestically, opposition on the part of the regional party chiefs and industry to economic reforms, developed by Speer's Ministry of Armament, significantly retarded the total mobilization of industry for war production. It also delayed the recruitment of German women into the labor force and foiled attempts to rationalize resource utilization. Underutilization of the existing stock of resources, human and material, and a tremendous diversion of energies from the goal of winning the war to interinstitutional rivalries were the results (Homze, 1967).

Essentially the same picture emerges from a study of the efforts to mobilize the resources of the Balkan countries for Germany's war effort. Again many institutions were involved. These stretched from the SS over various Reich Ministries, private industries, and even to ostensibly cultural organizations. The founding of a special organization, the Southeast Europe Corporation, did nothing to bring greater effectiveness to these efforts. On the contrary, the mere introduction of a new organization constituted an invitation to others to struggle for control over it or to attempt to abrogate its tasks. At the same time, the new organization concentrated more of its efforts to ward off these threates than on its ostensible purpose. The Southeast Europe Corporation "retaliated" against its enemies with the same methods they used. It too set out to infiltrate other organizations or tried to absorb them into its own structure. Here the creation of many "paper organizations" and the extensive use of impressively engineered public-relations shows in the form of conventions were additional techniques. These served the simultaneous ends of institutional and organizational defense and expansion at the expense of the war effort. Net imports from southern Europe declined throughout the war (Orlow, 1968).

Feuds in the service of organizational growth, regardless of the consequences to Germany, also characterized the relations between the Nazi Party and its organizational offspring. Party-SA relations, for example, by and large had been mutually supportive for the objective to gain executive power in society until 1933. Afterward, however, the SA grew very rapidly, to a size of 3½ million by early 1935. This growth resulted from the influx of former members of the Soldiers' League and other militias of Weimar. By that time the SA not only outranked the party by about a million members, but also the SA's social diversity, continuing militancy, and newly acquired relative purposelessness transformed this auxiliary force into a threat to the proclaimed principle of party supremacy in the state. Only about 24 percent of the SA were also party members. Not even the leadership cadres were all members of the party or "reliable" National Socialists (Bennecke, 1962:214). But the murder of the old SA leadership with the aid of the SS and the tolerance of the Army, the police, and the judiciary showed what was required for an actual "resolution" of a policy dispute. Apparently no less than a confluence of just sufficient legitimacy in terms of personalized fealty bonds, brutal force, and a favorable constellation of allegedly disinterested parties was necessary. Since no powerfully organized interests stood up for the SA, that combination of the tools of leadership dispatched it permanently into the shadow of political life, degrading it to a merely ceremonial function for the remainder of the regime. Resolving issues, however, remained a rare feature of politics in the Third Reich.

The pattern of ceaseless intra- and interinstitutional conflicts could be found also within the one organization that was ideal-typical of National Socialism, the SS imperium. Here the racialists opposed the pragmatists. The former, situated in the Reich Security Head Office, attempted to fulfill their special mission, the extermination of Jews, Gypsies, and other surplus populations. But they had to fight the pragmatists located in the SS Economic and Administrative Head Office and in various party and state offices whose interest was the exploitation of slave-labor power to the fullest. Furthermore, while one arm of the SS apparat proceeded with murder according to due instruction, another, the judicial branch, proceeded to prosecute the murderers in accordance with general regulations concerning discipline. While one branch, the educational institutions, turned out leadership cadres imbued with a specifically anti-economic orientation of "subjective heroism," the ideal of the fighter whose sole *raison d'etre* is to obey and to fight, the organization as a whole needed such cadres only in those combat SS formations actually deployed at the front. For most of its functions, police administrations, population resettlement, running the Holocaust Kingdom, domestic and foreign intelligence, and economic production, the SS actually needed the well-trained administrator and sound businessman as the function-appropriate leadership figure. Using a contemporary illustration, if you consider the organization in its entirety, a Harvard M.B.A. comes to mind as the most suitable preparation for an SS career. This becomes glaringly evident when one looks at the SS with a sociological perspective. In the language some sociologists use, "adaptation" refers to the ability of a formal organization to survive in a changing environment, to grow in it, and to do both without loss of autonomy. In these terms, the SS was one of the most adaptive bureaucracies in the history of formal organizations (Höhne, 1967:183–375). Being merely a personal bodyguard of Hitler at the beginning of the Third Reich, an SS presence had been established in most sectors of the division of labor in society by its end. For example, the SS "captured" as many economic enterprises as it could, establishing among other ventures a near-monopoly on soda-pop production throughout the whole territory of the Third Reich. While one department, the personnel office, did everything possible to restrict membership to the Aryan race in order "to lay a proper foundation" for the Order of the Deathhead as the Reich's future aristocracy, another, the combat SS, recruited among non-European populations in order to circumvent Army opposition and legal controls. The SS also competed with the Foreign Office over the control of foreign-relations conduct. The SS propaganda apparat battled with Goebbels' Propaganda Ministry over SS autonomy for its own newspaper. The SS intelligence service competed with Army and other intelligence services in an attempt to take over these organizations (Schellenberg, 1956). The SS domestic intelligence service clashed sharply with the party over the role of intelligence as a substitute for a critical press (Fraenkel and Manvell, 1965). But whether conflicts raged within the SS imperium or between one of its branches and outside organizations, none of these conflicts were regulated. In its inability to implement the leadership principle within its own domain and the multiplicity of conflicting goals pursued by its twelve departments, the SS was as much a microcosm of the Third Reich as in the diversity of its leading cadres. Here an illegitimate peasant son of Bavaria's backwoods could rise to generalship, as could a scion of Prussia's oldest Junker families. The university-trained, doctor-pedigreed children of Germany's bourgeois cultural elite could rise to elite status within the SS technocratic intelligentsia. The sons of Germany's erstwhile reigning houses under the Kaiser could bestow the glow of traditional legitimacy and prestige on the black uniform. Retired generals of the Austro-Hungarian Empire found their niches, as did adventurers of socially obscure and "racially doubtful" origins. In addition to genuine SS leaders, a title and uniform of "honorary SS leader" could be distributed to prominent people in the realm of industry, education, science, the arts, and diplomacy. Foreigners and even women were eligible. The wife of Count Ciano, for example, was an honorary SS leader. All of these seemed to enjoy a new elite status; none did so securely. Willingness to serve was all that counted, and the SS organization-conglomerate provided opportunities for virtually all manner of talent (Höhne, 1967:183–209, 240–69, 127).

Reading these case histories is like reading a litany. The same actors, the same pattern of mutual conflicts and evasions of objective goals appear again and again. The alignments in coalitions change, and relative to the earlier two regimes both intensity and frequency of conflicts seemed to have increased. But the basic pattern—the inverse relation between formal rationality of the organizations in society and substantive rationality of societal efforts as a whole—remains the familiar characteristic. In the absence of quantified studies in decisionmaking, illustrative material must suffice.

Goal-setting and the Production of Conflict

The Nazi regime propagated an image of the command society. One element in this image was a centralized administration where commands would flow from the *Führer* at the top to the last corner of the Reich. Toward this end the regime strengthened the internal controls in administration by stripping the *Länder* of their political autonomy. In addition, legislative and judicial constraints on bureaucratic officials were removed. These measures signaled a very clear goal specification: There was to be an unbroken chain of command. But this aroused the immediate resentment of various regional, religious, and class interests whose reality was in no way lessened by attaching the label NS. The net effect of the intended centralization of administration was the emergence of forty *Gauleiter* fiefs and widespread disobedience to any commands save those coming from the *Führer* personally. To counter the local satrapies again, the Berlin party bureaucrats tried to develop their own field organization in order to supervise governmental offices or usurp their tasks. This in turn, however, invited resistance from the field agencies of the governmental structures, the Army, and other NS organizations. It also severely restricted the capacity to get anything done with dispatch or uniformity, as the territorial units of the party administration, the government administration, and the Army recruitment areas did not coincide. Law after law, regulation after regulation, and daily order after daily order would rain down on party or government field agents, and their actual behavior would be governed more by the chance nature of personal relations than official channels (Jacob, 1963:149).

Concerning intraparty factionalism, personal ties of loyalty to the *Führer* not only permitted policy disputes, they also inhibited the exercise of leadership on the part of Hitler. According to Nyomarkay's (1967:145–50) analysis, there is an intrinsic inverse relationship between the charisma of personalized fealty and the capacity to lead in a modern society. Given an exclusive commitment to personalized charisma in the context of a differentiated society with naturally opposed interest, the leader cannot really decide on policy disputes and maintain his personal following. Every actual policy decision would amount to the injection of an additional element of ideological legitimacy to that based on purely personal fealty. Making a decision would constitute a precedent. It would be giving some content, however small, as to what National Socialism meant. As in common law, such decisions would cumulate and come to constitute a body of ideology that could serve as a source of legitimacy independent of the personal bond between the leader and his followers. Having only personalized charisma at his disposal before 1933 and being oriented purely to attaining executive authority at that time, Hitler took a fairly quantitative approach to charismatic legitimacy. He tried to maintain bonds of personal loyalty to the largest number possible, regardless of how diverse that following was. As has been pointed out, he also borrowed other legitimacy symbols by association with the military elite of the older order and kept his formal legal legitimacy of office incumbency intact at least until 1943. But personalized fealty bonds to critical bureaucrats in the SS, the Army, and the higher civil service, bonds not of shared convictions but of like interests in maintaining and expanding power, were the tools of implementing racial policies (Buchheim et al., 1965:I:133–71). In order to maintain this net of support, Hitler actually made very few fundamental decisions. Most of them dealt wholly with the drive for *Lebensraum*. To the extent that this feature of the "leadership principle" in action had become the mode of operations for lower-level echelons, the institutionalized disorder of Nazi domination can be attributed to Hitler's own exploitation of the German pattern of rule by interest constellation.

One of the basic factors underlying the conflicts in the labor program was the need to deny the real costs of the war, lest support for its conduct wane. This situation was not too different from that in the First World War when taxation had been avoided. The Nazi Party in its role as agitprop organization, however, was specifically charged with this denial during the Second World War. Consequently, the *Gauleiter* had to oppose restricting the production of consumer goods as well as drafting the females into the factories. For would such actions not necessarily interfere with their responsibility, which was the maintenance of an unshakable faith in final victory? Again, the attempts on the part of Speer's Ministry of Armament in providing the means for attaining that goal stood in opposition to the task of maintaining solidarity in a deeply divided society where maintaining everyone's effort in doing his duty demanded denial of the truth. The very need to maintain an impression of intrinsic superiority of German might interfered with creating even a level of adequacy.

If the goal of greater imports from the Balkans was to be attained through greater rationalization and coordination, then this above all called for clear jurisdictional responsibilities among a variety of agencies. Implementing such a strategy, however, would inevitably lead to the creation of a differential advantage of some agency or institution relative to others, which in turn would amount to a decision concerning its future role after the war. In a society where everything was politicized, such a policy decision had to be avoided lest the tenuous cohesion among powerful oligarchies and the very mobilization mechanism of "fulfilling the *Führer's* will" be upset.

The inherent contradiction between the demands of cohesion and cooperative effectiveness also characterized SA-party relations before 1933. If the SA was to be an effective fighting arm of the party deployed in a legalistic way—that is, with controlled rather than spontaneous violence—then hierarchical military controls seemed called for to keep the SA in line. Yet the more perfectly strict military controls would operate, the more these would endanger the principle of party supremacy. In an attempt to insure the latter, the SA used political education. The content of that education was to establish personalized charismatic bonds between leader and follower on the local level. However, that in turn lowered the effectiveness of the SA force as a pliant instrument of the party bureaucrats. Instead of becoming an instrument machined for instant obedience to party channels, it required Hitler's personal presence on the local scene to maintain allegiance in crisis situations (Nyomarkay, 1967:110–23). Thus while the development of traditional military controls was feared as a potential for autonomy of the SA from the party, the use of personalized charisma interfered with the effectiveness of deploying it.

After 1933 the party had to be made a legal creature of the state lest it remain completely ineffectual in "guiding" the administrative and judicial bureaucracy. Formal rational-legal mechanisms were the sole means to have the governmental apparatus perform, and so the party had to be adapted to this reality, rather than the other way around (Buchheim, 1965:I:13–30). This constitutes the best evidence of the weakness of value appeals in German society. Even a totalitarian revolutionary movement had to rely on formal legality in this merely formal nation-state in order to survive at all. But that very transformation made the party a less reliable instrument for "revolutionary tasks" such as the extermination of undesirables.

Similar to the development of the final solution of the Jewish problem, which had proceeded by a series of actions and reactions with a cumulative recourse to more radical means rather than according to a rational plan (Hilberg, 1961; Schleunes, 1970), the SS itself developed into a multifunctional organizational conglomerate without plan. In 1933 total SS strength was put at 52,000 men (Stein, 1966:XXVI). Toward the end of the war the SS imperium encompassed about 4 million men, if one includes the 2.8 million men of Germany's nationalized police force under the Minister of Interior, who was also the Reich Leader SS (Höhne, 1967:8–9). But the latter and wider definition is the more useful, for it calls attention to the fact that the SS imperium made use of three forms of legitimate authority. The SS could order men by rational-legal mechanisms—that is, call on them to perform in their capacity as employees of the Minister of Interior. It could also employ a variant, traditional military discipline, particularly in the combat SS. Last, one could also envoke the *Führer's* charismatic legitimacy and call on men as members of the Order of the Deathhead. The Reich Security Head Office, for example, used at least four types of stationery. Depending on the addressee and the business at hand it could issue written orders as an office of the Reich Leader SS, the Chief of the German Police, the National Crime Investigation Office *(Reichskriminalamt)*, or as an office of the Minister of Interior (Buchheim, 1965:I:78–79). Since the SS had not ever attained formal legal status comparable to that of the party, legally its Security Head Office was all or none of these, depending on what legal criteria one wished to employ. Practically, what it was depended for any one of its actions and agents on the strength of shifting opposing forces. In the recruitment of railroad stock for the transport of Jews across the face of Europe, the office used the stationery of the Minister of Interior. Such commands from one government agency to another succeeded unless an area Army command in the occupied territories interfered.

These multiple legitimacy principles both helped and hindered cooperation within the SS imperium. When the rigor of the eastern theater of war turned the propaganda notion of fighting "subhumans" into an obvious farce to those confronted with valor and technical competency on the part of the Soviet forces, one could rely on traditional military discipline where orders are orders. When toughness in the face of exterminations waned, one could do the same. At the same time, claims to superior charismatic insight, to superior command of rational legality as the sole basis of a modern order, and to matters of military discipline could be used in interorganizational feuds. While the SS worked hard first at voluntary, then at compulsory emigration of the Jews from Germany, the party and the Propaganda Ministry called on other countries to unite against "the world's archenemy" and close their borders. The SS "realists" here collaborated with the Zionists. Both tried their best to facilitate emigration to Palestine with financing from German Jews and the Jewish international community; and the SS argued a national interest, maintaining Germany's prestige abroad, and solving the Jewish problem "realistically" by ending the Diaspora through the creation of a Jewish nation. To the radicals in the party that course violated charismatic insights. In their eyes such a course would strengthen "the Jewish scourge on mankind," rather than "solve it once and for all" (Höhne, 1967:304–14). In the second phase, when repatriation and resettlement of Germans and expropriation and depatriation of Jews and Poles became SS policy, the SS became engaged in a continuous feud with party lords in the East who opposed the creation of a Jewish territory in "their" states, resisted the exportation of skilled Jewish labor from their area on economic grounds and, occasionally, even raised objections to extermination on human grounds (Höhne, 1967:285–342). Rivalry over the control of Jewish property engaged the SS with Göring's Four-year-plan Office. After the final solution had taken its definite shape in 1942, the Reich Security Head Office charged with its implementation emphasized death as the first priority; the SS Economic and Administrative Head Office continuously resisted, placing economic exploitation of captured labor resources ahead of destruction. As "owners" of the concentration camps, the "realists" in the economic branch here used rational-legal authority against the radicals in the security branch (Höhne, 1967:286, 358). Also, using traditional military legitimacy and the collaboration of their Army superiors, the combat SS generals disobeyed Himmler's charismatically backed orders whenever it pleased them (Höhne, 1967:444–47). Further, while some party circles preached the more old-fashioned nationalist gospel, superior SS charisma mingled with realism were the tools to propagate a supranational Germanic ideology. While the Reich Leader SS could dream of a non-German successor to his position, and SS intellectuals urged abandonment of a stupid conquest mentality and its replacement with realistic leadership attuned to the aspirations of other nationalities and their deserved place in the New Order, Hitler steadfastly refused to define the shape of things to come (Buchheim, 1958:58; Höhne, 1967:462–72). Last but not least, the inner divisiveness of the SS was also manifest in its involvement in the resistance movement. Here the genuinely charismatically committed to Hitler ruthlessly pursued those of their colleagues who opposed Hitler either on grounds of genuine humanism, realism, or sheer opportunism (Höhne, 1967:473–88).

The SS imperium constitutes the best microcosm of Nazi totalitarianism precisely because of its anarchical systemlessness. As the incarnation of the *Führer's* will, it had to be a mystical order, and it was that for some. As an unrestrained executive instrument, a machine tooled for instant obedience of any orders, it had to gain independence from other NS organizations and the state notably in its support base. In this respect it was at once a capitalist and a socialist enterprise. It was capitalist because its economic enterprises were the private property of the organization. It was socialist in that no individual owned the means of production or the output. The SS laid a claim to the status of an elite army, but had a supreme commander who was a soldier dilettante. It proclaimed to be the elite of the New Order but violated the fundamentals of elite formation by an indiscriminate personnel policy. It succeeded best where it had planned the least, in genocide; and it failed miserably where it had aspired the most, in creating a New Order.

The demise of the Reich demonstrates the apparently inevitable outcome of a regime that, situated in an active society, deprives extant social diversity of any legitimacy symbols without removing the diversity itself. Certainly, the presence of legitimacy symbols for dissent alone does not insure mechanisms that can set realistic national goals. But such symbols would seem to be prerequisites if an active and diverse society is to achieve any objectives at all. In the German case, where, finally, the will of the *Führer* became everything, that will also became nothing. The victims of the Holocaust engine aside, the *Führer's* will turned into a nebulous substance, graspable only in the means, the generation of more and more effort, but not in the ends, nor in coordinating the means. If the intentions of the Nazi regime lend themselves to any clear description, they were characterized by two mutually contradictory goals. According to Schoenbaum (1967), the most important and the first was the revision of Versailles. It meant the establishment of German hegemony in Europe, resuming the struggle begun under the imperial flag. And attainment of this goal required, above all else, the further development of Germany's industrial and technological resources with all the concomitants of social change that modernization involves. But on the other hand, the regime also aimed at the preservation of a preindustrial way of life, and it proclaimed to stem the tide of modernization. If anyone of significance had been serious about these objectives, the required policies would cover reversing the trend to urbanization, smashing big industrial trusts to liberate the people from the bureaucratic yoke, and the organization of economic life in line with some "Buddhist economics" where small is beautiful and decentralization the watchword of the organizers. In both respects the outcome was the opposite of the proclaimed intention.

Germany's defeat in the Second World War was more severe than in the First World War. Not only did she not gain a position of hegemony, but also her formal nation-state itself was dissolved, and about a third of her former national territory was lost.

Concerning internal societal development, "not a single clock was turned back" (Schoenbaum, 1967:245). Under the Nazis the flight from the countryside into the big city increased. The economy was industrialized faster than ever before. More women entered the labor force instead of remaining in "their appropriate realm of *Kinder, Küche,* and *Kirche.*" In fact, German society continued to follow the Western trend of greater income equalization, higher living standards, increased social mobility, and more participation even in political life. For many Germans the advent of National Socialism meant regained employment, above all else. Loss of one's political rights regarding the free expression of opinion hardly mattered. And in any case, for the small man there was the consolation that the former master, the white-collar salariat, had lost that right as well. While not democratic, political rights had been equalized (Schoenbaum, 1967:73–112; 234–74). The one indisputable accomplishment of National Socialism was the political mobilization of the people to unprecedented heights. If one can trust one regional sample as not entirely unrepresentative of the country as a whole, about 62 percent of the population was already "organized" on the eve of the war in 1939 (Heyen, 1967:335–51). Nearly two thirds of the entire population, from a baby to the oldest of the elderly, was affiliated with one or another Nazi organization. Deducting the children and those in retirement, this probably covered three quarters of the adult population in the labor force before the war, and their near total engagement during it. The single most important cause of this unleashing of the forces latent in modern German society was the Nazi *Weltanschauung.* It facilitated what the members of one-dimensional elites waited for: an opportunity for relentless resource competition and power expansion in the service of gaining a more secure foothold of status in society.

In mobilizing the population more than ever before but denying legitimacy to diversity, the Nazis only intensified the basic character of German political life. Mobilization of everyone's effort and societal failure had already been present in the Weimar Republic and in the empire. The failure of Weimar also indicates that a mere grant of formal legitimacy to political diversity is not enough to contain such self-contradictory dynamics as result from mobilization in a context of profound value dissensus and elite de-stratification. What the republic had suffered from, a real in contrast to a merely formal lack of legitimacy for the expression of political dissent, was increased under the Nazis, where all organizations in rivalry with each other became lobbies in a state that did not grant legitimacy to lobbying.

The question how such a system could have enjoyed any stability at all has a simple answer: war (Orlow, 1968:175–83). The war provided the multiple power-oligarchs in the party, the SS, the Army, industry, and government with an outlet for their competitive energies that promised each gains in the form of concrete assets to be secured in the East. The war therefore gave direction to mobilized and uncoordinated efforts. But the very lack of coordination that facilitated these efforts by leaving the future open, also deprived society of a chance of survival. Yet this answer remains somewhat incomplete. While applicable to rule under the *Kaiser* and the Nazi regime, the formula cannot apply to Weimar, which failed also because of an incapacity to regulate societal conflicts.

But a small alteration of Orlow's conclusion makes it applicable to all three national regimes. According to Orlow (1968:184–85, emphasis supplied), acceptance of the totalitarian political norms—that is, the overt goals of conquest—was an indispensable prerequisite for intrasystem success, but this "widespread acceptance by all institutional elites, agencies, and higher officials in the Third Reich in turn was a major factor in the system's overall failure to achieve its goals in dealing with extrasystem factors. In both the planning of policies and their execution the various German officials took into account *solely* the intrasystem impact of the extrasystem variables with which they had to deal." The consequence: "a bewildering array of petty feuds, political opportunism, and personalized rivalries among the various agencies." To make this statement on Nazism acceptable and at the same time generalizable to all three regimes in Germany, all one needs to do is remove the claim regarding shared goals of conquest. Then Weimar emerges as but an interlude in Germany's modern history and one in which the self-destructive forces inherent in the combination of value dissensus and one-dimensional elites were of the same kind but contained on a smaller scale.

It has been demonstrated in previous chapters that there was never a sharing of goals, if by that one means a shared commitment to a given type of society in its internal-organizational aspects. The "goal" of ruling over a *Mitteleuropa* or an *Osteuropa*, whether pursued under the imperial colors or the swastika, never constituted more than an opportunity set for multiple organized interests to grasp assets for themselves. Acting on the principle of the primacy of internal politics while keeping aloft the banner of national interest as a legitimation device had been the major factor in all the regimes' overall failure to achieve external and domestic-system goals. A pattern of unstable coalitions and fierce rhetorical struggles character-ized politics under the *Kaiser*. That pattern had stretched from the early days when the unstable iron-and-rye coalition dominated the scene, over the struggles about the Church and the socialist issues *(Kulturkampf* and *Sozialistengesetze)*, to the war-aims debates. The intensity of mutual opposition in these struggles was always fueled by the very self-conscious-ness with which Germans treated each other as ethical strangers. The utterly condescending response to the peace movement in Germany remains a vivid testimonial to a people whose intellectual groups were committed to the ideal that the fascinating aspects of the human species could never be found in what the species had in common but rather in how the members of different cultures differed from each other. Weimar democracy was also brought down by the same pattern of instability in coalitions and intensity of political emotions. In fact, it has been rather convincingly demonstrated that a veritable "merry-go-round" of interest groups delegitimated the intermediary power structure of the republic to a point where it virtually collapsed overnight when Hitler became a credible alternative (Lepsius, 1968). From this perspective the "system of system-lessness" that was Nazi domestic domination appears as a continuation of earlier patterns, however much one must credit the one really new institution, Goebbels' Ministry of Propaganda, with the effective enforcement of anti-Semitism and anti-Bolshevism as the one rhetorical line no one who cared to stay in the political game would dare to oppose. Therefore, the factual acceptance of the Nazi regime by the organized political forces in German society remains of interest primarily because of its moral implications. Beyond that there was nothing unique or new in the pattern, for most of the time throughout Germany's short-lived existence any serious interest in one's political efficacy there had demanded that one "accept the system." Even self-proclaimed revolutionaries did that. The effective forces that ran this modern society on its ruinous course had been "constitutionalists by reason," "republicans by reason," and "totalitarians 'by reason.' " It was a German reasonableness never to be identified in any personally, compelling way with a mere political regime. Hopefully, the evidence rendered in this and the preceding two chapters suffices to make that point. In the German understanding politics was struggle, the idea of the nation as an invitation to a common undertaking a mere propaganda tool to advance particularist interests. The moderation that is simply required if political conflicts in modern society are to be institutionalized forever eluded Germany's one-dimensional elites. That is why Orlow's (1968) insight regarding Nazi domination at home can be extended backward in time to the birth of the modern nation-state in 1871.

Orlow's "three layers of reality" concerning German political life were hardly unique attributes of the Nazi system. They had always existed. There was an outward façade. This changed with the nature of the regimes, from the monarchical constitutionalism of an authoritarian *Rechtsstaat*, over the appearance of institutionalized political conflicts during the democratic Weimar regime, to the monolithic façade of a totalitarian command society. Behind these façades lay a reality of intense and unregulated conflicts. In the main these were concretely manifest in the agitprop organizations of the empire, the private armies of Weimar, and finally the organizational chaos among and within the organizations of Nazi Germany. This first underlying reality had a constant as well as a variable aspect. The fact of unregulated conflicts was a constant. The intensity of the struggles, however, increased. An increasing recourse to violent means demonstrates the point. Beyond, however, was a third reality. This was organizational action in accordance with one uniform norm that might have read: Act so as to maximize your interests, assume that all others do the same, and legitimate your strategy, whatever it might be, by claiming to serve the whole better than any of your rivals.

CHAPTER NINE

Toward a Social Theory of Moral Indifference

A people accustomed to refined culture *and yet* capable to
withstand the horrors of war out there (which would not be an
achievement for a Senegal Negro!), and a people who then
return *despite all that* as basically decent as the vast majority of
our people, that is true humanity; this no one should ever
forget . . . this experience remains, whatever the outcome.
                    Max Weber to his mother in 1915
                    (Mommsen, 1974a:207)

Most of you know what it means when a hundred corpses lie
about, or five hundred, or a thousand. Having endured that
and, a few exceptions of human weakness aside, having
remained decent, that made us hard. This is and will remain an
unwritten page of glory in our history.
                    Heinrich Himmler to his
                    SS generals in 1943
                    (Höhne, 1967:335)

Less than a hundred years after her birth in 1871, modern Germany
expired as one nation-state in 1945. War had given birth, and war had
given death. At Versailles in 1871 Germans had stood triumphant. On
June 28, 1919, in that same Hall of Mirrors of Versailles Castle, Germans
stood in defeat and accepted the dictated peace in anger in order to
preserve their national sovereignty. No building of splendor marked the
occasion in 1945; only unconditional-surrender papers were signed, and
by men too exhausted for any emotion. In modern times collective
triumphs are but opportunities. That triumph at Versailles was an
opportunity for nation-building. As stated earlier, a nation is an invita-

289

tion, extended by the few to the many, for a collective undertaking, one that is to last from generation to generation. That presupposes the development of a shared collective identity, of values that bind men over and above the many interests that separate them. In Germany the invitation to nationhood was never accompanied by a respectful and caring concern for such values. The invitation remained a façade, and the opportunity was lost. Germany ended in ruins in a very literal way. In 1945, if you stood in Berlin or Hamburg, Dresden or Munich, you found yourself amid rubble stretching for miles, as far as the eye could see. Such moments in history are not moments of reflection. Your worries are biological, where to find something to eat, and a place to sleep. If you have social worries, these are utterly personal: how to find out about the fate of parent, spouse, or child. For the vanquished, months, perhaps years, would pass before the dawning realization that Germany lay in ruins also in a figurative way: That war had affirmed nothing because the "German" people shared nothing; that mountains of corpses were just so much dirt because they had been defined as sheer matter when still alive, *and for nothing* rather than any of the many shared ideals that men throughout history always managed to assign to their deeds of collective violence.

What, then, was the German "nation" in her short and mad history upon the stage of modern nation-states? One approximate answer can be gleaned from Max Weber's comparative work on the patterns of rationalization of human action. Schluchter (1980:134–69) demonstrated that Weber's abiding concern with the nature of modern capitalism led him to develop four types of the rational exploitation of property. If one were to search for an interpretive formula to characterize modern German history, what Weber called "politically controlled adventure capitalism" comes to mind. This would be a society organized to realize the acquisitive principle of profit accumulation by means of war and booty. It would be a whole society oriented to short-run opportunities and, in the spirit of a desperate gambler, willing to risk all rather than a capitalist society of the market-orientation type with its "disciplined greed" that subjects the profit calculus to long-run considerations. Such a formulation is tempting. It would be one full of irony. With Luther, Germany must be counted among the places where the Protestant Reformation was born; but in that country the "Protestant Ethic and the Spirit of Capitalism" never took root. However tempting, such a formulation would be misleading. The cases Max Weber used to construct his ideal type of political adventure capitalism were still human, however ruthless; still rational, however ambitious. Slaves, for example, were treated as a scarce factor of production rather than as matter with the character of an infinite supply. Imperial aspirations were guided by notions of the possible rather than fantasies of endless Darwinian struggles with projections of global domination, as in Hitler's "philosophy of history."

But there is a more important difference between modern Germany and possible historical antecedents to her history. That difference pertains to the contrast between tradition and modernity, one so much discussed in contemporary sociology. Contrasts emerge only on the background of at least one commonality. And so it is the latter that I have to address first. In addition, the difference with which I am concerned occurs in two forms, in a wider and in a narrower sense. I shall deal with the wider one first. And while some of the following may sound abstract and "academic," I ask the reader's indulgence, for some absraction is eminently practical if we are to understand the nature of modern sin, that moral indifference that men can carry to the point where they lose the constraint of common-sense self-interest, a point revealed in modern Germany history.

What then of this contrast between tradition and modernity? Starting with the common element, let me rely on Bellah (1964), who draws the dividing line between protohuman and human life with the aid of religious symbolization. I use the term "religious" in a very broad sense here. What is distinctive to the human species is the use of language for the satisfaction of a distinctively human need: the striving for comprehensive meaning in life and in dying. Only men can imagine patterns of meaning that transcend the immediacy of the situations they endure. With that capacity to transcend, men have a range of freedom in what they experience that has no parallels in other forms of life. Here is the way Bellah (1964:361) made the point: "Animals or prereligious men could only 'passively endure' suffering or other limitations imposed by the conditions of their existence, but religious man can to some extent 'transcend and dominate' them through his capacity for symbolization and thus attain a degree of freedom relative to his environment that was not previously possible." It would appear to follow that human *social* action always requires legitimation, beliefs shared to some critical extent among those who cooperate with each other. Put differently, legitimated action defines what we mean when speaking of the human condition in its social aspect. Bellah's evolutionary perspective on this distinctively human trait also made eminently clear that ranges of choice about meaning, and so about legitimation patterns have been tremendously enlarged over the course of human history. For example, while men in "primitive society" could not yet imagine society or the self as revisable entities, objects subject to fundamental change through human effort, both were certainly attributes of culture in "historical empire societies." Under the influence of monotheistic religious cultures models of some "new man" and a "better society" have been used to legitimate and delegitimate actual psychological and social reality for millennia. There is nothing new, unprecedented, or modern on this score. Critical for the tradition-modernity contrast is another point. It is this: However "revolutionary" in their aspirations traditional men have been—and this has varied impressively, encompassing the whole range from the "world-accommodating ethic" of the Chinese Mandarin to the "world-dominating ethic" of the Puritan (Weber, 1916; 1916–17; 1904–5)—they never dared to transcend the human condition itself by making a deliberate choice against the need to legitimate social action. That possibility emerged only with the Kantian Revolution, one that grounded the nature of religious life in the structure of ethics. Bellah used precisely this development as an evolutionary marker between tradition and modernity. By doing away with the need to locate symbols of ultimate meaning in any metaphysics claiming cognitive adequacy, modern man lives with the conviction that meaning creation is entirely human. Consequently, there are as many patterns of ultimate meaning as man can imagine. Man chooses his gods. There is no outer constraint. And so, in Bellah's (1964:371) felicitous phrase, the distinctive mark of modernity is the realization that the human condition itself has become a revisable entity, an "infinite possiblity thing." When Bellah found this evolutionary breakthrough to modernity he did not think of a possibility inherent in it. That possibility concerns the ending of the human condition. When men believe they can revise the human condition in infinite ways, they can indeed aspire to define it out of existence. Rather than continuing to define the human species as one that strives for comprehensive meaning, they can consciously endeavor to resist any transcendence, redefine the human condition into its opposite of an animallike state, and deem themselves "advanced." This was at the core of the SS ethic, which espoused the image of man the actor who dominates the world without the crutch of *any* belief (Nolte, 1965:402–54). In view of Bellah's (1970:230–57) later writing, one commits no cognitive heresy by making a direct connection between the notion of the human condition as an "infinite possibility thing" and Auschwitz, that haunting place in our consciousness. As everyone knows, *Arbeit Macht Frei* (work will make you free) was the slogan adorning the entrance to that camp. By now we appreciate that "To Hell with You, God" would have been a more apt expression of the unlimited arrogance that made up the essential core of the SS ethic. That ethic was a prototypical case of Bellah's (1970:244) "postreligious man, the cool, self-confident secular man . . . [who] is trapped in a literal and circumscribed reality that is classically described in religious terms as the world of death and sin, the fallen world, the world of illusion. Postreligious man is trapped in hell. The world of everyday reality is a socially and personally constructed world. If one confuses that world with reality itself, one then becomes trapped in one's own delusions, one projects one's wishes and fears onto others and one acts out one's own madness all the while believing one is a clear-headed realist." Only the modern condition provides the possibility to transcend the human condition. Clearly, there is no law that says this must happen. But it happened in Germany. So much for the tradition-modernity contrast in the wider sense.

In the narrower sense the tradition-modernity contrast of interest here bears on a point of political organization. Only modern polities have the universal franchise. Certain categories of felons excepted, every competent adult has a national citizenship role. Normatively, the citizen role crosscuts all other roles in society. With the ideal of one man, one vote, the citizen role is one of absolute equality. On the occasion of legitimating power in society we are all supposed to be each other's equals, no matter how unequal we may be as bearers of other roles such as social class, ethnicity, region, and so on. Whether votes actually put governors in their seats or unseat them and how is immaterial. Normatively, modern political rule is rule by popular consent. That is why what nations do as collective actors requires legitimation in terms of assertions about national interests. The legitimation problem is far larger than in traditional polities. Legitimate interests in modern societies are those of institutions rather than of persons; they are of a long-run nature typically outlasting by far the interests of persons in their finitude of individual lives. In stark contrast, personalized fealty bonds legitimate political authority in traditional polities (Weber, 1922:212–301). Therefore, a *traditional* "political adventure capitalism" does not necessarily lack internal legitimation when pursued in heedless disregard of consequences lying beyond the lifespan of the critical individuals involved. In modern polities where legitimation of the polity rests on law, or institutions, these fictitious "legal persons" and their presumed enduring interests, the same course of action is illegitimate by definition no matter how much actual political support it may have. Of course, the universal problem of finding some solution to the problem of succession implies that the distinction between person and office is universal. Nonetheless, in traditional polities one owed obedience to a master, some concrete person rather than an impersonal institution. Personalization of the office in the sense of a fusion of private and public interests was a requirement of legitimate traditional political authority. In modern polities such personalization lacks legitimacy; instead, leaders are required to identify with their offices, and followers with institutions such that all modern legitimacy—regardless of the type of political regime involved—rests on a complex mutuality in identifications with impersonal entities. As will be seen in a moment, the normative requirement of identification with an office on the part of officials provides one opportunity for moral indifference in any modern society. Suffice it to say here that the legitimation function requires far more effort, organization, and resources in modern than in traditional polities. That fact, seemingly, seduces scholars again and again to assign a legitimation function to genocide (Mosse, 1970; 1978a; 1978b; Fein, 1979). But there is too much continuity in the contentiousness with which Germans addressed the question of what is German, in their inability to regulate social conflict, and in their striving for world-power status to rest content with such an explanation of modern mass death.

With the Holocaust and the pursuit of empire in recent German history we encounter the *total* bureaucratic machine, the organization of a whole people toward *any* end because Germans generated no effective demand for legitimation regarding their imperialist aspirations nor the "final solution of the Jewish question." In Hobbes' (1881:91–96) original sociological conception of hell we still find a very human portrait, for his "war of all against all" was not only plausibly motivated, it was indeed the puzzling theoretical result that should have obtained from no less a source than man's ability to reason, the rational pursuit of self-interest. But serving neither the passion of belief nor the rational exploitation of the human factor of production, the Holocaust as a sideshow in Germany's drive for world-power status reveals one aspect that is constitutive of ultimate hell: the creation of meaningless suffering and the imposition of senseless death. In the narrower sense of Jewish genocide, the Holocaust served the personal whim of Hitler, not the legitimation requirements of the Nazi regime. In the wider sense of the goal of acquiring *Lebensraum* with the planned destruction of about thirty million Slavs in the East (Fraenkel and Manvell, 1965:115), the Holocaust served no discernible political legitimation function whatever. Rather than providing a posthumous service to some of the administrators of death who like Stangl (Sereny, 1974) strove so desperately to discover some meaning for their deeds afterward, it is time for sociology to face up to the possibility of the institutionalization of meaningless action. Minimally, the fate of the Polish people should make clear that the German state had become a tool that could be directed to the destruction of human life without any ideological justification. In the drive for empire the fate of nations was merely a matter of whether they might prove a useful tool or a hindrance. In the First World War Max Weber wondered how one could exploit Polish nationalism against the Russians (Mommsen, 1974a:224). As late as 1939 Hitler considered making the Poles an ally for the search of *Lebensraum* in the East (Hildebrand, 1973:33). When the Polish Government declined the opportunity, Poland was smashed in a very literal way.

Her leading strata in government, economy, and cultural life were shipped off to concentration camps, and the remaining population in the Generalgouvernement was dominated by so brutal a terror as to effectively "atomize" Polish society even below the level of the family as an effective unit of loyalty (Gross, 1975; 1979). When the German occupation authorities imposed the death penalty for any infraction of regulations, their aim was not to deter deviance. Their aim was the destruction of Polish society. Not the least one can learn from that story is that fact that modern law can grant a veneer of legitimacy even to rule by brute force. That modern man can live with façades of belief, ceasing entirely even to care about the realities of commitments and the moral ambiguities of life, remains Germany's contribution to world history. Interpreting it is our task.

The possibility of the emergence of amoral public policy is inherent in the very organization of complex and functionally differentiated modern societies. That possibility has been addressed in the critique of mass society in one version or another for decades. One finds assertions about the decline of community, the destruction of intermediary power groups, the immediacy of access of elites to masses and vice versa, and the fall of public man with the trivialization of charisma (Toennies, 1957; Kornhauser, 1959; Sennett, 1974). Such models only set up parameters. But they are not oriented to nation-specific societal characteristics; they remain too general to explain what happened in Germany. More, they get stuck with the aggregation problem of conflicting interests in complex societies. They do not define sharply enough the nature of amoral conduct. What turns out in its consequences to be amoral for society as a whole does not lack morality for some subunits in society, be these classes, or regions, or even families. The same is true of one other famous study of amorality at the societal level, and one quite rare in that it focused on a relatively traditional social order. This is Banfield's (1958) portrait of amoral familism. But the southern Italians he studied were not amoral persons. On the contrary, they were very moral. They only confined their caring concern to the most immediate and concrete unit of society, the family. They also did so for historical reasons that made such restriction of one's moral concern the most reasonable thing a man could do. Fortunately, a more cogent perspective on the nature of amorality is available. Drawing on the work of Simmel and Weber, on the one hand, and on her own empirical research on physicians on the other, Mayntz (1970a; 1970b) provides a useful definition of amoral conduct, two contrary role orientations that may produce it and, most importantly, a useful distinction between impersonality toward others as a personal attitude and as a normative obligation. Let us turn to details.

Since modern societies are characterized by high complexity in role structure, with many roles governed by quite different and even contradictory normative expectations, life in modern societies virtually invites amoral conduct. This becomes evident when one recognizes the nature of amorality. "Amoral role behavior can be defined as compliance with role expectations or specific (formally legitimate) orders without any evaluation being made by the actor of his behavior in terms of normative standards external to the role (Mayntz, 1970b:372). The external standards at issue are general moral standards, value standards applicable to behavior in any role and imperative for all members of a society. Consequently, it is "the abrogation of *moral* evaluation which defines the amoral role player" (Mayntz, 1970b:372). In formal organizations we know about this phenomenon in terms of "going by the book," a mindless following of formal rules in disregard of the common-sense understanding of the purposes of the organization. Sometimes such conduct is very mindful, as in a "go slow" on the part of employees who seek improvement in the conditions of employment. This tells us that the proper functioning of any formal bureaucratic organization demands more information than can be laid down in rules, and that saving information by the simple faithful following of official procedure is *one* mode of personalizing the office. But sometimes such conduct may be only mindless. Then, if sufficient guidance comes from the top, the organization and its members become a pure tool, one disposable toward good or evil, where "the role player may as well devote his energy conscientiously to caritative duties which he would not have been spontaneously motivated to fulfill, as he may help in the extermination of Jews in a concentration camp without harboring any feelings of personal hostility against them" (Mayntz, 1970b:372). It was the image of bureaucracy as a pure tool that fascinated, and frightened, Max Weber. He found bureaucracy fascinating because he saw in it the most rational device for cooperative efforts ever invented by mankind. That aspect of formal bureaucracy included the function that it liberates us from the bondage of various communal ties such as those of family, neighborhood, ethnicity, regional and class origin, and the like. Only so formal an organization with its iron-clad procedural rules segregating the task-relevant from the task-nonrelevant could wash off people's diverse social identities and permit them to cooperate with each other (Weber, 1922:217–26). The bureaucratization of a great deal of everyday life also frightened him. Formality and complexity in the organization of society also required a moral division of labor. And that very fact provided the opportunity for "a mechanized petrification" of all cultural development, one that might wither entrepreneurial spirits in all fields of endeavor in a society run by specialists with their certificates of competence produced by routinized education (Weber, 1904–5:182). Weber did not anticipate Treblinka; nor did he imagine that a modern nation-state could go on a suicidal rampage. But his ambivalence about bureaucracy remains a useful orientation because bureaucracy offers the most seductive opportunities for amoral conduct.

As Mayntz (1970b) has also shown, amoral role behavior has two sources. They are diametrical opposites of each other. Amoral conduct may result from overidentification with a role. It can derive from so exclusive an identification with one role that all one's obligations to other ones in effect vanish from the person's horizon of serious attention. The most prominent example from the repertoire of contemporary cultural complaints is the "workaholic," the man who knows but career and disregards his family. The other source is role distance, the complete absence of any personal identification with a role one performs nonetheless. Both these sources, it should be noted, apply far more to achieved roles such as work roles in formal organizations than to ascribed roles, such as sex, age, or ethnic roles (Mayntz, 1970b). The main reason is that achieved roles require more conscious individual learning and cognitive understanding of normative expectations than the typically more diffuse learning experience undergirding our entry into ascribed roles. It is the greater cognitive control on the part of the individual that enables him to overidentify with a work role or take the stance of the cool, distant, uninvolved mere role player who derives a sense of superiority over others precisely on the grounds of achieving occupational success without the cost of identification. Both cases share the critical feature of amoral conduct, the abrogation of a concern with moral standards supervening any given role. Important too is the recognition that the chances for amorality are unequally distributed in society. Consider a hierarchically organized formal organization. The higher you go up on the ladder of status, the less clear-cut and detail-specified are the role expectations. Toward the bottom you find little institutionalized uncertainty. There, most of the time, life is simple: You have to show up on time; you have to put out some acceptable quantity of work with some acceptable degree of quality. Time, quantity, and quality tend to be fairly well specified. Toward the top in the organization, life is not simple. You are supposed to exercise "leadership." Half the time nobody knows just what that means. The fruits of leadership often take a long time in becoming visible. Their stability is even less calculable, and worse yet, typically, they take abstract measures, discernible only by the specialist. Such measures of success may be some estimate of profit, some "advance in knowledge," the community's state of health in physical or mental terms, the state of the nation's security in international affairs. All these measures have technical meanings, none are understood by laypersons, and all are disputed by experts. Toward the top of any formal organization you find institutionalized uncertainty. Being a leader amounts to uncertainty reduction and in ways maintaining credibility with the experts just below you. Because normative expectations at the top tend to be abstract, because you are expected to exercise judgment and "leadership" but cannot be told in concrete detail just how to do either, Mayntz (1970b) suggests that overidentification with a role tends to be the more typical road to amorality in top positions in society, while nonidentification prevails more often at the bottom. For the incumbent of some top position, though, it is easy to imagine both paths to amorality, one succeeding the other over time. As a relatively young man, still struggling to get higher and ever higher, overidentification may be his lot; after the career levels off in midlife, nonidentification may set in as a reaction to having been a "workaholic" for so long. Important in all this is the direct link to modernity. The more dynamic, changing, and achievement-oriented a society is, and the more opportunities for upward mobility it provides, the more it also invites amorality among the most successful of its members. But to this point the problem of opportunities for amoral conduct has been examined only from the perspective of the insider in some functionally specialized work setting. Only internal legitimation problems have been recognized. This needs complementing with a focus on external legitimation problems.

Therefore, important also is one other point in the relationship between inequality and amorality. As Weber (1922:1,123) recognized, an ideal-typical large-scale bureaucratic organization *requires* a nonbureaucratic head. At the very top of the hierarchy the main task of the leader is the continuous legitimation of the organization vis-à-vis critical others in society on whose support the health of the organization depends. This is most easily appreciated in terms of whole institutional complexes in modern society rather than some one concrete firm, hospital, or government department. It is easier yet to visualize when one considers that the higher positions are manned by professionals. Laymen, as we all know, do not understand—indeed, cannot understand—the activities of professionals. Submitting oneself to professional counsel requires trust. Seen in this light, the main task of top leadership in the economic complex, the medical complex, the welfare complex, and so on is the management of trust. Doing that demands plain talk rather than technical jargon, and a credible assertion of common over divisive interests. In short, it calls for a performance that convinces a sufficient number for a sufficient time that contrary to Bernard Shaw's opinion "professions are not a conspiracy against the laity." The central importance of the management of trust can hardly be exaggerated. By a division of labor one means function specialization. Functionally specialized organizations are input-output-contingent creatures. And when such function-specialized activities are professionalized, none of the inputs can be acquired according to the free-market gospel of *caveat emptor* because none of the laypersons whence they come can be reasonably expected to know enough about their need and use. Only the insider can know something about that. But the outsider needs assurance. The critical role of the nonbureaucratic head, then, amounts to the management of trust between the two. Managing trust amounts to the coordination of internal and external legitimation demands. Modern society stands or falls with such management. And if the critical feature of such a role specialized for the management of uncertainty and trust must be its nonbureaucratic character—that is, the absence of concrete normative prescriptions specified in detail—it follows that the most important integrative roles in the larger society are also the ones providing the greatest opportunity for overidentification or non-identification, and hence for amorality in conduct. Regarding morality, therefore, modern society is characterized by a double jeopardy. Top-leadership positions invite amorality in two ways. One derives from the irreducible uncertainties in the management of internal legitimation; the other from the similarly irreducible uncertainties of external legitimation.

Finally among these preliminaries for understanding what happened in Germany, there is also a rather direct linkage among bureaucracy, impersonality, and amorality (Mayntz, 1970a). Ever since Weber's (1922:217–26) model of modern bureaucracy we are haunted by the administration of humans in an objective spirit, without passion and bias. We worry about our ability as modern men and modern women to administer the lives of concrete human beings as if they were matter. But as Mayntz (1970a) pointed out with cogency, it does make a very important difference whether the obligation to act on others in a spirit of impersonality is accepted as a norm or becomes pure habit, a psychological trait on the part of a people handler. In the former case, that one acts "unnaturally" remains a matter of consciousness. You know you are following rules. These rules *may* constrain your personal inclinations. Such knowledge provides a potential for breaking the rules. Watching yourself, you may in some given case decide that objectivity can also be carried too far, exercise moral judgment about your behavior, and "buck the system" in the name of supervening moral commitments that command exercising a caring concern for other people with more discretion than the rules permit because they are human. For the people handler to whom taking an impersonal attitude has become automatic second nature when acting in his occupational capacity, such a potential tool for moral self-correction does not exist. Whether he be a medical doctor, a social worker, or a clerk of the Internal Revenue Service, the person for whom impartial objectivity has become a sheer matter of habit does not feel *with* or *for* the lives he administers; at most such a person might feel irritated *about* them in terms of their recalcitrance in fitting into prescribed slots. In short, where the bureaucrats in the people-handling sectors of a modern society are perfect in their caring concern for formal justice, that society has correspondingly fewer resources to defend its humanity. Only a bureaucracy that permits some corruption here and there, some bending of the rules with special pleading retains its human face. Such an assertion does *not* amount to a wholesale indictment of bureaucracy as always and necessarily inhuman. Modern societies are also welfare societies. All have Social Security systems that transfer resources from the healthy, the younger, and the working to the ill, the older, and those no longer working. Obedience to impersonal law does eventuate in presenting gifts of a loving, caring concern to others, whether any particular giver likes it nor not. The connection between "a bit of corruption" and the human face of bureaucracy only alerts us to the familiar experience that no rule system, no matter how well intentioned, can ever capture the complexity of concrete human fate. And the distinction between acting with imper-sonal objectivity out of sheer habit or in compliance with a norm (one felt as an onerous burden on occasion) only alerts us to the fact that the normatively compliant bureaucrat does not constitute as much a resource for mindless compliance with orders and regulations as does the habitual one.

These sources of amoral conduct that modern society provides are general ones. As a potential of what may happen, they apply as much to the United States as to Great Britain, as much to France as to Germany over the last half century or even longer. But in distinction to the conepts employed in the critique of mass society from Toennies (1957) to Sennett (1973), they are more precise in their identification of the nature of amoral conduct. More, they lend themselves to explaining what happened in Germany by virtue of their relationship to specific features of German social structure demonstrated in earlier chapters and features that have not been demonstrated for other modern societies. The most important of these are the institutionalization of value dissensus and the consequent de-stratification of national elites under the impact of industrialization.

If incumbents of elite positions in modern societies have more opportu-nity for amoral role behavior than people in nonelite positions, as has been argued just now, such a differential opportunity should turn into a definite propensity for amorality in a context of institutionalized value dissensus in society. The reason is not diffiicult to see. *Institutionalized* value dissensus means that people expect to differ in their value commitments or standards of moral evaluation from all others in society who are not members of their "own circle," who were raised, that is, in primary socialization settings other than their own where basic values with a different content were taught. The relevant primary socialization scenes for basic values are the more communal bonds of kinship, neighborhood, social class, region, and religion. In modern society, elite positions are differentiated from these settings. Neither family origin, nor regional background, neither neighborhood, nor religious persuasion, not even social-class origin alone guarantee attainment of elite positions. Those who rise to elite positions are not likely to come from the same primary-group affiliations. In Germany this was best indicated by the "iron-and-rye coalition," which stood so prominently in political affairs at the beginning of her attempt at nationhood. The representatives of rye were Northeasterners; those of iron, Westerners. And as I have shown, the value commitments of these regions differed profoundly, not only for the regions in their entirety but also between the upper and the middle classes. As I have also shown, these two regions by no means exhausted the diversity of moral cultures prevalent among the Germans. Institutionalized value dissensus at the elite level in society means that members of various elites face each other as moral strangers. Consequently, there is a propensity for amorality in role behavior. Should you attempt to apply general moral standards to your conduct in office, such an attempt cannot be rewarded by some "significant other" in a different elite sector on whose support your own performance depends. The simple reason is the absence of commonly shared standards of evaluation. Where that is an appreciated fact of life, as it was in Germany, you would be very reluctant even to try to appeal to moral considerations. Given your knowledge that your peers are peers in position only but not peers in convictions, you know that your chances for earning derision or even contempt as a sentimental fool are far larger than the chances of gaining respect for such an endeavor.

Let me emphasize this first conclusion of the study. In modern German history one finds elites capable of a level of moral indifference to the suffering of concrete human beings that has scarcely its equal in human history generally. One of its sources was institutionalized value dissensus, a matter not only of perception but also of scientifically ascertainable fact, hence a matter of correct perception on the part of members of the national elite. Already Max Weber's early work on the social organization of the agrarian way of life lends itself to the distillation of three distinct value systems (Schluchter, 1980:134–69). One of these, in the Southwest of the country, was a *particularist* neighborhood ethic of simple reciprocity, *do et des*. Another, prevalent in the Northwest, was a *universalist* contract ethic. A third, prevalent in East Elbia, involved a mixture of two contrary economic ethics coexisting in a symbiosis that upheld seigniorial ideals while granting opportunities for the capitalist development of agraria. The former was a *particularist* patron-client ethic resting on grants to land use being exchanged for working the land of the landowner; another was a *universalist* contract ethic resting on the use of hired Polish migratory labor. But as shown in Chapter IV, this was but a pale shadow of reality in Germany. There was much more value dissensus than just three distinctive moral cultures. In Germany one finds value cleavages by region, by class within and between regions, and between the city and the countryside. These differences were so pronounced that Germans could make a cult of being forever contenious about that question of what is German. These are social conditions that invite men in elite positions to abrogate a caring concern with moral evaluations of their role performance. They act as self-conceived *Realpolitiker* instead. But the contentiousness of the question of what is German also permits them at the same time to conceive of themselves as "idealists," which conceals their moral indifference from themselves and from others.

Yet while most Germans were moral strangers to each other, one more common strand, one connecting at least the two most critical regions of East Elbian Prussia and the seat of modern industry in the West, was the unproblematical acceptance of the work ethic. In describing a middle-class character, Thomas Mann (1967:34) once expressed this commitment as follows: "Hans Castorp respected work—as how should he not have? It would have been unnatural. Work was for him, in the nature of things. . . . It was the principle by which one stood or fell, the Absolute of the time; it was, so to speak, its own justification." For members in elite positions this value simply had to reinforce the propensity to amorality. A work ethic, so unproblematical and taken for granted, drives men to overidentification with their careers in and of itself and quite apart from appreciated value dissensus in society. In Germany the work ethic functioned as a secondary reinforcer to amoral role behavior at the elite level.

This theme of activism in value orientations brings me to the third conclusion about the German propensity toward amorality at the level of national elites. As pointed out in Chapter III, on grounds of general theory pertaining to inequalities in society, one-dimensional elites are more active ones than status-consistent elites. If you have but control over one scarce resource in society—say, wealth—you will seek to gain a similar control over another—say, prestige. In contrast, status-consistent elites are satisfied in their claims to status resources. Other things being equal, if one compares only the status-inconsistent with the status-consistent elites, the former are dynamic social forces, the latter are conservative ones. As I have attempted to demonstrate in Chapter V, an unusually rapid process of industrialization saddled Germany with status-inconsistent elites at the national level. In contrast to the United States and Great Britain, modern Germany was a country "suffering" the fate of elite de-stratification through modernization. It was a country where the "merely wealthy" corporation executives confronted the "merely prestigious" but comparatively poor higher military officer corps. Both of these groups in turn confronted the "merely powerful" political elite in the executive branch of government, who typically lacked the corresponding prestige whenever they were not also professional soldiers, a condition prevailing after the disappearance of Bismarck. And both too confronted the primary bearers of cultural honor, the professoriat, who lacked wealth, power, and prestige in amounts even roughly corresponding to their role as presumed culture bearers, a role unchallenged until the Third Reich. Chapter VI through VIII demonstrated the relentless competition for resources among the German elites, a competition guided primarily by the pursuit of power as the royal road to status consistency. This prevented German society from developing effective mechanisms to institutionalize conflict in society; it also increased the intensity of conflicts as one moves from the founding of the nation to its demise. Imperialist goals were constantly fueled by these competitions. A politically engineered adventure capitalism held out the promise of winning the status game where no legitimate opposition prevailed, in the imagined empty spaces in the East. Creating the empty space, as the Nazi regime attempted, was merely the culmination of the modernization dynamics inherent in a society with institutionalized value dissensus and one-dimensional elites. The combination of one-dimensional elites and un-regulated social conflict was the most important structural source of amorality among Germany's elites. It amplified a shared work ethic normal in Western societies to abnormal levels of career opportunism. Critical too in this respect remains the fact that however nonbureaucratic in nature the heads of bureaucracies are supposed to be in the theories that sociologists design, they *are* heads of bureaucratic organizations. It is no accident that Weber attached so great an importance to the element of impersonality in bureaucratic relations. He did take the Prussian bureaucracy as his model. Creature of a "historical empire society," that administrative machine became the German one. So, given the persistence of status-inconsistent elites in society, one can also infer persistence in role overidentification, role distance, *and* the acquisition of an impersonal attitude toward the objects of administration as a habit, rather than a normative requirement experienced subjectively as an onerous burden. Of course, the three sources of amoral role behavior all involve motives. Such psychological data cannot be inferred from observed behavior. In a historical context such data are at best accessible through biographical information of specific persons in leadership positions. Sociological analysis remains too rough a tool for empirical verification on this point. But the question of which of the three sources of amoral role behavior or what combination was at work in generating that level of amorality that produced so much meaningless suffering and actually led this modern society to self-destruction does not matter much.

The variables of sociological analysis used here are universal ones, applicable to all societies. Every society has some value system; what varies is its degree of integration or the amount of value consensus in society. Every society has elites, and every modern one has national elites; what varies is the degree to which such elites make up an "establishment" or the degree of status consistency that elite members in different sectors enjoy. And so, finally, it is with conflict. No society is free of it, all face the task of conflict regulation short of violence; only the degree to which they succeed in this institutionalization of conflict varies. But in German society the values that obtained on these three variables took a form that produced multiple pressures for amoral role behavior among her elites and to an extent that, so far as known, has had no equal elsewhere in the modern world to date. These particular values were an unusually high level of value dissensus, a "system" of one-dimensional elites at the national level, and interelite competition for status resources eventuating in social conflicts ever increasing in intensity and without regulation, which sought an outlet in imperialism. Each of these three social structural conditions of German society made their own particular contribution to the amoral role behavior so prevalent among the German elites. Let us see how, tracing that story step by step by weary step.

Value dissensus pushed you towards an abrogation of morally evaluating your role performance. In his official capacity a reasonable man would not try to be also a moral man. His chances for finding a consensual echo for his caring concern about moral values among critical others were too slim. Given the one more commonly shared value, the work ethic, this particular characteristic pushed you toward overidentification with the work role in a context of profound dissensus on any other values. Further, had you a university education and consequently aspirations to be a cultivated man, you could also transform the sheer fact of value dissensus into an appreciated aspect of your life and times. You could elaborate fact into some kind of ideology about the "modern condition." Whether you went as far in this direction as did the SS ethic, with its aversion against any transcendence and its celebration of the pure man of action who acts with "dedication" but without the crutch of any belief, did not matter much. *Appreciated* value dissensus leads to role distance for elite incumbents. Here you take pride in your success, in your ability to perform in a leading position precisely on the grounds that you can do so without identifying with it. That surely grants a special sense of superiority. Ordinary people who succeed do so at the cost of becoming "workaholics," but you can do the same without that cost. You can be a success and remain completely aloof, as disdainful of mere work as some imagined aristocrat of old who only played, leaving work to minions. Finding yourself in a status-inconsistent position—with wealth but no power, or the reverse, with prestige but inadequate income, and so on—turned you into an activist. Here again the propensity toward either overidentification or role distance or both was amplified. And having generations of status-inconsistent models in leading positions of a bureaucratic kind in front of your eyes, development of an impersonal attitude toward the objects of administration as a personal habit was very likely. Surely, the combination of role distance with the bureaucratic mentality as habit produces an insurmountable amorality. Such a person lives in a world of abstractions and he makes a fetish of it, believing sincerely that any clear-headed person in a leadership position in modern society must be a strict constructionist about his functions and cannot possibly be asked to worry about the wider consequences of his action. And finally, because German society within its own confines had never developed the capacity to institutionalize conflict so that everyone could know with some assurance who the winners and the losers were in the relentless struggle for status consistency among the elites, the one great chance to break out of this cycle lay in the fortunes of war and some new order that might come afterward. More than any other conceivable alternative, war legitimated the accumulation of power resources. You could proclaim to serve the nation while pursuing in fact what was far closer to your daily concerns in office: advancement of institutional interests against all competitors. "Power corrupts, and absolute power corrupts absolutely," so we are told. Even a superficial acquaintance with the conduct of the German occupier of Poland suffices for the terrible truths lurking behind our verbal clichés.

So much as an answer to the question of what specific constellation of sociostructural elements produced a moral indifference of hitherto unknown proportions. But my story does not end here yet. Throughout this book I have assigned the Holocaust the status of a sideshow in Germany's drive toward empire. Since that attempt failed so spectacularly, it behooves us also to interpret the fact that a modern society can push the phenomenon of moral indifference among its leadership to the point of national suicide.

The common element between the meaningless suffering and death evident in the Holocaust and Germany's national suicide is the absence of adequate legitimation in collective action. Both events engaged the nation's resources. Such resources are managed in their allocation by elites. Usually elites can be expected to be more concerned with legitimation than the people at large. The reason for this is a simple one: Usually people in elite roles like the higher rewards associated with performance of such roles, and they also like to think that they deserve them. The apparent abnormality in the case of Germany's national elites is to be found in their seeming disregard for legitimation. A closer look at the ways in which modern, complex, and highly differentiated societies manage to act as collective actors, seeking to realize meaningful goals, can tell us that one-dimensional elites lack the tools to care effectively about problems of legitimation. Appreciation of the absence of the proper tools can tell us also about the loss of self-steering capacity in German society, a loss that led to the nation's demise.

In contrast to more simple forms of social systems, where members know each other in face-to-face familiarity, complex social systems attain self-steering capacity primarily through the operation of symbolic media. At the present time we certainly live in a media-conscious age. But it is not television, nor radio, nor newspapers that I have in mind. These are but channels through which communications flow. The concept self-steering through symbolic mediation refers to specific types of languages, to media in a more technical sociological sense. Understanding what these media are and how they are related to each other can help us in understanding how complex societies succeed or fail in self-steering.

Perhaps the most familiar of these media is money. Not only do we use it every day, but also many of us have learned something in introductory economics courses about the properties of money that make it a symbolic medium. So knowing about money instructs us a little about properties of symbolic media in general. Of particular advantage in this respect is the fact that we are all highly conscious about inflation, a situation where too many dollars chase too few goods and services, eventuating in rising prices. When inflation cheapens money and the expectation of continuity in such a trend goes beyond a certain threshold, people abandon money and seek refuge in gold. We may not know why trust in the exchange value of gold is so indestructible. But we do know that gold has functioned as the primary security base of money for ages and across many cultures. This suggests that use of a medium amounts to acceptance of quite enormous risks, and returning to its use after some severe disappointment may well be dependent on the belief that there is always a security base to fall back on if it fails. If this be the lesson of money, it behooves us to inquire whether other societal media have similar properties. And since we are more familiar with money, a brief, elementary, and selective review of some of its properties is a useful starting point for understanding the nature of self-steering through symbolic media in modern society.

First, money is utterly symbolic in that it has no value in use; you cannot eat it. It has value only in exchange. Another way to say this is that the symbol money represents, in the sense of stands for, utilities that have consumption implications. From this we learn that symbolic media represent some use values or "intrinsic satisfiers," as Parsons (1963b) called them. Second, so long as we keep money in a bank account or at home, we do save ourselves information. Only when we decide on spending do we need to know what we want and where to get it. "Liquidity," as Luhmann (1968:47) held, "is a substitute for information." Now, living in inflationary times, we are all aware of the fact that holding liquidity makes rational sense only if we feel fairly confident about price behavior in some foreseeable future of relevance to us. This tells us that our ability to save information by holding onto liquidity—that is, by holding claims to intrinsic satisfiers rather than securing control over them—is a course of action that makes sense only under conditions of sufficient trust in the monetary system's behavior. When trust crumbles, people abandon money and seek to secure gold, *the* classic security base of money the exchange value of which is always trusted. I have just said that with sufficient trust we can afford information-saving by keeping money in the bank or at home. Where we keep it makes a crucial difference. The centrally important role of a banker is *not* to act as a safekeeper for our savings. This brings us to the third important point about money. It is its credit function. When bankers loan money they create money in the process. More important yet, when they grant loans for productive purposes and the ventures financed on credit pay off, real economic growth results. With the proviso of a payoff in the extension of credit it is not just paper money that is added to what is already in circulation but also additional goods and/or services with effective demand. And this risky business of riding to success on one's debts highlights the fourth important point. The most important role of money is a double one. Money is a guidance mechanism for the economy and a motor in economic growth. This double role rests on enormous amounts of trust in the system. That should be obvious when we realize that it is our money that is put at the disposal of some entrepreneur venturing forth to test his innovative ideas in the marketplace. A given dollar does double duty, miraculously. The saver has a claim to his deposit, but the creditor has the money at his disposal for a specified time. Hypothetically, at any given moment in time a genuine banker is always broke. Should a run on the bank ensue, he could not satisfy depositors. And this aspect of trust undergirding the whole system highlights another important feature of symbolic media. The government tries to reduce risk somewhat by demanding that bankers hold reserve fractions in liquidity. That alerts us to the fact that the use of any symbolic medium rests on some code, a set of rules specifying permissible uses of the language. In the case of money this "operative code" is made up of governmental regulation and the law of property, more generally. Evidently, power backs up money.

Let me summarize some of the important lessons just learned from money. First, symbolic media represent or stand for some intrinsic satisfier, but they themselves have only value in exchange. Being intrinsically worthless, symbolic media are accepted despite the risks involved because they have their security bases. Security bases are other media (backup or crisis media, if you like), but in any event entities the exchange value of which is less doubted for whatever reason. Being languages, symbolic media have some operative code that specifies acceptable modes of using them. Second, holding liquidity rather than intrinsic satisfiers amounts, of course, to a sacrifice. If you hold money, you have sacrificed economic self-sufficiency. Rather than producing all you need for yourself, you specialize for the production of some values-in-use and leave the production of others up to other people. So money teaches us a central point about any division of labor. You always sacrifice self-sufficiency. Among many other reasons you do so is the fact that holding liquidity saves you information. Third and last, only trust in the system permits a medium to play its double role as a guidance mechanism and a motor in real growth of intrinsic satisfiers. The advantages of a division of labor depend on trust, a matter that is also contingent on complex patterns of media backing each other. Only if power backs money in a proper way to prevent inflation just enough to eventuate in real economic growth can men and women afford trust in the advantages of divided labor in society.

Turning now to the other three societal media, these are power, influence, and value commitments (Parsons, 1963b; 1963a; 1968b). Knowing about some of their features can enhance our understanding of the amoral conduct of modern elites in Germany.

As a symbolic medium, political power has been defined as the capacity to make decisions that are binding on others. Legitimate power is at issue. But legitimate power by no means guarantees intentions. A person in a position of authority may issue commands; subordinates may all be willing to comply. But these two conditions do not suffice to assure the attainment of some collective goal, which is the intrinsic satisfier of the power medium. It is an all too familiar story about directives getting stuck in communication channels of an organization, of policy directives being issued that subordinates lack the means to accomplish, and similar foulups in bureaucratic life that tell us that power is often only talk. A brief listing of some typical national goals in modern times should suffice to alert us to the symbolic nature of power and the complex nature of its dependency on other media in its operation. Modern governments set such collective goals as target rates of economic growth, somehow calculable levels of national security in defense postures, distributive-justice objectives in the welfare sector pertaining to health, education chances, and Social Security in old age. Many such goals take years, some decades or longer to accomplish. Most take money. Most also require persuasive powers or informed judgment to be set up in feasible fashion in the first place. These also require influence, which will be described below. The intrinsic satisfier, the realization of a societal goal through effective cooperation in society is, obviously, a highly contingent matter. Years may pass before anyone finds out whether power has had an effect, and what that effect is.

The operative code of power is the jurisdiction of office. Taking a nationally organized society as the unit here, the jurisdiction of office can be measured in terms of a concentration-dispersion ratio according to constitutional requirements. For example, in Britain and the Soviet Union power is far more concentrated than in the United States (Gilison, 1972); and so it has been in Germany. But such a formal measure hardly tells the whole story. If political leaders are to lead a nation, they need more than power. They need influence far more than power.

Second, what about information-saving and liquidity in the realm of power? Here the franchise is one outstanding example. Citizens possess it like some property; but they exercise it only on election day. In the interelectoral periods one can save information; only when you cast the vote are you really expected to know about issues, candidates, and parties. Furthermore, as every administrator knows, a deliberate nonenforcement of some regulations can save power and build up credit for effecting compliance with objectives he deems more important.

Third, power also has its credit function. A proper use of power at the national level can add to the medium and its intrinsic satisfier, effectiveness in cooperation in the nation as a whole. The process of legislation adds directives in a constant stream. Additions to the medium are made constantly. Indeed, the voluminous outpouring of law after law leads the newspaper reader to suspect that modern societies suffer enormous inflation of power. We do not call it by that name. We label the process overbureaucratization or overregulation. But we suspect that only a fraction of the intended results of this legislative activism is actually accomplished. Therefore, the specter of an "overgoverned" society is strictly analogous to an economy suffering from inflation. But this should not blind us to the phenomenon of real growth in collective effectiveness either. In historical perspective, there is simply no doubt that modern societies address a range of social problems that premodern societies simply were incapable of. The percentage of a nation's wealth that has become government expenditure is only a pale measure of this vastly enhanced ability to work together. That percentage has grown dramatically everywhere (Deutsch, 1970:67). Whether it is illness or accident, unemployment or educating our children, modern government has transformed a vast range of formerly private problems into social ones and therefore into public concerns, which opens the road to solutions through taxation. Only an understanding of power as a symbolic medium can help us understand this. Political power in modern societies is a highly generalized medium. One index of this can be found in a difference regarding the normative obligations of parliamentarians in premodern and in modern societies. In the former, Parliaments were only delegates' congresses. An M.P. was *not* to exercise judgment as to what might constitute the national interest; instead, he was to advance and defend the interests of his constituency in as direct and as *unmediated* a fashion as he could. A premodern parliamentarian was not a representative of "the people" but only of a particular part of them. In the normative sense, he was not to have any powers except those specifically delegated to him by his clients. In contrast, modern parliamentarians are supposed to represent the people as a whole. They are expected to define the national interest by articulating many local interests. They are granted *generalized* powers (Carsten, 1959). And whatever they accomplish in this respect can only be allocated to trust, or to the fact that a sufficient number of citizens rest content with the liquid franchise in their hands rather than engaging in the extraparliamentary politics of the street demonstration.

This just-mentioned possibility alerts us to what holding liquid power amounts to. Holding the franchise and waiting for judgment day at the ballot box amount to the relinquishment of coercive self-sufficiency, taking care of yourself with a gun in hand. Thus when power deflates, one communicates with ever more threatening forms of sanction, ultimately involving the means of violence. For the power medium the security base is force. So much for power as a symbolic medium.

Influence is a symbolic medium that represents or stands for the experience of belonging. The intrinsic satisfier is zero social alienation, as it were. You feel you know what your rights and obligations in your role set are, and you feel good as a social creature. That feeling is often the result of the receipt of advice, and having complied with it, advice of a superior trustworthy nature we ascribe to the influential. His particular language is influence, a medium of persuasion. The relationship between some influencer and an influencee involves a special kind of inequality. The former is supposed to know better than the latter what is in the latter's own best interest. The use of this medium rests also on a presumed consensus on ends. Only the means are regarded as problematic, and the influencer is supposed to have superior knowledge about them. That assumption gives him his advisory powers. Let me take the doctor-patient relationship as prototypical to describe influence. In suggesting a course of therapy, a doctor makes credible assertions about the patient's problem, assertions that *in principle* could be verified but are *in practice* not verified, certainly not to the patient's satisfaction. After all, attempting the latter would require sending the sick to medical school, hardly a very practical suggestion. The point is that he who is granted influence need not give detail justifications for the course of action he recommends and for the compliance he gets. His advice is trusted. One reason is that health is assumed to be better than illness, life better than death. The end is not in question, only the means are; and it is the doctor who controls them. Presumably, after an illness has been cured, the person can rejoin family, work associates, and playmates, and role strain attributable to his absence is reduced again. Reduced role strain amounts to enhanced solidarity, the intrinsic satisfier represented by influence. The example of the doctor-patient relationship points to modern professions as the primary bearers of influence in modern society. Professions are society's managers of uncertainty (Marx, 1969). The knowledge base of professions grows continuously, a process that produces uncertainty itself. The professional operates with a double consciousness about his precarious responsibility. First, he knows what is not known in the profession at large. Second, he knows that his own effort to keep up with new developments remains forever incomplete. Yet the client who comes to him with his problem demands expert solutions. To some extent both parties know that guaranteed success in solving the problem is beyond their powers. If nothing else, the clichés of uncertainty management make us aware of this. In medical practice the relevant cliché concerns the acknowledged fact that no diagnosis or prognosis can ever be 100 percent certain. In legal practice we find a similar belief, which can be captured in a lawyers' stereotyped remarks to a new client: "If another lawyer told you he can guarantee success in court for you, that man is either a fraud or incompetent." And the corresponding cliché on the clients' side that "only fools represent themselves in court" also tells us that dependency on professionals is acceptable despite acknowledged uncertainty about the outcome. Professions, better than any other role, tell us what acceptance of the influence medium permits the client to do. Accepting the medium with trust, a client can live with ignorance and impunity. Life in complex society requires no less, however much it worries us.

Isolating the professions as the primary bearers of influence and *the* example of the influence process par excellence serve to make a theoretical point. It is only in the ideal-typical modern society that professions have the necessary prestige to deserve that much trust. And prestige is the operative code of the influence medium. However much some real world may differ, the theoretical case, or the model, tells us what to look out for when it comes to the question of whether a society has institutionalized influence. The model tells us what kind of prestige we have in mind, and on what kind of prestige influence as a symbolic medium depends for its operation. Accordingly, prestige refers to "the criteria by which units in a [collectivity] are given *generalized* status-rank, one which transcends specificity of function or situation" (Parsons, 1969:435). This tells us that influence, as conceived here, can exist only in a stratified society, a society that has in fact generalized superiors, people looked up to by others regardless of the particular social situation of their encounter. This point is of central importance in understanding the helplessness of the German elites in preventing the suicidal dynamics of their society. Any modern society that suffers a deficit in institutionalized influence is one deprived of a very important self-steering mechanism.

In following the advice of influentials and making ourselves dependent on their judgment we sacrifice self-sufficiency in knowledge of the relevant facts that sometimes, as in the case of medical practice, have direct life-or-death consequences. That is true at the collective level of modern existence as well, and inevitably so, given the enormous advance in the division of labor. When trust crumbles here and influentials encounter credibility gaps, the security base is the family. As a reaction to repeated disappointments we become ever more reluctant to accept advice from strangers as to what may be in our own best interest and flee into the security of kinship bonds. They are our refuge at least so long as the old adage persists, "The family is the place where they have to take you in."

Abandoning the influence medium in public life typically follows some inflationary expansion of it. Claims were made that could not be verified in principle. Operating under acknowledged uncertainty, any modern influential can, even with the best of intentions, turn into some fool of hope and overestimate the efficacy of available knowledge to solve some problem. The risk of inflation is also inherent in the necessary resource competition among various sectors of the knowledge and development industries in modern societies. Legislative action, so we learn from the newspapers, virtually involves mountains of research and position papers for each new law. Seeing these on the TV screen, you ask yourself, can anyone properly digest all this information? Can so much really inform the creation of new power? Once again, one notes the intercontingency among symbolic media. If influence inflates, power may well suffer in efficacy. Inoperable laws may be passed. No doubt, there is a credit function in the operation of influence. Every occupation striving for professional standing, and succeeding, necessarily adds to the stream of influential information. More difficult to answer is the question of whether real additions to the intrinsic satisfier are conceivable. Can there be some real additions to net national solidarity in modern societies, social systems that still experience growth in functional differentiation? Let me leave the question open.

The last societal medium to be considered here concerns value commitments. The way in which modern people communicate such commitments typically takes the form of sociomoral rhetoric. The rhetorical symbols involved cover quite some range. One hears appeals to fatherland, socialism, "the just society," and similar slogans. Evidently, in their very form such slogans are intrinsically worthless. Such appeals have no direct consumption value. The intrinsic satisfier such talk represents is the experience of relational integrity we can enjoy as members of a morally tolerable society. This involves accepting the most general purposes of association patterns in society as unproblematically sound. Living with symbols in this area amounts to a life with conventional moral wisdom. You save yourself the trouble, and the likely failure, of trying to become your own Immanuel Kant. A life in accordance with formulas of conventional moral wisdom is again a life where liquidity substitutes for adequate information. Such a life is just as risky an existence as acceptance of the other media entails. But the consequences of failure may be more devastating to us personally. Failure may dehumanize us entirely.

Sociomoral rhetoric also has its particular operative code. But so far no satisfying definition of the code has been developed. Moral authority in social relations is the issue. Moral authority tells us what we owe to others, on what grounds, and what we are entitled to in turn. Illustrations demonstrating an unequal distribution of such authority come easily to mind. The institutionalized charisma of the Roman Catholic papacy can be mentioned. Moral brokers with some discernible effect on reform policies in society come to mind as well. In recent United States history Martin Luther King remains a case in point. Such figures have moral authority because the laity imputes to them a differential capacity to understand better than ordinary people what the central moral imperatives in some given historical situation are and require of us in our conduct.

The examples chosen illustrate the credit function. If all those who accept the moral message of some charismatic figure were to insist at one and the same time on detail proof just how going along with the ideals espoused might satisfy the experience of relational integrity in everyday life, the moral innovator would be broke. For when he mobilizes the people, the force of appeals rests on their generality. Were he even inclined to spell out the necessary detail for implementing values, the force of his appeal would have to vanish. This follows simply from the fact that in a highly complex and differentiated society, implementing new values, or implementing old ones but taking them more seriously than ever before, creates its own moral complexity and uncertainty. That is why our following the moral innovators in modern times has so often suffered the fate of moral inflation. Whatever their effects for good or for evil, charismatic dreams have been realized only through power, an admixture that necessarily diluted the original intentions. Nonetheless, charismatic figures can be usefully considered as moral entrepreneurs in a fairly strict analogy to the economic entrepreneur, the political broker, and the influence peddler. And what happens here when credulity crumbles, when the realization sets in that our desire to believe was naïve? What, in technical terms, is the security base of the commitments' medium? The answer derives from a presupposition that all going along with the moral wisdom of another entails. That is our ability to share values. But when we wake up with disappointment, that in turn registers in the individual experience as guilt. And only our ability to share guilt with others in society can assure us that we share values, even though in seeking their implementation in new ways we may utterly fail. A society where guilt cannot be shared at all, in no acceptable form that men and women deem appropriate, is a society with a fundamental flaw in the bases of its legitimacy.

Table IX-1   *Selected Characteristics of Societal Media*

Medium	Communication Mode	Intrinsic Satisfier	Operative Code	Security Base
Money	Inducement	Consumable utilities	Law	Gold
Power	Commandment	Cooperative effectiveness	Office jurisdiction	Force
Influence	Persuasion	Belongingness	"Prestige"	Kinship
Value commitments	Moral appellation	Experience of integrity	Moral authority	Shared guilt

To facilitate an overview, Table IX-1 presents the features of societal media just discussed. They are the tools for a macrosociological interpretation of Germany's collective suicide and the meaningless suffering and death that accompanied it.

In Chapter IV it was shown that German society was extremely divided in societal values. The main cleavages were regional. But the value commitments of social classes, the upper classes in particular, did not crosscut the regional divisions. Expressed in the theoretical language of values as a symbolic medium, this is a finding of several such media each with its own distinctive operative code. Consequently, German society was one equipped with competing moral authorities. In addition, in purely quantitative terms the work ethic of the middle and upper classes was one of the more commonly shared beliefs. But excessive diversity in all other respects left the nature of the good society that was supposed to be established by hard work an eternally contentious issue. Only within the segregated subcultures of region-specific social classes could one safely assume that one's partners shared one's own societal values. Only within these confined subcultures, therefore, could one float sociomoral rhetoric with some reasonable expectation to achieve a safe degree of intersubjective bindingness. For the members of the national elites, people of diverse regional origin, this meant the necessary privatization of social morality. They could share their beliefs in the circles of kinship and friendship only but not in their circles of occupational life.

Given the human propensity to interpret one's situation, one particularly prevalent among the educated, some elaboration of mere facts into principles of the modern condition was almost inevitable. One could make a virtue out of necessity and declare the necessary irrelevance of religiously tinged moral beliefs in the domain of public affairs of secular society. Men in elite positions in modern societies are, after all, men of affairs, not men of contemplation. Impressed perhaps by German historiography of a Ranke or a Meinecke, with its emphasis on the uniqueness of the great cultural traditions of mankind, the educated among Germans were certainly sensitive to values in the abstract. Man's history certainly demonstrated extraordinary variety in the construction of meaningful ethics. When coupled with an elaborately cultivated sense of genuine value relativism (and that was the only way you could live with yourself at peace when so dependent on moral strangers in other elite positions), commitments to values of one's own culture definitely became problematical. Having presumably also grasped the modern ideas of the infinite revisability of man, society, and culture, they were profoundly struck by the tremendous moral complexity that the modern condition presented. From the vantage point of history and the new vistas of an all-possibilities world, any simple evaluation of the morality of the conduct of nations seemed out of the question. Only romantic fools would deem themselves able to apply direct moral criteria to human behavior in this area. Committed both to value relativism and to that open-mindedness characteristic of self-conceived realists, and contemptuous of all political romanticizing, elites in Germany, in effect, banished societal values from circulation in the public realm.

For men of affairs the idea that morality had to be subjective and private rather than objective and social was also amply supported by the historical process that had led to the unification of Germany in the nineteenth century. And surely one had to learn from one's own history. That lesson showed what counted in the world. This was not the soft idealism of the dreamer about a nation as a societal community bound together by shared convictions and common citizenship responsibilities. Hard interests of power and money, of governmental bureaucracies and capitalist forces in the market sphere had forged the "nation" together. Germany had been constructed "from the top down." To the cold-blooded realist it remained an inescapable historical fact that Germany was "an instrumental-rational power association" (*ein zweckrationaler Machtverband*) rather than a nation that had grown "from the bottom up" on the basis of common bonds among citizens who shared a caring concern for a common undertaking. This meant that legality had become a substitute for legitimacy. And it carried a general lesson: the quintessential basis of authority in the modern age was *only* rational-legal. All the rest, like respect for tradition or pretensions to charisma, were simply pretensions. They were tools used by those who made laws for their interests. If you wanted to be part of the game, you had to adopt a purely instrumental attitude to matters of convictions. In a society where the values medium had been withdrawn from public circulation at the top, there was no alternative.

If Germany was a society with a structural deficit in societal values as a medium circulating in the public realm at the national level, the question arises as to how to categorize the extremist nationalist gospel that flooded her public communications channels in so recurrent a pattern. Nationalism had been rampant under the *Kaiser* in the prewar era of the First World War; during it, of course; toward the closing years of the Weimar Republic; and throughout the Third Reich when, however, it revealed completely its true face as a cover for imperialism. With values banished from the public sphere, this ferocious nationalist propaganda was influence, and an inherently inflated influence at that. Two additional reasons suggest this interpretation. On the one hand, de-stratification of a country's elites means the absence of a valid operative code for influence at the top of society. On the other hand, the dynamics of resource competition among relatively status-deprived one-dimensional elites leads each to latch onto the use of influence as the main tool in the striving for status congruence even though none of them possess influence in any secure way. The latter point should tell us that Nazism in particular was a form of middle-class extremism that went far beyond the sources of electoral support for the movement that had been known for a long time. Consider, ever since Bismarck the German elites were literally obsessed with the specter of a two-front war. Yet twice they engaged in one. And while entry into the First World War does lend itself to a "sliding into it" interpretation where incumbents in elite positions only knew that they were not doing enough to prevent war, entry into the Second World War was characterized by so persistent a pattern of aggression that deliberately risking war in East *and* West was the only conclusion the informed could draw. If there is a short formula by which to explain the collective suicidal drift of this modern society, it is to be found in the fact that Germany was characterized by middle-class extremism at the top. This is also a possibility inherent in any modern society, which is why German history has universal significance.

The withdrawal from circulation in the public sphere of societal values prevents the development of a deeper and more lasting societal identity than can be expressed in the more overt manifestations of national identity we find in bills of rights, constitutional principles, the *de facto* division of powers in society, and the like. This more covert but more permanent societal identity is anchored in consensus on stratification codes. In this connection let us firmly keep in mind a most important fact about American society. It is this: No matter how much Americans may think of their nation as a pluralist one in several respects touching on politics, race, class, region, and religion, all of them, irrespective of social class, *share* common standards of distributive justice (Alves and Rossi, 1978). And, whether they know it or not, they not only agree, for example, on the question of how much income inequality there ought to be in the nation, in recent history they have been able to practice what they preach. The actual U.S. income distribution in 1970 has been amazingly close to the normatively dictated one (Lipset, 1976:334). Distributive-justice norms bearing on income distribution are only a small part of the stratification codes of a society. Nonetheless, since money is the concrete thing that everyone can see, consensus on these norms contributes its share to a deeply felt national identity. That was utterly lacking in Germany. Stratification codes are norms regarding the unequal distribution of socially valued resources in society. Commonly, sociologists describe these resources in terms of wealth, power, prestige, and moral esteem.

Stratification codes prescribe how these ought to be distributed by specifying: (1) the amount of inequality deemed desirable; (2) the extent and nature of status congruence among them; (3) permissible types of exchanges between them and agencies controlling such exchange; and (4) above all else, legitimating reasons for the just-mentioned items (Eisenstadt, 1971). But a society, like the German, that had institutionalized dissensus on societal values is one that cannot generate consensus on any of these norms. Consequently, no consensus on the criteria for *generalized* status rank can emerge. Influence lacks a valid operative code. The use of influence inherently inflates the medium.

But use of a medium that lacks a valid code is only one condition that can lead to its inflation. Who uses it makes its own distinctive contribution to its inflation. By definition, one-dimensional elites have superior control over but one of society's unequally distributed resources. By assumption that scarce resources are valued ones that all desire to control, incumbency in a one-dimensional elite position condemns you to seek greater status congruence to acquire what you lack in resources. In the absence of any consensual normative controls on the unequal distribution of resources, such a search acquires a particular urgency, for in the absence of consensual stratification codes the world is one vast vista of opportunities for status advancement. Among the German elites three distinct reasons made the use of influence a particularly attractive tool in the striving for general status. First, one-dimensional elites are functional modern elites driven to an extreme of modernizing development. And functional elites are supposed to use influence on policymaking centers in society in order to secure the formulation of policies that work. Only experts can do that with responsibility, since only experts have the requisite knowledge. Second, the survival of a near-monopoly over high occupational prestige on the part of the Junker-military complex had shown how much could be accomplished by wielding this medium. Had they not always done well in their pursuit of special interests by waving the banner of national interests? And had they not done so well by managing to transform the historical source of their prestige through association with the crown into a more "modern" one by presenting themselves as *the* primary state-bearing group, regardless of the nature of the state, whether monarchical, republican, or totalitarian? But reliance on influence was dictated by more than just historical experience in advancing one's interests. Third, power and wealth had legal limits. Influence without constraints arising from consensual stratification codes had not comparable limits. Anyone could try to use influence without making himself ridiculous—anyone, that is, who had something of superiority to claim. Thus influence became the primary weapon by which the merely wealthy, the merely powerful, the merely prestigious, and the merely cultured tried to achieve more status congruence. And because influence had become the main weapon it had to be subjected to severe inflation.

But there was also a more personal or social-psychological source to influence inflation among the German elites. Incumbency in a one-dimensional elite position leaves you insecure. You cannot know whether you really deserve so much control over but one resource. Further, the very struggle for other resources and their respective symbolic media adds to status insecurity rather than reducing it. This results from the inability to regulate social conflict in society. The last three chapters have shown that a society with de-stratification at the top is one incapable of institutionalizing conflict. The demise of Weimar democracy should teach us a lesson on this score. That lesson is: Social structure is more powerful than political structure. A more accurate, if more cumbersome, formulation is that that structurelessness in inequalities at the top of society cannot be compensated for or neutralized by democratic rules of the political game, nor by any other political rules. Elite de-stratification generates conflict beyond the powers of a polity to regulate regardless of the nature of the political regime involved. If the modernization process entails a universal trend toward the emergence of the function specialist and the decline of generalized superiors in society, having a democracy provides false comfort. Unregulated conflict in the pursuit of status congruence generates so much social insecurity among "the best and the brightest" in modern society that rational collective action or self-steering capacity is severely undermined even in a democratic polity. Should increasing functional differentiation and the rise to prominence of the one-function specialist be associated with a level of value conflict that unravels consensual stratification codes, the oldest democracy may crumble in chaos.

An incumbent of a position of "one-dimensional eminence" who encounters random outcomes in conversion attempts finds himself in that Hobbesian hell that Inkeles (1954) described as institutionalized anxiety, a condition not confined to totalitarian rule. Whatever he tries, everything remains still possible, amazing success as well as utter failure. Further, under conditions of noninstitutionalized conflict, he knows only one thing: Nothing has endurance. The success of today may turn into the failure of tomorrow. Having only a one-dimensional status, such a person cannot rely on sound feedback from others concerning his sense of social self. And nothing can be quite as socially alienating as the combination of a performance ethic with institutionalized uncertainty about one's general standing in society. You are condemned to remain incomplete forever, like some *nouveau riche*. Aspiring to something more complete, you will inflate influence because anything you try is risky anyway. The questions who you are, can reasonably aspire to become, what you were yesterday, are today, and might be tomorrow are questions that remain forever open ones. This generates the kind of middle-class extremism represented in the figure of the achieving personality, the man who is, at any given moment in time, *only* the sum total of his successes and failures in his occupational life. The former he advertises constantly; the latter he tries to conceal from himself and from others, gaining perhaps the ultimate of "success" primarily on the latter point. But life in such a milieu is too stressful to last the whole adult life course for most. Age brings its toll and, unless you are a dullard, the cost in intellectual honesty associated with deceptions becomes too heavy to bear. And gradually you learn that there must be a better, a more secure way to protect the constantly bruised self. Eventually you cease trying to find an answer to the question of identity on the social plane. You shift gears, finding the answer as to who you are on the cultural plane instead. You move from over-identification with the role to role distance, without, however, letting go of influence attempts. Your mind stays on the social plane; only your heart moves somewhere else. Your mind has to stay in the social game because you do have responsibilities to family and children. Nonetheless, using art, "philosophy," or sociology, your sense of self, the one that you feel about becomes eventually utterly subjectivized and secure only by virtue of having become completely private. Desocialized, the sense of self looses its social constraint in normative terms. What you do becomes entirely a matter of the collision of interests; what you feel about your action becomes the sole private property you can ever hope to have. On the social plane you are but a careerist, following whatever opportunities for status advancement may offer themselves. No longer ethically controlled by social forces, you become incapable of responding to any offerings of more ultimate commitments with an inner-worldly relevance. For then, what matters ultimately to yourself has no relationship at all to what matters here and now, to your fellow human beings, in the finitude of life.

When such men occupy the leading positions in a modern society, the dynamics inherent in the media they have left to use deprive the system as a whole of effective self-steering capacity. With influence under long-term inflationary pressure, power tends to deflate, involving increased reliance on the security base of the medium, force, or rule by terror. The most important reason for this is the softening up of the operative code of power under the impact of inflated influence. Elites who constantly bombard the one-dimensional power controls with "better ideas" may leave the legal jurisdictions of office unaffected, at least in terms of illegal encroachments on power. But by virtue of the power holders' propensity to acquire the other media, the participants in policymaking increase, and multiple governors with dubious authorities arise. Orlow's (1968) account of the Nazis' economic policies in the Balkans provides most compelling evidence to the effect that inflated influence weakens power to a point where eventually influentials block each other's efforts, leaving only terror as a resource. But terror produces cooperation only under the limiting conditions of the prison or the concentration camp. Otherwise terror is but a tool that destroys organized resistance against illegitimate authorities. As evident in the case of the economic exploitation of southeastern Europe, an increasing reliance on terror produced the opposite of the intention, not development of economic resources for the Reich but their decay.

In theory symbolic media are the tools of leadership in complex, highly differentiated, and legitimate social orders. That theory specifies an order in the relationships among the media. The order is known as "a hierarchy of control." In this model values constrain the use of influence; influence constrains the exercise of power; and power controls money. This particular hierarchy is one way to conceptualize effective self-steering capacity in a modern society in a way that combines the moral responsibility of collective action at the national level with the flexibility and autonomy of the various institutional spheres as the economy, the science complex, the defense establishment, and so on, which a high division of labor in society requires. In German practice no such hierarchy was maintained or even attempted. One-dimensional in character, the German elites at the national level did not possess the requisite tools of leadership, and self-steering capacity of society was the victim. Three facts about the functioning of symbolic media tell us why. First, societal values had been withdrawn, and rather precipitously, from public circulation before use of the medium could even begin to do its job of legitimating the social order. Perhaps the first serious public debate about the nature of the good society in modern unified Germany was also the last one. Conducted toward the close of the century, this was the controversy about the nature, the desirability, and the possible inevitability of industrial society (Barkin, 1970). During the early years of the Weimar Republic one could still hope to find some respect in debating the issue of the compatibility of socialism and liberal democracy. But soon a seemingly much more "realistic" concern with collective effectiveness, "strong government," and *Realpolitik* undermined the respectability of any seriously caring concern with shared ideals. The ever-increasing militancy on the part of the private militias of right and left banished the values medium from public circulation for good. Second, influence assumed extreme levels of inflation to a point where nationalist messages turned into genuine word salad during the

Nazi era. Third, there was a drift toward power deflation in the sense of a growing reliance on "solutions by force" that accompanied the disbalanced functioning of influence and power.

This still did not mean that a skeptic, and one who cared about realistic national goals and the country's fate in pursuing them, had no means whatever at his disposal in his official occupational role. But having learned that one did not raise questions of moral principle, the skeptic could only raise doubts about efficiency of means. And this kind of consideration, the last that was publicly acceptable, confined him again to the use of influence. Yet all used that device and for the sake of corporate rivalry, the advancement of institutional or organizational interests. Thus even covert attempts at correction of the country's disastrous course had to remain ineffectual. They were seen by the addressee as something with which he was all too familiar, the attempt of another institutional interest to encroach upon his own turf and hard-won prerogatives. Rather than meeting receptivity, skepticism about the realism of national goals was greeted with defensive strategies. Deprived of the respectable use of values in the public arena, the skeptic could use moral concerns within the private realm only. And so, when worried about how it might all end, the Army officer could raise the question of the country's fate with his friend in the casino, a Navy commander might "commune" with his mate in the mess, an SS exterminator might succumb to drink with his cronies encapsulated within the delinquent community of the bearers of the highest "state secrets," and their executive counterpart in industry might take up the matter with his friend in the business club. Within the confines of these milieux there was little terror. Very little and nothing essential had changed or, as in the case of the higher SS leadership, official secrecy helped in disguising reality and decriminalizing crime with language euphemisms of abstractions. At any rate, the rare individual among the middle-class extremist elites of German society who still did care about the wider consequences of his actions was reassured, at the wrong place, on erroneous grounds, but reasssured nonetheless. Thus fortified, he could return to his job and just carry on.

In the German case it remains an irony that the one medium that once failed so spectacularly as to indelibly impress everybody with the risks of information-saving—namely, money, in 1923—was in general the best institutionalized medium throughout the short history of that "nation." But all the remaining three media functioned improperly. The German elites found themselves trapped in a vicious circle of inflationary influence pressures and deflationary power trends, a circle from which they could not escape because they had withdrawn societal values from circulation in the public realm.

Epilogue

No one knows when Germans will resume their task of nation-building, and how they will go about it. That they will do so seems likely. The age of nations shows no sign of ending. For decades intellectuals have written its epitaph. But the patient refuses to die. Books are so fragile instruments of learning about ourselves that one properly hestitates to express even hope of accomplishing anything beyond mere cognitive understanding. If one movie can move us more than thousands of pages of print, that still tells us only how we can be moved, and not whether we can change. The use of emotions for changing ourselves is only understood, and very imperfectly at that, in the clinical setting, in the encounter between therapist and patient who can share pain. Ten years ago the Mitscherlichs (1970) attributed the then persistent silence about the Holocaust in Germany to melancholia. The title of their book was a very telling one: *The Inability to Mourn*. Today we know that outside Israel the silence was near universal. And while the imperative of guilt reigns nowhere as compelling as it does among Germans, intellectually we have known for a long time just how much democratic societies, while proclaiming to fight evil, were mere bystanders. Perhaps it is worthwhile to contrast my intellectual understanding of that long-lasting silence with that of the Mitscherlichs. Theirs was a psychoanalytic argument, like most social-science theory, based on a model of man as a creature striving for meaning. But German society under the swastika was not entirely made up of young teen-agers with their usual proclivities to identify with charismatic figures. For that minority one *could*, conceivably, adopt an interpretation that keeps them in the human family regardless of the awesome size of the crime *because*, like historical humans, they deemed their deeds meaningful, however weird the meaning. Their silence, then, *could* be attributed to a diminished sense of self, resting in turn on "the lost object, Adolf Hitler." One could orient to them as people suffering from melancholia, and so as fellow human beings. But the German teen-ager did not know about Treblinka. The German generals did, and so did the elites in economic life and in the government bureaus, even though they

323

did not care to know. These elites earned themselves entitlement to a diminished sense of self far deeper and far more hopeless than any "lost-object experience" can generate. Amoral men, they failed to identify with anything of moral significance, and so they abandoned themselves as humans. Nothing human connects them with their victims, and their deeds remain beyond the powers of ordinary language discourse where the concepts of sin and forgiveness apply. If that can be granted, their children or their grandchildren face a difficult task before they can even aspire again to nation-building in a fashion that will permit their neighbors sleep at night. The children will have to learn to share pain and guilt in a civil manner and to mourn the deeds of their fathers. Mourning in civility may change us; no simple rejection of the father can.

APPENDIX:

Data and Method of Measurement of German Values

Prologue: A Note on Design

Without entering into a discussion of the problematic relations between super structure and substructure, this study treats the former as the independent variable and the latter as the dependent variable. However, this means only that I treat values as the givens and refrain from detailed inquiry as to their determinants. Concerning politics, I rely on secondary sources. Electoral data, studies on the parties in Parliament on the national and regional levels, and studies on important pressure groups constitute the main body of data in this area. Thus the only primary sources bear on values. The most important difference between these two sets of data is continuity in records over time for politics but only a restricted time span in the case of values, at least so far as quantified data are concerned. My primary data on values are confined to pre-World War I Germany, covering the period 1871–1914. This poses the problem of possible value change during the later periods, Weimar and Nazi Germany.

While certainly a significant departure from an ideal design, the absence of quantified evidence on value change does not appear too crippling. Three considerations seem to support this contention. First, empirically, values have been regarded as the most stable aspect of social structure even by a student of society who gained fame by his forthright assertion that change is ubiquitous. Dahrendorf's (1965) *Society and Democracy in Germany* implicitly argues for value stability throughout the modern period since 1871, conceding a possibility for real value change only to the impact of the Nazis. Second, just what happened to values under "Hitler's social revolution" can be gleaned from secondary sources. Third, my assumption of stability in value orientations between Wilhelminian and Weimar Germany is also paralleled by the fact of continuity in one aspect of political life: Electoral cleavages established during the empire remained stable until the end of Weimar (Lepsius, 1966a).

A study on the impact of values on politics must draw its data on values from sources that minimally satisfy two conditions. The first of these deals with the problem of "independence" between the two variables—here, values and political

325

action. The second involves satisfying the requirement of comparability of units. For national politics, data on German values as such appear requisite. For the political expression of the usual societal cleavages such as region, class, religion, and urban-rural setting, one would need data on the values of the groups composing these subcollectivities. Neither of these conditions were met perfectly; both, however, could be met just sufficiently.

Unfortunately, the independence criterion constitutes a kind of negative selction guide. It tells us what kind of materials on values one should *not* use rather than pointing to an adequate source. Satisfying the independence criterion between values and politics obviously precludes using any data loosely labeled political ideology. Thus party programs, election campaign material, policy papers, speeches in Parliament, and the like are ruled out. The reason is simple. Abstracting political norms from sources such as these, then "generalizing" common patterns among political norms "up the ladder" to more inclusive superordinate conceptions of the desirable—namely, values—and finally relating the values so gained "back to" political practice would constitute a circular-flow design at once too short and too closed to prove very illuminating. This tells us only that the source for material for values must be of a kind intrinsically considerably removed from the scene of political action. The second requirement of a match between the sources on values and the politically organized subgroups precludes the use of such "global" variables as Lutheranism as a source on values, unless one has data on the beliefs of Lutherans in different social classes, regions, and the like.

For a period before "the age of interviewing," not counting the census, one source on values that perfectly satisfies the first condition and comes close to filling the bill for the second is popular mass fiction. I use the kind of fiction just "plain" and perhaps "*kitschig*" enough to enjoy wide circulation among those less constrained by education but not so obviously "cheap" and "trashy" as also to meet with censorship by "the higher institutionalized wisdom of cultivated taste" that would restrict its circulation among the better-off. Realist fiction with mass circulation seemed to fill this requirement. At that time, novels of this kind were "populated" with Bavarians, and Rhinelanders, Prussians, and people in Baden. This fiction also depicted the wealthy and the poor, as well as city and rural people. One important variable, however, on which the stories proved uninformative was religion. There simply was not enough information permitting to code fictional characters on religious affiliation. What is more, though a regional or ethnic label lent itself as a religious indicator in some areas—as, for example, Upper Bavaria, which was practically completely Catholic—the Protestant-Catholic mix, not to mention confessional differences within Protestantism, was so dispersed in Germany as definitely to preclude using the regional label as an index of religious affiliation (Ravenstein, 1883). Thus value differences deriving from religious sources cannot be examined in this study.

The use of the novel—or, indeed, any other cultural product—for the analysis of societal values remains a problematical task. As Colby (1966) pointed out there are at least two basic problems. The first concerns the question just what the cultural product "reflects"—that is, what it means concerning the relation between author and audience. The second problem relates to the referent population: To whom do the "reflections" apply, the interests of the researcher, a user community in whole, or if not, what parts of the latter? Substituting novel for folk tale, the reflection problem has been most cogently stated by Colby (1966:381): "A [novel] is a complex cultural production. It may function as a catharsis, provide a world view, describe sanctions and prohibited behavior, liberate one from the immediacy of his own situation or describe various types of useful behavior or strategies." Obviously too, this catalogue of five ways a novel may be used is a mere beginning of listing the possibilities. As one might easily add a few more—for example, getting through a college course or serving as the basis of a five-o'clock ladies' tea—the question of a novel's use becomes progressively more complex. If the use of the novel is so problematical, then one might as well ask: Why use it at all? The answer is that for the study of values on a national and a regional level at the turn of the century the novel seems to be the least ambiguous source available for the analysis of values on a regional level. For apart from one national magazine serializing novels, nineteenth-century Germany also had quite a number of regional writers. Her *Heimatdichter*, living in different parts of the country, made it their business to describe "their own kind," such as Upper Bavarians or Berliners, and to contrast them with each other. Clara Viebig was such a writer, for example. In her works, East Prussians confront Rhinelanders, and people from the Southwest come into contact with Berliners.

The works selected also had to be "realistic." Here I follow criteria of ethnographic realism as developed by Martel and McCall (1964). The main points about these criteria can be listed as follows: (1) Stories are temporal in setting and permit identification of the readership with the fictional characters and their problems; (2) Tendentious material of a particular political or religious point of view is excluded; (3) Stories are widely read as reflected either in the type of medium—for example, a mass-circulation weekly—or the sales figures reached in a free market *without* help of some sponsoring organization with a mass membership. With the aid of a standard reference work on German literature before World War I (Nadler, 1912–18), 31 novels were selected according to the above criteria. These novels were written by 14 authors. Five of these were explicit regional writers whose works proved a smashing sales success as indicated by multiple editions or thousands of copies printed. Using a quota sample, 11 novels written by 8 authors were taken from the *Gartenlaube*, in Wilhelminian Germany the equivalent of the late American *Saturday Evening Post*. This material was intended as evidence of German values at the national level. The *Gartenlaube* was the only weekly devoted in part to "wholesome entertainment" with a truly national distribution at the time. It was a newspaper featuring novels in serial form. Later, I discovered that some of the regional writers had also started their careers by publishing in the *Gartenlaube*. In addition, the most popular German novel of the nineteenth century was included as well. That was Victor von Scheffel's *Ekkehard*. With a first appearance in 1855, this novel had reached 240 editions by 1904.

Originally I expected that the novels in the *Gartenlaube* would be "populated" with characters free of an ethnic label. These would have formed the source of German values. However, this expectation was quite wrong, as most of the fictional characters in the *Gartenlaube* novels turned out to be regional types. Thus by being a mirror of parochial plurality, this magazine failed to provide an integrative focus for Germans, at least in its entertainment section. Germans could not learn what constituted German characteristics by reading these novels; all they met with there were Bavarians, Prussians, Rhinelanders, and the like. At the same time this robs the study of any direct evidence on German values. There being no Germans in these novels, what constituted German values can only be inferred from orientations shared across the regions.

Also, although the matter does not appear too serious, the thirty-one novels do not satisfy requirements of a technical sample of popular literature. The universe constitutes the unknown. It proved impossible to get any firm idea as to the number of popular novels covering the period 1871–1914. All one can know, then, is that the novels selected enjoyed a very large readership, numbering in the tens and hundreds of thousands even under the most conservative assumption that each book was read by only one person. Only the novels selected from the *Gartenlaube* can be said to make up a sample. But one cannot assert that the novels serialized in it represent adequately the country's popular mass fiction. Next, while reliable knowledge of the regional, class, and sex composition of the readership is lacking, the only evidence I found on this point shows that the readership was indeed nationwide and not class-specific either. An analysis of letters to authors and the editors of the *Gartenlaube* showed that these kinds of novels were read by Junker ladies in East Prussia, *Kaffee-Klatsch* circles in bourgeois Berlin, southern conservative gentlemen, and servant maids everywhere (Zimmermann, 1963). As these examples show, regional and class biases were probably minimal, but sex bias cannot be eliminated entirely. Taken together, it would appear that the data suffer more from incompleteness than from misrepresentation of what the German people read.

The basic assumption underlying the use of popular realist fiction as a source on values was simply this: Whatever else a novel may have meant to its readers, one of its services was to assist the readership in the task of finding out who one was, and how and why one ought to be different from other Germans. A demand for such knowledge should be especially high during times of rapid social mobilization. As reflected in city growth and patterns of internal migration, Wilhelminian Germany was certainly such an age. Even though the use of realist fiction precludes obviously hostile ethnic portraits, one may well be dealing with stereotypes rather than "objectively correct" descriptions. However "understanding" or "loving," the authors may well have endeavored to bring out the "typically Bavarian" or the "characteristically Rhenish," etc., in their writings. Thus one might have data on acceptable auto- and heterostereotypes. At worst, this would exaggerate the differences one finds relative to "objective" conditions. At best (assuming that men live by stereotypes since they have neither the time nor the inclination to face complex reality) one obtains data more appropriate for politics than scientifically accurate portraits would be. Finally concerning incompleteness, if the basic assumption holds (that men learn about each other through the use of fiction, and what is learned can be approximately reproduced through coding the content), then the inference population is the readership's stereotyped images. This running into the tens of thousands would constitute vast oversampling.

Developing a coding procedure was guided by the following considerations. First, one tries to reproduce as much as possible the "learning experience" of the actual readership. Since one is after the components of stereotypes and such mental images are embodied in people rather than what they do, coding fictional characters rather than themes, plots, and plot resolutions seemed advisable. Second, any study on values useful for comparative purposes must concern itself with measuring identical dimensions among the different groups to be compared. Now, just about the only theme one could expect to occur with deadly regularity in popular mass fiction was the theme of love, a somewhat slim basis for the measurement of variations in values. On the other hand, popular fiction is full of people who can be seen as representing models of behavior. These characters are often presented in a simple, straightforward manner that permits unambiguous placement into the following: major and minor characters on the amount of exposure, and "good" and "bad" guys. Particularly the latter are not left in limbo. Where it is even vaguely possible that a shade of doubt could remain in the reader's mind as to where vice and virtue lie, the writer often resorts to fantastic plot resolutions to bring the morals in the story across (Zimmermann, 1963:26–30). Thus using popular literature as an empirical source on values is based on the expectation that if good guys and bad guys can be identified, if they differ, and if the way in which they differ can be specified, findings on these characteristics tell us something about the values of different groups classifiable by region, class, city and country setting, and so on.

Given a type of literature that presents people with a fairly clear message as to "how and what all good people *should* be and do, and what they *should not* be and do," the problem of measurement turns on devising a code of such characteristics —that is, stereotyped beliefs about goodness and badness. Therefore the unit of analysis is some moral belief. Coding consists of judging fictional characters analogous to the kind of impression an ordinary reader might form in some considerably more vague manner. The most important difference here to ordinary consumption of literature is the attempt to make explicit whatever stereotypic images the novels communicate. Thus coding involved ranking the degree of applicability of a series of statements to a fictional character.

Measuring Values

The code developed presents an attempt to operationalize some of the basic concepts of action theory. Proceeding from the idea that the value system of a society can be systematically analyzed on the basis of the four-functions paradigm (Parsons, 1959), the central assumption built into the code is: Given the assignment of first-order importance to one function, the ideal-typical solutions for all remaining functional problems should be slanted accordingly. For example, a society in which adaptation ranks highest in the attention scale will tend to develop different types of orientations to solving goal-attainment, integrative, and pattern-maintenance problems than one in which integrative problems rank highest. Which of the four functions becomes defined as of primary importance depends, given the idea of hierarchy of control, on the content of ultimate meaning concerns. Thus the basic solution to the pattern-maintenance problem "sets the stage," as it were, for the kinds of solutions probable for the remaining problems. Therefore, if it is possible to suggest four basic "directional approaches" to the meaning of life, each in such a way as to define one of the four functions as of primary significance, the different kinds of solutions most likely to be sought for the remaining three problems should be derivable.

To avoid a vast increase in complexity, this scheme was restricted to the first four "primary types"—"L-, I-, G-, and A-value systems" involving the relative primacy of the following pattern-variable combinations: universalism-quality, particularism-quality, particularism-performance, and universalism-performance, respectively. These correspond to "images of the good society," models of the appropriate society men and women are to uphold, build, cherish, and defend. I have labelled these models the communion model, the *Gemeinschaft* model, the corporatist model, and the market model, respectively. In fiction such images emerge from the predominant concerns of the fictional characters in the form of auto- and heterostereotypical social characters whose whole life is focused on: (1) problems of meaning and ideals, (2) problems of how to be well adjusted in getting along with each other, (3) questions of how best to cooperate toward the achievement of group goals, or (4) problems of how best to develop and make use of all conceivable means focused on self-advancement and status enhancement.

Now, using primary types only yields sixteen ideal-typical base-line solutions to the four problems of meaning, integration, goal attainment, and adaptation. Formulating sixteen different solutions at this point, however, obviously would have to be so general and abstract as to be virtually devoid of utility in the coding of fictional characters. In trying to rank the applicability of any one of the type solutions to the fiction hero, one coder would consider a different aspect than another, and reproducibility would approach zero. In short, there would be no useful measuring instrument.

Therefore, more attention must be given to what the characters do and say. As the code should be an instrument to measure value orientations rather than situation-specific norms, however, this means bringing the coding categories closer to "fictional reality"—that is, actions and sentiments of fictional characters —without giving them specific content. At first glance this procedure may well look like an impossible, because self-contradictory, task. However, use of the different "object levels" in action theory provided a solution yielding a useful level of reliability as well as satisfactory validity. Three elements in the "situation of action" serving as objects of orientation to the actor were used: (1) ideas (cultural level); (2) others, collectivities, and individuals (social level); and (3) self (personal level). Thus for each of the four functions three somewhat more concrete problems were posed. These with their four variable type-solutions yielded forty-eight statements applicable in varying degrees to the fictional character. Since the type solutions for the integrative problems could be formulated most readily in terms of conflict management, two additional more concrete problems concerning the meaning of conflict and the sources of a person's inner conflict suggested themselves. Finally, it also seemed useful to make an additional distinction concerning the social level of the adaptation function, which involves mode of orientation as distinct from mode of relation. Thus the final number of relatively concrete problem formulations for the four functions on three object levels came to fifteen. These with four variable type-solutions each resulted in sixty statements, each reflective of either L, I, G, or A primacy.

Turning to the pattern-maintenance function first, these more concrete problems were formulated as follows. On the cultural level the question of the character's basic philosophy of life is raised; on the social level the problem involves the way in which he defines his principal obligation to society; finally, on the personal level attention focuses on the way in which he defines his principal obligation to himself. Second, as concerns the integrative function, two problems have been stated as applicable on the cultural level. The first involves the ways in which the moral problem of right and wrong becomes defined. The second concerns the ways in which conflicts with others tend to be seen, or more specifically, the meanings attached to social conflict. On the social level, the problem relates to the basic modes of conflict resolution. On the personal level, the integrative function was somewhat more concretized into two problems again, the first relating to the principal sources of inner conflict, the second being devoted to the primary modes of self-discipline. Third, concerning the goal-attainment function, on the cultural level the problem turns on the definitions of the major goals in life. The ways in which controls by others are seen constitutes the more specific problem on the social level, with the personal level being devoted to the amount of personal energy displayed openly—that is, the question of the social valuation of "personality drive." Finally, concerning the adaptation function, the more concrete problems examined were as follows. On the cultural level, the question turns on the kinds of knowledge most highly esteemed. On the social level, the first problem deals with the ways in which the character orients himself to others—that is, the kinds of characteristics he uses most often to define the other as an object of orientation. The second question here deals with the primary modes of relating to others—that is, the major techniques of interpersonal adjustment. Last, on the personal level of the adaptation function, the more specific problem posed turns on the kinds of mental capacities valued as intelligence—that is, the kinds of cognitive abilities most appreciated as intellectual competence. For easy reference, Table A-1 provides a summary of these more detailed specifications of functional problems on three object levels.

Turning next to the four variable base-line solutions of each of these fifteen problems, these will be very briefly discussed by indicating the kinds of solutions most likely for a given type of functional primacy. Therefore the next few pages will be devoted to a discussion of the L-, I-, G-, and A-primacy types, respectively. With the total number of variable-type solutions being sixty,

Table A-1   Specification of Functional Problems on Three Object Levels

Function	Object level	Question number	Problem
L	Cultural	1	Basic philosophy of life?
	Social	2	Obligation to society?
	Personal	3	Obligation to self?
I	Cultural	4	Definition of right and wrong?
		5	Meaning of conflict with others?
	Social	6	Mode of conflict resolution?
	Personal	7	Source of inner conflict?
		8	Mode of self-discipline?
G	Cultural	9	Goals in life?
	Social	10	Controls by others?
	Personal	11	"Personality drive"?
A	Cultural	12	Kinds of knowledge?
	Social	13	Mode of orienting to *alter*?
		14	Mode of relating to *alter*?
	Personal	15	Kinds of intelligence?

restricting this discussion to the barest of outlines—even within the limits of those aspects of society most relevant for public affairs—seems a necessity, lest reporting on the construction of the instruments loses its instrumental significance.

Four Primary Types of Value Orientations

On the basis of some knowledge of German society, it appears permissible to restrict the considerations of an L-primacy type of values to the active version of idealism (Parons, 1959:664). In the communion model of the good society, then, the central purpose of life, the very focal point of one's existence, is seen to be the active fulfillment of one's highest ideals; one is supposed to have an *aktive Gesinnungsethik*. Everyday life tends to be permeated with a moralistic tinge. Pragmatic considerations are easily defined as crass opportunism. One must not only do the right things, one must also employ the right means. Any disturbances in the political realm in such a society have a high tendency to be escalated into value-movement action (Smelser, 1963). The classical imperative "You can because you ought" describes this basic philosophy of life particularly adequately. On the social level, the obligation to society tends to be defined as loyalty to an idealistic code of universal values best expressed in Kant's moral imperative. The primary obligation to the self inclines toward active self-improvement according to an internalized blueprint. In this respect the predominance of universalism quality would imply a high motivational force to develop a set of personal qualities. There is, in such a society, a press to do in order to be, which from a Taoist perspective must look like the height of misplaced energy. Obligation to the self then tends to be defined in terms of the pursuit of an ideal of perfection.

In the integrative sphere the question of right and wrong is most clearly one of deductive reasoning in a direction from general moral tenets down to the level of normative demands. Given the activist strain, the role of expertise in a society with L primacy not only involves getting special jobs done, but also and more importantly, defining what jobs must be done. In the political field this means that value questions tend to be defined quite often as technical questions subject to expert judgment. In fact, this tendency seems to be one of the major inherent breaks on the strain toward the generation of value movements mentioned above. In this type the solution to the question of right and wrong tends to take the assertive form so typical of uncompromising idealists: Right IS right. Partly as a consequence, the problem of conflict with others tends to be seen as one of evil, unnecessary ultimately, and something that must be solved and not simply accommodated to. On the social level, the major mode of conflict resolution thus has a tendency to be like the conversion of sinners. Therefore, attempts to bring the opponent to "truth" and free him from his misconceptions appear to abound rather freely. There also seems to be an inclination to search for the ultimate expert who "really knows" and can arbitrate the clash of different opinions. On the personal side, the major source of inner conflict gravitates toward the apparent coexistence of incompatible value demands or alternatively toward simple moral imperfection. Consequently, one major mode of self-discipline appears to be self-punishment and repression.

Concerning goals, the active idealist would be a person who serves a cause defined in value terms. He devotes himself to the realization of a *Weltanschauung*. As regards the goals likely to be set for the politically organized society these have an inherent strain toward the "total transformation of society" variety most conspicuous of revolutionary instances of the totalitarian kind. The principal and safest way of avoiding this kind of collective goal would be to refrain from defining collective goals too clearly altogether and to try for "government in splendid isolation." On the social level, control by others tends to be acceptable only insofar as these are "obviously" superior in value terms. On the personal level, the active idealist would be the kind of "high-drive personality" regarded as truly possessed, like a Dostoyevskyan character who *is* all missionary zeal.

Perhaps the most telling characteristic of the L-primacy type is the fact that pragmatism is a very limited phenomenon even in the adaptive sphere. On the cultural level, the kind of knowledge most ardently sought seems to be esoteric principles. On the social level, the primary mode of orienting to *alter* inclines toward seeing in him a bundle of qualities subject to evaluative scrutiny in terms of higher ideals. The question, Does *alter* belong to those who know the right path to truth, or is he one of the others, a potential saint, or still a sinner? tends to be of primary relevance. The chief mode of relating to *alter* inclines toward the immediate expression of who ego is and what he stands for. Consequently, a fairly high tolerance, if not a measure of appreciation, for idiosyncratic styles of interpersonal behavior appears to be present. Last, one of the major adaptive features of personality being cognitive capacity, what is being referred to as intelligence in this type tends to involve a high emphasis on the capacity to manipulate abstract symbols and appreciate theoretical relations—that is, understanding "universal truth."

Where the basic philosophy of life stresses getting along, interdependence, personal restraint, and champions an ideal of harmony, the I-primacy case of the *Gemeinschaft* model obtains. On the social level of the pattern maintenance base the obligation to society tends to be defined in terms of loyalty to law, custom, or traditional usage. The Confucian conception of filial piety is the classic empirical example in this respect. The most important obligation to the self is to maintain calm serenity, inner balance, and moderation.

In the integrative sphere right and wrong tend to be not so much conceptions subject to very sharply defined absolute standards that give a sense of finality to objects considered ends in themselves but are more often seen instead as of primarily instrumental significance, conventions necessary to maintain harmonious relations. Consequently, interpersonal and intergroup conflict tends to be defined as deriving from human errors of judgment. These of course may be all too human to bear, which leads on the social level to a mode of conflict resolution that maximizes bargaining procedures designed to resolve "misunderstandings" and to reconstitute the good will among the parties. In law itself, there should be some preference for restitutive action—that is, an attempt to re-create the status quo ante. On the personal level, being immoderate, loss of self-control, and most generally, doing something too much that is permissible and "quite human" in more modest doses provide the major sources of inner conflict. "Hanging onto good people" who can save ego from himself and protect him against himself may be the major mode.

On the cultural level of goal attainment the relative predominance of particularism-quality would imply the maintenance of propriety as a major goal. For the total society, the maintenance of its particular way of life against all potential threats may easily lead to a specially emphatic isolationist stance. On the social level, the problem of control by others tends to be managed by high regulation and basic acceptance as part and parcel of the human condition. That ego should be controlled by someone, first of all seems to be regarded as "in the nature of things, since without control life would obviously be strife and chaos." Second, however, authority tends to be parceled out among the population under this maxim: Each according to his station. Finally, the principal style of personal expression—that is, the typical answer to the problem of "How much drive?"—tends toward the preference for the muted, the controlled, the balanced, and the relaxed. Imperturbable calmness as a result of true inner balance rather than an enforced stance of intentional control tends to be the personality ideal.

In the adaptive sphere the kind of knowledge most admired are the principles of practical diplomacy—that is, that knowledge of man that has a most direct bearing on the management of smooth social relations. On the social level, the principal model of interpersonal orientation involves defining *alter* in terms of membership criteria—that is, mainly ascribed qualities. The chief mode of relating to *alter* tends to be highly stylized and stereotyped according to station. Finally, the kind of intelligence regarded as most desirable tends to be a kind of "human-relations wisdom"—that is, the intuitive capacity to grasp and harmoniously mediate all the complex forces influencing interpersonal relations. If wisdom is to know all that is human without being afraid of it, a wise person here is the one who "understands" and knows what is good for ego as a social animal.

Goal-attainment primacy appears to be the characteristic of societies in which the most widely shared elements of the basic philosophy of life stress such conceptions as duty, service, honor, and obedience. These are the hallmark ideals of the corporatist model. The relative predominance of the particularism-performance pattern implies a great emphasis on working for the greater glory of one's group. On the social level of reference, the obligation to society tends to be defined in terms of loyalty to authority and group leaders. Given a relatively great stress on achievement in this case, the major difference on this level relative to the I-primacy case would be the more open access to authority positions. Thus in this type loyalty is inherently subject to performance proof on both sides—that is, those in leadership positions as well as those outside. On the personal level, the principal obligation to the self would seem to involve the exertion of will power in the active pursuits of one's duties.

On the integrative side, the definition of right and wrong would incline toward the identification of right with that which serves the welfare of one's group. Conceptions of wrong, on the other hand, tend to be connected with what hurts the group, be it its social standing, influence, or material well-being. Interpersonal and intergroup conflict frequently becomes invested with the meaning of providing a test for one's fortitude in sticking to one's loyalties and commitments. Social conflict is therefore basically accepted as an essential part of life in this type, and regarded as a fate not to be avoided but faced in order to prove one's worth. On the social level the chief mode of conflict resolution tends toward extremes: Fighting to victory even at high costs, or acquiescent submission to superior power tend to be the prevalent modes. Whenever the conflict involves a question of honor, however, submission remains but a temporary retreat to await a more opportune constellation of forces and then to take double revenge for the slights suffered. On the personal level, the most prominent source of inner conflict seems to be the perception of selfishness. Egotism and egocentrism tend to be particularly sinful in this type. Consequently, one of the main modes of self-discipline involves one's redoubled efforts at rededicating oneself to one's duties. In contrast to the A-primacy type, this does not ordinarily involve an unusual amount of cognitive problems, since duties tend to be spelled out rather clearly wherever the virtues of order, service, and duty rank high; involved instead are sheer effort and will power.

Goal attainment provides the major focus of attention in this type. For the individual this would mean, above all, to serve his group faithfully. On the collective level, the society itself becomes the object of enhancement. Improvement of society in every conceivable respect, most prominently those subject to ranking in the international community, tends to be an end in itself to which incessant labor and all manner of resources are to be dedicated. Concerning the problem of control by others, such control would seem to be basically acceptable in this type without much question, so long as control originates from duly instituted authority or recognized group leaders, and so long as these maintain the performance standards that form part of the legitimation of their authority. The G-primacy type seems to be in need of active leadership if any stability of authority relations is to be maintained. On the personal level, the kind of "drive" that would appear to be most adequate in this type of society would be the oscillating type—that is, the person whose temperament predisposes him toward an alternation between "going all out in his duties" and then relapsing into self-indulgent pleasure as a reward for an exacting service faithfully rendered.

Within the problem of adaptation, the kinds of knowledge defined as most desirable tend to be technical, special, and practical. Dilettantism of all kinds seems to be inherently bound for proscription. From the perspective of the integrative ideal the expert in the present case always potentially appears humorless, possessed of an exaggerated sense of self-importance and pettily narrow-minded. Necessarily, from the perspective of his own values such assertions by outsiders seem unjust. On the social level the chief mode of orientation to *alter* involves viewing him primarily in terms of the positions he achieved in groups and organizations. The main mode of interpersonal adjustment seems to involve a set of sharply contrasting styles. One tends to be very formal and strict to superiors and outsiders yet feels free to very jovial informality and acting "like one feels" when among equals of one's own kind. The officers' barracks square-casino pattern of behavioral style provides the classic empirical example. On the personal level, the kind of intelligence most valued involves the capacity to manipulate people and situations. The intelligent man is, above all, he who manages to have his will prevail wherever he finds himself.

Finally, a society seems to be characterized by adaptation-primacy when the most pervasive elements of its members' philosophy of life contain the ideal of individual practical success. That is why the label "market model" seems appropriate. The individualistic strain inherent in the pattern combination universalism-performance suggests the phrase "go out and make thyself a success" as illustrative of a conception of man who is at any one moment in his life but the sum total of his achievements and failures and truly "makes" or "fails to make" himself. This appears to be part of a more general set of orientations summed up in the concept "instrumental activism." Given individualism, the definition of the obligation of society inclines toward that kind of other-directedness that, apart from embodying a fairly high degree of natural respect for the opinion of others, tends toward maximal utilization of these opinions in order to determine the directions most promising of the individual's maximum utility to society. On the personal level, the obligation to self gravitates toward a conception of incessant self-development throughout life not only as desirable but also as normal and indeed healthy (Dalton, 1964:43).

Within the integrative problem, the cultural definitions of right and wrong appear to involve primarily standards of pragmatic effectiveness. Put somewhat sharply, right is what gets results; wrong is what leads to failures in achieving one's objectives. The climate of opinion provides a framework, as it were, delimiting the ranges of feasibility. Interpersonal and intergroup conflicts are frequently seen as opportunities for competition that are to be engaged in to prove one's worth in getting ahead. Thus some social conflict seems to be basically accepted and viewed in a positive light as a means that—if properly used according to rules—insures progress. On the social level, the primary modes of conflict resolution incline toward regulation rather than "resolution" and frequently take the form of innovation and circumvention. "Rules exist in order to be circumvented" illustrates this kind of valuation of flexibility. On the personal level, the major sources of inner conflict tend to involve failure in achievement, while the main mode of self-discipline seems to involve a rational self-scrutinizing search aimed at the identification and elimination of "weak spots"—that is, sources of "unpreparedness."

Turning to the goal-attainment problem, the kinds of goals relevant for individuals would embrace a shifting and essentially endless series of pragmatic objectives symbolic of generalized success. The very instant one objective is attained, another one arises with equal attractiveness. The high concentration on the pursuit of pragmatic objectives so characteristic in this society frequently looks like crass materialism from the perspective of goal-attainment primacy, particularly where the general utility of the objectives is measured in terms of money. To the individual himself, however, and from the perspective of his philosophy of applied enlightenment, the direct opposite seems to ring more true: Success and wealth are primarily of symbolic significance. Goals proper for collective effort in this case are inclined to take the form of the maximization of society's resources utilization. A rising standard of living, the elimination of "wasteful pockets of poverty" may serve as more specific examples of the kinds of national goals likely to develop in this type.

On the social level, the authority problem leans toward a compromise solution, embracing acceptance of authority on the basis of utility to the recipient of commands on the one hand and his chance for some reciprocation on the other. In other words, ego will accept control by others so long as he believes he will gain thereby and can reciprocate in some manner. While the utility criterion needs no comment, the reciprocation element appears to derive from the particular conception of individualism inherent in the pattern combination universalism-performance. In sharp contrast to the cultivation of a private self as embodied, for example, in "secularized Lutheranism," this kind of individualism seems to involve independent efforts at self-realization through successful performance in social roles subject to universalistic and very visible measuring standards. Consequently, a too one-sided submission to authority in the public sphere, even if very profitable, tends to conflict with the ideal of *"making oneself."* The kind of solution of the level of "drive" that appears desirable in this case would be in the direction of general activism. The most ideal kind of person is the one who "works hard and plays hard."

Within the adaptation problem, the most highly valued knowledge would be

Table A-2 *Preferences for Value Orientation in Societies with Different Functional Primacies*

Function	Object level	Problem	L Primacy Universalism-quality	I Primacy Particularism-quality	G Primacy Particularism-Performance	A Primacy Universalism-Performance
L	Cultural	Philosophy of life?	You can because you ought	Be thyself complete harmony	Duty, honor, service	Make thyself a success
	Social	Obligation to society?	Loyalty to universal ideals	Loyalty to law	Obeying authority and group leaders	Using opinions of others
	Personal	Obligation to self?	Pursuit of an ideal of perfection	Inner harmony	Exertion of will power in doing one's duty	Incessant self-development
	Cultural	Definition of right and wrong?	Right IS right!	Right is balance	Right is what serves the group	Right is what gets results
I	Cultural	Meaning of conflict?	Evil problem of morality	Human errors of judgment	Test of one's fortitude	Opportunity to compete
	Social	Mode of conflict resolution?	Converting "sinners"	Clearing of "misunderstandings"	Victory or submission	Circumvention and innovation
	Personal	Source of inner conflict?	Moral imperfection	Being immoderate	Selfishness	Failure in achievement
	Personal	Mode of self-discipline?	Self-punishment and repression	"Hanging onto others"	Rededication to duty	Eliminating unpreparedness
G	Cultural	Goals in life?	To serve a cause	To maintain propriety	To serve one's group	To attain success
	Social	Control by others?	OK if *alter* = superior in values	"In the nature of things"	OK if *alter* = recognized and active authority	OK if ego profits and can reciprocate
	Personal	"Personality drive?"	Possessed of missionary zeal	Muted and relaxed	Oscillates between "going all-out" and relaxation	Generally energetic
	Cultural	Kind of knowledge?	Esoteric principles	Practical diplomacy	Technical specialty	Practical know-how and know-about
A	Cultural	Mode of orienting to *alter*?	As potential saint or sinner	As group member	As position-incumbent	As potential resource
	Social	Mode of relating to *alter*?	"Direct and idiosyncratic"	Stylized according to station	Oscillates between formality and informality	"Standardized" informality
	Personal	Kind of intelligence?	Understanding universal truth	"Human-relations wisdom"	Manipulating people and situations	Manipulating facts and figures

practical know-how and know-about. The simple idea here is that ultimately only that kind of knowledge is worth developing that can be used, the use again subject to universalistic criteria of assessment. The prevalent mode of orienting to the other, on the social level, would involve attention to *alter's* skills and abilities—that is, concentrate on what he can do. The most likely mode of relating would be comprised of that kind of "standardized informality" most conducive for maximization of effective adjustment. That is likely to be that style of interpersonal behavior that treats everyone more or less the same so that little adjustment capacity might be "wasted" by searching for clues that dictate the appropriate choice within a differentiated set of conventions. Finally, the kind of intelligence most likely to be valued primarily would be pragmatic intelligence, signifying a high capacity for high-speed manipulation of facts and figures, measurable by the test of effective application. For a more convenient reference these sixty type solutions to fifteen problems on three object levels of the four functions have been summarized in Table A-2.

The fifteen problems were phrased in terms of questions. For each of these, four answer statements were designed to reflect the variable type-solutions characteristic of the four primary functional types. This questionnaire constituted the instrument applied to fictional characters. It is reproduced below. Coding consisted in ranking the degree of adequacy of the four solutions posed for each question for a fictional character. Such ranking was done for each question *separately* and *independently* of the others.

Validity and Reliability

The first question to be asked about any instrument, of course, is: Does it measure in fact what it purports to measure? Obviously, the utility of the present approach would be drastically reduced if it should turn out that statements designed to measure integrative orientations would in fact be more indicative of another functional problem or relate to none of the conceptions employed here. Consequently, it seemed important to obtain an estimate of conceptual validity, and this will be reported here. The type solutions to the fifteen problems were drawn up in a scrambled fashion on the questionnaire in order to counteract possible tendencies to logical consistency on the part of the coders. The questionnaire was given to three students of action theory* with the request that they label the type solution according to which function they referred to. None of these "validity coders" had read any part of this description, which in fact did not exist at the time. The investigator explained the purpose of the instrument and simply referred to the "obvious variability of type solutions in societies with varying functional primacies." Conceptual validity was then measured in terms of percent agreement between coders and the investigator. As identification of one function could simply result from the residual left over after three statements had been labeled, a

*The help of my colleagues Jerry Platt, Victor Lidz, and Dean Hoge with validity coding and advice regarding revisions is gratefully acknowledged. The idea of the use of "object levels" was taken from Gordon and Gergen (1968; see chapter "Self-conception: Configurations in Content").

correction factor was applied in the simple manner of subtracting 15 from both numerator and denominator of the ratio, resulting in:

$$\text{percent agreement} = \frac{\text{no. of items agree} - 15}{\text{Total no. of items} - 15} \times 100$$

In cases of disagreement the investigator later obtained a reason why the coder identified the statement in question as he did. This procedure led to three revisions, which finally brought average agreement on concept validity to 89 percent, with a range of 83 percent to 93 percent among the three validity coders.

While the "jury opinion" approach seemed fairly adequate for the question of validity in this case, a conservative approach to methodology would require the exact opposite for reliability. One of the factors determining the efficiency of any instrument is the amount of training it requires to use it adequately. In a field such as this, where it would be fairly difficult to provide a list of instructions for the instrument (the best instruction of course being familiarization with action theory), an instrument that requires a great amount of training would not be very efficient and, nice numbers notwithstanding, neither would it be very reliable. For where coder training does not lend itself to clear specification, no good reproducibility by another investigator is to be expected. Training the coder amounts to little more than an essentially uncontrolled "brainwashing" procedure, whereby the investigator insures that the coder uses the instrument nearly as he does. Any reports of estimates of reliability based on such procedures at best insure the investigator against coding his material in a manner to support his research hypothesis but have little bearing on actual reproducibility. The present research relied essentially on the common-sense intelligence of a student of literature who had never had any introduction to sociological ideas for reliability coding. "Training" here amounted to exposing an intelligent person for 30 minutes to some of the basic elements of action theory. While certainly not reproducible in any controlled fashion, this "training" was exceedingly minimal. Given this approach, no one would expect any staggering results, but if any useful margins of reliability can be attained in this manner, both the efficiency and the reliability of the instrument should not be disproportionate to the numerical estimate of reliability. The latter was also measured in terms of percent agreement between coder and investigator who rank-coded fictional characters.

The reliability sample covered most of the authors and the relevant social categories of the characters. Thirteen novels and ranks on 62 characters were used for reliability purposes, amounting to about 27 percent of all 230 characters in 31 novels. As coding consisted in ranking the degree of adequacy of the 4 type solutions posed for each of 15 questions to the fictional character, the ranks were used as units measuring reliability. Coder-investigator agreement on the first rank came to a mere 60 percent, with the disagreements scattered over all questions and type solutions. Although this result constitutes fair departure from chance, which with four choices would be 25 percent, it was too low to present the results in any simple fashion. Therefore agreement on ranks 1 and 2 was measured. This measure yielded 78.88 percent reliability for the total set, involving 1,860 ranks.

Table A-3 The Accuracy of Measurement and Its Components in Coding Popular Mass Fiction
(in rounded percentages)

Category	Coder reliability (sa)	Absolute reliability (A.R.)	Validity (V.)	Total accuracy of measurement (A.R.) (V.)
Full set	79	88	89	78
Region				
Prussia	80	89	89	79
Rhineland	72	83	89	74
Southwest	77	86	89	76
South	79	88	89	78
Soc. class				
Upper	83	90	89	80
Middle	77	87	89	77
Lower	76	86	89	76
Sex				
Female	80	89	89	79
Male	78	88	89	78

Given this information, we can calculate the accuracy of measurement of the value data. First it should be stressed that simple coder-investigator agreement underestimates reliability. Such simple agreement (sa) covers two contingencies: Both may agree and be objectively right; this occurs with chance $(p) \times (p)$. Both may agree and be objectively wrong; this occurs with chance $(1-p) \times (1-p)$. Thus simple reliability sa $= (p) \times (p) + (1-p) \times (1-p)$. Solving the equation for p yields the absolute reliability (A. R.). This can be done according to the general formula $ax^2 + bx + c = 0$; where $a = 2$; $b = 2$; and $c = 1 - sa$. For the total set this yields a "p" or absolute reliability of 88 percent. Given two kinds of errors, one for reliability and another for validity, yields a total accuracy of measurement as the product of the two components. Table A-3 lists the components and the accuracy of measurement in our direct value data classified by region, social class, and sex.

The information in Table A-3 renders a simple rule of thumb in considering the results of content analysis of fiction. The highest amount of error in measurement occurred in the Rhenish figures. Here the figures suffer from 26 percent error. In all other cases the errors in measurement amount to 24 percent or less. Since these errors are evenly distributed among all questions and the 4 type solutions, any percentage figure on a given type of value orientation may be out by 6.5 percent to 6 percent. Assuming that the obtained figure lies at the center of the error range, this means that in comparing any 2 figures, the difference must at least exceed these figures before it becomes "interesting." Any differences smaller than 6 percent are at best "suggestive" but may involve nothing more than measurement error.

In closing, one additional test on the validity of the instrument going beyond the jury technique may be reported. This involved a check on possible sex differences in the measured orientations among the fictional characters. Assuming that sex differences in orientations of a population living in identical cultural milieux reflect *normative* (sex-role ascribed differences) rather than *value* disparities, testing for these would amount to validating the instrument on the question of whether it measures norms or values. Excepting the Rhineland, where a lower-class preponderance among the females prevented the test, the sex test with region and class controlled produced no significant differences in the orientations measured. On this basis therefore the instrument measures values rather than norms, as it was designed to do.

A listing of the novels used and a reproduction of the value questionnaire complete my story here.

Novels Used for the Analysis of German Values on a Regional Level

PRUSSIA

1. Fontane, Th. *Der Stechlin*. Berlin: A. Weichert Verlag (n.d.); first published, 1898; 16th ed., 1907; 36th ed., 1918.
2. ———. *Effie Briest* München: Nymphenburger Verlagshandlung, 1959; first published, 1895; 5th ed., 1896; 83,000 by 1923.
3. ———. *Frau Jenny Treibel*München: Nymphenburger Verlagshandlung, 1959; first published, 1892; 86,000 by 1920.
4. ———. *Vor dem Sturm*. München: Nymphenburger Verlagshandlung, 1959; first published, 1878; 24th ed., 1920.
5. Viebig, C. *Die vor den Toren*. Stuttgart: Deutsche Verlagsanstalt, 1910; 31,000.
6. ———. *Dilettanten des Lebens*. Berlin: E. Fleischel & Company, 1905; 4th ed.
7. ———. *Das Eisen im Feuer*. Stuttgart: Deutsche Verlagshandlung, 1925; first published, 1913; 22,000.
8. ———. *Das Schlafende Heer*. Berlin: E. Fleischel & Company, 1906; 20th ed.
9. ———. *Die Wacht am Rhein*. Berlin: E. Fleischel & Company, 1906; 18th ed.

1, 2, 4, and 8 deal with Prussian aristocrats; 3, 5, and 7 deal with Berlin bourgeoisie; 9 deals with Prussians living in the Rhineland; novels dealing with Prussians and Rhinelanders are listed under both regions.

WEST (RHINELAND)

1. Viebig, C. *Das Weiberdorf*. Berlin: E. Fleischel & Company, 1906; 20th ed.
2. ———. *Rheinlandstöchter*. Stuttgart: Deutsche Verlagsanstalt, 1922; 32nd ed.
3. ———. *Vom Müller Hannes.*Stuttgart: Deutsche Verlagsanstalt, 1925; 43,000.
4*———. *Die Wacht am Rhein*. Berlin: E. Fleischel & Company, 1906; 18th ed.
5.*———. *Dilettanten des Lebens*. Berlin: E. Fleischel & Company, 1905; 4th ed.
6.*———. *Das Schlafende Heer*. Berlin: E. Fleischel & Company, 1906; 20th ed.

*Already listed under Prussia, these novels portray the confrontation of Rhinelanders and Prussians; 1 and 3 deal with inhabitants of the Eifel mountains; 2, 4, 5, and 6 with inhabitants of the Rhine Valley and the Mosel valley.

SOUTH AND SOUTHWEST

1. Ganghofer, L. *Das Gottesleben*. Stuttgart: Verlag A. Bonz, 1905; 21st ed.
2. ————. *Der Klosterjäger*. Stuttgart: Verlag A. Bonz, 1905; 31st ed.
3. Rosegger, P. K. *Die Schriften des Waldschulmeisters*. Wien: Hartlebensverlag, 1894: 14th ed.
4. Auerbach, B. *Edelweiss*. Boston, Mass.: Roberts Brothers, 1869; 4th ed.
5. ————. *Barfüssele*. Stuttgart: Cotta'sche Buchhandlung, 1871, 3rd ed.; 6th ed., 1874.
6. ————. *Joseph im Schnee*. Stuttgart: Cotta'sche Buchhandlung, 1871, 3rd ed.; 6th ed., 1874.
7. ————. *Auf der Höhe*. Stuttgart: Cotta'sche Buchhandlung, 1878, 11th ed.

1 to 3 deal with inhabitants of the Deep South, 4 to 7 with those of the Southwest.

NATIONAL

Scheffel, J. V., von. *Ekkehard*. Stuttgart: Verlag A. Bonz, 1877, 22nd ed.; first published, 1855; 240th ed., 1904.

Die Gartenlaube sample:

1. Werner, E. "Am Alter," *Die Gartenlaube*, 1872, Nos. 1–17.
2. Marlitt, E. "Die zweite Frau," *Die Gartenlaube*, 1874, Nos. 1–21.
3. Wichert, E. "Ein kleines Bild," *Die Gartenlaube*, 1875, Nos. 12–20.
4. Temme, J. D. H. "Auf Waltersburg," *Die Gartenlaube*, 1878, Nos. 2–7.
5. Schmid, H., von. "Ledige Kinder," *Die Gartenlaube*, 1880, Nos. 1–7.
6. ————. "Trudschens Heirat," *Die Garterlaube*, 1885, Nos. 21–32.
7. Marlitt, E. "Das Eulenhaus," *Die Gartenlaube*, 1888, Nos. 1–14.
8. Elcho, R. "Weltflüchtige," *Die Gartenlaube*, 1892, Nos. 1–9.
9. Werner, E. "Fata Morgana," *Die Gartenlaube*, 1896, Nos. 1–25.
10. Heimburg, W. "Antons Erben," *Die Gartenlaube*, 1898, Nos. 1–26.
11. Robran, P. "Kampf ums Glück," *Die Gartenlaube*, 1900, Nos. 7–17.

The sample from *Die Gartenlaube* was selected on a quota basis. From the even years 1872–1900 the first full-length novel was taken. As the Harvard collection is incomplete, with the years 1876, 1882, and 1884 missing, the year before and after was taken alternately. No author was taken more than twice; in cases where the above procedure would have led to such selection, the novel was skipped and the subsequent one used instead.

Value Orientations Study
Coding Scheme for Fictional Characters

Author:_____

Title:_____

Publisher, place, year:_____

No. of editions, printings, copies:_____

Type of Story (circle): Exemplary;   Cautionary;   Both;

Other (specify):_____

Fictional Name:_____   Occupation:_____
Character: Sex:_____   Education:_____

Age:_____   Social Status:_____

Character Type (circle): Hero;   Villain;   Fool;

Good person;   Bad person;   Average person

Coder (name):_____

Date:_____

Time spent reading story:_____

Time spent coding this character:_____

Indicate (by number) the questions where coding this character was:
Very easy:_____   Fairly ambiguous:_____
Fairly easy:_____   Almost impossible:_____
Problematical:_____

A: For each of the listed general characteristics of a person, four alternatives are given. You are to select and rank order which of these characterizes X's attitudes and behavior MOST, FAIRLY, SOMEWHAT, and LEAST adequately, labeling your choice with Nos. 1 through 4, consecutively.

B: Where is the greatest distance on the ranking scale? Indicate by putting a / between the ranks—for example, 1/2-3-4 where the greatest distance is between the first and all the remaining alternatives, or 1-2/3-4 where it is between the first two and the last two.

C: Which of the alternatives, if any, does not apply at all? Indicate this by writing the rank or numbers in the designated space.

1. X's basic philosophy of life is:

   a. To live is to fulfill one's ultimate values and highest ideals. ☐

   b. To live is to be subject to the push and pull of a multitude of forces, some good, some bad; the main thing is to keep some balance and harmony. ☐

   c. To live is to be loyal to one's group and do one's duty for the sake of it. ☐

   d. To live is to work and utilize all opportunities as best as one can. ☐

   B: 1-2-3-4

   C: _____

2. X sees his principal obligation to society, or what he owes to others, in:

   a. Making use of the opinion of others in determining how he can be most useful in life. ☐

   b. Strict adherence to his ideals, principles, and/or to universal moral imperatives—that is, observing Kant's moral imperative. · ☐

   c. Obeying instituted authority and group leaders. ☐

   d. Respecting the rights of others and maintaining peace and harmony. ☐

   B: 1-2-3-4

   C: _____

3. X sees his principal obligation to himself, or what he owes to himself, in:

   a. Maintaining his ideals in the face of an "imperfect world." ☐

   b. Developing himself in as many ways as possible so long as he lives—that is, development of all his potentialities to their fullest capacity. ☐

c. Being at peace with himself the way he is and/or developing a balanced, harmonious personality according to what is appropriate to his station. ☐

d. Exerting his will power to direct himself in doing his duty and maintaining self-control. ☐

B: 1-2-3-4

C: ‾‾‾‾‾‾‾

4. The principal ways in which X defines what is right and what is wrong are:

a. Right is what contributes to peace and harmony among men; wrong is what makes for strife and conflict. ☐

b. Right IS right according to and as logically derived from universal absolute principles; wrong is what is logically contrary to them. ☐

c. Right is what gets practical results, subject only to what others think about it; wrong is what leads to failure in making the most of one's opportunities. ☐

d. Right is what serves the welfare of one's group; wrong is what hurts their well-being. ☐

B: 1-2-3-4

C: ‾‾‾‾‾‾‾

5. X regards conflicts with others predominantly as:

a. Deriving from the fact that some others lack in their commitment to universal absolute principles, and therefore solvable in principle by making sure that everybody believes what is right. ☐

b. An important part of life itself that exists in order to test one's will power in sticking to one's loyalties and commitments to others. ☐

c. Either a real evil or mere human errors of judgment, which are to be avoided and quickly resolved when they occur. ☐

d. Competitions to be won and an opportunities to demonstrate one's skills and capacities in getting ahead.

☐

B: 1-2-3-4

C: _____

6. X's principal mode of resolving conflicts with others involves:

a. Asserting his rights or circumventing adversaries through the use of all possible effective means to their fullest capacity.

☐

b. Attempting to bring the opponent to "truth" through exhortation and/or setting the right example, and once this fails, suppressing them by force if possible.

☐

c. Denying the existence of real conflict by declaring it a "misunderstanding" and clearing this up through compromise bargaining that reconstitutes the good will among the parties by having everyone maintain his proper station.

☐

d. Fighting to victory over them, and when that fails, submitting to their superior power but only temporarily, waiting in fact for a better chance to win in the future.

☐

B: 1-2-3-4

C: _____

7. The predominant source of X's inner conflict is:

a. Realizing his selfishness and failing to do his duty as a group member.

☐

b. Failure in the successful use of his skills and abilities, and/or finding out that he is insufficiently prepared.

c. Realization of his own imperfections and/or moral weaknesses.

☐

d. Realizing that he is getting into trouble with others through excess—that is, being immoderate or unbalanced (for example, by noticing that he tends to do something too much that is OK in more modest doses). ☐

B: 1-2-3-4

C: _____

8. X's principal mode of self-discipline involves:

   a. Repression of his "bad" urges and being a 100 percenter—that is, a pure and truly moral person. ☐

   b. Employment of a utilitarian calculus to diagnose his weak points and maximize his chances in the future. ☐

   c. "Scolding himself" for being so foolish as to let himself go and forming closer ties to "good" people of his kind who protect him against himself. ☐

   d. Getting his primary loyalties and obligations as a group member straightened out and abiding by this maxim: Duty first, pleasure later. ☐

B: 1-2-3-4

C: _____

9. X's major goals in life are:

   a. To serve a cause or "represent" an ideal defined in value terms—that is, a *Weltanschauung* (for example, religious, political, philosophical, artic-expressive). ☐

   b. To be a generally successful individual as measured by wealth and/or prestige by others. ☐

   c. Doing his duty in contributing his share to the welfare of some specific group of which he is a member. ☐

   d. To live harmoniously with others and doing his part to maintain law and order everywhere. ☐

B: 1-2-3-4

C: _____

10. In what he does, X tends to view control by others as:

    a. Acceptable if he can control them in turn, and/or a "nuisance" to be put up with so long as he can clearly profit thereby. □

    b. Acceptable only if these others are clearly superior in terms of his ideals. □

    c. "In the nature of things," since without control life would be chaotic and full of strife. □

    d. Acceptable so long as these others are duly instituted authority and/or recognized group leaders. □

B: 1-2-3-4

C: _____

11. X is the kind of person who is:

    a. "Going all out" in pursuit of things he regards as his duties as a group member, but otherwise relaxed so that his behavior oscillates between strenuous exertion of energy and easygoing, self-indulgent pleasure. □

    b. Never trying to excel and doing what is normally done by others he considers his equals. □

    c. Generally energetic in everything he does and making the most of all his capacities—that is, he "plays hard and works hard." □

    d. Possessed of a driving, all-consuming sense of mission and pursuing his tasks with relentless energy. □

B: 1-2-3-4

C: _____

12. The kind of knowledge X values most is:

    a. Esoteric, abstract principles that only the "few elect" understand. ☐

    b. *General* practical knowledge; all that is or could be useful to get ahead in life—that is, practical know-how and know-about. ☐

    c. *Specific* technical knowledge directly relevant to his major duties in life. ☐

    d. Knowledge about human relations—that is, the principles of practical diplomacy. ☐

    B: 1-2-3-4

    C: _____

13. X's predominant mode of orienting to others—that is, the way he regards them—is:

    a. Based primarily on how useful they can be to him in terms of what they can do—their abilities and skills. ☐

    b. Based primarily on their achievements as group members—for example, how far they got in their profession, what positions they hold in organizations, etc. ☐

    c. Based primarily on whether or not they share his ideals, values, and *Weltanschauung*. ☐

    d. Based primarily on who they are in terms of group memberships—for example, a family, occupational group, as a fellow villager, etc. ☐

    B: 1-2-3-4

    C: _____

14. X's predominant mode of relating to others—that is, the way he behaves toward them—is:

    a. Geared toward maximum effective adjustment through the skillful practice of "standardized informality." ☐

b. Moving between two poles—namely, formality
to superiors and outsiders on the one hand, and
on the other, intimate, relaxed, self-indulgent
"naturalness" to peers when in their exclusive
company.   ☐

c. Dictated by the ideals he works for or represents; thus his manners are geared to communicating directly who he is or what he stands for.   ☐

d. Geared to his station in life and the rights and
obligations that go with it: thus his manners
involve a differentiated set of etiquettes designed
to treat others appropriate to their station.   ☐

B: 1-2-3-4

C: _____

15. The kind of intelligence X values most is:

a. "Wisdom"—that is, the capacity to "intuitively
grasp" and harmoniously mediate all the com-
plex forces in interpersonal relations.   ☐

b. "Political intelligence"—that is, the capacity to
manipulate situations and people so that his will
prevails.   ☐

c. "Pragmatic intelligence"—that is, the capacity to
ascertain quickly all the relevant facts in a situation and manipulate them for effective action.   ☐

d. "True understanding of the text"—that is, a
conceptual command of abstract principles.   ☐

B: 1-2-3-4

C: _____

References

Adler, H. G. 1955. *Theresienstadt, 1941–1945: Das Antlitz einer Zwangsgemeinschaft.* Tübingen: J. C. B. Mohr.

———. 1974. *Der Verwaltete Mensch: Studien zur Deportation der Juden aus Deutschland.* Tübingen: J. C. B. Mohr.

Adorno, T. W.; Frenkel-Brunswik, E.; R. N. Standford, and D. J. Levinson, 1950. *The Authoritarian Personality.* New York: Harper & Brothers.

Aigner, Dietrich. 1978. "Hitler und die Weltherrschaft," pp. 49–69 in Wolfgang Michalka (ed.), *Nationalsozialistische Aussenpolitik.* Darmstadt: Wissenschaftliche Buchgesellschaft.

Allen, Sheridan Wm. 1965. *The Nazi Seizure of Power.* Chicago, Ill.: Quadrangle Books.

Almond, Gabriel A., and Verba, Sidney 1963. *The Civic Culture: Political Attitudes and Democracy in Five Nations.* Princeton, N.J.: Princeton University Press.

Alves, Wayne M., and Rossi, Peter H. 1978. "Who Should Get What? Fairness Judgments of the Distribution of Earnings," *American Journal of Sociology* 84:541–64.

Arendt, Hannah. 1951. *The Origins of Totalitariansim.* New York: Harcourt, Brace & Company.

———. 1963. *Eichmann in Jerusalem.* New York: The Viking Press.

Askenasy, Hans. 1978. *Are We All Nazis?* Secaucus, N.J.: Lyle Stuart.

Banfield, Edward C. 1958. *The Moral Basis of a Backward Society.* Glencoe, Ill.: The Free Press.

Barkin, K. D. 1970. *The Controversy over German Industrialization.* Chicago, Ill.: University of Chicago Press.

Barnard, Chester I. 1938. *The Functions of the Executive.* Cambridge, Mass.: Harvard University Press.

Bauer, Yehuda. 1978. *The Holocaust in Historical Perspective.* Seattle, Wash.: University of Washington Press.

Bechtel, H. 1956. *Wirtschaftsgeschichte Deutschlands.* München: Callway Verlag.

Bellah, Robert N. 1957. *Tokugawa Religion.* Glencoe, Ill.: The Free Press.

———. 1964. "Religious Evolution." *American Sociological Review* 29 (June):358–74.

———. 1970. *Beyond Belief.* New York: Harper & Row.

Ben-David, Joseph. 1971. *The Scientists' Role in Society: A Comparative Study.* Englewood Cliffs, N.J.: Prentice-Hall.

Bendix, Reinhard. 1965. "Jacob Burckhardt and Max Weber," *American Sociological Review* 30, 2 (April): 176–84.

Bengtson, Robert J. 1962. *Nazi War Aims.* Rock Island, Ill.: Augustana College Library.

Bennecke, Heinrich. 1962. *Hitler und die SA.* München: Günter Olzog Verlag.

———. 1968. *Wirtschaftliche Depression und Politischer Radikalismus.* München: Günter Olzog Verlag.

Berger, P. 1970. "On the Obsolescence of the Concept Honor," *European Journal of Sociology* XI, 2:339–47.

Berghahn, Volker R. 1966. *Der Stahlhelm: Bund der Frontsoldaten, 1918–1935.* Düsseldorf: Droste Verlag.

Beyerchen, Alan D. 1977. *Scientists under Hitler: Politics and the Physics Community.* New Haven, Conn.: Yale University Press.

Binion, Rudolph. 1976. *Hitler Among the Germans.* New York: Elsevier.

Blau, Peter M. 1977. *Inequality and Heterogeneity.* New York: The Free Press.

Boberach, Heinz. 1965. *Meldungen aus dem Reich: Auswahl aus den Geheimen Lageberichten des Sicherheitsdiensts der SS.* Düsseldorf: H. Luchterhand Verlag.

Böhme, Helmut. 1966. *Deutschlands Weg zur Grossmacht.* Köln: Kiepenheuer & Witsch.

Bokolsky, Sidney M. 1975. *The Distored Image: German Jewish Perceptions and Germany 1918–1935.* New York: Elsevier.

Born, Karl E. 1966. "Der soziale und wirtschaftliche Strukturwandel Deutschlands am Ende des 19. Jahrhunderts," pp. 271–84 in H.-U. Wehler, (ed.), *Moderne deutsche Sozialgeschichte.* Köln: Kiepenheuer & Witsch.

Bracher, Karl D. 1955. *Die Auflösung der Weimarer Republik.* Villingen: Ring Verlag.

———. 1970. *Die deutsche Diktatur.* Köln: Kiepenheuer & Witsch.

Bracher, Karl D.; Sauer, Wolfgang; and Schulz, Gerhard. 1960. *Die Nationalsozialistische Machtergreifung.* Köln: Westdeutscher Verlag.

Bramsted, Ernest K. 1964. *Aristocracy and Middle Classes in Germany.* Chicago, Ill.: University of Chicago Press.

Broszat, Martin. 1970. "Soziale Motivation und Führerbindung im National-Sozialismus," *Vierteljahresschrift für Zeitgeschichte* 18:392–409.

Buchheim, Hans. 1958. *The Third Reich.* München: Kösel Verlag.

Buchheim, Hans, et al. 1965. *Anatomie des SS-Staats,* Bd. I. Freiburg i. Br.: Walter Verlag.

Büsch, O. 1962. *Militärsystem und Sozialleben im Alten Preussen.* Berlin: Walter de Gruyter.

Carsten, Frederic L. 1959. *Princes and Parliaments in Germany.* Oxford: Clarendon Press.

———. 1966. *The Reichswehr and Politics: 1918–1933.* Oxford: Clarendon Press.

Cash, W. J. 1941. *The Mind of the South.* New York: Alfred A. Knopf.

Chary, F. B. 1972. *The Bulgarian Jews and the Final Solution.* Pittsburgh, Pa.: University of Pittsburgh Press.

Chickering, Roger. 1975. *Imperial Germany and a World Without War: The Peace Movement in German Society, 1892–1914.* Princeton, N.J.: Princeton University Press.

Colby, B. N. 1966. "The Analysis of Culture Content and the Patterning of Narrative Concerns in Texts," *American Anthropologist* 68, 2 (April): 374–88.

Converse, Philip E. 1964. "The Nature of Belief Systems in Mass Publics," pp. 206–61 in David E. Apter (ed.), *Ideology and Discontent.* London: Macmillan.

Conway, J. S. 1968. *The Nazi Persecution of the Churches 1933–1945.* New York: Basic Books.

Craig, Gordon A. 1964. *The Politics of the Prussian Army.* New York: Oxford University Press.

Crozier, Michael. 1964. *The Bureaucratic Phenomenon.* Chicago, Ill.: University of Chicago Press.

Dahl, Robert A. 1958. "A Critique of the Ruling Elite Model," *American Political Science Review* 52:463–69.

———. 1961. *Who Governs? Democracy and Power in an American City.* New Haven, Conn.: Yale University Press.

Dahrendorf, Ralf. 1959. *Class and Class Conflict in Industrial Society.* Stanford, Calif.: Stanford University Press.

———. 1965. *Demokratie und Gesellschaft in Deutschland.* München: Piper.

Dalton, M. 1964. *Men at Work.* Homewood, Ill.: Dorsey Press.

Dawidowicz, Lucy S. 1975. *The War Against the Jews.* New York: Holt, Rinehart & Winston.

Der Spiegel. June 15, 1970

———. January 29, 1979

Des Pres, Terence. 1976. *The Survivor: An Anatomy of Life in the Death Camps.* New York: Oxford University Press.

de Tocqueville, Alexis. 1954. *Democracy in America.* New York: Vintage Books.

Deutsch, Karl W. 1953. *Nationalism and Social Communication.* Cambridge, Mass.: MIT Press.

———. 1970. *Politics and Government.* Boston: Houghton Mifflin Company.

Dicks, H. V. 1972. *Licensed Mass Murder: A Socio-psychological Study of Some SS Killers.* New York: Basic Books.

Dietrich, Richard. 1966. *Kleine Geschichte Preussens.* Berlin: Haude & Spenersche Verlags-buchhandlung.

Dittmann, Wilhelm. 1945. *Das Politische Deutschland vor Hitler.* Zürich: Europa Verlag.

Donat, A. 1963. *The Holocaust Kingdom.* New York: Holt, Rinehart & Winston.

Dore, Ronald. 1973. *British Factory-Japanese Factory: The Origins of National Diversity in Industrial Relations.* Berkeley, Calif.: University of California Press.

Dronberger, Ilse. 1961. *The Political Thought of Max Weber: In Quest of Statesmanship.* New York: Appleton-Century-Crofts.

Drucker, Peter. 1978. "The Monster and the Lamb," *The Atlantic Monthly* (December):82–87.

Dumont, Louis. 1970. *Homo Hierarchicus: An Essay on the Caste System.* Chicago, Ill.: University of Chicago Press.

Eckstein, Harry. 1961. "A Theory of Stable Democracy." Center for International Studies, Princeton University, Research Monograph No. 10.

————. 1966. *Division and Cohesion in Democracy.* Princeton, N. J.: Princeton University Press.

Eisenstadt, S. N. 1963. *The Political Systems of Empires.* New York: The Free Press.

————. 1971. *Social Differentiation and Stratification.* Glenview, Ill.: Scott, Foresman & Company.

Enselling, Alf. 1962. *Die Weltbühne, Organ der Intellektuellen Linken.* Münster: C. J. Fahle.

Erikson, Erik. 1959. *Identity and the Life Cycle.* New York: International Universities Press.

Espe, Walter M. 1934. *Das Buch der N.S.D.A.P.* Berlin: Schoenfeld's Verlagsbuchhandlung.

Eyck, Erich. 1962. *A History of the Weimar Republic.* Cambridge, Mass.: Harvard University Press.

Fein, Helen. 1979. *Accounting for Genocide.* New York: The Free Press.

Feldman, Gerald D. 1966. *Army, Industry, and Labor in Germany, 1914–1918.* Princeton, N.J.: Princeton University Press.

Fest, Joachim C. 1973. *Hitler.* München: Propyläen.

Fischer, Fritz. 1967. *Germany's Aims in the First World War.* New York: W. W. Norton & Company.

Fleischner, Eva. 1977. *Auschwitz: Beginning of a New Era?* New York: Ktav Publications Company.

Fox, Renée. 1978. "Why Belgium?" *European Journal of Sociology* 9, 2:205–28.

Fox, Thomas, and Miller, S. M. 1966. "Intra-Country Variations: Occupational Stratification and Mobility," pp. 574–81 in Reinhard Bendix and Seymour M. Lipset (eds.), *Class, Status, and Power.* New York: The Free Press.

Fraenkel, Ernst. 1958. "Parliament und öffentliche Meinung," pp. in Fraenkel, Ernst (ed.), *Zur Geschichte und Problematik der Demokratie.* Berlin: Duncker & Humblot.

Fraenkel, Heinrich, and Manvell, Roger. 1965. *Himmler.* Frankfurt/ Main: Ullstein.

Friedrich, Carl J. 1954. "The Unique Character of Totalitarian Society," pp. 47–60 in Carl J. Friedrich (ed.), *Totalitarianism.* New York: Grosset & Dunlap.

Gabler, H. 1934. "Die Entwicklung der deutschen Parteien auf landschaftlicher Grundlage von 1871–1912," Inaugural dissertation, Friedrich-Wilhelms Universität, Berlin.

Galtung, J. 1966. "Rank and Social Integration," pp. 145–98 in J. Berger,; M. Zelditch, Jr.; and Bo Anderson (eds.), *Sociological Theories in Progress.* Boston, Mass.: Houghton Mifflin Company.

Gay, Peter. 1968. *Weimar Culture.* New York: Harper & Row.

Geiss, Immanuel. 1966. "The Outbreak of the First World War and German War Aims," *The Journal of Contemporary History* 1, 3 (July): 75–91.

Gellner, Ernst. 1967. "Democracy and Industrialization," *European Journal of Sociology* 8, 1:47–70.

Germino, D. 1959. *The Italian Fascist Party in Power.* Minneapolis, Minn.: University of Minnesota Press.

Gilison, Jerome M. 1972. *British and Soviet Politics: A Study of Legitimacy and Convergence.* Baltimore, Nd.: The Johns Hopkins University Press.

Goldstein, B. 1949. *The Stars Bear Witness.* New York: The Viking Press.

Goodman, Norman, and Marx, Gary T. 1978. *Society Today.* New York: CRM/Random House.

Gordon, C, and Gergen, K. J. 1968. *The Self in Social Interaction.* New York: John Wiley and Sons.

Groh, D. 1966. "The Unpatriotic Socialists and the State," *The Journal of Contemporary History* 1, 4:151–77.

Gross, Jan T. 1975. *A Society Under Occupation: Poland 1939–1944.* Ann Arbor, Mich.: University Microfilms International.

———. 1979. "Terror and Obedience: A Society Under Occupation," *European Journal of Sociology* 20, 2:333–42.

Gurr, Robert T. 1974. "Persistence and Change in Political Systems: 1800–1971," *American Political Science Review* 63, 4 (December):1482–1504.

Gurr, Robert T. and McClelland, Muriel. 1971. *Political Performance: A Twelve-nation Study.* Comparative Politics Series No. 01-018, Vol. 2. Beverley Hills, Calif.: Sage Publications.

Guttsman, W. L. 1963. *The British Political Elite.* London: McGibbon and Kee.

Haffner, Sebastian. 1978. *Anmerkungen zu Hitler.* München: Kindler Verlag.

Halpern, William S. 1965. *Germany Tried Democracy.* New York: W. W. Norton & Company.

Harrower, Molly. 1976. "Were Hitler's Henchmen Mad?" *Psychology Today,* July:76–80.

Heaven, P. L. 1977. "Do Authoritarians Hold Authoritarian Attitudes? *Journal of Psychology* 95:169–71.

Helmreich, Ernst C. 1979. *The German Churches under Hitler: Background, Struggle, and Epilogue.* Detroit, Mich.: Wayne State University Press.

Heyen, Franz J. 1967. *Nationalsozialismus im Alltag.* Boppard: Harald Boldt Verlag.

Hilber, Raul. 1961. *The Destruction of European Jews.* New York: New Viewpoints Franklin Watts 1973 edition.

———. 1971. *Documents of Destruction.* Chicago, Ill.: Quadrangle Books.

Hildebrand, Klaus. 1973. *The Foreign Policy of the Third Reich.* Berkeley, Calif.: University of California Press.

———. 1978. "Innenpolitische Antriebskräfte der nationalsozialistischen Aussenpolitik," pp. 175–200 in Wolfgang Michalka (ed.), *Nationalsozialistische Aussenpolitik.* Darmstadt: Wissenschaftliche Buchgesellschaft.

Himmler, Heinrich. 1943. "Rede vor den Reichs-und Gauleitern in Posen am 6.10.1943," pp. 162–82 in B. F. Smith, and A. F. Peterson, *Himmler Geheimreden 1933–1945.* Frankfurt: Propyläen.

Hintze, Otto. 1962. *Staat und Verfassung,* Vol. 1. Göttingen: Vandenhoeck & Ruprecht.

Hobbes, T. 1881. *Leviathan.* Oxford: James Thornton.

Hoffmann, P. 1970. *Widerstand, Staatsstreich, Attentat: Der Kampf gegen Hitler.* Frankfurt: Ullstein Verlag.

Hoffmann, Stanley. 1963. "Paradoxes of the French Political Community," pp. 1–117 in S. Hoffmann, et al., *In Search of France.* Cambridge, Mass.: Harvard University Press.

Höhn, Reinhard. 1935. *Reichsgemeinschaft und Volksgemeinschaft.* Hamburg.

———. 1963. *Die Armee als Erziehungsschule der Nation.* Bad Harzburg: Verlag für Wissenschaft, Wirtschaft und Technik.

Höhne, Heinz. 1967. *Der Orden unter dem Totenkopf.* Gütersloh: Sigbert Mohn Verlag.

Homze, Edward L. 1967. *Foreign Labor in Nazi Germany.* Princeton, N.J.: Princeton University Press.

Horkenbach, Cuno. 1930. *Das Deutsche Reich von 1918 bis heute,* Vol. 1. Berlin: Verlag für Presse, Wirtschaft, und Politik.

Höss, Rudolph. 1959.*Commandant of Auschwitz.* Cleveland, O.: World Publishing Company.

Huber, Ernst R. 1963. *Deutsche Verfassungsgeschichte seit 1789,* 3 vols. Stuttgart: W. Kohlhammer Verlag.

———. 1966 *Dokumente zur Deutschen Verfassungsgeschichte,* 3 vols. Stuttgart: W. KOHL-HAMMER Verlag.

Hunt, Richard N. 1964. *German Social Democracy, 1918–1933*. New Haven, Conn.: Yale University Press.

Hunter, Floyd. 1959. *Top Leadership, U.S.A.* Chapel Hill, N.C.: University of North Carolina Press.

Hüttenberger, Peter. 1976. "Nationalsozialistische Polykratie," *Geschichte und Gesellschaft* 12, 4:417–42.

Inkeles, Alex. 1954. "The Totalitarian Mystique," pp. 88–108 in J. C. Friedrich (ed.), *Totalitarianism*. New York: Grosset & Dunlap.

Inkeles, Alex, and Rossi Peter. 1965. "National Comparisons in Occupational Prestige," *American Journal of Sociology* 61 (January):329–39.

Inkeles, Alex, and Smith, David H. 1974. *Becoming Modern*. Cambridge, Mass.: Harvard University Press.

Jacob, Herbert. 1963. *German Administration Since Bismarck*. New Haven, Conn.: Yale University Press.

Jones, George F. 1959. *Honor in German Literature*. Chapel Hill, N.C.: University of North Carolina Press.

Kaim-Caudle, P. R. 1973. *Comparative Social Policy and Social Security: A Ten-country Study*. New York: Dunellen.

Kaltefleiter, Werner. 1968. *Wirtschaft und Politik in Deutschland*. Köln: Westdeutscher Verlag.

Kayser, Christine. 1961. "Calvinism and German Political Life," unpublished Ph.D. dissertation, Department of Social Relations, Harvard University.

Kehr, Eckart. 1965. "Zur Genesis des Königlich Preussischen Reserveoffiziers," pp. 51–63 in Eckart Kehr, *Der Primat der Innenpolitik*. Berlin: Walter de Gruyter

———.1966. "Zur Genesis der preussischen Bürokratie und des Rechtsstaates: Ein Beitrag zum Diktaturproblem" pp. 37–54 in Hans-Ulrich Wehler (ed.), *Moderne deutsche Sozialgeschichte*. Köln: Kiepenheuer & Witsch.

Keller, Suzanne. 1963. *Beyond the Ruling Class: Strategic Elites in Modern Society*. New York: Random House.

Kersten, Felix. 1952. *Totenkopf und Treue*. Hamburg: Robert Mölich Verlag.

Kluckhohn, Clyde, et al. 1951. "Value Orientations in the Theory of Action," pp. 388–433 in T. Parsons and E. A. Shils (eds.), *Toward a General Theory of Action*. Cambridge Mass.: Harvard University Press.

Kofler, Leo. 1966. *Zur Geschichte der bürgerlichen Gesellschaft*. Berlin: Luchterhand Verlag.

Kohn-Bramstedt, Ernst. 1937. *Aristocracy and the Middle Classes in Germany*. London: P. S. King.

Kornhauser, William. 1959. *The Politics of Mass Society*. Glencoe, Ill.: The Free Press.

———. 1966. "Power Elites and Veto Groups," pp. 210–18 in R. Bendix and S. M. Lipset (eds.), *Class, Status, and Power*. New York: The Free Press.

Koselleck, Reinhart. 1966. "Staat und Gesellschaft in Preussen: 1815–1848," pp. 53–84 in Hans-Ulrich Wehler (ed.), *Moderne deutsche Sozialgeschichte*. Köln: Kiepenheuer & Witsch.

Koszyk, Kurt. 1966. *Die Presse der deutschen Sozialdemokratie*. Hannover: Verlag für Literatur und Zeitgeschehen.

Kraus, Theodor, et al. (eds.) (no date). *Atlas des östlichen Mitteleuropa*. Bielefeld: Velhagen & Klasing.

Kriesberg, Louis. 1979. *Social Inequality*. Englewood Cliffs, N.J.: Prentice-Hall.

Kruck, Alfred. 1954. *Geschichte des Alldeutschen Verbands, 1890–1939*. Wiesbaden.

Krummacher, F. A. 1964. *Die Kontroverse Hannah Arendt, Eichmann und die Juden*. München: Nymphenburger Verlagshandlung.

Langbein, Hermann. 1972. *Menschen in Auschwitz*. Wien: Europa Verlags A.G.

Lasch, Christopher. 1978. *The Culture of Narcissism*. New York: W. W. Norton & Company.

Lebovics, Herman. 1969. *Social Conservatism and the Middle Classes in Germany, 1914–1933*. Princeton, N.J.: Princeton University Press.

Lendvai, P. 1971. *Anti-Semitism in Eastern Europe*. London: Macdonald & Company.

Lenski, Gerhard E. 1966. *Power and Privilege*. New York: McGraw-Hill Book Company.

Lepsius, Rainer M. 1966a. "Parteiensystem und Sozialstruktur: Zum Problem der Democratisierung der deutschen Gesellschaft," pp. 371–93 in W. Abel et. al. (eds), *Wirtschaft, Geschichte und Wirtschaftsgeschichte.* Stuttgart: Fischer Verlag.
———. 1966b. *Extremer Nationalismus.* Stuttgart: W. Kohlhammer Verlag.
———. 1968. "The Collapse of an Intermediary Power Structure: Germany 1933–1934," *International Journal of Sociology* 9, 3 and 4:289–301.
———. 1978. "From Fragmented Party Democracy to Government by Emergency Decree and National Socialist Takeover: Germany," pp. 34–79 in J. J. Linz and A. Stepan (eds.), *The Breakdown of Democratic Regimes: Europe.* Baltimore, Md.: The Johns Hopkins University Press.
———. 1979. "Die Entwicklung der deutschen Soziologie nach dem Zweiten Weltkrieg," pp. 25–70 in Günther Lüschen (ed.), *Deutsche Soziologie seit 1945.* Köln: Westdeutscher Verlag.
Leuner, H. D. 1966. *When Compassion Was A Crime.* München: Wilhelm Heyne Verlag.
Levy, Marion J. 1964. "A Revision of the Gemeinschaft-Gesellschaft Categories and Some Aspects of the Interdependencies of Minority and Host Systems," pp. 233–66 in Harry Eckstein (ed.), *Internal War.* New York: The Free Press.
———. 1979. "Modernization Exhumed." Paper read at the Annual Convention of the American Sociological Association, Boxton, Mass.: August.
Lewy, Guenter. 1964. *The Catholic Church and Nazi Germany.* New York: McGraw-Hill Book Company.
Lidz, Victor. 1979. "Secularization, Ethical Life, and Religion in Modern Societies." *Sociological Inquiry* 49, 2 and 3:191–217.
Lijphart, Arend. 1968. *The Politics of Accommodation: Pluralism and Democracy in the Netherlands.* Berkeley, Calif.: University of California Press.
———. 1969. "Consociational Democracy." *World Politics* 21, 2 (January): 207–25.
Lindenberg, Christoph. 1978. *Die Technik des Bösen: Zur Vorgeschichte und Geschichte des Nationalsozialismus.* Stuttgart: Verlag Freies Geistesleben.
Linz, Juan. 1964. "An Authoritarian Regime: Spain," pp. 291–341 in Erik Allardt and Y. Littunen (eds.), *Cleavages, Ideologies, and Party Systems.* Helsinki: Academic Bookstore.
Lipset, Seymour M. 1960. *Political Man.* Garden City, N.Y.: Doubleday & Company.
———. 1963. "The Value Patterns of Democracy," *American Sociological Review* 28, 4:515–531.
———. 1976. "Equality and Inequality," pp. 307–53 in Robert K. Merton and Robert A. Nisbet (eds.), *Contemporary Social Problems.* New York: Harcourt Brace Jovanovich.
Loewenberg, Peter. 1971. "The Unsuccessful Adolescence of Heinrich Himmler," *American Historical Review* 76, 3:612–41.
Lowie, R. H. 1945. *The German People: A Social Portrait to 1914.* New York: Farrar Rinehart.
Luhmann, Niklas. 1968. *Vertrauen.* Stuttgart: F. Enke Verlag.
Macridis, Roy C. 1963. "France," pp. 137–265 in Roy C. Macridis and Robert E. Ward (eds.), *Modern Political Systems: Europe.* Englewood Cliffs, N.J.: Prentice-Hall.
Maguire, Daniel C. 1975. *Death by Choice.* New York: Schocken Books.
Mann, Reinhard. 1978. "Everyday Life in National Socialist Germany," Paper presented at the Third Annual Meeting of the Social Science and History Association. Columbus, O.: November 3–5.
Mann, Thomas. 1967. *The Magic Mountain.* Harmondsworth, Middlesex: Penguin Books.
Mark. Ber. 1975. *Uprising in the Warsaw Ghetto.* New York: Schocken Books.
Martel, M. U., and McCall, George J. 1964. "Reality Orientations and the Pleasure Principle: A Study of American Mass Periodical Fiction," pp. 283–336 in Lewis A. Dexter and David M. White (eds.), *People, Society, and the Mass Communications.* New York: The Free Press.
Marx, John H. 1969. "A Multi-Dimensional Conception of Ideologies in Professional Arenas: The Case of the Mental Health Field," *Pacific Sociological Review* 12, 2 (Fall):75–85.
Marx, Karl. 1852. "The Eighteenth of Brumaire of Louis Bonaparte," excerpts, pp. 318–48

in Lewis S. Feuer (ed.), *Marx and Engels: Basic Writings on Politics and Philosophy*. Garden City, N.Y.: Doubleday & Company, Anchor Books, 1959.

Mayntz, Renate. 1970a. "The Nature and Genesis of Impersonality: Some Results of a Study on the Doctor-Patient Relationship," *Social Research* 37, 3 (Autumn):428–46.

————. 1970b. "Role Distance, Role Identification, and Amoral Role Behavior," *European Journal of Sociology* XI, 2:368–78.

McClelland, David C. 1964. "The United States and Germany: A Comparative Study in National Character," pp. 62–92 in David C. McClelland, *The Roots of Consciousness*. Princeton, N.J.: Van Nostrand Company.

Merkl, Peter H. 1975. *Political Violence Under the Swastika*. Princeton, N.J.: Princeton University Press.

Merton, Robert K. 1957. *Social Theory and Social Structure*. Glencoe, Ill.: The Free Press.

Miale, F., and Selzer, M. 1976. *The Nuremberg Mind*. New York: Quadrangle Books, The New York *Times* Book Company.

Michalka, Wolfgang. 1978. *Nationalsozialistische Aussenpolitik*. Darmstadt: Wissenschaftliche Buchgesellschaft.

Milgram, Stanley. 1974. *Obedience to Authority: An Experimental View*. New York: Harper & Row.

Mills, C. Wright. 1951. *White Collar*. New York: Oxford University Press.

Mitscherlich, A., and Mitscherlich, M. 1970. *Die Unfähigkeit zu trauern*. München: Piper Verlag.

Mommsen, Hans. 1966. *Beamtentum im Dritten Reich*. Stuttgart: Deutsche Verlagsanstalt.

Mommsen, Wolfgang J. 1974a. *Max Weber und die deutsche Politik*. Tübingen: J. C. B. Mohr.

————. 1974b. "Universalgeschichtliches und Politisches Denken," pp. 97–143 in Wolfgang J. Mommsen (ed.), *Max Weber: Gesellschaft, Politik und Geschichte*. Frankfurt: Suhrkamp.

Moore, Barrington, Jr. 1966. *Social Origins of Dictatorship and Democracy*. Boston: Beacon Press.

Moore, Gwen. 1979. "The Structure of a National Elite Network," *American Sociological Review* 44, 5 (October):673–92.

Morse, Edward L. 1976. *Modernization and the Transformation of International Relations*. New York: The Free Press.

Mosse, George L. 1964. *The Crisis of German Ideology*. New York: The Universal Library, Grosset & Dunlap.

————. 1970. *Germans and Jews*. New York: Howard Fertig.

————. 1975. *The Nationalization of the Masses*. New York: Howard Fertig.

————. 1978a. *Nazism: A Historical and Comparative Analysis of National Socialism*. New Brunswick, N.J.: Transaction Books.

————. 1978b. *Toward the Final Solution: A History of European Racism*. New York: Howard Fertig.

Most, Otto. 1915. "Zur Wirtschaft und Sozialstatistik der höheren Beamten in Preussen," *Schmollers Jahrbuch für Gesetzgebung, Verwaltung und Volkswirtschaft* 39, 1:181–218.

Müller, Christian. 1970[?]. *Oberst i.G. Stauffenberg*. Düsseldorf: Droste.

Müller, Klaus J. 1969. *Das Heer und Hitler*. Stuttgart: Deutsche Verlagsanstalt.

Musmanno, Michael A. 1961. *The Eichmann Kommandos*. Philadelphia, Pa.: Macrae Smith.

Nadler, J. 1912–18. *Literaturgeschichte der Deutschen Stämme*. Regensburg: J. Habbel Verlag.

Nakane, Chie. 1970. *Japanese Society*. Berkeley, Calif.: University of California Press.

Neuhaus, G. 1913. *Die berufliche und soziale Gliederung des Deutschen Volkes*. Mönchen-Gladback: Volksvereinsverlag.

Neumann, Sigmund. 1965. *Die Parteien der Weimarer Republik*. Stuttgart: W. Kohlhammer Verlag.

Nipperdey, Thomas. 1961. *Die Organisation der deutschen Parteien vor 1918*. Düsseldorf: Droste Verlag.

————. 1966. "Interessenverbände und Parteien in Deutschland vor dem ersten Weltkrieg," pp. 369–88 in Hans-Ullrich Wehler (ed.), *Moderne deutsche Sozialgeschichte*. Köln: Kiepenheuer & Witsch.

Nishio, H. 1965. "Political Authority Structure and Development of Entrepreneurship in Japan," unpublished Ph.D. dissertation. Berkeley, Calif.: University of California.

Nolte, Ernst. 1965. *The Three Faces of Fascism*. New York: The New American Library.

———. 1970. *Theorien über den Faschismus*. Köln: Kiepenheuer & Witsch.

Nyomarkay, Joseph. 1967. *Charisma and Factionalism in the Nazi Party*. Minneapolis, Minn.: University of Minnesota Press.

Obler, Jeffrey; Steiner, Jürg; and Dierickx, Guido. 1977. *Decision Making in Smaller Democracies: The Consociational "Burden."* Comparative Politics Series No. 01-064, Vol. 6. Beverly Hills, Calif.: Sage Publications.

O'Neil, Robert J. 1966. *The German Army and the Nazi Party, 1933–1939*. London: Cassell.

Oppenheimer, Heinrich. 1923. *The Constitution of the German Republic*. London: Stevens & Sons Ltd.

Orlow, Dietrich. 1968. *The Nazis in the Balkans*. Pittsburgh, Pa.: University of Pittsburgh Press.

———. 1969. *The History of the Nazi Party*. Pittsburgh, Pa.: University of Pittsburgh Press.

Palmore, Erdman. 1975. *The Honorable Elders*. Durham, N.C.: Duke University Press.

Parsons, Talcott. 1942a. "Democracy and the Social Structure in Pre-Nazi Germany," *Journal of Legal and Political Sociology* 1:96–114.

———. 1942b. "Some Sociological Aspects of the Fascist Movements," *Social Forces* 21:138–47.

———. 1945. "The Problem of Controlled Institutional Change," *Psychiatry* 8:79–101.

———. 1946. "Certain Primary Sources and Patterns of Aggression in the Social Structure of the Western World," *Psychiatry* 10:167–81.

———. 1951. *The Social System*. Glencoe, Ill.: The Free Press.

———. 1953. *Working Papers in the Theory of Action*. Glencoe, Ill.: The Free Press.

———. 1959. "An Approach to Psychological Theory in Terms of the Theory of Action," pp. 612–711 in Sigmund Koch, (ed.), *Psychology: A Study of a Science*, Vol. III. New York: McGraw-Hill Book Co.

———. 1961. "An Outline of the Social System," pp. 30–79 in T. Parsons, et al. (eds.), *Theories of Society*. New York: The Free Press.

———. 1963a. "On the Concept of Influence," *Public Opinion Quarterly* 27 (Spring):37–62.

———. 1963b. "On the Concept of Political Power," *Proceedings of the American Philosophical Society* 107, 3:232–62.

———. 1964. "Evolutionary Universals in Society," *American Sociological Review* 29, 3 (June):339–57.

———. 1968a. "The Position of Identity in the General Theory of Action," in C. Gordon, and K. J. Gergen (eds.), *The Self in Social Interaction*. New York: John Wiley &Sons.

———. 1968b. "On the Concept of Value Commitments," *Sociological Inquiry* 38 (Spring):135–60.

———. 1969. "Postscript to Chapter 15," pp. 430–38 in Talcott, Parsons, *Politics and Social Structure*. New York: The Free Press.

Passow, R. 1922. *Die Aktiengesellschaft: Eine wirtschaftswissenschaftliche Studie*. Jena: G. Fischer Verlag.

Pauker, Arnold. 1968. *Der jüdische Abwehrkampf*. Hamburg: Leibniz Verlag.

Peterson, Edward N. 1969. *The Limits of Hitler's Power*. Princeton, N.J.: Princeton University Press.

Pfohl, E., and Friedrich, E. 1928. *Die deutsche Wirtschaft in Karten*. Berlin: Verlag von Reimer Hobbing.

Plessner, Helmut. 1959. *Die verspätete Nation*. Stuttgart: W. Kohlhammer Verlag.

Pletsch, Carl. 1979. "The Socialist Nation of the German Democratic Republic or the Asymmetry in Nation and Ideology Between the Two Germanies," *Comparative Studies in Society and History* 21, 3:323–45.

Poliakov, Leon. 1949. "Mussolini and the Extermination of the Jews," *Jewish Studies* XI (July):249–58.

———. 1954. *Harvest of Hate*. New York: Syracuse University Press

———. 1974. *The Aryan Myth*. London: Chatto and W. Heinemann for Sussex University.

Poliakov, Leon, and Wulf, Josef. 1955. *Das Dritte Reich und die Juden*. Berlin: Grunewald Verlags.

Preller, Ludwig. 1949. *Sozialpolitik in der Weimarer Republik*. Stuttgart: F. Mittelbach.

von Preradovich, Nikolaus. 1955. *Die Führungsschichten in Österreich und Preussen 1804–1918*. Wiesbaden: F. Steiner Verlag.

Pride, Richard A. 1970. *Origins of Democracy: A Cross-National Study of Mobilization, Party Systems, and Democratic Stability*. Comparative Politics Series No. 01-012, Vol. I. Beverly Hills, Calif.: Sage Publications.

Protokolle des Preussischen Landtags, Haus der Abgeordneten, 1897, Bd. III.

Puhle, Hans J. 1966. *Agrarische Interessenpolitik und Preussischer Konservatismus im Wilhelminischen Reich: 1893–1914*. Hannover: Verlag für Zeitgeschehen.

Pulzer, P. G. J. 1964. *The Rise of Anti-Semitism in Germany and Austria*. New York: John Wiley & Sons.

Putnam, Robert D. 1976. *The Comparative Study of Political Elites*. Englewood Cliffs, N.J.: Prentice-Hall.

Ravenstein, L. 1883. *Spezialkarte des deutschen Reichs*. Leipzig: Bibliographisches Institut.

Rehms, H. 1912. *Deutschlands Politische Parteien*. Jena: G. Fischer Verlag.

Reinhardt, Kurt F. 1962. *Germany: 2000 Years*. New York: Frederick Ungar Publishing Company.

Reitlinger, G. 1961. *Die Endlösung: Hitlers Versuch der Ausrottung der Juden Europas 1939–1945*. Berlin: Colloquium Verlag.

Ringer, Fritz K. 1967. "Higher Education in Germany in the Nineteenth Century," pp. 123–38 in Walter Laqueur, and G. L. Mosse (eds.), *Education and Social Structure in the 20th Century*. New York: Harper & Row.

———. 1969. *The Decline of the German Mandarins*. Cambridge, Mass.: Harvard University Press.

Ritter, Emil. 1954. *Die Katholisch Soziale Bewegung und der Volksverein*. Köln: Bachem Verlag.

Ritter, Gerhard. 1965. *Staatskunst und Kriegshandwerk*, 2 vols. München: Oldenbourg Verlag.

Rohe, Karl. 1966. *Das Reichsbanner Schwarz-Rot-Gold*. Düsseldorf: Droste Verlag.

Röhl, J. C. G. 1967a. *Germany Without Bismarck*. London: B. T. Batsford Ltd.

———. 1967b. "Higher Civil Servants in Germany, 1890–1900," pp. 101–21 in Walter Laqueur, and G. L. Mosse (eds), *Education and Social Structure in the 20th Century*. New York: Harper & Row.

Rokeach, Milton. 1960. *The Open and the Closed Mind*. New York: Basic Books.

———. 1968. "A Theory of Organization and Change Within Value Attitude Systems," *Journal of Social Issues* 24, 1:13–33.

———. 1979. *Understanding Human Values: Individual and Societal*. New York: The Free Press.

Röpke, W. 1946. *The Solution of the German Problem*. New York: G. P. Putnam's Sons.

Rose, Arnold M. 1967. *The Power Structure: Political Process in American Society*. New York: Oxford University Press.

Rose, Richard. 1971. *Governing Without Consensus*. Boston: Beacon Press.

Rosenberg, Alfred. 1964. *Das politische Tagebuch Alfred Rosenbergs*. München: Deutscher Taschenbuchverlag.

Rosenberg, Arthur. 1931. *The Birth of the German Republic*. London: Oxford University Press.

Rosenberg, Hans. 1966. "Die Pseudodemokratisierung der Rittergutsbesitzer Klasse," pp. 287–308 in H.-U. Wehler, (ed.), *Moderne deutsche Sozialgeschichte*. Köln: Kiepenheuer & Witsch.

Rostow, Walt W. 1960. *The Stages of Economic Growth*. Cambridge: Cambridge University Press.

———. 1963. *The Economics of Take-off into Sustained Growth*. New York: Macmillan, St. Martin's Press.

Roth, Günther. 1963. *The Social Democrats in Imperial Germany*. Totowa, N.J.: Bedminster Press.

Rubenstein, Richard L. 1975. *The Cunning of History: Mass Death and the American Future*. New York: Harper & Row.

Sauer, Wolfgang. 1966. "Das Problem des deutschen Nationalstaates," pp. 407–36 in H.-U. Wehler (ed.), *Moderne deutsche Sozialgeschichte*. Köln: Kiepenheuer & Witsch.

Schad, Susanne P. 1963. "Anti-democratic Tendencies Among the University Professors of Constitutional Law in the Weimar Republic," unpublished M.A. thesis. New York: Columbia University.

Schellenberg, Walter. 1956. *Memoiren*. Köln: Verlag für Politik und Wirtschaft.

Schleunes, Karl A. 1970. *The Twisted Road to Auschwitz*. Urbana, Ill.: University of Illinois Press.

Schluchter, Wolfgang. 1980. *Rationalismus der Weltbeherrschung*. Frankfurt: Suhrkamp.

Schmalenbach, Herman. 1961. "The Sociological Category of Communion," pp. 331–47 in T. Parsons et al. (eds.), *Theories of Society*. New York: The Free Press.

Schoenbaum, David. 1967. *Hitler's Social Revolution*. Garden City, N.Y.: Doubleday & Company, Anchor Books.

Schoeps, Hans Joachim. 1964. *Das Andere Preussen*. Berlin: Haude & Spenersche Verlagsbuchhandlung.

———. 1966. *Preussen: Geschichte eines Staates*. Berlin: Propyläen.

———. 1970. *Bereit für Deutschland*. Berlin: Haude & Spenersche Verlagsbuchhandlung.

Schramm, Wilhelm von. 1964. *Aufstand der Generale*. München: Kindler.

Schulz, Gerhard. 1963. *Zwischen Demokratie und Diktatur*, Bd. 1. Berlin: Walter de Gruyter.

Schweitzer, Arthur. 1964. *Big Business in the Third Reich*. Bloomington, Ind.: Indiana University Press.

Schwend, Karl. 1954. *Bayern zwischen Monarchie und Diktatur*. Müunchen: Richard Pflaum Verlag.

SDR = Statistik des Deutschen Reiches.

Selzer, M. 1977. "The Murderous Mind," *New York Times Magazine*, November 27:35ff.

Sennett, Richard. 1974. *The Fall of Public Man*. New York: Random House, Vintage Books.

Sereny, Gitta. 1974. *Into That Darkness*. New York: McGraw-Hill Book Company.

Seton-Watson, C. 1967. *Italy from Liberalism to Fascism*. London: Methuen Company.

SJDR = Statistisches Jahrbuch für das Deutsche Reich.

Smelser, Neil J. 1963. *The Theory of Collective Behavior*. New York: The Free Press of Glencoe.

Smith, B. F., and Peterson, A. F. 1974. *Himmler Geheimreden 1933–1945*. Frankfurt: Propyläen.

Solzhenitsyn, Aleksandr I. 1973. *The Gulag Archipelago I*. New York: Harper & Row.

———. 1975. *The Gulag Archipelago II*. New York: Harper & Row.

Sontheimer, Kurt. 1962. *Antidemokratisches Denken in der Weimarer Republik*. München: Nymphenburger Verlagsbuchhandlung.

Speer, Albert. 1969. *Erinnerungen*. Berlin: Propyläen Verlag.

Stein, George H. 1966. *The Waffen SS*. Ithaca, N.Y.: Cornell University Press.

Steiner, Jean-François. 1967. *Treblinka*. New York: Simon & Schuster.

Steiner, John M., and Fahrenberg, Y. 1970. "Die Ausprägung autoritärer Einstellungen bei ehemaligen Angehörigen der SS und der Wehrmacht," *Kölner Zeitschrift für Soziologie und Sozialpsychologie* 22:551–66.

Steiner, Jürg. 1974. *Amicable Agreement Versus Majority Rule: Conflict Resolution in Switzerland*. Chapel Hill, N.C.: University of North Carolina Press.

Steinert, Marlis G. 1977. *Hitler's War and the Germans*. Athens, O.: Ohio University Press.

Stern, Fritz. 1965. *The Politics of Cultural Despair*. Garden City, N.Y.: Doubleday & Company, Anchor Books.

Swanson, Guy E. 1967. *Religion and Regime*. Ann Arbor, Mich.: University of Michigan Press.

Taviss, Irene. 1968. "The Technological Society: Some Challenges for Social Science," *Social Research* 35, 3 (Autumn):521–39.

The Jewish Black Book Committee. 1946. *The Black Book: The Nazi Crime Against the Jewish People*. New York: American Book Stratford Press.

Thies, Jochen. 1978. "Hitlers Endziele: Zielloser Aktionismus, Kontinentalimperium oder Weltherrschaft?" pp. 70–91 in Wolfgang Michalka (ed.), *Nationalsozialistische Aussenpolitik.* Darmstadt: Wissenschaftliche Buchgesellschaft.

Thorwald, Jürgen. 1975. *The Illusion: Soviet Soldiers in Hitler's Armies.* New York: Harcourt Brace Jovanovich.

Tillion, G. 1975. *Ravensbrück.* Garden City, N.Y.: Doubleday & Company, Anchor Books.

Toennies, Ferdinand. 1957. *Community and Society.* East Lansing, Mich.: Michigan State University Press.

Tomasson, Richard F. 1970. *Sweden: Prototype of Modern Society.* New York: Random House.

Trevor-Roper, H. R. 1969. *The European Witchcraze of the Sixteenth and Seventeenth Centuries and Other Essays.* New York: Harper & Row, Torchbooks.

Turner, Henry A., Jr. 1963. *Stresemann and the Politics of the Weimar Republic.* Princeton, N.J.: Princeton University Press.

Waite, Robert J. 1952. *Vanguard of Nazism.* Cambridge, Mass.: Harvard University Press.

Waite, Robert L. 1977. *The Psychopathic God: Adolf Hitler.* New York: Basic Books.

Weber, Eugen. 1964. *Varieties of Fascism.* New York: D. Van Nostrand Company.

Weber, Max. 1895. "Der Nationalstaat und die Volkswirtschaftspolitik," pp. 1–25 in Max Weber, *Gesammelte Politische Schriften,* ed. J. Winckelmann. Tübingen: J. C. B. Mohr, 1971.

———. 1904. "Objectivity in Social Science and Social Policy," pp. 50–112 in Max Weber, *The Methodology of the Social Sciences,* tran. E. A. Shils and H. A. Finch, Glencoe, Ill.: The Free Press, 1949.

———. 1904–5. *The Protestant Ethic and the Spirit of Capitalism.* New York: Scribner's Sons, 1958.

———. 1905. "Critical Studies in the Logic of Cultural Sciences," pp. 113–88 in Max Weber, *The Methodology of the Social Sciences,* (trans. E. A. Shils and H. A. Finch). Glencoe, Ill.: The Free Press, 1949.

———. 1906. "Capitalism and Rural Society in Germany," pp. 363–85 in H. H. Gerth and C. Wright Mills (eds.), *From Max Weber: Essays in Sociology.* New York: Oxford University Press, 1958.

———. 1915. "Religious Rejections of the World and Their Directions," pp. 323–59 in H. H. Gerth and C. Wright Mills (eds.), *From Max Weber: Essays in Sociology.* New York: Oxford University Press, 1958.

———. 1916. *The Religion of China,* trans. and ed. H. H. Gerth, New York: The Free Press, 1951.

———. 1916–17. *The Religion of India.* New York: The Free Press, 1958.

———. 1917a. "National Character and the Junkers," pp. 386–95 in H. H. Gerth and C. Wright Mills (eds.), *From Max Weber: Essays in Sociology.* New York: Oxford University Press, 1958.

———. 1917b. "Parliament and Government in a Reconstructed Germany," pp. 1, 381–1, 469 in Max Weber, *Economy and Society.* Totawa, N. J.: Bedminster Press, 1968.

———. 1919a. "Politics as a Vocation," pp. 77–128 in H. H. Gerth and C. Wright Mills (eds.), *From Max Weber: Essays in Sociology.* New York: Oxford University Press, 1958.

———. 1922. *Economy and Society.* New York: Bedminster Press, 1968.

Wehler, Hans-Ulrich. 1966. *Moderne deutsche Sozialgeschichte.* Köln: Kiepenheuer & Witsch.

———. 1973. *Das Deutsche Kaiserreich 1871–1918.* Göttingen: Vandenhoek & Ruprecht.

Wertheimer, Mildred S. 1924. *The Pan-German League, 1890–1914.* New York: Longman & Green.

Wiesel, Eliezer. 1960. *Night.* New York: Hill & Wang.

Williams, Robert C. 1966. "The Russians in Germany: 1900–1914," *The Journal of Contemporary History* 1, 4:121–45.

Williams, Robin, M., Jr. 1979. "Change and Stability in Values and Value Systems: A Sociological Perspective," pp. 15–46 in Milton Rokeach, *Understanding Human Values: Individual and Societal.* New York: The Free Press.

Winckelmann, J. 1952. *Legitimität und Legalität in Max Webers Herrschaftssoziologie.* Tübingen: J. C. B. Mohr.

Winkler, Heinrich A. 1968. "Bürgerliche Emanzipation und nationale Einigung. Zur Enstehung des Nationalliberalismus in Preussen," pp. 226–42 in Böhme Helmut (ed.), *Probleme der Reichsgründungszeit.* Köln: Kiepenheuer & Witsch.

Zapf, Wolfgang. 1966. *Wandlungen der deutschen Elite.* München: Piper Verlag.

Zborowski, Mark 1953. "Cultural Components in Responses to Pain," *Journal of Social Issues* 8:16–31.

Zimmerman, M. 1963. *Die Gartenlaube als Dokument ihrer Zeit.* München: Heinemann Verlag.

Zorn, Wolfgang. 1966. "Wirtschafts und sozialgeschichtliche Zusammenhänge der deutschen Reichsgründungszeit," pp. 254–70 in Hans-Ullrich Wehler (ed.), *Moderne deutsche Sozialgeschichte.* Köln: Kiepenheuer & Witsch.

Zunkel, Friedrich. 1962. *Der Rheinisch-Westfälische Unternehmer.* Köln: Westdeutscher Verlag.

———. 1966. "Industriebürgertum in Westdeutschland," pp. 304–41 in Hans-Ulrich Wehler (ed). *moderne deutsche Sozialgeschichte.* Köln: Kiepenheuer & Witsch.

Index